POLO

THE GALLOPING GAME

POLO

THE GALLOPING GAME

AN ILLUSTRATED HISTORY OF POLO
IN THE CANADIAN WEST

TONY REES

Published by
Western Heritage Centre Society
Box 1477, Cochrane, Alberta

Design and Production: Karo
Project Management: Callisto Ltd.

Cover photo: Polo at High River, c. 1907 (detail)
Glenbow archives, NA-394-2

Canadian Cataloguing in Publication Data

Rees, Tony, 1948-
Polo, the galloping game

Includes index.
ISBN 0-9685962-1-5

1. Polo – Canada, Western – History. I. Western Heritage Centre Society. II. Title.
GV1011.6.C3R43 2000   796.35'3   C00-911236-7

To the players and patrons of polo who,

for more than a century,

have sustained the game in

the Canadian West.

Fred Mayer, World Polo Associates

City of Victoria archives, 98009-003-7634

"Going for the Hook" by Rich Roenisch

BC archives, G-07990

ST. JAMES'S PALACE

It is not widely known that polo has been played in the Canadian West continuously since the 1880's. Moreover, there are many families where the fourth generation is now playing. Their inherited passion for the sport is one which I certainly share.

My own family has been associated with the game since its introduction into Britain in the 1860's. First came my great great uncle, the Duke of Connaught who took up polo as a young army officer. My great grandfather, King George V, was a member of a Royal Navy team in Malta in 1886-8 while his older brother, the Duke of Clarence, played in the 10th Hussars. My grandfather, King George VI, and his three brothers were devoted to polo, as was my father, The Duke of Edinburgh, and my great uncle, Lord Mountbatten. I am proud to say that this family tradition is being carried on by my two sons, William and Harry.

We also have had links with the game in western Canada. The Duke of Connaught was on his way to Kamloops to present the first Kamloops Challenge Cup when the First World War broke out in 1914. Prince Henry, later Duke of Gloucester, played in Vancouver in 1929. The Duke of Windsor, when Prince of Wales, had a ranch in Alberta and was Honorary President of the High River Polo Club.

When polo was first played in the West, horses were a part of everyday life and man's connection with animals was synonymous. Today, sadly, for most of us this link has been loosened. However, success depends as much on the fitness, training and skill of the horse as it does on the qualities of the rider. Polo players must learn to value their ponies and respect them for their instinctive knowledge of the game. In my opinion, the close bond which develops between polo pony and its rider is one of the great attractions of the game.

As a physical contest, polo provides a refreshing break from even the most absorbing of sedentary occupations. The truth of this can be witnessed in its growth in Calgary and its resurgence elsewhere in the West.

Two themes in this fascinating history are typical of successful polo: the continuity of family associations and the dedication of its enthusiasts. I am delighted to see that the principles of tactical skill, training, discipline, horsemanship and team work, exemplified by great Canadian players such as Frank Ward and George Ross, continue to be the focus for their successors today.

MY WARMEST CONGRATULATIONS to those who had the breadth of vision and cared enough about polo to preserve its history in this intriguing book. As one would expect, it describes the game's arrival in the Canadian West, the rise and decline of polo clubs, how they weathered the crises of war and economic depression, and tells of tournaments and significant games.

But the book gives more than its title suggests. It is a unique record of the period when polo held sway as a 'cowboy' sport, the focus of social life in the widely separated communities of the early West, and of its players who came to a new country and contributed to the birth of its distinctive culture.

As a former naval officer myself, I was glad to discover that polo had been initiated in Canada by the Royal Navy. As the daughter of a naval officer who was an ardent player, I have followed the game throughout my life. Though I played 'stick and ball' with my family at home and my mother joined a ladies team in Malta, I was never able to progress to competitive polo in England mostly because of the advent of the Second World War. I am glad to see what women have achieved in the Western Canadian game and that they now compete at all levels.

During the last twenty-five years, I have been a frequent visitor to Western Canada and on four occasions since 1989, have been invited to present The Earl Mountbatten Memorial Plate in memory of my father at the Calgary Polo Club. Each time, I have been impressed by the quality of play, and by the growth in the Club's playing and social memberships. Its facilities have been enlarged and developed imaginatively: the warmth of its hospitality is well known. All seems well with this Club which is reputed to be the oldest in continuous existence in North America.

What gives particular pleasure is the news that the sport is growing in popularity and that polo is being played once more in other towns from Winnipeg to Victoria. May we look forward to the day when they will once again be playing for a true Western Canadian championship.

Mountbatten of Burma

The Countess Mountbatten
of Burma, CBE, CD, JP, DL
11/11/00

POLO, THE GALLOPING GAME was conceived some ten years ago to be a history of polo in southern Alberta. When research revealed that local teams regularly competed in Manitoba, Saskatchewan and British Columbia, the scope of the project was widened to chronicle the game throughout the Canadian West.

It may seem paradoxical that a sport, often seen as an expensive pastime, should take such a firm hold in the rough new world of the Canadian West and flourish there for more than a century. The answer lies in its affinity with a populace whose daily life involved horses and horsemanship, and in its unique accessibility.

While polo clubs in Winnipeg and Vancouver were closer in style to those in England and the eastern United States, the game put down its deepest roots in the small ranch towns of the Alberta foothills and in the grassland valleys of the B.C. Interior. It was Pincher Creek that saw the creation of Canada's first polo club: there were at least a dozen such in southern Alberta by the time the Great War began. All were open to anyone who wanted to play and while their rosters include the English-born ranchers and Anglo-Irish nobility one would expect, the great majority were cowboys, homesteaders and clerks.

The thrills and pleasures of polo were treasured by those whose stories the book contains. Their devotion to the game sustained it in times of adversity and inspired them to widen its appeal. Their enthusiasm extended to their families and friends, bringing them together in a society which, unique in the sporting world, enjoyed both the game itself and the pleasure of each other's company. They deserve the gratitude and emulation of polo supporters today.

Universal dependence on the horse has ended and, without the ranches upon which polo was based, centres of competition beyond major cities have disappeared. The centre of the sport has devolved upon the Calgary Polo Club, which has inherited the traditions of the game in Alberta with the responsibility to sustain and promote it.

When we watch a high-goal match with all that it entails — our best players, strings of fine ponies, meticulous training — we see only the polished surface of the sport. Accessibility to polo should not be limited by playing skills nor competitive ambition. As it was the key to its survival in its first hundred years, accessibility remains vital to its future. To flourish for another century, the demands of high-goal tournament polo must be balanced with the needs of players, young and old, who wish only to play a game they love with their families and friends.

Fred P. Mannix
President
Calgary Polo Club

THIS BOOK IS BASED ALMOST ENTIRELY on new research into original sources. It owes its existence to the dozens of individuals and organizations who opened their collections and their memories and were so generous with the assistance they provided.

In every town where the game was played, long-time residents still know where their polo grounds were located and can remember the names of the men and women who played there. In countless conversations, I never spoke with anyone who was indifferent to the part that polo had played in their lives or in the lives of their families. In fact, many could easily recall, as if it were yesterday, the details of a particular match from fifty years ago or more. This book is for them and I can only hope it does justice to their place in the history of their game.

Thanks must go first to Jeffery Williams. A fine author and historian in his own right, his research into the British roots of the Canadian game was invaluable. Also, his rich knowledge of military history has ensured that Canada's Armed Forces can take their rightful place in the story of western polo. Jeffery was also a meticulous and patient editor and invariably provided an encouraging and steadying influence on the project.

Jennifer Ough undertook the early research in Alberta and was the first to confront the mind-numbing task of reading endless rolls of scratchy microfilm, hunting for any and every reference to western polo. It was Jennifer who began to build the foundation on which this book rests.

A special debt is owed to Desmond Deane-Freeman. A fine gentleman and a congenial host, he undertook a great deal of personal research and provided a unique insight into the Millarville, High River and Lord Strathcona's clubs and their players. The special section on the great polo traditions of the Deane-Freeman family could not have been written without his help.

Sincerest thanks to Jill and Tony Yonge who graciously shared their home and their memories of British Columbia polo in the post-war era. Their only failing was an excessive modesty when it came to the part they have played in keeping the West Coast game alive.

Penny Wilmot provided access to her irreplaceable collection of family photographs and documents and cheerfully answered any number of follow-up questions about her grandfather's crucial role in the birth of western Canadian polo and her father's long, distinguished career in the game.

For sharing their memories and their knowledge of prairie polo, I am indebted to Harry Irving, Warren Hunt, Clint and Rob Roenisch, Tim and Tony Gregg, Byron Palmer, Rob Peters, Steve Benediktson, Don and Shannon Cross, Betty Bacon, Jane Hetherington and Cassie Thorburn, Donna Wilson, Sydney Turner, Bill Wolley-Dod, Gordon and Gloria Sellar, Dr. Marmie Hess, Don Watson, Joan Gunn Allard, Sally and Doug Connelly, Mike Milvain, Shirley Lush of the St. Charles Club in Winnipeg, Pat Dix of Spokane, Washington, Bob Tate of Sheridan, Wyoming and Molly Akers of Palmerston North, New Zealand.

For their help in exploring the history of British Columbia polo, my thanks to the family of Ross Hett (especially to his daughter, Diana Hett Palmer), to David Wallace, Herb Cripps, Ian Tyson, John and Sidney Madden, Sherri Porter and Marilyn Kynaston.

Western Canada's archives, museums and libraries contain a wealth of unique material bearing directly and indirectly on the history of polo, but without the help of their dedicated, professional staff, much of it might have remained hidden. A very special thank you to: Lindsay Moir, Doug Cass, Ellen Bryant and the staff of the Glenbow Library & Archives in Calgary and to Glenbow's chief photographer, Ron Marsh; to Jennifer Bobrovitz, local history librarian at the Calgary Public Library; Dianne Vallée and Bill Holmes of High River's Museum of the Highwood; Warrant Officer Darryl Crowell, curator, and Corporal Lee J. Ramsden, archivist, of the Regimental Museum, Lord Strathcona's Horse (Royal Canadians); Elisabeth Duckworth and Susan Cross of the Kamloops Museum & Archives; Sue Baptie of the Vancouver City Archives; Joan Seidl of the Vancouver Museum; Donna Johnson, archivist at the Kelowna Museum; Linda Wills of the Greater Vernon Museum & Archives; Annette Milot of the Sam Waller Museum in The Pas, Manitoba; Nancy Gale Compau of the Spokane Public Library's Northwest Room and the Coronado Historical Association Archives.

For their assistance in smoothing my way through any number of practical and technical matters, I am grateful to Lucile Edwards and Tim Mills at the Calgary Polo Club and to the staff of the Mancal Corporation, especially Sonja Norgaard, Ann Clipstone, Deryck Bodnarchuk, and Anita Mills.

I am pleased to acknowledge the financial support of David Arnold, trustee for the High River Polo Club Limited.

I must also express my personal thanks to Donna Kynaston for her help with the research and for her always astute reading of the early drafts, to Chuck Stormes for sharing his unrivalled expertise on all things equestrian and to Bob Spaith for the use of his cabin at Pekisko, within sight of the old Gee-Bung polo grounds.

Finally, this project began as an exploration of the history of polo in southern Alberta. However, as the research progressed it became clear that the Alberta game was only a part of a far broader story that stretched across the whole breadth of the Canadian West and involved much more than just the history of a sport. It was only through the unwavering support and generosity of Fred P. Mannix and Bill Turnbull that I was given the time and the resources to follow the research wherever it led. No author could ask for more.

Tony Rees
Calgary, Alberta
October, 2000

CHAPTER 1

PERSIA
TO
PINCHER CREEK

FROM THE MOMENT of its introduction to Alberta's Rocky Mountain foothills, the grand and ancient game of polo spread across the ranchlands like a prairie grass fire. Within three years of Captain Edmund Wilmot's return from a trip to England in 1889, bringing with him to his Pincher Creek ranch the first decent sticks and balls, the game had gone from a rough Sunday diversion for cowboys to a series of well-organized, disciplined clubs, playing Hurlingham Rules for elegant sterling cups and even travelling, ponies and all, on the new transcontinental railway from Calgary to the Pacific coast for a weekend tournament in Victoria, British Columbia.

Although the game, as it came to Canada, was a recent craze, born only a few years earlier on the drill field of an English light cavalry regiment, its true origins stretch back thousands of years to the broad plains of southwestern Asia and its mounted warrior herdsmen. There are references in the great Persian epics as far back as 600 B.C. and the game, fully recognizable, is depicted in the rich illuminations that surround their texts. But myriad forms of this simple stick and ball game must have existed almost from the first contact between man and horse.

From a Persian manuscript, 16th century.

Persian pitcher with polo scenes, Kashan or Rayy, 12th-13th century.

From Persia, where it was called "chaugán" (after the four-sided shape of the playing field), the game spread east and west along the old trade and war roads, eventually appearing in ancient chronicles from Byzantium to China and Japan. Everywhere in between, wherever the horse was the foundation of a society, some regional variation of polo took root and held fast.

Polo, in its original form, flourished across Asia until well into the sixteenth century when a combination of political and social change led to its precipitous decline. After more than two millennia, it all but disappeared from Persia, Afghanistan and northern India.

But it did not die out entirely. The game managed to survive in small, isolated pockets along the Indian frontier from the Hindu Kush to Bhutan.

The most reliable account of how polo began in England is related by one who was present at the event. In his book *Chances of Sports of Sorts*, Colonel T.A. St. Quintin (who went on to become one of the great players of the early era) relates the following:

It is ancient history now that one day in 1869, when the 10th Hussars were under canvas at Aldershot for the summer drills, "Chicken" Hartopp, lying back in a chair after luncheon, reading "The Field", exclaimed, "By Jove! this must be a good game in India." Some five or six of us who were in the tent then and there sent for our chargers, and routed up some old heavy walking-sticks and a chicker-ball, and began to try to knock the ball about — a somewhat difficult thing to do properly, as may be imagined, on a tall horse with a short stick, as, of course, we could not reach the ball.

And, where the Indian border juts in a mountainous wedge between China and Burma, polo (or "kanjai" as they called it) remained the national sport of the Manipuri.

Though there seemed few formal rules of play, the size of the field (about two hundred twenty-five yards long by one hundred ten yards wide and surrounded by a low berm), the shape of the sticks and placement of the goals tied it to the ancient game of the Persians rather than to the differently evolved matches played by the Chinese. This was the game that would eventually find its way to Pincher Creek, Alberta.

About the middle of the nineteenth century, as the British Raj grew steadily toward the height of its power over India, English indigo planters and government officials based in the district headquarters at Silchar (between the Burmese border and present-day Bangladesh) watched the Manipuri play their national game and soon began to join in. They called it "hockey on horseback" and by the mid-1850s they were fielding their own teams and, in the year after the upheaval of the 1857-58 Mutiny, started the first formal polo club in the British Empire.

It is often asserted that modern polo was a game discovered, and taken up, in India by the British military and brought back to the homeland by returning regiments and retirees. Contemporary accounts, however, tell a slightly different story.

From the isolation of Silchar, the game found its way to Calcutta where a club was established in 1863 and the game took firm hold among colonial officials and planters alike. Still, it remained a local or regional phenomenon and any military presence was largely a matter of individual interest. While the game that came to England was indeed the Manipuri's kanjai, it was introduced not by returning cavalry, but rather by way of an article in a sporting journal.

St. Quintin goes on to relate a tale of the Hussars acquiring a string of smaller, quieter Irish ponies, improving equipment and a summer spent practicing the fundamentals on a newly made field at their home base in Hounslow. Later that year, a challenge was issued to the 9th Lancers and England witnessed its first chaotic approximation of a polo match.

One year later, the game was finding favour, if not outright passion, among British cavalry regiments and that year saw the involvement not only of the 9th Lancers and 10th Hussars, but of the Blues and the 1st Lifeguards as well.

In 1872, the 10th Hussars were posted to India where they were a major influence in the rapid spread of military polo. Clearly, they were a force to be reckoned with for several years and, in 1877, played in the finals of the first Indian Inter-regimental Tournament. Their opponents were the same as in that first game at Hounslow: the 9th Lancers.

The military game, as practiced by its early adherents, was a riotous affair. With up to eight or even

Courtesy of J.N.P. Watson, *The World of Polo*

nine players a side and no rules to guide them, the result was inevitable. St. Quintin described England's first polo match as follows:

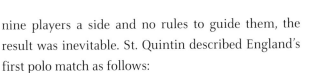

We tried to put some sort of organization into the game, which we rather based on that of a football team...but, as you may imagine, in about two minutes the two sides were mingled up anywhere, all jammed together, ramming into each other, generally at a walk, with little idea as to where the ball was, like a football scrimmage, and the only two people remaining in their places were the two goalkeepers, sticking religiously to their respective posts.

Whatever else it might have been, St. Quintin reports it was "...grand fun, and a very cheery, good game."

But the chaos and the "grand fun" of 1870 were not long a part of English polo and, by the end of that decade, it had taken on much of the character that marks the modern game.

Polo came to the cavalry at a time when soldiering was increasingly being seen as a profession. According to T.F. Dale, one of the finest of the first generation of polo writers, "A cavalry commission was then becoming a career for a man and not merely the pleasant prolongation of his school days." It was inevitable, then, that polo should come to be seen as an extension of the cavalryman's training in horsemanship, discipline and team play. It had certainly been seen that way by the ancient Persians: a useful and educational diversion.

Very quickly, British cavalry regiments adopted a severely disciplined approach to the game. Ball control and precision passing were emphasized at the expense of the headlong rush. Every man knew his position and was expected to play it to the letter. Defence was considered to be of paramount importance, to the point where scoring was severely curtailed. It was not uncommon for a game to end in a goalless draw and still be considered, from a tactical perspective, to have been a great success.

Early polo match at Hurlingham (detail).

As the popularity of polo spread rapidly through the Army (and the Royal Navy), so it also caught the attention of the civilian sporting class. Though there is some debate about which was the very first private polo club in Britain, one name came quickly (and permanently) into prominence: Hurlingham.

Founded in 1868 as a fashionable social club (with a specialty in pigeon shooting), Hurlingham constructed its first polo field in 1873 in response to the remarkable popularity of the game and the need to find a use for its grounds during the shooting off-season. The first players, most already associated with the club, were a mix of landed gentry, cavalry officers (both active and retired), London businessmen and anyone else who could afford the stiff membership dues.

Hurlingham soon established itself as the centre for polo in England and, to all intents and purposes,

Courtesy of J.N.P. Watson, *The World of Polo*

for the rest of the world as well. In the decades between its founding and the outbreak of the Great War, nearly every major player and manager had once called Hurlingham home. It played host to most of the major tournaments (including, eventually, the regimental championships) and, for teams from around the globe, a win at Hurlingham was as close to a world title as there was.

But what truly put Hurlingham at the centre of the polo world were "the Rules."

By 1874, within a year of building their first polo field, the members had, through a powerful subcommittee, done away with the grand melee that had been the principal feature of St. Quintin's game. Although modified and expanded over the years, the seventeen original Hurlingham Rules and their accompanying bylaws still define the game of polo wherever it is played.

Their language was simple and clear; their purpose straightforward. The Rules set the size of the ponies and the field, standardized sticks and balls, established codes of conduct and dress and formalized the hitherto ad hoc rules of play. The appended bylaws defined the length of a game and number of players.

Where there had once been eight or more players per side, now there would be five (four in the military). Where the periods of play (and the rest time between those periods) had been uncertain and irregular, now they would be fixed at three of twenty minutes each with a five-minute break in between. Hooking an opponent's stick was permitted (though not over or under his horse); "riding off" was allowed, but crossing an opponent's path while he was in possession of the ball was not.

By their wording and their simplicity, the Rules sought to regularize the game, but not to rob it of its friendly, informal atmosphere. Umpires were nominated by each side but, while certain acts were deemed unacceptable, there were no specified penalties for misdeeds. Obviously, the players were expected to abide as much by the spirit of the Rules as by their letter.

When the guns of August, 1914 brought polo's first great era to a close, the Hurlingham Rules had expanded to some forty in number, absorbing such regional and national variations as seemed to benefit the game while rejecting those which served only to slow it down or make it unnecessarily complicated. They have not changed dramatically since.

In 1874, when the Rules were first introduced, the game of polo was restricted to a few cavalry regiments, the Navy and a small number of private clubs in England and Ireland. With the exception of the isolated remnant Indian game, it was a British sport. Over the next two or three decades, as polo spread rapidly around the world, two things remained constant: its profoundly English character and its Hurlingham Rules.

Polo arrived in Australia in 1876 and in New Zealand soon thereafter. Indeed, that first Australian club was founded at Warrnambool by none other than T.A. St. Quintin, late of the 10th Hussars. Polo spread across the English Channel to Spain and France and Belgium. It was played in north, east and South Africa; in Turkey and the Middle East; in Singapore and, of course, in India. Polo came to the Argentine in about 1883 and was even reintroduced to Persia. It was brought to the eastern United States in 1876 and, soon after, to California. And, it came to Canada.

With the exception of the United States (where the game was introduced by American Anglophiles who had seen it played on their regular business and social trips to England), the names that made up the memberships of the first polo clubs in continental Europe, in the Middle and Far East were British names. They were diplomats and government officials; businessmen, military attachés and those who could afford a residence away from the chill of an English winter.

Fred Mayer/World Polo Associates

Everywhere they went, whether former private club players, Hussars or Lancers, they carried a bag of sticks and balls and they carried the Rules. And, because of those rules, wherever they established new clubs, the game they played was essentially the same.

In the Argentine and the Dominions — Australia, New Zealand, South Africa and Canada — polo was an export that accompanied the millions of pounds of British investment capital that moved around the world as the Empire grew to the apex of its power toward the end of the nineteenth century.

The attraction of South Africa lay primarily in its mineral wealth, but in Argentina, Australia, New Zealand and Canada, what drew the syndicates of British investors was livestock: cattle and sheep to feed its fast-growing population. And it was through these investors and their sons that the game of polo found its way to Canada's West Coast, to British Columbia's interior valleys and, most dramatically, onto the vast grasslands of the Prairie West. ▓

1889
AND
ALL THAT

THE BIRTH OF THE CANADIAN GAME

CHAPTER 2

Lieutenant (later Rear-Admiral)
Sir Robert Arbuthnot, c. 1893 –
An early member of the Warspite's
polo team, he was later killed at
the Battle of Jutland.

WHEN POLO ARRIVED IN CANADA it was still a new phenome-
non, not yet a decade old. And here, as in England, it was the military that
led the way.

The first Canadian match has been dated to the summer of 1878, and it
featured members of the British Garrison stationed at the East Coast port of
Halifax, Nova Scotia. Although it was a beginning, polo did not then take root
and was not heard of again until more than a decade later.

In September of 1889, the *Halifax Recorder* reported that, during the
past summer, the game had regained some popularity and a mix of military
and civilian players had secured the enclosure of the Halifax Riding Grounds
for the purpose of playing polo. A gang of workmen had converted its
rough turf into a splendid field and well-attended matches were held regularly
each Tuesday and Friday at 4 p.m.

Looking west into the heart
of Alberta's foothills country —
Not much has changed since the
first great ranches were established
in the mid-1880s.

On the West Coast, too, 1889 was an important year and again the military provided the catalyst for the introduction of polo. In the spring of that
year, a team of officers of the Royal Navy's Pacific Station at Esquimalt issued
a challenge to the sporting gentlemen of neighbouring Victoria.

Although details of the match itself are unknown, history has recorded
the names of the players and the fact that they were "suitably equipped"
(meaning proper sticks and balls in lieu of the folkloric broom handles and
cricket balls that invariably marked "first matches" elsewhere).

The Navy was represented by lieutenants George Warrender and
T. Thynne, Dr. Pearson and Captain Lambton (in command of H.M.S. *Warspite*).
They played a Victoria foursome comprising Messrs. M.G. Drummond,
H.A. Barton, H.F. Newton and C.W. Ward. The final score is not known and
it seems to have been a one-time event, but it did mark the beginning of
what would be a unique, if brief, contribution to the history of polo. It was

only in Victoria that the British military made a formal and substantial contribution to the success and popularity of the game in Canada.

One could be forgiven for finding it odd that the Royal Navy had even the remotest interest in the thoroughly terrestrial game of polo. And yet, the officers of what was then the greatest expression of Britain's global hegemony may well have been more responsible for developing the international character of polo than their mounted counterparts from the army.

That was certainly the case as far as lifelong sailor Lord Mountbatten was concerned. A fine player and chronicler of the game (usually writing under the pen name "Marco"), Mountbatten has described the worldwide influence of Britain's naval polo teams in the game's earliest years. Polo was a feature of Royal Navy life on the island of Malta as early as 1874, making that club a near-contemporary of Hurlingham. Teams from ships of the Mediterranean Fleet played at bases everywhere from Gibraltar to Cairo while, across the Pacific, Australia, New Zealand, Fiji and

Samoa all saw games staged by the crews of visiting warships. The same was true for China and the Far East, for coastal Africa, the West Indies and the West Coast of the Americas.

With Esquimalt's importance as a British naval base, it is not surprising that the first game in 1889 was initiated by naval officers or, given their experience with the game, that it was played with proper equipment. No surprise, either, that at least one of those officers was more than just a hack player. In a 1936 article,

Mountbatten records that, on Malta in 1886, a four-some from H.M.S. *Dreadnought* won the first Army versus Navy match. On that team were a Lieutenant H.R.H. Prince George (later George V) and a Lieutenant (later Admiral) George Warrender.

The next recorded match took place in the summer of 1891. A Victoria newspaper of July 20th reported the following:

An enjoyable game of polo was played at Beacon Hill yesterday afternoon between the Victoria team and one from H.M.S. Warspite. Messrs. Cecil Ward, H.F. Newton, H.A. Barton and B. Powell played for Victoria and the Navy was represented by Lt. Sir Robert Arbuthnot, Lt. A.P. Ethelston, Dr. Pearson and Mr. C. St.A. Pearse. The game ended 7-5 in favor of the latter.

The *Warspite* must have departed Victoria soon thereafter since, according to Mountbatten, its polo team was active in Valparaiso and Santiago, Chile by 1893.

Many of the early Navy poloists went on to important careers in the Senior Service. Lieutenant Alfred Ethelston was promoted to commander and, in 1899, landed in South Africa with the Naval Brigade. He was killed in action at Gras Pan two months later. The Honorable Sir Hedworth L. Lambton, GCB, KCVO, the captain of the *Warspite,* rose to the rank of admiral of the fleet and served as commander-in-chief at Portsmouth during the Great War.

Sir Robert Arbuthnot (both a polo player and captain of the *Warspite's* cricket team) went on to command the 3rd Destroyer Flotilla before rising to the rank of rear-admiral, second-in-command (under George Warrender) of the 2nd Battle Squadron. He was killed in action at the Battle of Jutland and awarded the KCB posthumously.

Then-Lieutenant Warrender had perhaps the greatest career of them all. He had joined the Navy in 1873 and, after service in the Mediterranean and with the Pacific Station, he was promoted to captain in 1899. The following year he was largely responsible for Royal Navy operations during the Boxer Rebellion in China.

By June, 1914, he was a vice-admiral commanding the 2nd Battle Squadron of the Grand Fleet and, in 1915, he was commander-in-chief at Plymouth. Ill health would force his retirement the following year. Sir George John Scott Warrender (7th Baronet), KCB, KCVO, died in January, 1917.

Matches between the Royal Navy and the Victorians became a regular feature for the balance of the summer and fall and throughout 1892, the year in which the Victoria Polo Club was formally created. In that year, too, Victoria first played host to a visiting team as a foursome from Calgary, Alberta arrived for an August weekend of polo.

Since no formal records have survived from the early years of the Victoria Polo Club, any history of the game on Vancouver Island must rely on the vagaries of local newspaper coverage. Such sources indicate that the game was growing in popularity. Certainly there was a team in the Cowichan Bay area just north of Victoria, centred on the British enclave at Duncan, and at least one polo match was played there in September of 1893.

There is no mention of polo in the local press for 1894, but this is probably due more to a lack of significant matches than that the game was not being played, for in June of 1895, the Victoria Polo Club was reported to be readying itself for a season of matches with the blessing of no less a patron than the lieutenant-governor. Thirty-five members had paid their $5 subscription fee and regular play was scheduled for Tuesdays and Fridays.

The first match of the 1895 season was played between a combined team from the Victoria and Cowichan clubs and a foursome fielded jointly by the Army and Navy. The game, won by the military, was

played at Beacon Hill Park on Victoria's waterfront and special transport was scheduled to bring spectators from the city and surrounding area. Along with light refreshments there was entertainment by the band of H.M.S. *Royal Arthur* and, according to the press, the complete success of the day was a tribute to the club's "thoroughness in management."

In 1893, while based at Coquimbo in Chile, The *Royal Arthur* had become flagship of the Pacific Station. In an indication of how seriously the Navy took its polo, permission was immediately sought (and obtained) to bring the ponies of the ship's polo team along to its new base at Esquimalt, a passage of some thirty-four days' duration.

The game of polo seemed well on its way to becoming an integral part of the social and sporting life of a burgeoning provincial capital.

If the presence of a British army and navy were the driving force behind the introduction of polo on Canada's East and West coasts, such was not the case out on the grasslands of the Prairie West. Again, 1889 was the genesis year, but almost nothing else was the same.

Without benefit of well-mounted light horse regiments, country clubs or a tradition of playing team sports (indeed, without any real traditions of any kind), polo took hold in southern Alberta as it did nowhere else in Canada. The roots it put down in those first few years would prove deep and strong enough to sustain the game through the uncertainties of a boom and bust economy, through two world wars and periods of profound social change. While the popularity of polo waxed and waned in concert with forces beyond its control, from the moment it was established in the eastern slope foothills of the Canadian Rockies, it has never gone away.

Captain E.M. Wilmot is quite properly credited with founding the first polo club in Canada in 1889,

but the honour could as easily have gone to any of the other Englishmen who had gathered for a social visit at the Chinook Ranch the previous summer. As the story was told some forty years later by Maria Clarkson, who was present at that gathering, the idea of playing polo had been planted by a magazine article (most likely in *Land and Water*), in much the same way that it had been with the 10th Hussars.

From a historical perspective, Wilmot's good fortune in being accepted as the founder of prairie polo rests on his being the first of those assembled at the Chinook Ranch to have returned home for a visit. It could as easily have been Brooke, Garnett or any of the others. Certainly, whoever was first onto the train would have had strict instructions to bring back proper replacements for their rake handles and cricket balls.

Nevertheless, when Wilmot returned with his bag of polo sticks and balls (and, no doubt, at least one copy of "the Rules"), the effect on his hired hands and neighbouring ranchers was instantaneous. Within a year or two, there were at least four well-organized, disciplined foursomes based within a few miles of Wilmot's Pincher Creek ranch and practice games were already underway more than one hundred miles to the north around the booming cowtowns of High River and Calgary.

The question is "Why here?" Why did polo become so popular so quickly in southwestern Alberta? What is it about this foothills country that has sustained the game for more than a century when it has proved so transitory elsewhere?

The answer lies in the timing and nature of the first substantial wave of settlement to come into the country. Before the arrival of the first contingent of Mounted Police in 1874, there were, to all intents and purposes, no permanent white settlements across the breadth of Canada's southern grasslands. This land held little interest for the Canadian fur traders who long before had occupied the parkland and boreal forest belts to the north. Even the Americans, with their early development of steamboat traffic on Montana's upper Missouri, evinced little interest (save a thriving whisky trade with the resident Blackfoot) in the country that lay north of the river. Indeed, at the time the

Hurlingham Rules Committee was sitting down for its first meeting in England, the precise location of the international boundary across North America's western plains had not officially been established.

The decade of the 1870s set the stage for what would be the utter transformation of the high plains west (both American and Canadian). In the period following the end of the American Civil War, the countless herds of buffalo were all but eradicated, the resident Native populations were subdued and the first transcontinental railways had made their way across the empty heart of the continent.

Two things moved quickly to fill what amounted to a multi-million-acre vacuum. First came cattle as huge herds of semi-wild longhorns were driven north out of Texas to the railheads of Kansas and on north into the empty grasslands of Nebraska, Wyoming, the Dakotas and Montana.

And, following hard on the heels of those first cattle drives, was money; millions of dollars worth of investment capital looking to cash in on the coming boom.

Businessmen and speculators were lured by tales of great wealth produced from minimal (and almost risk-free) investment. The stories were circulated through newspapers and such books as General J.S. Brisbin's 1881 bestseller *Beef Bonanza: or How to Get Rich on the Plains.* They promised profit margins of twenty-five to fifty per cent and, remarkably, many of the stories they told were actually true. While eastern Americans made up many of the investment syndicates, there was also a tremendous interest on the part of English and Scottish capitalists, flush with the profits from a brilliant Empire. Fast-growing urban populations in both the United States and Britain, coupled with the new railways and even newer refrigeration technology, seemed to guarantee burgeoning markets and soaring profits.

The development of the Canadian plains lagged a decade or so behind America's and

Glenbow archives, NA-644-28

was not generally characterized by the fever pitch of the progress south of the newly surveyed 49th Parallel. With no permanent settlements other than those surrounding the new Mounted Police forts and no railway to move cattle to eastern or overseas markets, the first Alberta ranches were modest affairs. Often started by retired Mounties, they produced only enough cattle to feed the forts and fill federal government orders for the treaty beef promised to southern Alberta's Native populations in return for their signatures on Treaty #7 in 1877.

By 1880, though, things began to change rapidly. America's open ranges were already filled beyond their capacity, showing the strain of rampant overgrazing, and many of the large corporate ranching operations were looking

Sons of England Benevolent Society of Calgary on their annual coyote hunt, May 1895.

north toward the still-empty Canadian grasslands. By 1880, too, it was known that Canada's transcontinental railway — the Canadian Pacific — would follow a southern route across the Prairies and into British Columbia. In advance of the railway, the government began to encourage settlement and large-scale cattle ranching was considered the ideal catalyst.

Canada's close post-colonial relationship with the British government, coupled with the prospect of cheap grazing land and assured markets, proved irresistible to British (and eastern Canadian) capital and it began to flow freely into the Prairie West.

The stamp of approval for western development came from Canada's Governor General, the Marquess of Lorne. In 1881, he had travelled widely across the southern Prairies and duly reported his thoroughly positive impressions of the country and its prospects. Though he wistfully expressed his own aspirations for a ranching life, it was his entourage (particularly his secretary, Sir Francis De Winton) who returned full of enthusiasm to Ottawa and England and began the work of assembling moneyed syndicates.

The names of these early investors read like a who's who of Canadian and British wealth. With De Winton were Lord Shannon, Sir John Walrond Walrond and Lord Clinton, Montreal steamship magnate Sir Hugh Allan, Alexander Staveley Hill, the Earl of Lathom (later Lord Chamberlain of England), and a hundred others. The Quorn Ranch, established at the height of the boom in 1885, was owned by a syndicate from the Quorn Hunt Club in Leicestershire and even harebrained schemes like the ill-fated Military Colonization Company Ranche managed to find substantial infusions of English and Canadian capital.

With the promise of the railway and the political influence to secure their huge leases, the big corporate ranches moved to establish themselves in southwestern Alberta. Stocked with thousands of cattle purchased from Montana and from across the Great Divide in Idaho or Oregon, by 1885 the great ranches stretched, one six-hundred-forty-acre section upon another, in an unbroken patchwork from the Bow River Valley north of Calgary down the foothills belt almost to the American border.

There were smaller, family-owned operations, too, founded by American cowhands and trail bosses, retired Mounties and eastern stockmen drawn by the promise of abundant land and a new life in the West. From this mix, a unique society began to emerge, cobbled together from the familiarities of home and the practicalities imposed by a demanding new country.

In popular histories, much is made of the American influence. Southern Alberta, they

Fort Macleod, 1894 – This bustling town enjoyed a brief heyday as the capital of Alberta's "Cattle Kingdom."

Glenbow archives, NA-3287-1

Glenbow archives, NA-2084-1

assert, was settled by American longhorn cattle, managed by southern cowboys who first drove them north out of Texas and decided to stay and build their own personal empires. It is a nice, romantic connection to the "Wild West" of dime novels and Hollywood movies and it is the image which has sustained Calgary's annual Stampede Week celebrations since before the Great War. But, while there were Americans — even Texans — involved in the birth of Alberta's foothills ranching society, their influence was much less prevalent than generally believed. The flagpoles that marked the isolated ranch houses did not display the Stars and Stripes; they flew the Union Jack.

At the height of the cattle boom in the last two decades of the nineteenth century, voices on the dusty streets of Calgary, High River or Fort Macleod were less likely to exhibit the Texan's drawl than the Scottish brogue, the flat, "unaccented" cadence of Anglo-Montreal or the elegant speech that signalled an English public school education.

Many of those public school accents, polished at Rugby, Eton or Winchester, were likely to belong to a group of newcomers known as the "Remittance Men." Traditionally the second or third sons of English or Anglo-Irish gentry, they began to appear in southern Alberta from the birth of the big ranch era. Some were sent into the West to look after their father's or older brother's ranching investments; others were promised a regular stipend — their "remittance" — for as long as they stayed away from their family's affairs. Others simply came in search of a great adventure.

Their reputation among other settlers and townspeople was, to say the least, mixed. One oft-quoted Calgary newspaper article declared them "too lazy to plough, and too shiftless to own cattle," while others made great fun of their dress and their manners.

Alison Emde/Planet Photography

Brood mares at the Quorn Ranch, c. 1893 – The Quorn Ranch was one of several early Alberta ranches that were originally more interested in fine horses than in cattle. Owned by members of the Quorn Hunt in Leicestershire, the ranch had a brief but extravagant life. By the late 1890s, expenses had far outstripped revenues and the operation was finally sold in 1906.

Branding calves at the Pincher Creek Roundup, 1886.

Cecil Douglass, 1898 — Douglass was a long-time regular with the Millarville Polo Club. The photograph taken in England at around the time he left for Canada.

One ranch manager complained often to his investor-owners back in England as their sons spent summers on the ranch doing little except wearing out the horses, annoying the cows and, in his opinion, eating and drinking up most of what would have been the syndicate's profits.

Many remittance men were true to their reputation, spending only a few months in the country before moving on to greener pastures or returning to England (usually after their first hard prairie winter). Others stayed until the era of the big corporate ranches came to a close in the first decade of the twentieth century. But many, many others made permanent homes in Calgary and its surrounding foothills, starting their own ranches or businesses and leaving descendants who live in southern Alberta today.

And, with whatever else they achieved, a few of the remittance men brought the game of polo to the eastern slope of Canada's Rocky Mountains.

While it was scions of well-to-do English families who introduced Hurlingham's game to the Prairie West, their enthusiasm alone could neither have made it so widely popular nor sustained it for so many years. It had a far broader appeal.

Although Captain Wilmot is widely credited with founding the first organized polo club in Canada at Pincher Creek, he must have been only one of a number of Englishmen who brought at least a familiarity with the game to southern Alberta. How else can

one explain its almost spontaneous appearance in such widely spaced, isolated communities? There is simply nothing in the historical record to connect Wilmot directly with the teams that emerged almost simultaneously in Calgary and High River. And just how many sticks and balls could he possibly have had in that bag?

While there is little record of the game in Alberta between 1889 and 1892, a high level of behind-the-scenes activity was occurring on several fronts. H.B. Alexander is credited with forming the Calgary Polo Club in July, 1890, while Colin George Ross, who emerged as the most significant force in the early game, was holding practices on his ranch south of High River. The *Fort Macleod Gazette* announced the organization of a club in July, 1891 with the following terse release:

There was a meeting at the barracks on Tuesday evening for the purpose of forming a polo club. Serg. Wright acted as secretary. The organization was completed, and the sticks ordered to be sent for. The club starts with a large membership, including both police and citizens.

By mid-1892, four southern Alberta teams — Calgary, High River, Fort Macleod and Pincher Creek — were sufficiently well-organized to begin playing their first tournaments. One of the earliest took place not in Pincher Creek or Calgary, but far to the west on Vancouver Island.

A Victoria newspaper published the following report on the team's arrival:

The members of the Calgary Polo Team, who have travelled westward hundreds of miles over prairie and mountain for the sole and express purpose of playing the Victoria Club, arrived with their ponies — strong, close-knit little brutes — by last night's Yosemite [a ferry from the mainland]. The visitors were met at the dock by members of the home club and escorted to the Union Club, whose hospitality they will enjoy during their stay in the city. The ponies have been stabled at the Jockey Club grounds and will be given a little practice work this morning.

The game took place on August 25th on the grounds inside the racetrack at the Willows on the outskirts of the city. Victoria was represented by an experienced Navy-civilian squad of Pearse, Arbuthnot, Ward and Ethelston while Calgary fielded a team made up of D.H. McPherson, T.S.C. Lee, H.R. Jamison and H. Samson. At the last moment, Samson was replaced by a Mr. L.V. Cuppage, reported to be "one of the best players in Canada."

As was often the case, after covering pre-game activities in some detail, the Victoria papers neglected to publish the results, but, according to polo historian Daphne Lodwick, "it is believed that Calgary won."

The Calgary team (actually made up of players from both Calgary and High River) returned home quickly, in time for a major tournament to be held in Calgary the first week of September.

If the Victoria match of 1892 was just the beginning of a century-long tradition of southern Alberta polo, it represented a highlight in the brief early history of the game on Vancouver Island.

The success of the 1895 season in Victoria had continued into the following year, although the club was said to have hosted more races and gymkhanas than polo matches during the summer. Then, in late September, 1896, the polo club hosted its first (and last) multi-team tournament.

Under the joint patronage of Lieutenant Governor Dewdney and Admiral Palliser (and with the provincial Premier in attendance), a four-team, six-game round-robin began on the 23rd of the month at the Driving Park. Joining the hosts and neighbouring teams from Cowichan and the Esquimalt Naval Base was a foursome which had travelled all the way from Nicola Valley in the province's interior.

The tournament closed on the 28th and newspaper reports praised the close, exciting games and the quality of play by all involved. In the final analysis, however, the press delivered a mix of caution and enthusiasm:

The only weak feature of the tournament was the light patronage of the public. Provided a reasonable degree of encouragement be extended to the enterprising Victoria Club, there seems nothing in the way of securing an international match next year between representatives from California and British Columbia teams.

The hopes for an international tournament were never realized and Lodwick offers this terse obituary for Victoria polo: "The ships that were at Esquimalt at the time were ordered to sea and the club ceased to exist."

Glenbow archives, NA-993-6

The Millarville cricket team, 1897 – Cricket enjoyed a brief popularity among English settlers and the Millarville team was rated one of the best in the district. Polo players Norman Willans and "Dublin" Rodgers are seated in the middle row, first and second from the right.

NO PRETTIER GAME TO WATCH

1892–1900

IN THE THREE SHORT YEARS between 1889 and 1892, the game of polo put down deep roots in Alberta's foothills ranchlands. That foundation would support the game for more than a century and keep it strong while everywhere else in Canada, it drifted in and out of fashion with little continuity from one period to the next.

Most writers on the subject of early sports and leisure in Canada (especially in the West) tend to assume the obvious when it comes to polo. They accept it as an old and integral part of English sporting life — in much the same way they see cricket, croquet and fox hunting — which was naturally exported, along with its adherents, to a new land. Further, they see a game which remained, as it had in England, the preserve of the well-to-do.

Glenbow archives, NA-1129-3

Polo at Fort Macleod, 1894 – Early games were played on the flats beside the Oldman River which is visible in the background.

However, more recent studies, like those of Calgary historian John Varty, have challenged both of those earlier assumptions. Polo, of course, was not a long-established game at the time it came to the Canadian West; it was barely two decades old. Further, though it may have been imported along with other English sports, it quickly outstripped such things as cricket and fox hunting, neither of which ever found much enduring favour on the Prairies. Not that the early English ranchers didn't try.

There were some attempts to create a prairie variation of the hunt with the local coyotes substituting for the fox. Rather than the traditional pack of foxhounds, the dog of choice (or necessity) was a large, shaggy coursing hound that looked three parts Irish wolfhound and one part heaven-knows-what. The results were lamentable. If the idea was the sport of the hunt, the coyote was simply too uncooperative, usually opting to draw the dogs into a high-speed flat race over miles of open country. If the idea was varmint control, it was quicker and far more efficient to shoot them (though in neither case was the word "efficient" really appropriate).

The Fort Macleod polo team, winners of Alberta's first tournament, Fort Macleod, 1892 – (left to right) Montagu Baker, Stanley Pinhorne, Edmund Wilmot, A.E. Browning.

There is no question that in most of Canada polo did remain a sport for the privileged few. The nature of the game as it appeared in Toronto, Montreal and Vancouver was a reflection of its British origins: restricted to exclusive clubs whose membership represented the moneyed élite.

The Mounted Police team, Fort Macleod, 1892 – (left to right) George Ross, Major Davidson, Sergeant Sam Heap, Captain White Fraser and Inspector Montagu Baker. George Ross, never a member of the force, is obviously visiting for a game. The other players were all part of the garrison at Fort Macleod, but surprisingly, polo was never officially encouraged or sanctioned by the Mounted Police.

Throughout the early period, many of the early English players either returned home or moved on to other "opportunities." Several would leave at the turn of the century to fight in the Boer War and never come back to Canada. Others simply dropped from sight. Still, the loss of several founding players did little to slow the game's popularity or progress.

There was never a formal military presence in the Canadian Prairie West. There was no equivalent to the United States cavalry or to the British army in India. But the Mounties were here, even before the first settlers, and their presence was a constant and substantial influence on the country's early development.

The Mounted Police was a new force when it came west in 1874 to close the whisky forts that were flourishing just north of the newly surveyed international boundary along the 49th parallel. They established the posts which would grow into the cities of Fort Macleod, Lethbridge and Calgary and many early policemen took their retirement and stayed in the country to establish some of the first ranches, principally to supply cattle to the new Native reserves.

Fort Macleod emerged as the first "capital" of the new territory. What government there may have been was administered from the town and businesses that grew up around the police barracks to serve both the force and the burgeoning ranches that stretched west toward the mountains. It was hoped — even assumed — that the C.P.R. would come through town, choosing the Crow's Nest Pass as its route through the Rockies.

By 1890, however, the country had changed dramatically. The transcontinental railway had gone through Calgary rather than Fort Macleod and the town soon lost its place at the centre of the ranching empires. Calgarians were even requesting the transfer to their city of Justice James Macleod, the man who had helped lead the Mounties west and given both towns their name.

In southern Alberta (and, a few years later, in the British Columbia Interior) the game may have been introduced by remittance men, but they did not, for more than a moment, keep the field to themselves. Varty has examined the minute books of the various foothills clubs and discovered, in their membership rolls, the local heavyweight names one would expect: the prosperous ranch owners and managers, the retired Army officers, bankers and lawyers. But he also finds the lists leavened with the names of store clerks, farmers and cowhands. Such was obviously not the case in Victoria; neither would it ever be in Vancouver, Toronto or Montreal.

This broader participation acted as a buffer against the effects of the essentially unstable population of remittance men.

It is unlikely that any in the first Mounted Police contingents had played polo in England (though some had seen service in the British army), but later recruits included members of the same "squirearchy" that had spawned the remittance men. When the first polo clubs were springing up in southwestern Alberta, the Mounted Police presence was already in decline. Still, the garrison remained the social centre of Fort Macleod. It was at the garrison that the organizational meeting of the polo club was held in 1891 (with Colonel Macleod as its president) and it was the Mounties versus the civilians when they began to play the game on the flats beside the Oldman River.

The following notice appeared in the *Fort Macleod Gazette* of April 21, 1892:

Col. Macleod has kindly presented a cup to be played for by polo clubs this and succeeding years...to be played [for] the first time at Macleod at the time of the race meeting. ...Another cup will also be played for on the 1st and 2nd of June. This is a cup presented by Macleod people.

With this announcement, the first era of tournament polo in Alberta was born and at the beginning of June, teams from Pincher Creek, High River and Calgary came to town to join their host foursome in trying for the new cups.

The trophy rules were simple and straightforward. The Colonel Macleod Cup would first be played for in Fort Macleod at a tournament open to any and all polo clubs. In subsequent years, the games would be held on the home ground of the defending champion. Any club which could win the cup for two years in succession would keep it.

Matches for the Macleod Cup would be played in Fort Macleod at a time decided by the hosts. It, too, would be open to all-comers and become the property of any club that could capture it twice in a row. Individual cups were promised to the players on the winning teams.

The tournament would settle the first winners of the trophies through a four-game elimination, to be followed by a separate championship game for each cup. The June 9th issue of the *Gazette*, though presumably reporting its first polo matches, offered not only the hard results, but added a remarkably sophisticated critique of the level of play, including several quite specific observations on the individuals involved.

The first game of the tournament pitted the hosts against Pincher Creek. "Play was rather slow," opined the *Gazette*, attributing it to a lack of practice by the Pincher Creek squad. Fort Macleod won the game 4-1.

Game two saw Calgary against High River, "In the opinion of many, one of the best in the tournament, [with]...many brilliant pieces of individual work." The Calgary team was obviously not up to its potential (Tom Critchley played the entire match with only one pony) and High River came away with a 4-3 win.

On day two, it was winners versus losers with High River dispatching Pincher Creek 5-2 and Fort Macleod handling Calgary with ease.

Next day saw the final for the Macleod Cup and the *Gazette* waxed eloquent on the quality of the play and reaction of the large crowd:

The first final, that for the cup presented by the citizens, was played on Saturday morning and brought out a large number of spectators. It was a splendid exhibition of polo, and, as the time neared the end, and the play became, if possible, harder and faster, the enthusiasm of the crowd knew no bounds.

(left to right) H.B. Alexander, Frank Macnaghten, Tom Critchley, T.S.C. Lee, Calgary, 1894.

That Fort Macleod emerged with a 6-4 win over High River might have accounted for at least some of the high excitement.

That same evening, the two foursomes rode out again, this time to contest the Colonel Macleod Cup. The *Gazette,* tersely this time, records a 5-0 "walkover" for High River. The paper offered an odd rationalization for the home team's poor play: "The Macleod men seemed to be demoralized by their victory of the morning."

All in all, this first Alberta tournament was judged a thoroughgoing success and the *Gazette* could not resist taking to its bully pulpit:

The games were watched by large crowds, and when play was close and exciting, as it most frequently was, the enthusiasm of the spectators rose to a high pitch. It is little wonder that the game has caught on here, for there is no prettier game to watch, and the qualities that go to make a good polo player — dashing horsemanship, courage, quickness and sureness of eye, and strength of wrist and arm, are those which are especially dear to the western heart.

The roster of players who came for this first major tournament offers an interesting look at the kind of men who built the foundation for the prairie game.

Pincher Creek's Louis Garnett was one of the first remittance men to settle in the area, arriving with his brother, Jack, in 1879. His place in local history is secure, based upon his insistence on appearing every night for dinner in full evening dress. He said it was to "keep from reverting to savagery."

Garnett's teammate, Herbert Rimington Mead, was a pioneer doctor in the district, starting his practice about 1886. A true child of the Raj, his father was assistant surgeon to the Indian army and head of the Bombay Hospital. He was widely respected in Pincher Creek for his compassion and humanity, things which may have cost him his life. He died of pneumonia in 1898 after treating workmen who had fallen victim to a diphtheria epidemic during the construction of the Canadian Pacific's Crowsnest Pass line.

Two members of the host team from Fort Macleod were H.S. Pinhorne and Edmund M. Wilmot. Although Wilmot is generally credited with starting polo in the Pincher Creek area, he never appeared on that team's list of players at any tournament. Indeed, his presence at the Macleod Cup matches is the only record of his participation in any Alberta tournament whatsoever.

The story of Stanley Pinhorne would have been well-known to everyone in the southern Alberta ranching community. He was the nephew of Alexander Staveley Hill, an English lawyer and M.P. who was principal investor in the Oxley Ranche, one of the area's largest (and most troubled). Stanley had been sent from England to act as his uncle's eyes and ears in what became a protracted series of lawsuits between Hill and his resident manager. The suits dragged on for five years until, in 1890, Pinhorne found himself installed as manager of a reorganized New Oxley Ranche.

Popular among his peers, he was an active member of the stockmen's association (and a dedicated polo player). But the years of acrimony, the pressures of running a large ranch and, probably, the loneliness of a single man's life took their toll and Pinhorne took to drink. In early October, 1892, he was found dead in his bed, a pistol in his hand. He was not yet forty years old.

Among the players from High River was Herbert Samson. An Oxford-educated remittance man from a banking family, he was co-founder of the Bar XY Ranch and a respected officer of the Alberta Stockgrowers Association. He travelled with the Calgary team to Victoria in 1892 and became a mainstay of High River polo, appearing regularly in tournaments until at least 1896.

At the turn of the century, he left to fight in the Boer War and never came back to Alberta, deciding instead to remain in South Africa to begin a new ranching enterprise. In a 1901 letter to a friend, Samson says the decision grew from his distaste for the increasing numbers of homesteaders then flooding into the High River district.

From Calgary came two of the Critchley brothers, Tom and Oswald, in the first expression of a family passion for polo that would be a dominating force in the Alberta game for more than twenty years.

It is interesting to note that Calgary did not send a full complement to the tournament, relying instead on a Macleod player, Mounted Police Staff Sergeant Sam Heap, to complete their roster. This, and the fact that Tom Critchley played the same pony through at least one entire match, give a good indication of how difficult it was in those early days to travel the distances necessary to attend a tournament. A good many newspaper accounts from the period take pains to point out how far one team or another had travelled to make the game. A network of railway spurs would eventually make the transportation of men — and especially of ponies — a much easier proposition. At the time of the first Macleod tournament, however, the line from Calgary through High River to the Fort was still several months from completion.

The Calgary Polo Club held its first tournament in early September, 1892, but the team had been busy since its visit to Fort Macleod in June. Just before making the long trek to Victoria, a Calgary foursome had accepted an invitation to play in a three-team tournament during the annual exhibition and race meeting at the territorial capital in Regina. Arriving in early August, Oswald and Tom Critchley, together with Jamison and Cuppage, won both their matches against teams from Regina and the Qu'Appelle Valley. Although there was obviously some strong early polo activity in what would become the province of Saskatchewan, the inconsistent appearance of teams from Regina, Qu'Appelle and Indian Head over the next decade suggest that the game never really took a firm hold.

It has been said that Victoria was one of the participants at the first Calgary tournament, but there is no hard evidence they had followed Calgary back from their West Coast match only ten days earlier. Pincher Creek would certainly have been invited, but perhaps the travel was too much for them and they failed to appear. So it would be Calgary, Fort Macleod and High River playing for the Calgary Polo Club's new Challenge Cup.

As at Fort Macleod, many of the players were on their way to becoming fixtures of the game in southern

Alison Emde/Planet Photography

The Calgary Challenge Cup – Presented at the first Calgary tournament in September, 1892, the sterling silver trophy has been in continuous play ever since, making it probably the oldest such prize in North America. The engraved plate on the front of the trophy was copied from a photograph of the team which had won the first western Canadian tournament held three months earlier in Fort Macleod.

Alberta while others would make only a brief mark on the record. There was also evidence of the players' changing allegiances, something which would continue to be a characteristic of club membership throughout the period.

Calgary was again represented — as it nearly always was — by a Critchley, in this case, Tom. His brother Oswald, who had played earlier in Fort Macleod, was perhaps already on his way back to England after the death of his first wife. Also playing for the host team were club founder H.B. Alexander, H.R. Jamison and Louis Cuppage; for the latter two, a final appearance.

Albert Browning was back for Fort Macleod, as was Mounted Police Inspector Montagu Baker. They were joined by Hugh Davidson and Staff Sergeant Sam Heap, Calgary's borrowed fourth from the previous June.

High River sent three of its Colonel Macleod Cup-winning team: C.G. Ross, Herbert Samson and Duncan McPherson. William K. Humfrey (one of the Pincher Creek "originals" of 1889) substituted for Harry Robertson.

The *Calgary Herald,* enthusiastic about the prospects, asserted that the teams, who could be seen "...cantering round the streets on handsome little ponies," were "...without doubt the finest polo players in Canada."

According to the *Calgary Herald,* the tournament was a three-game affair opening with Calgary versus High River, to be followed by the winner versus Fort Macleod. High River defeated Calgary and then, in front of a large crowd, rode out to hand Fort Macleod a 10-0 thrashing and claim the Challenge Cup.

Published tournament accounts for the years 1893 and 1894 are, to say the least, confused and even contradictory. In those years, there were three trophies officially in play in Alberta — the Colonel Macleod Cup, the Macleod Cup and the Calgary club's Challenge Cup — but who won what and from whom is difficult to ascertain with any certainty.

Adding to the profusion (and confusion) of polo trophies, Calgary made another trip to Regina in mid-August, 1893 to play for the Hayter Reed Challenge Cup, said to represent polo supremacy of the Territories. Facing teams from Regina, Qu'Appelle and Grenfell, Saskatchewan, Calgary swept through undefeated, even beating an all-star team in the closing match. What happened to the Hayter Reed trophy is unknown, but, in the erratic history of Saskatchewan polo, it is never again referred to by name.

In mid-September, 1893, a five-day tournament and gymkhana was advertised for Calgary stating that the Calgary and Colonel Macleod trophies would be up for grabs. It may have been the only Alberta tournament of the year. Again, it was Fort Macleod and High River who came to town.

In the first game, a High River foursome played Fort Macleod. After a scoreless first quarter, Macleod drew first blood, but ultimately they were no match for High River who prevailed 6-3.

Alberta's uncertain weather challenged the next day's game, as the *Gazette* reported the story:

---- •-||-╪◆♦◊♦◆╪-||-• ----

It snowed so hard during the morning that there did not seem to be a possibility of getting the game off. The snow stopped about noon however, and at four o'clock, although the west half of the ground was still white, it was decided to start the game.

---- •-||-╪◆♦◊♦◆╪-||-• ----

Glenbow archives, NA-460-6

Calgary managed five quick goals in the first quarter and defeated Fort Macleod by a final score of 6-4.

Some speculation is necessary to make sense of the results. The rules for the Macleod Cup stated that it must be played for at a tournament in Fort Macleod, but there were no matches reported there in 1893. A later article in *Polo* magazine states that Macleod lost its cup to Calgary in 1893, so it is possible that they brought it north that September and put it up for play. If they did, the newspapers make no mention of it.

Press coverage of the tournament was spotty, but the last two games, at least, were recorded in detail. The name High River was engraved again on the Calgary Challenge Cup for 1893 following a 4-1 win over the host team. Calgary then responded with a 4-3 defeat of High River to take the Colonel Macleod Cup.

While reporting of the matches was thin, the *Gazette* went to some length to cover the social aspects of its team's Calgary trip:

On Sunday night the teams were invited to a grand ball in the new opera house. This was an immense success.... Crowds of pretty and nice dressed women, a splendid floor and a charming little supper. On the whole, the members of the Macleod team say they were treated right royally, and would gladly make the trip over again.

The most intriguing match of the 1893 Alberta polo season may have taken place in Mitford, a small foothills community west of Calgary. Calgary and High River were invited to play a couple of matches (with each team winning one), after which there was to be a game staged between Natives from the Sarcee and Stoney tribes. Unfortunately, details of the match are not recorded. Certainly, there is no evidence that polo ever became more than a brief curiosity among the Treaty #7 nations.

Weak newspaper coverage leads again to confusion about 1894. There was a tournament at Calgary in mid-July again pitting the hosts against Macleod and High River. High River must have been off its game since the name Fort Macleod is engraved on the Calgary Cup. The Fort team probably won the Macleod Cup, too, since the *Gazette* reports that it was on display in a Fort Macleod store in August. Calgary took the Colonel's trophy for the second year in a row and, according to the rules, was entitled to keep it. Whether they exercised that privilege is not known, but the Colonel Macleod Cup was never played for again and has since vanished.

In that year, there was to be a tournament at Fort Macleod toward the end of September, perhaps at its usual time in conjunction with the annual agricultural fair. According to the *Gazette,* a new field had been established in August. Laid out inside the racetrack, it was one hundred forty-four by two hundred eighty-five yards and said to be "...a good one."

What happened on that new field is open to speculation; indeed, a full tournament may not have been held. Calgary did come to play and it must have been a one-sided affair.

New polo field or not, Fort Macleod polo had run into trouble. Despite its earlier Calgary and Macleod cup wins, the *Gazette* ran an editorial on October 5th which strongly criticized the local effort against Calgary:

The polo season...wound up a few days ago at Macleod when Calgary beat the home team in a very decisive way. We cannot account for the crushing defeat of the Macleod representatives on previous form, and must suppose that the simple reason lay in the fact that the north was stronger by a good deal.

But the editorial went on to discuss something of more importance than the town's wounded civic pride. It seems that during the tournament there was talk of forming an Alberta polo association with definite headquarters and official delegates from the seven extant clubs. According to the *Gazette,* this association would arbitrate all disputes (and, presumably, ensure consistent rules of play).

What concerned the paper most, however, was the problem of players having allegiances to more than one club. The *Gazette* would like to see the new association register players with a single club at the start of the season to ensure that each team could count on fielding a well-disciplined, practiced foursome for major matches.

Talk of an association went nowhere during the tournament, and one can sympathize with the paper's frustration. It had touched on an issue which would profoundly affect southern Alberta polo in the next decade. More than any other club in those early years, Fort Macleod suffered the divided loyalties and outright defection of several good players. While teams like Calgary and High River could draw on a steadily growing pool of well-established talent, the Macleod club never seemed able to carry a strong core of leading players from one tournament to the next. Over the years, personnel changed often as the Mounted Police reassigned staff elsewhere and others, like Wilmot, left the area. In the tournaments of 1893 and 1894, Macleod had been led by Albert Browning and Sam Heap, but the other two positions rarely saw the same names. The team used founding member Dr. George Kennedy (the garrison's surgeon from 1878 to 1887), Browning's brother and Michael Holland, another player "on loan" from the Pincher Creek district.

Perhaps it was a reflection of the town's general decline as a thriving centre for the ranching community but, after 1894, Fort Macleod was no longer a factor in southern Alberta polo. The game's obituary appeared in the *Gazette* on July 9th, 1897:

In view of the recent polo tournament at Pincher Creek, in which four clubs competed, it seems a pity that the interest in polo should have so died out in Macleod that it has no team to represent it, nor has had for the past two seasons. The Macleod Agricultural Society will be holding their annual fair this fall and a polo tournament between the different clubs in the district would prove a great attraction. Such a tournament was advertised last year, but eventually fell through. Some of our local polo enthusiasts should take the matter up.

Apparently, what local polo enthusiasm still remained was not enough to rekindle the flame.

There would be new Fort Macleod teams in the new century and the Macleod Cup would again be up for play but, by 1895, the team's greatest years were over.

As Macleod declined, so the Pincher Creek district flourished as a centre for first-class polo. Those ranchers and wranglers who first joined Edmund Wilmot on the Alberta Ranche in 1889 had continued their fierce attachment to the game. Although they were not often seen at tournaments in Calgary, High River or Macleod during the early years, the Pincher Creek players had enough competition among themselves to sustain four permanent teams and any number of necessary alternate combinations.

The story of the rise of polo in the Pincher Creek district clearly shows features that characterized the southern Alberta game, especially where player mobility and the formation of new clubs are concerned.

Polo at Beaver Creek, 1894 –
(left to right) Robert Milvain,
Michael Holland, P.L. Briggs and
Billy Humfrey.

A group of young "Remittance Men" at the Beaver
Creek Ranch, 1894 – Billy Humfrey (back row, right) and
the ranch's co-owners Robert Milvain (back row, second from
left) and Michael Holland (front row, centre) were among
the first polo players in the Pincher Creek district.

Brandy and soda race at the Calgary Polo Club gymkhana, 1895 – The figure in the left foreground is a Mounted Police sergeant in full dress uniform.

The charm of local legend notwithstanding, Wilmot's early adherents were not entirely a gaggle of rough cowboys learning an elegant game from a recently arrived member of England's landed gentry. Neither were they simply a collection of rich wastrels with Oxbridge accents and too much time on their hands. Rather, those who first gathered on the Alberta Ranche represented the variety of settlers who built the foundations of a new society.

Wilmot certainly had money. Considering the size of the operation and the other names in the syndicate, his family's investment in the Alberta Ranche must have been substantial.

Lionel Brooke apparently had more money than he knew what to do with. The Oxford-educated son of Sir Reginald Brooke, he was at best an amateur rancher but his extensive family ensured a steady and substantial series of inheritances which he used to indulge his passion for foreign travel and painting. Brooke served in the Boer War and eventually left the district to spend several years on Vancouver Island. Still, he returned often to Alberta, once, according to his obituary, by hiring a taxicab to drive him all the way from Victoria. He died in 1939 at the home of friends in Pincher Creek at the age of seventy-nine.

The Garnett brothers, Louis and Jack, were among the first to come into the country, building an

impressive mansion known as "The Grange" and dressing for dinner, but they succumbed to the lure of the Klondike gold rush, leaving what they called their "white elephant" to burn to the ground a year or two later.

When the great house burned, it was in the possession of former Mounted Policeman Sam Heap. Sam was from Lancashire. Sent to Iowa as a "farm student," he soon left to tour the western states with a stock theatre company. In 1888, he was drawn to the romance of life in the Mounted Police and ended up posted to Fort Macleod.

Holding the rank of staff sergeant, he was a founding member of the Macleod polo team, playing regularly in all the early tournaments. He married the local schoolteacher in 1897 and left the force to take up residence at the Garnett place. His brother, Thomas, one of Wilmot's originals, lived nearby. Sam did not take to ranching and rejoined the Mounties for a time, eventually retiring to become Fort Macleod's postmaster. He lived until 1948.

Charles Kemmis was born in New Brunswick in 1874 and settled in the Livingstone country north of Pincher Creek. He worked at a succession of ranches until 1899 when he left for Calgary to study law. Called to the Alberta bar, he was eventually appointed solicitor for the town of Pincher Creek. D.G. Plunkett, too, worked for the town, serving as secretary, deputy sheriff and police magistrate until his death in 1940. Both men continued their association with the Pincher Creek polo team until well into the next century.

Two of the early Pincher Creek players founded families which, to this day, figure prominently in the history of the province. The first of the Lynch-Stauntons and the Milvains arrived in the West in the late 1870s. While both had some money behind them, neither really met the test of the true remittance man.

A.H. Lynch-Staunton came west from Ontario in 1877 with the Mounted Police. His father was a Dominion land surveyor who spent some years in the Prairie West drawing his perfect lines across the open grasslands. At eighteen years of age, A.H. was assigned to build a police post and horse-rearing operation just east of Pincher Creek. He lasted with the force only a couple of years before taking his leave and setting up a small ranching operation in the district. He was joined in 1883 by his brother, Richard, who had come west as a chainman on his father's survey crew and, eventually, by a third brother in 1896. They built a strong ranching operation near the Oldman River north of Pincher Creek and the family remains a presence in that country to this day, boasting an Alberta lieutenant governor among its members.

Although these Lynch-Stauntons came from England to Ontario some years before, there was another branch of the family that went even farther afield. One Lynch-Staunton was a member of a top-flight polo team from Argentina that made a well-publicized tour of England in 1912.

Robert H. Milvain arrived in the Pincher Creek district in 1878, the first of three brothers to come to Canada. By 1888, when brother James arrived, Bob Milvain and his partner Michael Holland (said to be the son of a Canterbury Cathedral canon) were ranching in the Beaver Creek area of the Porcupine Hills northeast of town. For a few years, Jimmy cowboyed for a number of spreads in the area, including the old Walrond, until he went into partnership with Irishman Harold Mackintosh. All four were fiercely dedicated to their polo.

In about 1897, Robert Milvain dissolved his partnership and headed for the Klondike. He is said to have amassed a decent fortune and returned to England after the First World War. His brother Jimmy married Mackintosh's sister, Winnifred, and they ranched together until his death in 1945. Their first son, James Valentine Milvain, studied law and rose to become the first native-born Albertan to serve as chief justice of the province.

A.H. Lynch-Staunton, Holland and the elder Milvain were "originals." Though Holland played for Fort Macleod in the 1893 Calgary tournament, in that year he founded his own club at Beaver Creek. In August, 1894, the team hosted a tournament and gymkhana on the flats beside the creek.

Visiting teams came from Fort Macleod and Pincher Creek, the latter being matched against the host foursome in first day's draw. For Pincher Creek, it was Garnett, Dr. Mead, Geddes and retired Mountie R.B. ("Chappie") Clarkson. Their hosts were Holland, Philip Briggs, Robert Milvain and W.K. Humfrey. Beaver Creek triumphed by 7-3, with Humfrey accounting for six of the goals.

The next day it was Beaver Creek against Macleod. It was one of Fort Macleod's last games and they acquitted themselves well. Dr. Kennedy, the Browning brothers and Sam Heap played Beaver Creek to a 6-goal draw at the end of regulation time and it took seven minutes before the hosts could score the winner. According to the *Gazette,* the game was "a corker...all through it was for blood."

Beaver Creek captured all the silverware on offer that day: the Pincher Creek Challenge Cup, the Garnett brothers' tankards and their own Beaver Creek Cup. From the account of the game, they probably owed much of their success to the play of W.K. Humfrey.

William Keys ("Billy") Humfrey was involved in nearly every early match and tournament. He played for Pincher Creek at Fort Macleod in June, 1892 and for High River in Calgary later that year. His name appears twice on the Calgary Cup, first for High River in 1892 and again for Macleod, the 1894 winners.

Irish-born to a landed family, Humfrey was the proprietor of the "Roodie" Ranch just west of Pincher Creek and polo was clearly one of the great loves of his life. He always seemed able to find the time to travel considerable distances for the sake of a good match and many photographs of polo matches and gymkhanas on the field at the Roodie survive.

(left to right) George Ross, Frank Macnaghten, O.A. Critchley and Addie Hone were four of the finest players and patrons of the first era.

Humfrey had all the earmarks of the classic remittance man, probably using family money to establish his ranch in the mid-1880s. His widowed mother, Maria, and at least one sister joined him there in 1886. Maria eventually married Chappie Clarkson and they took over the operation of the ranch. Billy Humfrey was not among the players at a major local tournament in July, 1897, so it is reasonable to assume that he must already have left the district. He later served in the Boer War and then remained in South Africa where he joined the South African constabulary.

The growth of polo in the Pincher Creek district was typical of the way in which it developed in the Canadian West (and in the states of Washington and Idaho as well). The game would begin at some specific centre, drawing a few players from a wide area. As it took root (and the need for competition increased), a player from an outlying ranch would convince his neighbours or hired hands to give it a try and a new team might be born.

Isolated from the rest of the province, the small group of Pincher Creek players quickly divided and subdivided into at least four — and sometimes five or six — teams, each one developing its own identity. The result was easier, more regular practice and much less travel for a good, competitive match. For tournaments outside the area, the pool of available talent was much deeper and a strong foursome could usually be conjured from the best in the district. More teams also meant greater access to quality mounts and, for a tournament, the best string of ponies could be assembled in much the same way as players. It also meant that older (and wealthier) players could provide real assistance to young up-and-comers who might not otherwise be able to afford top quality ponies or cover the cost of a ticket to Calgary or even Spokane.

Glenbow archives, NA-5554-10

In 1895, Allan Kennington organized another subdivision of the Pincher Creek core. With the first Sunday afternoon practices at his ranch on the north fork of the Oldman River, he assembled a small group of players which became the strongest (and longest-lived) club in the southwest. The names, at first, were familiar: Jimmy Milvain and the ubiquitous Billy Humfrey, together with W.E. Smith and Kennington himself. With Humfrey's early departure, Harry Gunn would be tapped to complete the foursome.

The core of the original North Fork team appeared at Pincher Creek's Dominion Day tournament of July 1st and 2nd, 1897. The *Fort Macleod Gazette* (in the same issue in which it bemoans the lack of interest in its own team) provides a brief account of the scores and a complete list of the players for each of the four competing teams.

The list is instructive since it reveals an association clearly in transition. North Fork was present, but Beaver Creek was gone, along with its founders Bob Milvain and Michael Holland. The Pincher Creek team comprised four names — Hogan, Heard, Kuntz and Holloway — that had not been seen before (and only rarely seen again). There was also a South Fork team, the presence of Chappie Clarkson indicating that it was probably based at the Roodie Ranch.

The fourth team, called the "Freebooters," was clearly a pick-up assemblage of senior players who may have got together to fill out the draw and enjoy one last swing at the ball with old friends. Their name was taken from an English all-star team of the same period, which surely indicates that someone in the district was keeping abreast of the game in the homeland. Louis Garnett was probably captaining his last team before heading for the Klondike and riding out with him were then-retired staff sergeant Sam Heap and A.H. Lynch-Staunton.

South Fork, under Clarkson, had Sam's brother Tom and the peripatetic Lionel Brooke, while Kennington, Gunn and Milvain formed the heart of the North Fork team.

If anyone thought the Freebooters were simply along for the ride, the scoring clearly suggests otherwise. In the first game, South Fork beat Pincher Creek 7-4 while the old-timers outlasted North Fork by 4-3. On the second day, the Freebooters ran South Fork hard and handled them easily, 7-1, South Fork declining even to contest the fourth quarter.

In the early spring of 1897, the association for which the *Gazette* had lobbied a few years earlier finally came into being. The Southern Alberta Polo Association appointed representatives from each of its member teams and managed to draw up and publish a set of bylaws and regulations. Dr. Mead was elected the association's first president, but it was likely the only polo highlight in that last year of his life. He had broken his leg early in the season and was still confined to his home some months later.

Glenbow archives, NB-9-4

H.B. ("Harry") Alexander – Irish-born rancher, adventurer and first president of the Calgary Polo Club.

How long the fledgling southern Alberta association lasted is not known, but by the close of the decade, nearly all of Wilmot's "originals" were retired from the game or gone from the country. But with the start of the new century, there would be another generation of players ready to lead the North Fork polo team through its greatest years.

In the years before the Canadian Pacific Railway transformed the small Mounted Police outpost of Fort Calgary into the booming centre of the foothills ranching country, most early settlers and their first herds of cattle came into the country not from the east but up from the south along the old ox-team supply road from the Missouri River steamboat terminal at Fort Benton, Montana.

The small community of High River grew at a point on the trail where it crossed the Highwood River about fifty miles south of Calgary. The town lies at the edge of the foothills belt with the great original ranch leases strung out behind it to the west and the broad, flat expanse of prairie stretching away before it to the east.

Although High River was a strong presence at the very first tournaments, it would be eight years before the town had a "proper" polo club with its own grounds. From the start, however, High River and its players established a remarkable record of top-flight tournament play. Much of that success can be attributed to George Ross. The first games and practices were held on his ranch and, while several other local ranch owners were skilled players, Ross' position as team captain was never challenged. Almost from the very first practices, he also managed to attract a number of young cowboys

to the game. It was these Alberta-raised players who would become the backbone of the great High River teams of the next two decades.

From the beginning, there were close connections between Calgary and the High River area. Before the Calgary & Edmonton Railway built its line south to Fort Macleod in 1892, the fifty miles between them meant that most major High River ranchers kept some sort of secondary residence in Calgary. For some, Calgary was home base and the High River ranch more an investment and prairie equivalent to a "country estate."

The welter of business, social and family relationships among the ranching and business communities of both towns makes for some heavy sledding when trying to sort out exactly who's who. That complexity carried over onto the polo field, especially in the early years. Billy Humfrey seems to have played for everyone at one time or another, but there were several others, too, whose allegiance was more to the joy of the game than to a particular club. Harry Alexander, for example, played a few games for High River while still a leading light of the Calgary club. In the mid-1890s, there were several matches and tournaments where club affiliations were set aside and everyone simply chose up sides as if it were a sandlot softball game.

Even with all the comings and goings, High River had two strengths in the early years. One was certainly George Ross and the other was a deep pool of talent which ensured that whatever particular foursome assembled on any given day, it would have to be reckoned a favourite. In addition to Ross and Herbert Samson, there were two names of particular significance in those formative years: D.H. McPherson and A.H. Eckford.

Duncan McPherson came into the High River area around 1887. The son of a British general with experience in India, McPherson may already have known something about polo. He had been in the West for some time and risen to the rank of inspector in the Mounted Police. His father was a major investor in Eckford's High River Horse Ranch and he probably came to High River to manage the property. Duncan likely joined Ross for the first practices at the Little Bow and he played for the team in both 1892 tournaments and in the Calgary matches of 1893. He obviously had the passion (and the money) to make the long trip to Victoria in 1892. Though his early impact was considerable, he was not in the country very long. For reasons unknown, he returned to England mid-decade.

In 1887, A.H. Eckford was working on the ranch as a common hand for thirty dollars a month. He had been in Canada since about 1884 and is said to have been involved in the Northwest Rebellion. He may have been working for room and board, but he was no common hand. His father, Major Haldane Eckford, was major shareholder in the place, together with his partners, the lords Strathcona and Mount Stephen and General McPherson. When his father died in 1896, Herbert became sole proprietor of the nearly 7,500 acres that comprised the High River Horse Ranch. In one year, it is said, Eckford's ranch handled 2,300 head.

Eckford first appeared for High River in the 1893 Calgary tournament and, from that day forward for more than a decade, he was a regular with the team. After nearly thirty years in the district, he sold out in 1914, returned to his family estate in Ayrshire, Scotland and served, with the rank of major, in the Great War.

The transfer of the ranch was big news at the time, its American purchasers paying $100,000 cash to acquire the property. Calgary's *Albertan* played the story as follows:

The money has been paid in and the papers turned over. It is one of the biggest real estate deals that has been put through in Calgary for a long while, and the best part of it is that it is a real sale, and not one based on two per cent coin and 98 per cent promises to pay.

The new owners, operating the property under the name Round T Ranch, would continue Eckford's involvement with polo after the Great War. And Eckford himself would later play an important role in trying to save the High River Club from the ravages of the Great Depression.

By 1898, the sixteen miles between Ross' place and the town was proving an impediment to regular practice and he obtained ten acres of land a mile south of town. The owners, the Holmes family, were another name closely associated with High River polo.

On that new field, complete with a pavilion and a pole with a flag that read "High River Polo Club," Colin George Ross and his players set to serious practice. The result would be some of the finest polo teams of that or any era in Canadian polo.

He does not often appear in the record of tournament polo in southern Alberta, but Alfred Ernest Cross was the almost-invisible man at the centre of the game in Calgary from its beginnings in 1890 until well into the new century.

Cross was anything but a remittance man. Though his family had emigrated from Scotland to Montreal, that had been in 1826 and what the family had it had earned in Quebec. Cross had come west in 1884 after attending the Ontario Agricultural College in Guelph and graduating from Montreal's McGill University veterinary school. He had a job waiting at the Cochrane Ranch just northwest of Calgary, but he did not stay with it for long, preferring instead to file his own homestead claim in the foothills country southwest of High River. With some family money from Montreal, Cross was on his way to building the majestic "a7" Ranch. Formally founded in 1886, it is today one of the largest ranches in Canada and still firmly in the Cross family's hands.

Cross' first friends in Alberta came from among those who, like himself, had taken up ranching in the great boom of the 1880s. Their names appear on the early member lists of Calgary's Ranchmen's Club, on the city's first hospital board and, most important in terms of longevity, as investors in a local brewery. Their names are also well-represented on those first polo trophies.

Always an "Alberta first" booster, A.E. Cross noticed the lack of a decent brewery anywhere west of Winnipeg. Sensing the growth that was to hit Calgary, he borrowed from the bank, sold some shares and, in December, 1891, launched the Calgary

Brewing & Malting Company. Among those present at the first official meeting in April, 1892 were Herbert Samson, Herbert Eckford and Duncan McPherson. They would soon be joined by T.S.C. Lee, H.B. Alexander and the Honorable F.A. Macnaghten.

About Thomas Somerville Charters Lee, comparatively little is known. He joined Cross and Alexander on the early spring roundups down near the a7, but he was no cowboy and only seems to have dabbled occasionally in stock rearing. T.S.C. Lee was a real estate agent, land speculator and builder and his string of dreams and schemes would involve most of his friends (and his friends' families) for years. His most substantial contribution to the Calgary landscape was the Alberta Hotel, an elegant three-storey sandstone structure in the centre of the city. Boasting the longest bar in Alberta, it was the ranch and business community's preferred watering hole until 1916 when prohibition closed it down. It has been a commercial block ever since.

Lee's real estate ads appeared daily in the *Calgary Herald* for several years, offering for sale a mix of large ranches and residential properties. He was the first (and longest serving) president of the Ranchmen's Club and a member of the Calgary hospital's first board of directors. As for his polo, he was in Victoria in 1892, played for Calgary in 1893 and appeared in the 1895 and 1896 tournaments and occasionally thereafter, but did not seem to develop the passion for the game that marked several of his peers.

Henry Bruen Alexander, first president of the Calgary Polo Club, led a life that seems the perfect subject for romantic fiction. He came to Alberta from Fircroft, Ireland early in 1888 and founded the Two-Dot Ranch south of High River. Local legend says he had ridden an Irish Derby winner before he came west. He may also have played some polo in Ireland, under the guidance of John Watson, the game's first great star. The Two-Dot was primarily a horse rearing operation when Alexander owned it and he imported several thoroughbreds (including "Silk Gown"). Their descendants were a strong presence on western tracks for years afterwards. He was also the one-time owner and trainer of "Bendigo," the most storied polo pony ever bred in Canada.

While he played some early polo with Ross at High River, he seems to have spent most of his time in Calgary playing the real estate market and building some of the city's most impressive sandstone commercial buildings (the "Alexander Block" still stands on the city's 8th Avenue across from Lee's Alberta Hotel). He was often in partnership with his cousin, George (builder of the city's first waterworks) and had extensive landholdings in Calgary (including, possibly, the Polo Club field just north of the Bow River in present-day Hillhurst). He was also heavily involved in early mining ventures in British Columbia's Kootenay country.

Alexander travelled regularly between Alberta, British Columbia and his home in the British Isles and his later appearances with the Calgary polo team were irregular. He sold the Two-Dot in 1902 and left the district, but he was back and playing again in 1906, said to have just returned from a trip to South Africa, though not as a participant in the Boer War. Perhaps he was visiting his old friend Samson.

A founding member of the Ranchmen's Club and habitue of Cross' "Wolves' Den" (the club's precursor — an old railway boxcar, complete with men's club decoration and a large barrel of whisky in the corner), Alexander missed the first Stampede in 1912 as he was then involved in mounting an expedition to the North Pole. He served in the first war, driving an ambulance for the French army, and made it back to Calgary for the Victory Stampede of 1919 (hitching a ride across the Atlantic, it is said, on a British battleship).

Harry Alexander died in Kenya in 1932 at the age of seventy-one. Always looking for a new adventure, he had moved there a decade before to establish a coffee plantation.

The Honorable Francis Alexander Macnaghten was born in 1863, the second son of the 4th Baronet Macnaghten of County Antrim, Ireland. Eton-educated, Macnaghten first came into the country to the Oxley

Captain Meopham Gardner, c. 1900 – Gardner's ranch at Pirmez Creek was one of the earliest in the area northwest of Calgary. His son, Clem, would become a world-champion rodeo star and Calgary polo stalwart between the wars.

Glenbow archives, NA-1942-1

Glenbow archives, NA-2913-5

Ranche in the 1880s and eventually bought a small place on the western outskirts of Calgary. He was a founding member of the Ranchmen's Club and an almost permanent fixture with the polo club, appearing in nearly every major tournament until the First World War.

In 1905, Macnaghten married Beatrice Ritchie, daughter of Canada's chief justice and, in 1916, through a tragic series of events, succeeded to his father's title. His father had died in 1913 and passed the title to Francis' older brother, Edward, who died the next year. Both of Edward's sons were killed in action within three months of each other and Frank (as he was always known) became the 8th Baronet in 1916. He finally left Calgary permanently in 1923 and lived at the family estate until his death in 1951.

Alexander had about eight members on his original Calgary polo club roster and they made up the various foursomes contesting the major tournaments of 1892-94. High River had about the same, all learning the game and playing at various levels of competence. But beginning in 1895 and 1896, something new was added to the Alberta game.

Mid-decade saw the first of an intermittent series of popular games generally said to be played in the "American style." These matches — including the Ladies' Cup and "Irish versus the World" — were usually held as an added feature to an annual club tournament. "American style" meant that the club players were divided up among a group of designated captains (perhaps according to some generally accepted, informal handicapping

system) with play carrying on during the afternoons or mornings when the club teams were off the field.

The attraction of such matches was obvious. Even where a tournament drew only three clubs, enough games could be scheduled to fill a full three days. Everyone, including the crowd, would get their money's worth. Players who might have travelled substantial distances, investing a good deal of time and money to get to the tournament would be guaranteed to play in more than just one or two games (especially if their club team was knocked out of contention on the first morning).

The Irish versus the World matches were especially interesting, pointing out an important fact about the earliest remittance men and those who came later. In most histories, the remittance men are said to have been sent out from "England," but there was a substantial number of Scots (including T.S.C. Lee) and even more came from Ireland. They were Anglo-Irish, to be sure, sons of the landed gentry whose fathers had joined London-based investment syndicates and many of more modest means. Still (for the purposes of a good match at least), they seem to have retained

their distinct identity. And polo has a history in Ireland as long as it has in England. Some of the earliest clubs started there and it was from Ireland that the 10th Hussars secured their first string of ponies.

The tournaments and individual matches of 1895 and 1896 were a watershed for several reasons. They showed that southern Alberta and the game of polo were changing. The years were marked by a string of new names and new clubs emerging on the scene.

The invitational matches not only reflected the growing number of high-quality players, but also the spread of polo into new areas around High River and Calgary. It was the same "hiving off" of skilled players from the centre to the surrounding districts that had given the Pincher Creek area such vitality. Plus, these "satellite" teams were attracting new players from among the growing rush of homesteaders.

In early August, 1895, Calgary and a new team from Pine Creek returned to Regina to play in a tournament held in conjunction with the annual territorial exhibition. Calgary defeated a team from Regina while Pine Creek had little difficulty with a foursome from Moosomin, a town near the Manitoba border.

Through the middle and late 1890s, the character of southern Alberta was beginning to undergo profound changes. The era of the huge, corporate ranches was drawing to a close; no new ones were being created. In the 1880s, the first investor syndicates would have purchased a comparatively modest homeplace from which to manage the tens of thousands of acres they held under lease from the federal government. By the mid-1890s, there were few new leases to be had and many of the older parcels had been withdrawn and sold off by the quarter- or half-section.

The railway line from Calgary southward down the foothills to Fort Macleod had opened the country to farmers and small ranchers, cutting the big corporate operations off from their summer grass to the east. Some ranchers bought up as many of these homestead parcels as they could, but the cost was high and the price of beef was down substantially in the depressed economy of the 1890s.

Clearly, the federal government now believed that the future of the West lay in large numbers of small landowners rather than in vast areas of thinly populated grazing lands.

Pine Creek was a small settlement (no more than a post office and general store) perhaps ten miles south of Calgary. A couple of miles closer to the city were the communities of Midnapore and Fish Creek. South and west of town, the villages of Millarville and Priddis were growing as the rush of homesteaders increased. To the north and west, up the Bow River, the town of Cochrane would come into its own after the turn of the century, supporting its own small satellites like Glenbow and Grand Valley.

Together with the older towns of Calgary and High River, these new communities gave new momentum to the game of polo as it moved toward a new century.

The effect of the changes sweeping the foothills was on full view at Calgary in August, 1896. Seventeen riders came to the matches to play for two trophies and, through a long series of games, they divided and subdivided themselves into at least seven different configurations. The old guard was there in force, but there was an ample representation of the newcomers who would dominate the game in the next decade.

Play for the Ladies' Cup was between four teams, none of which represented a particular club. On "Mr. Ross's Team," the old High River captain was joined by his neighbour Herbert Eckford, James "Dublin" Rodgers and another newcomer, Walter Hooley from Pine Creek. In their first game, they were matched against a Stapleton Ranch team composed entirely of Critchleys: Oswald, Tom, Harry and brother-in-law Tom Holt. It took overtime for Ross to win by 4-3.

Next to play were "Mr. Samson's Team" and "Springbank." Samson was playing with two Calgary originals — Frank Macnaghten and T.S.C. Lee — and Robert Milvain, up from Pincher Creek.

Springbank was an emerging area on the western outskirts of Calgary. Polo never coalesced there and local players came into Calgary or, in later years, travelled either the short distance west to Cochrane or south to Millarville. This pick-up team was led by A.C. Fraser, supported by Addison ("Addie") Hone, Herbert Lott and Captain Meopham Gardner.

Fraser was an early, though occasional player from just west of Calgary who seemed to have left the country by the turn of the century. The same was true of Lott, who married and raised five children in the Springbank area but left for the West Coast in 1907 and did not return. Meopham Gardner, however, did put down roots. He first came into the Pirmez Creek area near Cochrane during the Rebellion of 1885 and decided to return and establish a homestead. He continued to build on his "Burgie Ranch" property for years, raising cattle and prize saddle horses (and organizing another of those ill-fated "coyote hunt clubs"). He died in Calgary in 1944 at the age of ninety-two. The captain's son, Clem, would figure prominently in Calgary polo circles between the wars.

While the teams for the Ladies' trophy worked toward the final, the players were also competing for the Calgary Challenge Cup.

The Springbank players remained together, but the other teams dissolved and recombined as Pine Creek, Calgary "A" and Calgary "B." Robert Milvain dropped out in favour of another new name that would continue to appear in subsequent years: Wolley Dod.

In the first game, Pine Creek's Wolley Dod, Hooley, Rodgers and Ross prevailed over Springbank 5-4, but only after twenty-five minutes of overtime. Later, the Calgary "B" team of Holt, Eckford, Tom and Harry Critchley proved it was aptly named, getting thrashed 12-2 by the "A" team's Macnaghten, O.A. Critchley, Samson and Lee. Calgary "A" then went on to take the cup with a close 3-2 win over Pine Creek.

This tournament was covered extensively in the January, 1897 issue of *Polo* magazine and its commentary on the Samson-Springbank match reads as follows:

This was an instance of a strong hitting team on a rough ground holding [up] a much better team (that is a team that played real good polo and kept their places); but none of Samson's team were hard hitters. Springbank were all first class hitters, but played all over the ground.

Its analysis of the Calgary trophy final pulled no punches either:

* ◆◇◆ *

Pine Creek deserve credit for the manner they played. Hooley plays a good number two, but is inclined to come back too far, not trusting his back. O.A. Critchley has the same fault, but rides such good ponies he makes up the lost time very quickly. Macnaghten at number one is hard to beat; Samson at number three is very good; Lee is correct, but too slow for a back. Ross is a sure back and a very hard hitter.

* ◆◇◆ *

All in all, the magazine's reporter was impressed by the quality of the play:

* ◆◇◆ *

This [the Calgary trophy final] was the greatest game of polo played in the West, and to the last moment it was anybody's game. Calgary were better mounted than Pine Creek, and classing the two teams it looked ten to one on Calgary.... [In] the last quarter, five minutes before time, Ross broke his stick, and before he could get back, Critchley got started on Pete and made the third goal for Calgary.

* ◆◇◆ *

Most of the new players represented the new reality of settlement in the southern Alberta foothills. They were not the sons of the investment syndicates that had so dominated the early development of the country. They were not managing vast leaseholdings and waiting for their next cheque from home. They were homesteaders; farmers or small ranchers trying to make a go of it on their own. With a few notable exceptions, if they had money from home, it was not much.

Addie Hone and his brother George (always known to his neighbours as "Pie") were born at Ballymacad north of Dublin and came to the Millarville-Priddis area southwest of Calgary in the early 1890s. They homesteaded together until Addie moved to Midnapore in 1908, remaining there until he returned to Ireland in 1918. George stayed at Priddis until 1915 when he and his wife left for Vancouver Island. From mid-decade on, the Hones figured regularly with the new teams then organizing in the Millarville and Pine Creek areas.

The Hones made their own contribution to the confusion of family relationships which have always marked southern Alberta's polo community. Addie and George had three cousins — the brothers Herbert ("Mick"), Joe and Nim Hone — who were also playing in Midnapore at about the same time.

The Hones likely came by their passion for polo at home in Ireland. Theirs is a common surname around Dublin and, while a specific connection cannot be clearly established, they were probably related to one Captain T. Hone of the 7th Hussars. According to T.F. Dale, Captain Hone was the only man in the early years to have engraved his name on both the Champion Cup and the Interregimental trophy. He was also a member of the Hurlingham team that made the first visit to the United States in 1886.

James "Dublin" Rodgers was born in Northern Ireland, one of a family of ten, nine of whom came to Canada, with six living in the Millarville district. What their Irish background was is not known, but it does not seem to have been particularly privileged. Dublin and his brother Joe walked into the country in 1885 as roustabouts for one of the last ox-team supply wagons from Fort Benton (after the railway came through Calgary, the need for the Montana trail diminished). After a brief stint with the Quorn Ranch, Dublin homesteaded in the Sheep Creek district southeast of Millarville in 1886.

Rodgers was known for the hospitality of his "Hillside" ranch, for the polo ponies he bred and for his fine play. Sadly, the game he loved would cost him his life. He died as the result of injuries received during a match in about 1902. Most unfortunately, a serious blow to his head was not immediately fatal. "Robbed of his reason," as the newspapers tactfully put it, Rodgers spent two years in Montreal undergoing treatment before he finally succumbed in August, 1904.

Two of Dublin's five children carried on the Rodgers polo tradition. William Jasper (known as "Jappy") and Robert Hugh ("Paddy") both played in the Calgary area between the wars.

Walter Hooley was another settler with an obscure background and a brief, slightly mysterious, life in southern Alberta. He arrived in the Pine Creek area from England about 1887 with his brother, Charles, his sister-in-law, their children and a couple of servants. One of the first families in the district, they were apparently the cause of some curiosity among their neighbours.

Walter was a mainstay of the Pine Creek polo and pony clubs from their founding in the mid-1890s, appearing regularly on the polo field and in the gymkhanas that became an annual feature for a few years. He is said to have spent some time in the Klondike, returning in time to see the rest of his family sell out and move to the West Coast. He married a woman from Millarville in 1912 and, one year later, his body was found floating in the Bow River near his home.

A.G. Wolley Dod was a founding member of the Pine Creek Polo Club which had begun play in 1895, and his surname added its own twist to the confusing welter of names that often confounded the press (and frustrated the historian). Though spelled "Wolley Dod," it was pronounced "Wooley Dod" and that is how the newspapers regularly printed it. Compounding the papers' problem were Walter Hooley and long-time club secretary H.G. Wooley.

A.G. was born in England in 1860, the son of Rev. Charles Wolley Dod, a long-time master at Eton where A.G. himself was educated. He first came to North America in 1882 where he spent a few years working at various jobs in the U.S. Midwest. Following a return to his English home, 1887 saw him travelling across Canada on one of the C.P.R.'s first transcontinental passenger trains, visiting Vancouver and finally settling on 800 acres of Canadian Pacific homestead land just south of Calgary at Pine Creek.

There he continued to ranch and play polo until 1909, when the pressures from the new homesteaders proved too much. He sold out and moved into a fine new house in Calgary's Elbow Park.

During his time at Pine Creek, A.G. was joined by his younger brother. Frederick Hova Wolley Dod played a little polo, too, and eventually bought his own place nearby where his gardens quickly became the show place of the district. An avid lepidopterist, Hova left his butterfly collection to Canada's National Museum in Ottawa where it can still be seen today. He died of a fever contracted in Turkey during the Great War.

Over the years, Wolley Dod emerged as one of Calgary's leading citizens. An early member of the Ranchmen's Club, president of the Exhibition Board and long-time director of the Horticultural Society, he remained active in the polo club long after his playing days were over. Like so many of his generation, he also fulfilled his military obligations.

He enlisted as a sergeant in the Canadian Mounted Rifles when it was formed after the Boer War and, when the C.M.R. was absorbed by the 15th Light Horse, he was commissioned in the new regiment. Despite being well over fifty years of age when the Great War began, A.G. joined the 82nd Battalion of the Canadian Expeditionary Force with the rank of major and later joined his son, William, in the 31st Battalion. He saw active service both in France and England. Following the war, he rejoined the 15th Light Horse and, with the rank of lieutenant-colonel, commanded the regiment for several years.

Arthur George Wolley Dod continued to live in Calgary until his death in 1936.

Millarville made its first "official" appearance at the 1897 Calgary Cup Tournament. Calling itself "Sheep Creek" (from the name of the creek that flowed near the village), the foursome was made up of Dublin Rodgers, Addie Hone and the Moseley brothers.

Glenbow archives, NA-998-1

One of the first of the great North Fork teams, 1898 – (left to right) W.E. Smith, Jimmy Milvain, team founder Allan Kennington, Harry Gunn.

William and Harry Moseley lived briefly in the area, both leaving for Vancouver around 1903. Still, they made their contribution to the game, appearing with either Millarville or Pine Creek. The brothers also joined the 1901 "Irish versus the World" invitational match.

Sheep Creek faced Calgary and High River for the 1897 Calgary Cup (eventually won by Calgary 6-4 over High River) and then divided up for the Ladies' Cup matches. The Calgary foursome was notable since it marked one of A.E. Cross' infrequent appearances in tournament polo. He picked a good time to come out, putting his name on the Calgary Cup and, as a member of O.A. Critchley's pick-up team, on the Ladies' Cup as well.

The Ladies' Cup matches have caused more than one recent historian to slip. Millarville's local history, in its enthusiasm for the high quality (and new equality) of women's athletics in the West, is pleased to report that Mrs. Maude Rodgers, Dublin's wife, had played in the Ladies' Cup games of 1897. While women would begin to play the game formally after the Great War, the Ladies' Cup was in fact first presented for play in 1896 by the wives of a few of the players. It was always a men-only trophy.

Held as usual in conjunction with the annual fall exhibition, the Calgary tournament of September, 1899 was noteworthy for several reasons. A team from Qu'Appelle, Saskatchewan made an appearance, the first visit by a non-Alberta foursome. They had travelled some five hundred miles via the C.P.R. for the privilege of losing both their games.

Also attending was the team from North Fork, near Pincher Creek. Still under the leadership of their founder, Alan Kennington, the foursome was making a rare visit to Calgary.

Even after the railway was opened between Calgary and Fort Macleod, the North Fork area remained isolated. In its account of the tournament, the *Calgary Herald* reports that the team had come nearly one hundred and fifty miles across the prairie, driving fifteen ponies. Despite the difficulties, the North Fork foursome was obviously developing a taste for travel. In the new century, it would emerge as one of the great teams in Canadian polo history, regularly appearing at tournaments in Winnipeg and Spokane, Washington. Two of the players who would form the nucleus of those fine teams — Jimmy Milvain and Harry Gunn — made the trip to Calgary.

Filling out the four-team roster were Calgary and Sheep Creek. Calgary (the eventual tournament winner) was represented by O.A. Critchley, Frank Macnaghten and A.C. Fraser. Their fourth was High River original Herbert Samson, making what must have been a farewell appearance before leaving for South Africa.

The Sheep Creek-Millarville team was a pick-up collection. Joining regulars Dublin Rodgers and Addie Hone was P.L. Briggs.

Philip Lemuel Briggs seems to have been another of those "itinerant" players whose name appears for a number of different clubs over the years. He played for the Beaver Creek team in 1894 and probably for Fort Macleod that same year. Sandhurst-educated, he came from England in 1893 to join George Ross' Little Bow outfit. A local history remembers only that he kept a few racehorses and a pack of English foxhounds with which he tried to hunt the local coyotes. Tracking by scent rather than sight, the hounds were badly outmatched and Briggs is said never to have caught so much as a single coyote.

Though a regular on polo fields with several different teams, his real love seems to have been his racehorses. His name appeared (together with Critchley's) on the winners list of the Winnipeg races in 1896 and he was the secretary for at least one of the Calgary club's gymkhanas in the late 1890s.

Briggs brought his new wife to Alberta in 1898, but after the loss of two infant children, they returned to England in 1903. Briggs died in 1947.

Briggs must also have been an avid photographer. Recently, his only surviving child, Christopher, who now lives in Australia, sent three albums of his father's photographs from the High River area (including pictures of his horses and foxhounds) to Calgary's Glenbow archives.

Sheep Creek's fourth player in the 1899 tournament was sixteen-year-old Justin Deane-Freeman. While there are unconfirmed reports from earlier years, 1899 is the first documented appearance of a young man who, in the course of a brief, brilliant career, came to be known as perhaps the greatest polo player ever to emerge from southern Alberta.

The brief, mercurial era of the remittance men was closing fast and the great ranches with which they were associated would soon be things of the past. Most of the vast holdings which survived the depression of the mid-1890s and the subsequent onrush of the homesteaders would be finished off by the killing winter of 1906. Many of those first young men had already gone from the country and others had settled down to a life of near-respectability in a more civilized society. But for many others, the century would close with the promise of one last great adventure: the Yukon and the Klondike gold rush.

To the aging remittance men, first drawn to the West by the promise of an exciting new life, the lure of the North proved irresistible. Among them, Pine Creek's Walter Hooley succumbed, as did High River rancher W.G. Hanson.

The Garnett brothers and Bob Milvain left their Pincher Creek holdings and made for the goldfields, with a stop in Edmonton on the way. The *Edmonton Bulletin* reported their departure in August, 1897:

R.H. Milvain and J. Garnett...arrived on Monday's train Yukon bound by the great river route. They have arranged for a boat to be built by John Waters, 25ft long, 6ft beam, 2ft 9in in depth. This boat is sharp at both ends and is rigged with mast and sail, two sculls and a sweep. The weight will be 800 pounds and the cost $60. This style of boat is particularly recommended ...for the trip down the Mackenzie, being moderate in cost, having a large carrying capacity and being suitable for navigation in still water...in rapids or on portages.

The *Calgary Herald*, which reprinted the *Bulletin* piece, closed with the following: "Messrs. Garnett and Milvain are being sent by a Pincher Creek and Calgary syndicate." The names of those backers have been lost, but one can well imagine it was something which would have appealed to the members of the Ranchmen's Club, especially the Wolves' Den alumni. It would be nice to know if their investment ever paid a dividend, although it is unlikely they really cared.

While new players and new clubs brought a vitality to the country surrounding the traditional Calgary-High River axis, Calgary polo itself was, at century's end, still dominated by nearly the same cast of characters that first brought the game to life a decade earlier. O.A. Critchley and his brothers, Frank Macnaghten, T.S.C. Lee and the rest could always be counted on to field a strong team, but there seemed little in the way of fresh faces. And even the old guard would be reduced at the turn of the century as Lee's name dropped from the tournament play lists and O.A. Critchley sold the Stapleton Ranch and took his family back to England. His brother Harry's house was also put up for sale.

Critchley would not come back for a decade. And when he did, it would be to a different place in a very different world. ▧

VENI, VIDI, VICI

THE PRAIRIE WEST
1900-1914

Auto polo – This wild and obviously dangerous "sport" was popular at annual fairs and exhibitions across Western Canada and the United States.

CHAPTER 4

IT IS TEMPTING, in writing the history of polo in Western Canada, to look for specific connections with Britain; to look for the regiments or public schools where the early remittance men might have learned the game. But poring through school enrollments or regimental lists rarely yields much of value. Captain Wilmot was only briefly at Rugby School, too early to have seen the game played there, and he was unlikely to have played polo as a part-time soldier with his territorial infantry battalion. George Ross was a major, but his regiment was High River's own 15th Light Horse. He was only twenty years of age when he came to High River, hardly old enough to have developed his remarkable skills before emigrating. The same is probably true for the Critchley brothers, Bob Newbolt and most of the rest of the early players.

There is evidence — anecdotal and circumstantial — that a few men had played the game before they came to the West. The Royal Navy teams in Victoria were clearly experienced, even transporting their own ponies up and down the West Coast to their various anchorages. Louis Cuppage, who appeared briefly for Calgary in the early 1890s, was acknowledged to be a superb player: "the best in Canada." He must have brought his skills with him. Arthur Barrett, a fixture with Millarville just after the turn of the century, is said to have played polo with the British army in India before emigrating and Calgary's Harry Alexander probably had the best training of them all. He learned his polo in County Carlow, Ireland, under the firm hand of John Watson,

Alison Emde/Planet Photography

the first great star of the game. But these gentlemen were clearly the exception.

So, if most western players did not learn the game in Britain, where did they first play polo? The answer is that they learned it here in Canada. Whether in Victoria or Kamloops, Calgary or High River, they would all have known how to ride well and, given their families' social position in Britain or their avocation here, they would have owned a number of good saddle horses. The great foothills ranches were certainly stocked with a wealth of fine horseflesh. In fact, many of them (the Quorn and the Eckford, for example) were more committed to raising horses than cattle.

Finally, polo, in its fundamentals, is like any good game: it is dead simple. Give a decent horseman a patch of flat ground, a stick and a ball and he will quickly grasp the basics. After all, the 10th Hussars and the gentlemen ranchers of Pincher Creek were both inspired by a magazine article.

There may be some uncertainty about the polo roots of many of the early sportsmen, there is no doubt whatsoever as to where three of the Canadian game's greatest players of the pre-war era learned the game. Harry Robertson, Marston SexSmith and Justin Deane-Freeman were all entirely homegrown.

Harry Robertson is remembered as one of the most gifted players ever to wear the High River scarlet. He is also an excellent example of how the prairie game expanded beyond the confines of the exclusive country club to include players with more talent than money.

(left to right) Joe and Mick Hone, Justin Deane-Freeman and Addie Hone, c. 1905 – This was one of the "Irish" teams that played a regular series of matches against "the rest of the world." They were a popular added attraction at many turn-of-the-century Alberta tournaments.

Spectators at a Calgary polo match, c. 1900 – (left to right) Unknown, Mrs. Herbert Eckford, Lady Macnaghten, A.E. Cross, Nell Cross and Frank Bedingfield.

If the Robertson family had old country money behind it, there certainly wasn't much. Three Robertson brothers left England in the late 1880s and settled at Shoal Lake, northwest of Brandon, Manitoba. Harry came to High River around 1890, followed eventually by his brothers. He cowboyed around for a time — perhaps he worked for Ross or Eckford — and made his first recorded appearance on the polo field with the Colonel Macleod Cup-winning High River team of 1892.

At the turn of the century, Robertson opened a livery and feed store in town and continued to play polo under Ross' tutelage, becoming an integral part of a series of High River foursomes that were, on their record, arguably the best teams Alberta (and perhaps all of Canada) ever produced. By mid-decade, he could consider himself one of Canada's first "professional" players.

Born in Gatineau, Quebec, just east of Ottawa, Marston SexSmith was only two years old when his family homesteaded in High River. He grew up on horseback, eventually working for a number of outfits, including George Lane's legendary Bar-U. He began to appear on the polo field for High River around the turn of the century, quickly becoming an important element in a number of great foursomes. SexSmith played into the 1920s, was appointed provincial brand inspector and died in Edmonton in 1938.

Joseph Deane-Freeman from County Cork, Ireland settled near Millarville in 1886, one of the earliest to homestead in the district. His wife and five children joined him a year later and two more children would be born after they arrived. Before the end of the decade, Joseph had completed the building of "Monea," a large and graceful log house named for a property owned by his wife in Ireland. The house quickly became the social and sporting centre of the community, boasting a cricket pitch, tennis courts and, most important to their third child, Justin, a polo field.

Justin was born in Ireland in 1882, came with his mother to "Monea" and eventually took out his own neighbouring homestead in 1899. By 1903, he was a ranch foreman near Cochrane and worked for rancher and meat packer Pat Burns in 1906-07.

But what he really did was play polo, and he played it extraordinarily well.

This new trio, together with three or four homegrown players from the Pincher Creek district, not only came to dominate the local tournament scene, but would also find themselves in demand to join teams in Eastern Canada and the United States.

The new century opened to the same regimen of tournament polo established in the previous five years. Over the next few seasons, the player pool would deepen and widen, allowing Calgary, High River and Millarville to field high-quality teams at both the junior and senior levels. Pine Creek ceased to play as a club, but most of its riders found new homes with Calgary and Millarville, bringing both to near-parity with the powerhouse at High River. The continuing series of Ladies Cup tournaments and Irish versus the World matches remained a popular showcase for individual talent and, taken with the new junior games, gave the Calgary-area polo scene a richness it had never before enjoyed.

New tournament trophies were put into play at Sheep Creek-Millarville and at High River and the names engraved on them in their first years are a clear indication of how closely matched the clubs really were.

If the game was strong on the field at the beginning of the new century, it was equally strong as a social presence. Both High River and Calgary regularly hosted dinner-dances to close their tournaments and those occasions soon became the major social event of the year. Newspapers in both towns gave the balls full-page coverage, indulging in breathless descriptions of the ladies' dresses and the tunes they danced to, often until first light. Calgary's Polo Ball of 1903 was attended by over one hundred guests with every name dutifully recorded by the *Calgary Herald.* Those names constitute a comprehensive "A" list of Calgary society at the time; everyone who was anyone was there.

The 1903 Calgary tournament in mid-August was typical of the state of the game in the new century. There was another victory for the Irish and a three-way draw among Calgary, Millarville and High River (including a match between junior teams from the latter two). The games were close and the crowds enthusiastic.

Calgary's captain was the tireless F.A. Macnaghten, well into his second decade as the club's most consistent performer. He was supported by William Toole, Pine Creek original A.G. Wolley Dod and enthusiastic part-timer A.E. Cross. Millarville's G.H. ("Ted") Noton, Justin Deane-Freeman and emerging regular Herbert Anderson rode out under the direction of Addie Hone.

The most important new addition among the senior players was Frank B. Ward, a recent arrival in the High River district from British Columbia, where he had played for Victoria against the Royal Navy in 1896. He and his partner J.D. Pemberton (who also appeared in the junior match) had just purchased the

Two-Dot Ranch from H.B. Alexander, beginning a six-year stay in Alberta during which Ward would often wear the scarlet jersey. After returning to British Columbia in 1908, he would dominate the game in that province.

The junior games were significant since they marked the first tournament appearance of a fifteen-year-old Millarville player who would figure prominently in the years leading up to the Great War and then, especially, in the difficult times of the 1920s and 1930s. The young man was Justin's younger brother, W.E. ("Willie") Deane-Freeman.

High River, too, had begun to host its own annual tournament in 1903. It was usually scheduled to precede the Calgary meeting by a few weeks and it quickly took its place as a major event.

The 1904 High River tournament team was an example of how deep their player pool had become. A.H. Eckford was making yet another appearance for a team with which he had been associated from its very inception. Frank Ward played second with Harry Robertson at third and George Ross playing back. With over 20 paid-up playing members, the club could have fielded any number of quartets and still been a strong contender. Even the High River "B" team, which beat a new squad from Pekisko at the tournament, was anything but second-string. High River in 1904 was clearly showing the power that would make it the pre-eminent Canadian team of the period.

The Calgary tournament of 1904 marked an important point in the evolution of the western game as the teams began to play six periods of ten minutes each rather than the traditional fifteen-minute quarters. In that same match report, the following sentence appears: "There was plenty of scoring in the fourth rokar." It is hard to know exactly what was meant by a "rokar." Since the word "chukker" did not appeared in English usage until 1900 (and had not been used by the *Calgary Herald* in any polo report to date), one is seeing an editor's first fumbling attempt to use a term that was new to him. The tournament was held at the club's old grounds just across the Bow River to the north and west of the city's downtown. The grounds had been in use for more than a decade, but in that time, Calgary had undergone tremendous change.

The Millarville Polo Club, c. 1910.

Though the boom expected immediately after the arrival of the railway had not materialized, as the century closed the young city hit its stride and entered a long period of sustained growth. The 1891 census had recorded some 3,800 residents, a number that would increase by only six hundred in the following decade. However, by 1905, the year in which Alberta became a province, Calgary boosters could boast (loudly) of 10,000 citizens, a number that would increase more than four-fold by the start of the Great War.

Though the most of the city's initial growth had been to the south of its business centre, away from the natural barrier of the Bow River, the new century saw houses and neighbourhoods being established on the valley flats along the north shore. Soon, the

broad expanse of the Calgary polo field, too, would become valuable residential property and, in about 1906, it was lost to the club. Today, the old grounds are hidden beneath the community of Hillhurst, the earliest houses of which date from the latter part of the decade. From the loss of the Hillhurst field until a new, dedicated facility was opened southwest of the city in 1914, the Calgary Polo Club was without a permanent home.

Although much is made of the depth of High River and the experience of Calgary after the turn of the century, the Millarville Polo Club, at its best, could easily match its two main rivals in both the number and quality of its players.

Millarville today is a mixed community of family ranches and a steadily increasing number of small acreages held by people who make their living in Calgary. At the turn of the last century, it was homestead country, a patchwork of small holdings carved out of the great ranch leases. Without a railway nearby, the area was one of a string of communities that remained largely reliant on Calgary and smaller satellite towns like Okotoks (a small town midway between Calgary and High River) and Turner Valley. The area has always been prime horse country and home to a large number of serious breeders and trainers. Millarville's fairgrounds and half-mile racetrack, built just after the turn of the century, are still the social centre of the community, with a Canada Day race meeting that has been held nearly every year since the track was built.

The 1906 Millarville club accounts showed thirty paid-up subscriptions, including two of the late Dublin Rodgers' brothers, Harry and Alfred, a pair of Douglasses, three Hones and a number of individuals who formed the core of the playing members through the club's greatest years.

Herbert ("Specky") Anderson arrived in the district with his father and brother, filing on his homestead in 1889. He was probably a founding member of the Millarville club (few records exist for any year prior to 1906) and

served on its executive in a variety of positions every year from 1906 to 1912, the year in which he died prematurely at the age of only forty-one.

Moutarne Langland ("Montie") Fraser came to Canada in 1905 and by 1906 was a paid-up member of the polo club (as he would be until 1914). The polo field was just a fence away from Fraser's property and his wife remembers that he always kept five good ponies ready for play. In 1914, he was appointed Millarville's captain, capping a fine career as a steady team player. Fraser enlisted in 1914 and found himself in a tank crew. Severely gassed at the Somme in 1916, he returned to Canada and joined his wife and children who had relocated to Vancouver Island during his absence. He never fully recovered his health and died there in 1926.

Little is known of Ted Noton except that, even seventy years after he left the area, the Millarville local history describes him as "An Englishman of means who had the reputation of being exceedingly rude; his Irish wife, Annie Kennedy, is remembered with more affection."

Rude he may have been, but he was also a renowned cricketer and a fine polo player, travelling with a succession of Alberta foursomes to Montreal, Toronto and California. He was captain of the Millarville polo team every year from 1905 to 1912, when he and his wife left the district.

A.C. ("Condie") Landale went to sea from his native England at the age of 12 and rose to command his own ship in the China tea trade. When he came to the Millarville area is uncertain, but he was secretary of the polo club in 1905. In 1909, he purchased "Monea" from the senior Deane-Freemans and lived there, raising Shorthorn cattle and polo ponies, until shortly before he went overseas in 1914 in command of the 15th Light Horse.

After the war, Landale and his family returned to southern Alberta and settled at the Bearspaw Ranch on the Bow River just west of Calgary, where he became a regular player for Calgary and for the fine Cochrane polo teams of the 1920s.

Together with these founders of Millarville society, the club could also boast a pair of the characters who gave remittance men their questionable reputation in southern Alberta.

Arthur Barrett and Edward Melladew were both on the membership list for 1906 and continued to appear periodically for the next few years. They were great friends and both are the stuff of myriad local legends.

Barrett was the nephew of a British admiral and came out to Western Canada just after the turn of the century. Although he did own property southeast of Millarville, he was not what one could call either a homesteader or a serious rancher. What land he had was probably given over to the keeping of his polo ponies and racehorses, of which he is said to have had a number. Mostly, though, he seems to have drifted about the countryside staying with friends and trying to slake a prodigious thirst. He was almost certainly living on his remittance, the monthly stipend from home that would ensure his continued absence from his family's affairs in England. But whatever he was receiving, it was not enough: one friend recalls being asked by Barrett to write to his family telling them of his death and requesting a cheque for $650 to cover the cost of a suitably lavish funeral.

Though the tales of his taste for whisky may be exaggerated, it is certainly what people have remembered most about him. "Never too drunk to sit on a horse" goes one cryptic reference and Frank Ward recalled that Barrett was not much use as a polo player unless he had quite a few drinks under his belt.

Edward Melladew seemed cut from the same cloth. His family were prosperous cotton manufacturers in Liverpool and Melladew, too, was living on his remittance, first at the Bradfield College Ranch north of Millarville and then on his own place nearby. He was easily a match for Barrett both on the polo field and in his thirst. One acquaintance remembers them both dressed in their best cowboy outfits — chaps, boots, spurs and all — well into their cups and wagering which of them could swim a rain-swollen Sheep Creek in full regalia.

Melladew's life around Millarville was as brief as it was colourful. In 1911, he "accidentally" shot himself in the head at the Grand Central Hotel bar in nearby Okotoks. His friend Barrett stayed in the area a while longer but eventually went back to England. He is said to have been killed in the Great War.

The years from 1904 to 1908 marked another of the periodic upheavals that characterized southern Alberta polo from its earliest days. The pool of top-flight players in those years was remarkable. High River, already fielding two strong teams, gained further strength in 1904 with the formation of its own satellite, the Gee-Bung Polo Club from the small foothills ranching community of Pekisko. While Pine Creek had ceased play, its members shifted their allegiance either to Millarville or Calgary, to the distinct benefit of both.

And yet, while the clubs were reaching their greatest strength in both number and quality of players, they began to be undermined by the emergence of the individual "star" and the formation of a series of what, in modern parlance, would be called "super-teams." While the Ladies' Cup or the Irish versus the World games had always proved popular, they had been an added attraction at

the annual tournaments and a chance for players to supplement the one-a-day club matches. Newspapers certainly gave the impression that such "American style" play was lighter and less intense than the competition for the Calgary or Sheep Creek challenge cups. Beginning soon after the turn of the century, however, the combination of widely varying levels of ability, easier travel and money began to divide the members of the southern Alberta clubs into "haves" and "have-nots."

In 1885, it had taken considerable effort and dedication to move a polo team and its ponies from Calgary or High River to a tournament in Fort Macleod (or even from High River to Calgary itself), but by the end of the first decade of the new century, southern Alberta's teams and individual players had become regular attractions at tournaments from Montreal to California.

When Alberta teams first began to make their cross-country treks is not certain. A recent history of the Montreal Polo Club says High River played in a Toronto, Ontario tournament as early as 1902. While that date cannot be confirmed, a *Calgary Herald* article from August, 1906 does say that George Ross was making ready to take his fourth team to Eastern Canada.

The first trip east was probably in September, 1903. Although reports are sketchy, it seems the invitation had come from the Toronto Hunt Club following the visit, earlier that year, by one H. Middleton. He was a horse rancher and sometime polo player from Okotoks who had taken a string of forty ponies to Toronto where they had proved easy to sell to the new team in the Ontario capital.

He joined Ross, Macnaghten and Addie Hone and, playing under the nickname "Free-booters," they rode out against teams from Rochester, New York; Toronto and Montreal. Although Rochester won the tournament, the trip was a success for the Calgary players and

Middleton managed to sell another string of twenty ponies for an average price of $170.

The first eastern tournament for which there was extensive coverage in the Calgary press was held at Toronto's Sunlight Park during the second week of September, 1905 and showcased teams from Toronto, Montreal and High River as well as American teams from Buffalo and Rochester.

The Toronto and Montreal clubs were newcomers to the game but Buffalo had been organized as early as 1877 and was ranked one of the top teams in the East. It didn't matter much to High River which scythed its way through the opposition in game after game. Toronto fell by 10-7, Rochester by 13-1 and Buffalo by 12-4. What High River did to the Montreal squad was mercifully unreported, but when High River's Harry Robertson replaced an injured Montreal player in their game with Toronto the result was 14-4, the newspapers giving Robertson full credit for the win.

September, 1906 reckoned to be more of the same. Both the *Calgary Herald* and *High River Times* sent the team off with the highest expectations. The Calgary paper pointed out that in three previous trips, Ross' teams had yet to lose, while the *Times* was especially fulsome. Its headline read: "Veni, Vidi, Vici. The Champions Leave for Further Victims. New Laurels for Our Polo Boys."

The tournament, held at Montreal's St. Lambert grounds, was to include Toronto and Kingston, Ontario as well as the "Myopias" and the "Dedhams" from Massachusetts but the American squads did not seem to appear.

High River took up where it had left off the year before, beating a new Kingston club easily and then drubbing Montreal by 14-1. The *High River Times* was effusive. Under the front-page headline "Greater Victories, High River Polo Team Wins Fresh Laurels" came the following:

From present indications the team will meet with even greater success than they did in 1905, and there is very little doubt but that they will again win the championship.

That report was clearly tempting fate and a few days later both the *Calgary Herald* and the *Times* had to publish the awful news: "Our Polo Boys Meet With Defeat at the Hands of Toronto."

The score was 7-2 and, with their third win, Toronto took the tournament. There was some complaining about Toronto's habit of changing personnel for every match, but the press had to acknowledge that the westerners were off their form and were simply beaten by a better effort.

The teams that travelled to Toronto and Montreal, though called "High River" or "Calgary" in the press, were anything but club teams. Rather, they were true all-star foursomes. In 1905, it was George Ross, Harry Robertson and Marston SexSmith of High River, joined by Ted Noton of Millarville. In 1906, Ross and Noton went again, but this time they were accompanied by Calgary original Harry Alexander and the talented Justin Deane-Freeman of Millarville.

Alexander was a bit of a surprise since he had not been seen on the field for some time, but the rest of the players were the characteristic mix of young and old that marked the game in the new century. Characteristic, too, was the mix of money and modest means. Clearly, Ross always had the funds to indulge his passion for polo and horses, as did Harry Alexander with his Calgary real estate and British Columbia mining interests. Little is known about Ted Noton's finances, but he seems to have been able to afford his love of polo and cricket. While Deane-Freeman, Robertson and SexSmith would all go on to play professional polo, none would then have had the means to cover the cost of train travel for themselves and their ponies followed by a week or more in a city like Toronto or Montreal.

One can see the hand (and purse) of George Ross in this. Always committed to encouraging young polo talent, he was no less willing to ensure that such talent was exposed to the widest possible audience. Deane-Freeman, Robertson and SexSmith would all spend time teaching and playing for pay in Montreal or Toronto and they probably had George Ross to thank for those clubs being able to see them perform first-hand.

For Ross and Middleton, though, Toronto and Montreal were not entirely pleasure trips. They were clearly in the horse (or, more properly, the pony) business. In its announcement of the 1906 team's impending trip, the *Calgary Herald* had this to say about Ross:

The majority of polo ponies now playing in Montreal, Toronto and Kingston have been bought from [Ross'] stable and it speaks well for his judgement that he has been chosen as judge of ponies at both Toronto and Montreal shows. [He] takes twenty ponies in his car this year, and it can truly be said that he never took a better bunch.

One wonders about the chance that any of the ponies the western team rode in the tournament ever saw Alberta again. The tournament record alone was advertisement enough of their quality.

There was another Alberta team that began to travel widely in 1905. North Fork was the most prominent and skilled survivor of what had been, in the 1890s, a thriving and competitive Pincher Creek-Fort Macleod group of clubs. The North Fork team, always the class of the district, was not particularly deep in numbers of players available to it, but its core of five regulars — Harry Gunn, Bert Connelly, Harry Evans, Jimmy Milvain and Rollo Burn — supplemented by three or four occasional players, was second to none in the West.

The area was relatively isolated from the rest of the province and the Pincher Creek club's record of appearances at matches in Calgary or High River was inconsistent and unpredictable. But even without the benefit of regular high-quality opposition or the discipline of top-flight tournament play, when the North Fork foursomes came out at mid-decade, they began to amass a collection of silverware that was the equal of any other Alberta club.

North Fork was invited to Winnipeg in mid-June of 1905, becoming the first Alberta team to make what would become a regular pilgrimage in the years leading up to the Great War.

Polo was first introduced to Winnipeg as a feature attraction at the annual horse show. A field had been laid out (presumably at the fairgrounds) and local newspapers were enthusiastically reporting the arrival of the teams while assuring that Winnipeg, too, would have a strong representative. Under the bold headlines, "Polo Players Are Here Now" and "Three Western Teams Reach the City for Big Polo Matches," the *Winnipeg Tribune* of June 13th was clearly excited by the prospects:

The big polo matches which will be pulled off tomorrow and Thursday afternoons in connection with the Horse Show will easily prove one of the most interesting and spectacular features of the show. Four teams will take part in the tourney and from all indications the contests should prove the most entertaining and spirited which have been seen in Winnipeg for some time. The training of the ponies figures just as largely in the result as the skill of the players so that the games will be watched with no little attention.

The three outside teams to take part in the tourney reached the city this morning. Indian Head, Qu'Appelle and Gillingham, Alta. are the places that have specially sent representatives to the show, while Winnipeg will also have a strong team to go on the course. Animated tests of skill are thus assured for both tomorrow and Thursday. The party to reach the city this morning included twenty people, the wives of a number of players and their friends accompanying the teams.

The ponies reached the city this afternoon, and are by long odds the best class of horses of this kind which have ever been seen in this city. There are thirty-two in all, and everyone a high-priced animal of blood. The draw for the tourney will be made tomorrow morning.

The "Gillingham" referred to was the small post office closest to the home ranches of Alberta's North Fork team. The papers will also call them "Norfolk," but there is no doubt as to their origin.

The polo field that the *Tribune* reported to be "almost as smooth as the green baize on a billiard table" turned out to be every bit as rough as it was short, but Allan Kennington, Jimmy Milvain,

Tom Heap and T.B. Jenkinson swept past Qu'Appelle by 13-2. Then, after heavy rain had washed out their match against Indian Head, they returned the next day to best a combined Saskatchewan foursome by 7-2.

In the end, Winnipeg did not manage to put a team on the field, but J.A. Cantlie, Jr. announced the purchase of two of those "high-priced animals of blood" and promised that the host team would not disappoint again. Top breeder Jenkinson's presence with North Fork was an indication that the trip from Alberta was as much a matter of business as pleasure and he was the likely source of Cantlie's new ponies. They were probably not the only ones to change hands during the visit.

As was so often the case with new teams and tournaments, the bright promise of 1905 did not carry over to the following year and there is no record of a 1906 polo meeting in Winnipeg.

As Alberta's players and teams began to include travel plans in their annual tournament schedule, there were still matches to be played at home. The only game of 1905 that received serious attention from the press, however, was Calgary's June visit to High River. It was a wildly popular event with over one hundred spectators taking a special train down from Calgary. The town of High River, it was reported, "went out of business temporarily for the game, business houses closing and everyone adjourning to the grounds about a mile out of town." Betting was slow, though, apparently caused by some nervousness about the quality of the visiting team.

While the High River fielded its "A" side of Ross, Robertson, Ward and Eckford, the Calgary team was from Calgary in name only. Even the *Calgary Herald* had to acknowledge that this was a hand-chosen quartet: "The Hon. F.A. Macnaghten had undertaken to pick a team which could show George Ross' High River team they were not invincible." And so he did. Macnaghten, Addie Hone, Justin Deane-Freeman and Ted Noton managed a late goal and then hung on for a 5-4 win in what was enthusiastically reported as a "splendid contest."

Then, in 1906, George Ross and Harry Robertson put any vestigial thoughts of High River's invincibility to rest once and for all. Robertson went off to play in Montreal and Ross moved to Calgary.

Ross was not abandoning High River entirely. He had always moved freely between the two centres; always been a regular fixture for both clubs. Still, High River was losing his tireless promotion of his game and his strict, disciplined approach to the development of younger talent. Although there was some continued success on the field, High River would never again be such a dominant power in southern Alberta polo.

Despite the defections, High River remained the centre of polo activity for 1906, hosting at least three significant events. Their season began in mid-June with a military sports tournament hosted by the 15th Light Horse, the regiment led by Major George Ross. Amidst the spectacle of a musical ride, tent-pegging, tug-of-war and wrestling on horseback, Calgary and High River played a spirited six periods of polo with Calgary posting a 4-3 win (the winning goal being scored by Macnaghten after stunning his opposite number's pony with an accidental mallet blow to the head and riding in unopposed).

In a late June match against a visiting Millarville squad, the High River team had changed again with Eckford and Ward supported this time by Pekisko's F.R. Pike and A.C. Shakerley, but Millarville sent its best side and came away with a narrow victory. That made it two losses in a row for the post-Ross club with the main event still to come.

In late July, 1906, the fourth annual competition for the High River Challenge Cup drew four visiting teams. Calgary and Millarville were there, seeking to repeat their earlier victories, and they were joined by two new teams featuring some old faces.

"Livingstone" was the name chosen by a one-event pick-up team from north of the Pincher Creek district. It was headed by North Fork founder Allan Kennington and one of his premier players, Jimmy Milvain.

The Sheep Creek Challenge Cup – This trophy was awarded to the winner of the annual Millarville Tournament from 1903 until about 1914. Like other trophies from clubs which did not survive the Great War, it was played for occasionally in the 1920s and 1930s and is now in the collection of a Calgary museum.

The Fish Creek club had a more complicated origin. The presence of Addie Hone and Walter Hooley connect it with the old Pine Creek teams. Today, the Fish Creek area has been swallowed up by the city of Calgary but at that time it was a small rural area that lay between the city and Pine Creek. In the years after Calgary first lost its regular grounds to urban sprawl, players congregated there for practices and the occasional game. When George Ross bought a place at Fish Creek in 1907, the club flourished and, briefly, became synonymous with the Calgary Polo Club. With Ross' departure for greener pastures and the creation of a new Calgary polo facility in 1913, the name Fish Creek disappeared from the polo scene for many years.

The draw saw Livingstone's superior ponies carry them to a win over Fish Creek while Millarville took another victory from High River. After a win over Livingstone, Calgary faced Millarville and, by eight goals to three, won another shield on the High River Challenge Cup. And High River had lost its third home stand in a row.

Ross' relocation was coincidental with the Calgary club's move to the city's old racetrack just south of the business centre on the Elbow River. The property was owned by T.S.C. Lee who had made some serious investments in the property, building a new polo field in the middle of the track and surrounding it with a golf course and club house. The players tested the field in June with another of Macnaghten's Irish challenges and then mounted the annual tournament for the Calgary Cup. The home club succeeded in holding on to its trophy against teams from High River, Millarville and Fish Creek.

If the club thought it had found its new home, it was a brief hope. The 1906 tournament was the only major event to be held at Elbow Park. Later that year, Lee offered to sell the land to various club members for $5,000 but, when they declined, apparently believing they could continue to rent the field for a nominal charge, the property was sold to a residential developer (whose ads later trumpeted "Buy Lots in Elbow Park, the Old Home of Polo and Golf").

In 1907, the Calgary club, again without a permanent grounds, negotiated the use of the playing fields at Mewata Park for its matches and in June, opened their season with a special match. Calgary and Fish Creek rode out to play in front of Japan's Prince Fushimi, then on a cross-country goodwill tour. The ground was undersized and irregular and the Prince had to leave before the match was over, but a crowd estimated at about a thousand enjoyed what was described as "whirlwind playing."

The park was used later in the summer for the Ladies' and Calgary cup matches but other demands on the field from local baseball and football teams meant that Mewata could not be counted on for regular practice or scheduled matches. Again, Calgary would be homeless for 1908.

High River versus Indian Head, Saskatchewan, at the Chipman Cup Tournament in Winnipeg, 1907.

The balance of the 1907 Alberta season saw a rain-soaked Millarville tournament and a five-team gathering in High River at the end of July. The hosts were joined by Pekisko, Fish Creek, Calgary and Millarville. High River was to end its two-season losing streak and won its first match against Pekisko, but then lost a close contest to a Calgary team which went on to claim the High River Challenge Cup with a win over Fish Creek.

High River's 1907 season would not be without one bright light. Although it had recently shown itself the weakest sister among the principal southern Alberta clubs, the team travelled to Winnipeg in September with high expectations. Joining teams from the revitalized Pincher Creek district, Indian Head, Saskatchewan and two foursomes from the host club, High River considered itself the favourite to take the new Chipman Cup. Anticipating the formation of a Western Canada Polo Association, C.C. Chipman, then in charge of the Hudson's Bay Company's Winnipeg operations, had presented the trophy to the Winnipeg Polo Club, intending that it become symbolic of western Canadian polo supremacy.

Beginning in 1907, and continuing without serious interruption until the outbreak of the first war, the city of Winnipeg, with its polo club based at the St. Charles Country Club and a strong military presence at Fort Osborne Barracks, would become a major centre for western Canadian polo.

The matches opened on a soft, wet field (leading a Winnipeg newspaper to suggest the players might be well-advised to carry a "niblick" to dig the ball out of the deep divots), with Pincher Creek going down to the Winnipeg "Moonlighters" in a close game and then finding themselves surprised (and beaten) by the previously uninspiring team from Indian Head.

High River had no difficulty in the preliminaries, giving lessons in team play to the enthusiastic but undisciplined Winnipeggers. For the *High River Times,* "It was strategy versus speed and strength and strategy won." Though George Ross had left his old team, the lessons he taught had obviously been well-learned.

In the final, Indian Head reverted to form and handed the Chipman Cup to High River by 10-3. In further testament to their team balance, High River got goals from all of its players with SexSmith and Holmes scoring three apiece and Limoges and Anderson each adding a pair.

This team showed the nucleus of the "new" post-Ross High River. Although long-time regular J.R. Anderson, the manager of the Union Bank, was playing his last match before leaving the district and Marston SexSmith would spend several seasons in Toronto and Montreal, Bill Holmes and Pastro Limoges would lead the team through to the outbreak of the war.

Both had deep roots in the town. Limoges' Montreal-born father, Joseph, was the town's leading retailer and long-time honorary president of the polo club. Pastro's brother, Gus, also played for the team on occasion. Bill Holmes was born in High River, the son of a homesteader on whose land the first permanent polo grounds were built. He was the club captain for several years and, after serving in the Great War with the 15th Light Horse, he became a strong voice in the effort to re-form the club in the mid-1920s. He remained one of High River's leading public figures until his death in 1956.

The 1907 Winnipeg tournament did indeed see the birth of a Western Canada Polo Association. There had been earlier talk of such an association as teams began to travel outside their local areas, but this seems to have been the first serious meeting. Patrons were appointed from the three Prairie provinces and the Hurlingham Rules were adopted as the standard of play. The Hurlingham restriction on the size of ponies was adopted, too, but any horse which had been played in a tournament before September, 1907 was exempted from the 14-2 height limit. It was agreed that another tournament would be held in 1908, with invitations going to eastern and American teams. Winnipeg, equidistant from East and West, clearly saw itself as the coming centre of Canadian polo.

The 1908 Alberta polo season showed the cumulative effect of the changes which had been taking place over the previous three or four years. Calgary and Fish Creek were appearing as separate teams, but the real strength was clearly with Ross, Macnaghten and Justin Deane-Freeman at Fish Creek.

George Ross himself had added a new dimension to Alberta polo in the winter of 1907-1908. He escaped the northern cold with a trip to California and established what would become a second home for a number of local players and, eventually, a permanent one for himself.

Ensconced at Riverside, just east of Los Angeles, Ross wrote a glowing letter to the president of the High River club:

———— ❖ ————

This is simply a heavenly place, the climate is grand and the polo is good, and further, I have shown that I can play with anybody in the South. If I had our old High River team, well mounted, I could win the international cup worth $5000. It is gold. The big tournament is the second week in March. They pay your transportation for horses, grooms and players. In fact during the tournaments you are not allowed to spend anything, and for a month it is polo tournaments and polo racing.

———— ❖ ————

Despite enthusiastic encouragement from the *High River Times,* the rest of Ross' old team did not make it to Riverside in 1908, but he had begun a tradition of snowbird polo that remains an important part of the Alberta game to this day.

Without permanent grounds for 1908, Calgary's tournament became an event at the annual exhibition in early July and four teams played for the Calgary and Ladies' cups and for a new trophy, the American Day Polo Championship cup. Joining the host team and Fish Creek were Millarville and Pekisko. For the first time in the history of the Calgary tournament, the High River scarlet was not seen on the field.

Perhaps it was the uncertainty about the home club's situation or just that the city had grown large enough that polo was no longer the town's premier sporting event, but the 1908 tournament barely rated a mention in the *Calgary Herald's* coverage of the exhibition. If the club had hoped to attract new attention to the game by playing in front of the huge exhibition crowds, it was a miscalculation. Where the annual matches and their attendant soirees had once been the social event on the Calgary calendar, polo at the exhibition was just another attraction, lost in the noise of a hundred others.

The new trophy, presented by the American Association of Calgary, was intended to become a part of the fair's annual "American Day" celebrations on the Fourth of July. The game led off the tournament with Pekisko matched against Calgary. The Gee-Bungs were expected to win easily, but it was a little-known Calgary foursome that carried the day by a narrow two goals to one. The American cup, placed on display at the Ranchmen's Club, would not be seen again until 1975 when the Calgary Polo Club put it back into play.

Learning much about the other games is difficult. Ross' team won the Ladies' Cup and his Fish Creek team probably won the Challenge Cup, too, beating both Pekisko and Millarville. Ross may have been getting on in years, but he was still the acknowledged master of disciplined team polo.

There was probably a Millarville tournament in 1908 (the club's account book shows the usual $5 surcharge in addition to the

members' annual subscription) but no detailed account of the matches can be found. It can be assumed that Ross' Fish Creek team won the trophy since Millarville was reported to be in Fish Creek early in August playing "a return game" against "the Champs" (and beating them by two goals). Fish Creek also hosted another of Macnaghten's Irish challenges, but the result was not reported.

That left the High River tournament in mid-September to close the 1908 Alberta season. The club's minute book offers no details, but the *High River Times* reported the following on August 6th:

———— ❖ ————

At the polo meeting held...on Saturday last...all present were unanimous in holding a tournament in September. The meeting decided to hold a tournament under the American system which is as follows: Teams to be picked by a committee of members of the High River from various players in attendance at the tournament.

———— ❖ ————

Once-powerful High River seemed to be a club in disarray. The team had not been much in evidence during the season and now its own tournament had been radically altered.

Ken Woo

The American Day Polo Championship trophy – This silver cup, with its art deco handles, was created by the American Association of Calgary to be played for during the Calgary Exhibition & Stampede's annual "American Day" celebration. The cup was contested only once — in 1908 — before it was brought back onto the field by the Calgary club in 1975.

The *Times* had already expressed its distaste for the "American system" in an editorial which appeared immediately after the 1908 Calgary matches:

Nothing will destroy the game of polo in Alberta more quickly than the formation of a team of four ex-captains and four of the strongest players in Canada, to wit: Messrs. Ross, [Deane-]Freeman, Alexander and Hone. Amateur teams like Pekisko, Millarville and Calgary will not stand the slightest chance to win amongst such a strong team and it was a mistake to allow this team to compete for the American cup.

The editorial is confusing inasmuch as this foursome never appeared together at the Calgary tournament (there is no evidence that Alexander was even in attendance), but there is no mistaking the paper's position. On September 10th, the *Times* took another shot:

While many would prefer polo as played in the past, yet under [the] prevailing circumstances it is well that the American system was adopted. At any rate we are to witness a week of exciting polo contests.

In the days before the September 15th draw, thirty-two entries had been received by the club secretary and the *Times* was promising a full week of top-flight polo. On the day of the draw, however, only sixteen players appeared.

The four teams drawn were a mix of players, familiar and occasional. With Shakerley were Barrett, Macnaghten and Masterman; with Ross it would be Gornall, Melladew and Fraser (all from Millarville). Deane-Freeman would play with Jamieson, Landale and Pekisko's Snowden while Millarville's Specky Anderson captained Ward, Wolley Dod and North Fork's Jimmy Milvain. Obviously, the host club had taken the *Times'* concerns to heart and tried to balance the teams as much as possible.

Jamieson came the farthest for the games, travelling down from the Buffalo Lake area just east of Red Deer. How he was connected with southern Alberta polo is not clear, but he might well be the same Jamieson who played briefly for Calgary back in 1892. He may also have been responsible for a brief flourish of polo activity in the district town of Alix. Calgary travelled there for a pair of games in September, 1908. The newspapers' notoriously inconsistent spelling of surnames does not help to establish his identity with any certainty.

The weather was perfect and attendance was good. Even the *Times* seemed to put aside its concerns and reported the matches with enthusiasm. In the end, all the handicapping mattered little as Ross' team swept into the final and defeated Shakerley by 7-0 to take the new Lane trophy, presented by George Lane himself.

A pair of front-page headlines appearing in the *High River Times* on September 17th give a clue to the source of the apparent troubles within the High River club. One read "This is Polo Week — Polo Tournament in Full Swing — Only Sixteen Contestants Playing." Next to it, but higher up the page and closer to the centre, was another that read "Polo at the 'Peg — The Winnipeg Free Press Loud in its Praises of High River Polo Players."

Limoges and Holmes, together with Pekisko's Carlé and a twenty-three-year-old named Frank McHugh (about whom more will be heard in years to come) had gone to Winnipeg to defend the Chipman Cup. The fledgling Western Canada Polo Association had done a poor job of coordinating the various tournaments and it will not be the only occasion when Winnipeg will prove difficult.

Pincher Creek, too, had gone back to Winnipeg but did not have a good time of it. They were beaten 5-2 by High River in a match that cost Pincher Creek's Bolster the life of his best pony (he had already seen his second best destroyed only the day before due to the same cannon bone injury). And they lost to their hosts, with the final for the Chipman Cup played by Winnipeg and High River.

At the previous year's tournament, High River's Marston SexSmith had said that Winnipeg possessed great raw polo talent and needed only strong discipline and good competition to make it into a great team. They had obviously taken his advice to heart and won the 1908 Chipman Cup final with a 6-4 victory over the defending champions. It was to be St. Charles' only significant victory of the pre-war era.

Pincher Creek's second straight appearance in Winnipeg was another sign that polo had made a comeback in that district. After a few years of relative inactivity and the failure of the Fort Macleod club, there seems to have

(left to right) Bill Holmes, Frank McHugh, referee Harry Gunn, Richard Carlé and Pastro Limoges, High River's Chipman Cup team, Winnipeg, 1908.

been a general polo revival in that southwestern part of the province that had first given life to the prairie game. While North Fork would garner most of the press, reborn teams from Pincher Creek, South Fork (and eventually even Fort Macleod), together with a couple of new organizations, breathed new life into the game.

There may not have been much coverage in the Calgary or High River papers, but the little *Pincher Creek Echo* tried hard to keep its readers up to date, reporting not only on their team's visits to Winnipeg, but also on the local matches in the area.

The earlier pattern of "spinning off" a number of teams from one centre was at work again. In 1905, the *Echo* reported on a match between Pincher Creek and Stand Off, a small community at the western edge of the sprawling Blood Indian Reserve just east of the town and directly south of Fort Macleod. There had been vague reports of polo activity there in the 1890s but, between 1905 and 1909, the team became a regular participant at area matches. In 1909, Stand Off played in a July tournament at Pincher Creek and then, in August, the same foursome appeared, wearing new jerseys, as the host team in a match at Fort Macleod, signalling the return of polo to that town.

The Pincher Creek team of 1905 showed that several of Wilmot's originals had continued to play the game. A.C. Kemmis, D.G. Plunkett and A.H. Lynch-Staunton were still active, with Kemmis and Plunkett leading the team to Winnipeg in both 1907 and 1908.

There was a small tournament at Pincher Creek in July, 1906 involving the hosts, Stand Off and North Fork. With a victory over the home team, North Fork retained the Pincher Creek cup. First contested in 1894, it is not known exactly when the old trophy came back into play.

Cowley is a small town west of Pincher Creek and the closest community to the North Fork ranches. In the next few years, the names "Cowley" and "North Fork" would be used almost interchangeably (even, on occasion, fielding separate foursomes) as the team found a permanent home ground in the town. In June, 1907, North Fork and Pincher Creek played a match for the Cowley Cup. The *Echo* reported that North Fork had retained it so it must have been in play before, though there is no record of its first presentation.

There was at least one other trophy up for play in the Pincher Creek district during this period. A "Henderson Cup" was played for at Pincher Creek in July of 1909. Again, Pincher Creek, Stand Off and North Fork were involved and again it was North Fork that took the silverware home.

Other than adding to the confusion of trophies in the district, the tournament showed that Tom Heap,

Winnipeg's St. Charles club, 1908
Chipman Cup winners – (left to right)
George Killam, Wilford Lemon,
Captain Cope, J.A. Cantlie, Jr.

another original, was still enjoying his polo, although he left the area permanently two years later. A new name on the North Fork roster was Hugh Pettit. He had grown up with the other young players who succeeded the originals and went on to make the names of Pincher Creek and North Fork synonymous with top-flight polo in the second decade of the twentieth century.

On August 10th, 1909, Fort Macleod marked its reappearance on the scene by hosting a match with Pincher Creek. The "rebadged" Stand Off foursome made an auspicious return with a closely played 2-1 victory. But the highlight of the district's busy 1909 polo season was Pincher Creek's third foray to Winnipeg in early September.

The team was an all-star aggregation with Gunn and Jimmy Milvain from North Fork, Harry Evans of Macleod and Pincher Creek's Bolster, probably out to avenge the loss of his two prize ponies the year before. As it had been in 1908, the only competition for the two Alberta teams (a combined High River-Pekisko quartet also made the trip) came from their hosts at the St. Charles club. Indian Head, Saskatchewan failed to appear at the last minute for the second year in a row. As it had in 1908, the Winnipeg club divided itself into two squads for the preliminaries but would field its best foursome should it manage to get through to the finals.

The teams would be vying for two trophies: the Chipman, in its third year of play, and some new silverware presented to the Winnipeg club by the Earl of Winterton. While the Chipman represented the championship of Western Canada, the Winterton was intended to become the St. Charles club's "home trophy," played for each year in Winnipeg.

Neither Pincher Creek nor High River-Pekisko had any trouble with their subdivided Winnipeg rivals. As the *Echo* reported it:

It was another sorry day for the Winnipeg teams at the polo grounds yesterday for both went down to defeat, leaving the visitors to fight it out for the Winterton Cup this afternoon. Pekisko was 6 to 1 and Pincher Creek 6 to 3.

The Winterton final was a closer affair with the High River-Pekisko team taking the new cup from Pincher Creek in a 3-1 game that was more even than the score indicated.

The best Winnipeg foursome came out to face Pincher Creek for the Chipman Cup and although the home team was, on the evidence, reckoned to be stronger man-for-man, Pincher Creek seemed determined finally to win in Winnipeg. In a game described as being "...by no means of the spectacular kind," they fashioned a workman-like victory by 10-3.

Meanwhile, one hundred miles to the north of Pincher Creek, the 1909 season had been inconsistent and uncertain. For the first time in two decades, the name "Calgary" was missing from the tournament lists. Still without a home field or strong leadership, the club also suffered the loss of several of its new, younger players from the previous seasons. Indeed, three of the American cup-winning team of 1908 had left the city and the fourth, Frank McHugh, elected to sit the year out.

What proved to be a rather unstable year opened with an announcement in the *High River Times:*

Arrangements have been completed for a polo match to be played at High River, on Friday afternoon May 14th, between Montreal's crack polo team and an equally clever team from Millarville.

The "Montreal" team was, in fact, High River's Harry Robertson and Marston SexSmith and one bona fide Montrealer, Oscar Beaudry. Montreal club founding member Major Frank

Meighen was scheduled to play, but his place had been taken by Pekisko's A.C. Shakerley.

Robertson and SexSmith had been playing for pay with the eastern club for two or three years and, a week after this match, they were scheduled to return to Montreal for the 1909 season. Montreal club regular Oscar Beaudry had not come 3,000 miles just to play in an exhibition polo game. During his visit, he negotiated the purchase of the Eden Valley Ranch, 6,000 acres of prime foothills cattle country on the Highwood River west of town. When the players returned to Quebec, they also took a carload of new ponies.

George Ross began the 1909 season in top form, having spent another winter playing in California, this time at San Diego's Coronado club. In an April interview with the *Calgary Herald,* Ross clearly felt that the prospects for the coming Alberta season were bright. Millarville would have over twenty playing members and he expected his Fish Creek club to be up from its sixteen of 1908. He was confident that Alberta would again be well-represented in Winnipeg, but was doubtful about making another trip to Toronto or Montreal. In fact, although at least three Albertans had played with the clubs in the recent past, the surprise loss to Toronto in 1906 marked the last time a foursome from Alberta would be seen in Eastern Canada for nearly a century.

Ross' pre-season optimism seemed unwarranted as the Millarville tournament got underway in mid-July. Only two "A" teams — Millarville and Fish Creek — were present. It was certainly the first time since serious tournament polo began in southern Alberta that neither High River nor Calgary had appeared. The host's "B" squad was matched against teams from Fish Creek and Pekisko.

Appearing for Fish Creek, along with their captain, George Ross, were regulars Joe and Addie Hone and Frank Macnaghten. For Millarville it would be Barrett, Landale,

Hulme and, for the last time, its greatest star, Justin Deane-Freeman.

After spending two seasons with Ross at Fish Creek and playing for Montreal in 1907, Deane-Freeman had decided to move to the Coronado club at the end of 1909. As the *High River Times* reported:

Justin Deane-Freeman is leaving the country to take up a position in California. He decided not long ago to finish his polo career in this country at Millarville. He learned all his polo playing with this club when he first started and he decided to end his time here with the club that taught him. As he is considered one of the best players Alberta has ever seen, the distinct gain to Millarville is apparent.

Millarville, playing without Deane-Freeman, had emerged as the strongest of the Alberta clubs. With him, they had no trouble handling an experienced but ageing Fish Creek team. They played them twice in two days and took both games by a combined score of 16-4.

At the 1909 High River matches, while the *Times* may have claimed that "...those who attended were unanimous in saying that it was the most successfully conducted tournament ever held in the west," something was decidedly amiss. Not only were Pincher Creek and the reborn Macleod club last-minute cancellations, but High River itself was almost a no-show at its own tournament. The *Times* referred to the hosts as "the High River-Pekisko team" but only William Holmes was a High River regular. Shakerley, Carlé and Snowden, while they might have held memberships in the High River club, represented the heart of the Pekisko Gee-Bungs.

The High River Challenge Cup came down to a three-way draw with Fish Creek defeating Millarville for the right to play Pekisko in the final. The town of High River could take at least some comfort in the fact that the Gee-Bungs' 9-7 victory kept its silverware close to home.

The second half of the tournament saw play for the George Lane trophy. Five teams played a fierce schedule of ten games in two days with a final on the third. Ted Noton's foursome captured the Lane trophy on what must have been very tired ponies. The Lane Cup matches were also significant since they saw the reappearance of Harry Robertson, back in the district after his final season in the East.

The 1909 High River Challenge Cup was the second triumph of the year for the "combined" Pekisko-High River team. Only three days before the start of the High River meeting, they had arrived home from Winnipeg after defeating Pincher Creek for the new Winterton Cup.

As was frequently the case in the history of Canadian polo, as one team declined, another appeared to breathe new life into the game. Such was the case in 1909.

While several southern Alberta teams wobbled through their season with a non-existent Calgary, a shaky

High River and a number of high-profile defections, polo came to life around the small, prosperous ranch town of Cochrane.

Like many western communities, Cochrane owed its life to the Canadian Pacific Railway as it wound its way west from Calgary toward the Rocky Mountains in the mid-1880s. The original townsite lay along the Bow River in the deep scenic valley that was part of Senator Matthew Cochrane's huge leasehold ranch.

When Cochrane gave up his leases near the end of the decade, smaller cattle outfits and homesteaders slowly began to fill the land around the village which grew accordingly to supply their needs. By 1900, Cochrane could boast its own brickyards, stone quarries, sawmills and lumberyards and would grow quickly until the outbreak of the Great War.

The town also spawned a number of surrounding loose-knit ranching communities like Glenbow and Grand Valley. And it was from such places the *Cochrane Advocate* reported signs of what was to grow into a thriving and long-lived centre for first-rate polo:

The Cochrane Polo Club met at the Union Bank on Friday last.... The subscription was fixed at $5.00 and a suitable ground has been located on the second flat between the village and the Bow River on the east side of the road to the steel bridge. The first game is to take place on Saturday afternoon and the members will welcome the attendance of all interested in the sport.

While they were all born horsemen, the men who first played polo in the Cochrane district in 1909 had little of the remittance men about them. They were small ranchers and cowhands who came into the district from England, Eastern Canada or the United States (and places much farther afield), but they would inherit no titles or estates and there was no great pool of British capital to pay for their leases, stock their ranches or cover their overdrafts. Some had connections to the first great ranches in the district, but most would have to face the hardships of the

The Grand Valley Ranch, 1914 –
Owned successively by the Bell-Irving
family, R.W. Meiklejon, O.A. Critchley
and Gilbert Rhodes, the ranch enjoyed
a long history as the centre for polo
in the Cochrane district.

coming booms and busts with little but their own tenacity to see them through.

The first reported polo match took place between Cochrane and Glenbow on June 19th, 1909. Glenbow, referred to (perhaps facetiously) by the *Advocate* as "the rising town of the west," never became anything like a town. It was the name of an early ranch and a signpost on the C.P.R.

That first Cochrane team showed no evidence of previous experience with the game. Howard Abell took a small homestead in Grand Valley and remained in the district for the rest of his life. R.W. Widdes was the town's banker. In 1884, young English-born Osborne Johnson homesteaded in central Alberta before moving south to the Cochrane area. He remained a bachelor, raised fine show horses and lived in the area until his death in 1960. Of Angus McPherson, nothing more is known.

For the Glenbow Ranch, it was Walter Hutchinson, the brothers Harold and Edward Payne Le Sueur and Victor Saunders. Hutchinson had come into the district in 1906 via Argentina after spending most of his life in New Zealand. He raised cattle and horses and lived in the district until his death in 1953 at the age of eighty-one. The Le Sueur brothers arrived from the island of Guernsey via a coffee plantation in Brazil and homesteaded west of Cochrane. Their later fate in the country is not recorded.

Vic Saunders did have his remittance. Provided with a classical education in England, France, Germany and Russia (where his father had substantial business interests), he was sent out to the West and provided with a homestead in the Jumping Pound Creek area just southwest of Cochrane. In 1910, he married into the Kerfoot family, one of the oldest in the district and another of southern Alberta's great polo families.

The *Advocate* reported an exciting match (with a couple of spills but no serious injuries) and a 5-2 win for Glenbow.

In late August, 1909, the third of the district's young teams made its first recorded appearance against Cochrane. Grand Valley stretches north and west from the Bow River into the Wildcat Hills and was home to the Bell-Irving Ranch, one of the oldest in the Cochrane area and one that came to figure prominently in the history of Cochrane polo.

The Grand Valley team included one of the remaining Bell-Irvings (the original owner, William, had sold out in 1900 and bought a ranch in Cuba), R.W. Meiklejon, the current owner of the place and two young men named Kerfoot. Duncan and Adrian ("Pat") Kerfoot were the first of a name that would be synonymous with Cochrane polo for as long as it survived in the district.

The brief season of 1909 closed with a banquet, replete with endless toasts, fine cigars, songs, stories and a promise to be back for hard practice next year.

That spring of 1910 saw a dramatic turn of events that would propel Cochrane's neophyte players into the very centre of southern Alberta tournament polo, then take them even farther afield. In 1910, Oswald Asheton Critchley swept back into Alberta and settled in Cochrane.

Critchley had spent nearly a decade in England, seeing to the education of his five sons. His three eldest sons were either already back in Canada or would soon arrive. With his partner, Gilbert ("Dusty") Rhodes, Critchley purchased the old Bell-Irving from Meiklejon and went back into the cattle (and polo) business.

The southern Alberta polo season of 1910 began under a terrible cloud. On March 12th, Justin Deane-Freeman, generally acknowledged to be the finest player ever produced in the Canadian West, was killed during a match at his new club in Coronado, California.

Although George Ross had announced he would not play in Alberta in 1910, preferring to remain at Coronado, he changed his mind after Deane-Freeman's death and appeared with his Fish Creek team at the annual High River tournament in late July.

Reporting of the 1910 season in the Calgary area was thin. Other than a notice of the beginning of practice at Fish Creek in May, the High River tournament was the only event that received any attention from the local press.

The *High River Times'* reporting of the tournament again suggested a High River club in turmoil. Only a few days before the games, the polo ground had been flooded by heavy rainfall and there was some doubt that it could be used. The first game proved heavy going, with the field shortened to avoid the worst patches, but it drained quickly and the following matches were faster. There were two trophies up for play: the High River Challenge Cup for "A" teams and a new trophy, the Van Wart Cup, for "B" sides.

Pekisko had decided not to defend the trophy they had won the year before or to try for the new prize and, in the coverage of the "A" competition for the Challenge Cup, there is no mention of High River. Given their record over the past two years, it is possible they did not field a team to play for their own trophy. In what must have been an anticlimactic match (despite the *Times'* claims to the contrary), Fish Creek's old reliable foursome of Hone, Hone, Macnaghten and Ross downed Millarville 3-1.

The new trophy, presented that year by Calgary Sheriff Van Wart, was intended by its donor to encourage young players and, for that reason, High River decided that it should be played for annually among the "B" sides of the major teams. The cup final matched Fish Creek against a High River "B" side that included Holmes and Limoges, both well-established and well-travelled "A" level players. Even with the edge in experience, High River could not prevail and went down by a score of 7-5.

Meanwhile, farther south, Pincher Creek, Fort Macleod and North Fork continued their regimen of regular matches and at least two tournaments. Pincher Creek hosted a meeting at the beginning of July, 1910, which resulted in a rare win over the always-dangerous North Fork and then a victory over Macleod in the final.

At Fort Macleod in August, the home side went through to the final but North Fork proved the better squad and took the Henderson trophy by 4-1. With their victory, North Fork also took possession of the old Macleod Cup, back in play after resting in Fort Macleod since it was last contested in 1894.

It was perhaps the fitting finish to a sad and uncertain Alberta season that none of its teams

The Fish Creek Challenge Cup – Created in about 1906 by George Ross' new club just south of Calgary, the trophy was the main prize at the club's annual tournament until 1914. Following the war, it was only occasionally put into play at Chinook Park but, since the late 1970s, it has again become a regular part of the Calgary club's season.

travelled east to Winnipeg for what had become almost the traditional year-end tournament.

The 1911 season opened with higher expectations. In early April, at the annual meeting of the High River club, "a number of enthusiastic members" re-elected Bill Holmes as their Captain and welcomed several new playing members. The annual tournament was scheduled for July 26th-28th and, best of all, the club announced that Harry Robertson and Marston SexSmith were back from Montreal to take their place on the "A" team.

The original Montreal club had disbanded at the end of 1910, leaving only the newer Back River club to carry on. Just before it folded, however, Montreal hosted the first visiting team from England ever to play in Canada.

On September 24th, 1910, a foursome from Ranelagh that had been on a tour of the eastern United States came north to play a series of matches against picked Canadian teams at the grounds of the Montreal and Back River clubs. Ranelagh was represented by Lord Rocksavage, F.A. Gill and the legendary Grenfell brothers. The Montreal club sent out four of its best, including Robertson and SexSmith.

It was no contest. Ranelagh took the match by 14-2, but perhaps the humbling experience was tempered somewhat by the Canadians' knowledge that they finally had the chance to play against some of the best.

At the conclusion of the match, the Grenfells' older brother presented a beautiful trophy, to be known as the Grenfell Cup, with the intention that it become the Canadian polo championship trophy. It became a symbolic tribute to his brothers, too, when they were both lost to the Great War, one receiving a posthumous Victoria Cross.

The Osler Challenge trophy – First presented in Winnipeg in 1912, the trophy was part of the great North Fork sweep and was next played for at their 1913 tournament in Cowley. Won by Cochrane, it was subsequently put up as the prize for the first polo match at Calgary's new Chinook Park grounds in 1914. The Osler has recently been brought back into play at the Calgary club.

The cup, which alternated annually between the Toronto and Montreal tournaments, came to represent the championship of Eastern Canada and was played for until 1939. It now rests in Canada's Sports Hall of Fame. Robertson and SexSmith remain the only western players to be associated with the Grenfell Cup matches.

In mid-April of 1911, representatives from the Calgary area gathered in the city to try again to form an association of the western clubs. What happened to the organization created at Winnipeg in 1907 is not known, but the confusion of 1909 and the lack of a Winnipeg tournament in 1910 suggest that it had never really been an effective influence. Again, Winnipeg promised to attend. Again, they did not and the local clubs went on to set their own tournament dates without St. Charles (or the Pincher Creek district). Still entertaining hopes for an association of all the western clubs, it was announced the matter would again be discussed during the High River matches. There is no evidence this follow-up meeting ever took place.

Rules were on the agenda at the meeting, too. While the clubs did not like a proposal to reduce the six periods of play from ten to seven and a half minutes each, they did agree to eliminate the offside rule.

The *Calgary Herald's* brief report on the rules of play is interesting because it happened so rarely. With the exception of the formal adoption of the Hurlingham Rules at Winnipeg in 1907, the Calgary meeting represents the only publicly reported mention of a decision regarding the rules. Earlier, when the

clubs began to play six periods rather than four, the result of that decision had simply appeared, without comment, in the reports of the matches. In the few minute books that have survived, there are no motions regarding rules and one must assume that such things were settled informally among the members of the various clubs (probably over drinks during one tournament or another).

It is not that dropping the offside rule comes as a surprise: even Hurlingham itself did away with it. The surprise is that the Alberta clubs had ever used it at all. American clubs had never enforced offside, leading to the development of the wide-open hit-and-run game that eventually became the worldwide standard. Although the Canadians remained resolutely English in most things, knowing those first rough, enthusiastic matches were played under the stricture of the offside rule seems to work against the natural impression of a wild, headlong, cowboy game.

In 1911, Fish Creek and Calgary were still playing as two teams, both using the former's ground about six miles south of the old city limits. Despite Ross' continued assertions that he would be staying in California, he opened the season for Fish Creek, losing a match to a visiting Millarville foursome. He would also play later for Calgary against a visiting team from Pekisko.

Cochrane, under O.A. Critchley, continued its regular schedule of practices and pick-up games, but on a new field. In early May, the club's Grounds Committee investigated several possible sites in and around the town. The original field had been deemed unacceptable for further play due to its proximity to the Cochrane "nuisance ground," the condition of which was reported by the *Advocate* as being "a disgrace to any civilized community." The new field was located within Cochrane's racetrack and it was ready for practice by the end of May.

At the Fort Macleod tournament in mid-July, North Fork retained the Macleod Cup for the second year in a row with a close, overtime win over their hosts.

In reporting the match, the Fort Macleod paper began using the term "chukker." It was still not in regular use among the other papers and, when they did use it, it appeared in any of a half-dozen spellings from

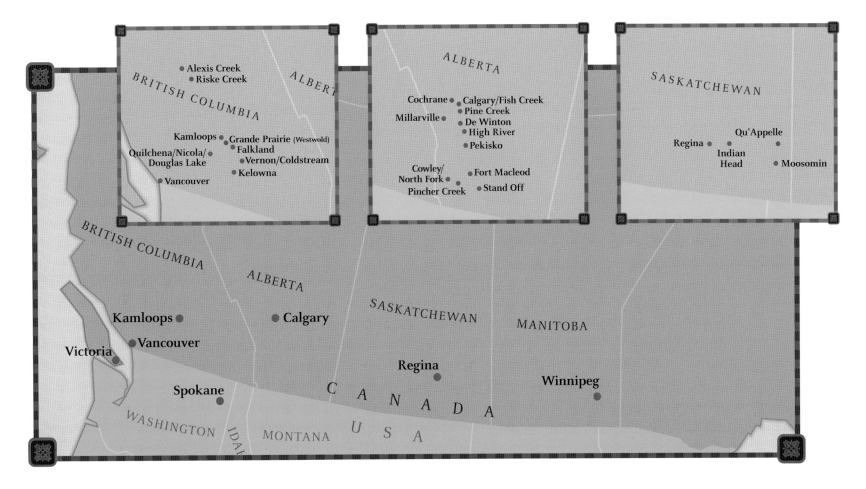

"chukka" and "chukkah" to "chucka" and "chucker," often within the same report. The use of the term became standard in Alberta by the 1920s, though its spelling continued to be creative until long after that.

The 1911 Millarville tournament took place in early July, with the host's "A" team losing to a Robertson-enhanced Pekisko squad. The result of the "B" game was the same with Millarville going down to the Gee-Bungs by 5-4. The event also marked the first appearance of the new Cochrane team at a southern Alberta tournament.

The Millarville meeting was also significant since, only one year after the death of Justin Deane-Freeman, it featured two of his brothers. Willie played for the "A" team, his first tournament appearance since his auspicious debut in 1903. Riding out for the "B"

side was the youngest of the Deane-Freemans, twenty-year-old Brudenell. According to the *High River Times,* they both showed their late brother's potential for greatness on the polo field.

The High River tournament was scheduled for July 26-28 and, as late as July 6th, the *Times* was still advertising that both Winnipeg and Cochrane would be sending a team, but neither finally appeared.

The tournament pitted "A" teams from Calgary, Fish Creek, Millarville and Pekisko against each other for the Challenge Cup; for the Van Wart trophy, it would be "B" sides from High River, Pekisko and Millarville. What happened to the earlier-touted High River "A" team, featuring Robertson and SexSmith, is anyone's guess.

Calgary took the "A" tournament over Millarville while High River captured the Van Wart Cup with an easy 8-2 win over Millarville "B." A pair of "exhibition" matches

followed the tournament, but not, as previously advertised, an all-star match captained by Ross and Robertson.

The players showed the usual amalgam of young and old with a liberal admixture of Hones, but one squad in particular bears mention. With the exception of Condie Landale (who seems to have settled in with Calgary between his longer stints with Millarville and Cochrane), the Calgary team harkened back to the very beginnings of the prairie game: Frank Macnaghten, George Ross and Oswald Critchley. One could be reading a tournament report from 1892. It was the last time they ever played together.

The 1911 season closed with High River travelling west to Pekisko but the Gee-Bungs' hopes for their first multi-team tournament were dashed as Millarville did not show.

Again, no Alberta team made the trek to Winnipeg, leaving hopes for a true championship of Western Canada unfulfilled for another year. In 1912, that would change in dramatic fashion.

Polo activity in Winnipeg was not restricted to a single annual tournament. There may not have been a western championship tournament every year and Alberta was not always represented, but the St. Charles field was the site for the typical rounds of regular practice and intra-club matches, interspersed with occasional visits from outside clubs. Newspaper reports are sketchy for anything other than big events, but they do indicate that the game was flourishing.

In 1909, for example, the St. Charles club put on an exhibition match for the benefit of six hundred or so members of the British Association (a scientific association that was holding meetings in Winnipeg at the time). The City provided special transportation to the club grounds and the band of the 18th Mounted Rifles provided the entertainment. Similar events are recorded in most of the pre-war years.

However, what marked the Winnipeg polo scene as different from any other area of the country before the war was the strong presence of the military. The city was home to a number of militia regiments, including cavalry, but the most important was Lord Strathcona's Horse. Based at Fort Osborne Barracks since its reformation in 1909, members of the regiment began appearing on the club grounds as early as 1910 when Lieutenant

A.E. Shaw (a former Mountie and sometime Calgary player) led a team of St. Charles players at an intra-club match in August of that year. From then until the outbreak of war, members of the Strathcona's and other Fort Osborne staff officers made their individual or team presence felt at every turn.

In July, 1911, the *Winnipeg Tribune* reported on a match at the country club that showed the beginnings of the brief, but important career of the first Strathcona's polo team. A foursome from the country club (featuring a visitor from High River, Pastro Limoges) faced a team clearly identified as "the Garrison." Although two of the players were not Strathcona's — Claude Bulling and Lieutenant Price Montague were both St. Charles regulars — the other two were lieutenants A.E. Shaw and A.C. Critchley, the core of the great team that would emerge over the next three years. The Garrison won the match by 5-3 and the players were presented with small cups donated by club supporter Captain Hugh Osler of the 79th Cameron Highlanders.

In early August, 1911, another Garrison foursome was back on the field and, again, the Strathcona's did not constitute the entire team. A.E. Shaw was supported on that occasion by a British exchange officer, Major Louis Lipsett, St. Charles member Stanley Morse and, most important, by the Strathcona's commanding officer, the imposing Colonel (later General) Sir Archibald Cameron Macdonell. His presence on the field was an indication that Strathcona's polo had unequivocal (if unofficial) support at the highest level. Again, the Garrison was victorious; again it was by 5-3.

The Alberta season of 1912 unofficially began on New Year's Day with the news from San Diego that the "famous Alberta polo team" had arrived at the Coronado club to open its 1912 season. The team was made up of Fish Creek's Addie Hone, Millarville's Ted Noton and Condie Landale, Kenneth Snowden of Pekisko and Major Colin George Ross, late of High River, Calgary and Fish Creek. The team remained in California, probably mostly at Ross' expense, until at least the middle of March. On March 18th, it closed the Coronado season with a narrow win over a visiting English squad comprising the lords Gower, Tweedsmouth, Herbert and Burke.

Hone, Landale and Snowden were home in time for the start of play in Alberta. But Ted Noton, a fixture with the great Millarville teams of the past decade, never returned to the province.

And, for the first time since he arrived in the small cowtown of High River more than twenty-five years earlier, George Ross, the great general of Alberta polo, was missing from the lists. After two or three years of announcing his retirement, he became the highly paid secretary of the Coronado Polo Club and remained in California.

In mid-July, Pekisko's strong "A" foursome of Shakerley, Carlé, Harper and Snowden won the Fish Creek tournament, defeating an inexperienced (and now leaderless) host team by fourteen to two and then posting a 1-goal win over Millarville.

If there was a Millarville tournament in 1912, it was not reported by the Calgary or High River press. Six teams visited High River for their annual meeting at the end of July, but the weather was foul and heavy rains caused all but two games to be cancelled. There was a "Married versus Single" match and one try for the Van Wart Cup. Whether the trophy was awarded on the strength of that is not recorded.

With Calgary, Fish Creek, Cochrane, Millarville, Pekisko, Fort Macleod and High River all in town at the same time (only North Fork and Pincher Creek were not represented), losing at the High River tournament to the weather was truly unfortunate. It would have been as close as Alberta had come, since the early 1890s, to crowning a true provincial champion.

In the south, too, there was not much polo news in the *Echo* or the Fort Macleod papers for early 1912. There was talk that a new team had been formed on the South Fork (perhaps at the Roodie Ranch again), but there is no evidence that such a club ever amounted to anything more than a rumour. Talk was strong, too, about the forthcoming tournament at Fort Macleod in mid-September and for a while it looked as if the provincial championship, rained-out High River, might actually come to pass. The Macleod papers were even promoting the Macleod Cup as again being emblematic of Alberta polo supremacy.

When the tournament opened, however, the expected seven teams were reduced to only three: Macleod, North Fork and a Critchley-led aggregation that called itself Cochrane. In fact, only Critchley and Gilbert Rhodes were Cochrane regulars. At this meet, they were supported by Pekisko's Ken Snowden and High River's premier itinerant professional, Harry Robertson.

The Chipman trophy – Presented in 1907 by C.C. Chipman, head of the Hudson's Bay Company in Winnipeg, the cup was always intended to symbolize the championship of Western Canada. Last played for in Winnipeg in 1913, when it was won by the Strathcona's, the trophy was probably taken to Calgary by the regiment when it moved there after the war. The Chipman was next put up for play in 1925 at the first post–war western championship and has remained at the Calgary club ever since.

After twenty years of tournament polo in southern Alberta, a second generation of players was beginning to appear on the field. One of the Macleod team was Dr. Allan Kennedy. His father (who served as timekeeper for the tournament) was Dr. George Kennedy, former Mounted Police surgeon and one of the Fort Macleod originals from 1891. At the aborted High River meeting six weeks earlier, the Van Wart Cup match had seen a pair of Critchleys on the same team for the first time since the turn of the century. In this case, though, they were not brothers but father and son: Oswald and Walter. Two more Critchley sons — A.C. and Jack — were already in the Strathcona's at Winnipeg and making a mark with their polo team.

The Macleod tournament came down to Cochrane and North Fork for the Macleod Cup. North Fork had held it for two years and had the bye into the final. Cochrane first beat the host team 10-5 and then, to the surprise of many, took the trophy away from North Fork with by an easy seven goals to two.

If North Fork were not up to their usual standard, it may have been because the modest 1912 Macleod tournament seemed an anticlimax. In mid-July, Bert Connelly, Harry Gunn, Rollo Burn and Harry Evans had pulled off the greatest single-tournament silverware sweep in the history of Canadian polo.

After a two-year absence, North Fork joined High River in Winnipeg for a four-team tournament with the St. Charles club and the Fort Osborne Barracks.

High River sent a foursome of Bill Holmes and one of the sometime-regular Nelson brothers together with Millarville's Willie Deane-Freeman and T.B. Jenkinson, a horse rancher from the Medicine Hat area

who would make his mark after the war, raising top-quality ponies and playing polo from his Virginia Ranch base near Cochrane.

The St. Charles club did its usual division and subdivision to fill out the draw but, more significantly, the 1912 Winnipeg meeting saw the first major tournament appearance of A.E. Shaw, Douglas Cameron and Oswald Critchley's son, A.C. With the later addition of A.C.'s brother, Jack, they built the pre-war foundation for what would become the great post-war polo traditions of Lord Strathcona's Horse.

From the historian's perspective, the 1912 Western Canada Championship was a confusing affair. With so much silverware at stake and a key injury, the St. Charles club was forced to mix and match its available talent in order to field the best teams for each of the three trophy series.

For the Winterton and Osler matches, Fort Osborne Barracks played as a team, the first all-military aggregation to appear in Winnipeg. Shaw, Critchley and Lipsett were joined by twenty-one-year-old Lieutenant A.D. Cameron who had joined the Strathcona's in 1911. Though Cameron made it through the Winterton Cup matches, his introduction to tournament polo was cut short in the Osler final as he took a bad fall in the third chukker. Unable to continue due to a broken collar-bone, his place was taken by High River's Willie Deane-Freeman. It was not the only serious injury during the tournament. High River's Claude Lonsdale had already broken a shoulder blade during a Winterton match.

For the Chipman Cup matches that closed the tournament, Winnipeg "A" included lieutenants Shaw and A.C. Critchley, Major Lipsett and St. Charles original Charles Killam: it was the Barracks team, minus Cameron. The "B" team would all be from St. Charles: Crossin, Winans and the Montague brothers, Ray and Price.

In the end, it didn't matter who played with whom; North Fork was simply unbeatable.

Playing a fierce two-a-day schedule (sometimes in the presence of Canada's Governor General, the Duke of Connaught), North Fork won six matches in a row and captured not only the Winterton and Chipman trophies, but the new Osler Challenge Cup as well.

Press coverage was unprecedented. Papers in Winnipeg, High River, Pincher Creek and Fort Macleod devoted long columns to chukker-by-chukker descriptions of nearly every game. North Fork's "hometown" of Cowley staged a celebratory evening for the team in mid-August. Between the dinner and the dance (which went on until dawn), a long round of toasts was proposed and answered as the three trophies, filled with champagne, made their way from hand to hand around the hall.

It would be sixteen years before another Alberta team visited Winnipeg and the St. Charles Country Club.

It went almost without notice that the 1912 Alberta season closed with the first tournament to be hosted by the town of Cochrane.

Toward the end of September, a large number of players from area clubs descended on the new racetrack field to play in a revival of the Ladies' Cup matches of a decade earlier. While the results of the various matches are of no real significance, the tournament did establish that Cochrane had both the facilities and the community support to stage a major tournament. One year later, after much lobbying by O.A. Critchley, the town would play host to one version of the 1913 Western Canada Championship.

While Critchley did not (as some stories suggest) introduce polo to the Cochrane area,

there is no question that without his boundless enthusiasm for the game, Cochrane would never have progressed as far as it had in such a short time.

Again in 1913, the first news of the new season came from California. A carload of seventeen Alberta ponies, under the care of Harry Robertson, left for Coronado at the end of November, 1912, with the rest of the team scheduled to leave in time to get in some practice before the first match on New Year's Day. Playing with Robertson would be Pekisko's Carlé and Snowden and Cochrane's O.A. Critchley. Team sponsor, George Ross, let it be known that he would be happy to play with the team should any of them be injured.

Although the team lost its opening day match against Pasadena, it acquitted itself well for the rest of the season, competing for as many as five different trophies at various tournaments. One headline from the tour perfectly represents how much the world had changed in the two-and-a-half decades since Wilmot dumped his bag of sticks and balls onto the rough grass of the Alberta Ranche: "Pekisko Lose to Hawaiians."

In general, the 1913 Alberta season seemed a quiet affair. It is not clear whether this reflected the real level of activity or simply that the press (especially in Calgary) was not paying as much attention to the game as it used to. Millarville had over twenty subscriptions, with at least a dozen paying the $5 surcharge for playing members, but there is no entry at all in the High River club minute book for 1913. Pekisko's subscription list had dropped substantially in the past couple of years, but they were still talking about hosting a tournament. There was no word from the polo grounds at Fish Creek.

The season really amounted to two tournaments, both of them claiming to be a western championship. In mid-July, Cochrane hosted the "Western Canada Polo Association Tournament" and, a month later, Cowley

put the Osler cup into play during what they expected to be a major gathering of the western teams.

At Cochrane, the turnout was impressive, if not comprehensive. Five teams were announced — Macleod and Cowley from the south; Fish Creek, Millarville and Cochrane from the local area — and they would play for the Van Wart Cup. North Fork was a last-minute cancellation and there was no word at all from High River or Pekisko. A series of Ladies' Cup matches would fill out the week.

While significant teams were missing, the Cochrane tournament came closer to fulfilling the decade-old desire to draw all the major clubs together than any before it. The newspapers opined that it would, "...in coming years be made the greatest tournament in the Dominion." The events of less than a year later made everyone wish that it could have been accomplished sooner.

In a full slate of preliminaries, it was Cochrane over Macleod and Fish Creek over Millarville. Fish Creek then beat Cowley for the right to meet the hosts for the main prize. The Ladies' Cup was captured by a foursome under the leadership of Fort Macleod's Dr. A.H. Kennedy. The Macleod papers were quick to report on the "splendid victory" of this second generation player. Less than a month later, those same papers covered the death of his father, Dr. George Kennedy, pioneer Mounted Police surgeon, founding member of the polo club and the town's leading citizen.

The final for the Van Wart trophy was not a particularly close affair. Fish Creek was able to run the Cochrane ponies into the ground in the later stages of the game and cruised to a 10-4 win.

While the tournament showcased most of the best players of the time, including Willie Deane-Freeman, Condie Landale and Harry Robertson, in the end it was three old Fish Creek familiars who carried the day. Frank Macnaghten, Addie Hone and his cousin Mick showed them all that they still knew how to play the game.

One of the conditions of the Osler cup, won the year before by North Fork, was that it be played for in the hometown of the current holders. Using the Osler as a drawing card, the town of Cowley went all out in preparing to host its first major tournament.

The *Lethbridge Daily Herald* put the price tag for the tournament at $6,500, most of it spent on preparing the grounds at the South Alberta Country Club. Seven teams were expected and games would be played in front of Alberta's lieutenant governor. Immediately following the tournament, several of the teams were scheduled to travel to Spokane, Washington to try for the new Western States Championship.

On their way to Cowley, Cochrane stopped off in Fort Macleod to defend the Macleod Cup. The town had been hoping for bigger things, previously announcing that Millarville and Pekisko would also be joining in, but it came down to a one-game affair between host and defender.

Even with hired gun Harry Robertson, Macleod was no match for Critchley, de la Vergne, Rhodes and Landale and Cochrane retained the Macleod Cup by 7-4.

One week later, the Cowley tournament also failed to meet that town's high expectations. Of the seven teams promised, only four arrived. Joining North Fork, Cowley and Fort Macleod, Cochrane was the only team from outside the immediate area. To make matters worse, the weather did not cooperate, keeping the hoped-for crowds to a minimum on some days and causing the final match to be delayed by twenty-four hours.

It was North Fork over Macleod followed by Cochrane over Cowley, leaving what were clearly the best two foursomes in the tournament (perhaps even in the province) to play for the Osler cup. If the tournament did not entirely live up to its promise, the final match certainly did. It took a full twenty-five minutes of overtime before Cochrane could score the winner and add to its rapidly growing collection of silverware.

The tournament concluded with a Ladies' Cup match and an "English versus Everyone Else" all-star finale. Following the presentation of trophies by the lieutenant governor and a dinner dance, all four teams left for the Spokane Interstate Fairgrounds.

The 1913 tournament in Spokane was designed to stimulate public interest in the game of polo in eastern Washington and neighbouring Idaho. The board of the Interstate Fair had offered to pay all expenses for the Canadian teams and, to add to the attraction, a splendid new trophy would go to the winners. That trophy, presented by Spokane businessman Thaddeus S. Lane, would come to be known as the Northwestern International Challenge Cup and would be played for regularly over the years by teams from the United States' Pacific Northwest and Western Canada.

The tournament was, by all accounts, a great success, with Cochrane and Macleod eventually playing for third-place honours. Macleod managed to exact a measure of revenge and ended the Cochrane winning streak with a solid victory. North Fork, back on form, managed to make it to the final where they lost to a team from Portland, Oregon by a single marker. North Fork's would-be tying goal missed by an inch just moments before the timer's bugle ended the game.

The tournament was a success in more ways than one. Spokane, together with Boise, Idaho and Portland, soon became known for their top-flight polo. And, probably as a result of their exposure to those emerging teams, Jimmy Milvain, Bert Connelly, Harry Robertson and Hugh Pettit would all find themselves playing professional polo in the northwestern United States.

That first Spokane tournament marked the end of a frustrating year for Alberta polo. Although Calgary-Fish Creek had won the Cochrane meeting, it was not a season where the traditional powerhouses had triumphed often. Indeed, it was Cochrane itself, in only its fourth year of serious play, which emerged as the dominant Calgary-area team, travelling widely and winning more than its share of matches against a series of credible opponents. In the south there had been a new enthusiasm for the game and, had it not been for the failure of teams like Millarville, Calgary and Pekisko-High River to appear as promised, Alberta could well have had at least three major tournaments that would have settled the matter of provincial supremacy once and for all. In short, 1913 was a season of lost opportunities; opportunities that would never present themselves again.

Compounding an already confusing 1913 tournament schedule, Winnipeg hosted a fall meeting that also laid claim to being the Western Canada Championship.

The 1913 Winterton Cup tournament at the St. Charles club was largely a local affair. The Alberta clubs that might have thought of travelling east (including the defending champions from North Fork) had gone south instead to play in Spokane. A team from Regina provided the only outside competition. 1913 was also the year in which the Strathcona's first appeared as a team entirely in their own right.

The tournament began at the end of the first week in September with a four-team round robin involving Regina, the Barracks and two teams from St. Charles.

The soldiers quickly showed themselves to be the class of the field, winning all three of their matches, followed by Country Club "A," Country Club "B" and Regina, which failed to win a game.

The Winterton Cup-winning team was an all-Strathcona's foursome with Shaw, Cameron and

Polo at Cochrane, 1913 – (left to right) Dick Brown, Oswald Critchley and Gilbert Rhodes.

Glenbow archives, NA-2924-6

A.C. Critchley joined by A.C.'s brother, Jack who had been posted to the regiment in 1911. It did not start out that way, however. The tournament began with Louis Lipsett in the saddle but, in the first game, he had collided heavily with teammate A.C. Critchley and been knocked unconscious. That put Cameron into the match and he remained on the team for the duration. Again, Lipsett's was not the only injury in what were apparently a spirited series of matches. In an opening-day game between Regina and St. Charles' "B" squad, Winnipeg's Mr. Justice Metcalfe had lost several teeth to a blow from a mallet. Polo matches at the St. Charles always seemed to produce a steady stream of more than trifling wounds.

The 1913 tournament marked the final appearance of Major Lipsett. A British officer attached to the headquarters at Fort Osborne, on mobilization in 1914, he chose to stay with the Canadian Forces. After commanding the Royal Winnipeg Rifles in the desperate battles around Ypres, he rose to the rank of major-general in command of the 3rd Canadian Division. He was killed at the Battle of Mount Sorrel in 1916.

It has often been claimed that the 1913 Winnipeg tournament gave the Strathcona's the Western Canada Championship, their only such win until they repeated the feat in Calgary in 1931. The Winterton trophy, however, represented only the St. Charles club's championship. The western Canadian cup was the Chipman and newspaper accounts of the tournament made no mention of it being up for play in 1913. To add to the confusion, a photograph of the 1913 Strathcona's team — posed behind a table jammed with their season's haul of trophies — clearly shows the Chipman Cup sitting at the front on the right-hand side.

In the final analysis, the problem with establishing who was the 1913 western Canadian champion rests with the Western Canada Polo Association itself. The organization's fundamental weakness allowed three tournaments to claim that theirs was the "real thing." Cochrane, Cowley and, apparently, Winnipeg, all believed they were hosting a western championship (and Cochrane actually had the largest number of teams competing). But, while Cochrane offered the Van Wart Cup and Cowley the Osler, only Winnipeg had the Chipman. Since the Chipman Cup was acknowledged as symbolic of western Canadian polo supremacy, the 1913 champions were Lord Strathcona's Horse.

It is far too easy to say the momentous events of August, 1914 slammed the door on the first great era of polo in the Canadian West. While the outbreak of war certainly brought the game to a shuddering stop, it was not solely responsible for the confusions and disappointments which characterized that final season. The record of the years leading up to the spring of 1914, and of that last year itself, show that western polo was already in the throes of another of its frequent upheavals and transitions.

The 1914 season had opened in mid-April with the Calgary meeting of the Western Canada Polo Association where the tournament schedule for the year was presumably settled. Unfortunately, records of these meetings have not survived so it is difficult to know which clubs were still taking an active role. Fort Macleod was present and so was High River. Calgary-Fish Creek would certainly have been there, probably with Millarville and Cochrane, too. Pincher Creek, though, had fallen quiet again and North Fork-Cowley, not generally represented at the association's meetings, might still have been smarting from the losses incurred at its high-priced association-supported tournament the previous year.

The Cochrane papers reported the beginning of regular practice in mid-May while, at the same time, Fort Macleod announced that it would be the site of a major association-sanctioned meet to begin on July 14th. A week later, the *High River Times* reported that the local club would host a fall tournament with up to twelve clubs competing. To live up to an association stipulation that the grounds must be in first-class condition, the club hired a crew to level and irrigate the field.

The biggest news of the year should have been that the Calgary club, after nearly ten years without a proper home, would be playing on a new, permanent field just southwest of the city at Chinook Park.

Although the new polo grounds were officially opened on Saturday, June 20th, the day was not marked by the kind of tournament that one might have expected for such a major event. The crowds were reported to be the largest ever to watch polo in Alberta, but they were cheering for only two teams: Fish Creek and Cochrane.

The match was touted as the Western Canada Championship, based largely on the fact that Cochrane was putting the Osler cup up for play. They had won it in 1913 at Cowley and, although the rules stated that the cup should be defended at the home ground of the winning team, Cochrane had agreed to bring it to Calgary. There was a good deal of pre-match publicity in the press, special buses were booked to take the crowds out to the new grounds and the starting time was delayed so as not to interfere with the unveiling of Calgary's Boer War Memorial earlier in the day.

And, there would be one additional feature at the match. It would be refereed by Major Colin George Ross, back from Coronado for a visit.

Cochrane was represented by its best foursome of O.A. Critchley, Condie Landale, de la Vergne and Rhodes. Fish Creek came with its 1913 Cochrane-winning team of Frank Macnaghten, Addie and Mick Hone and a fast-developing second-generation player named Dick Brown.

The score was close through much of the first half, with Fish Creek holding a steady lead and, apparently, able to rise to any threat from the Cochrane four. In the second half, Fish Creek pulled out to a comfortable 11-4 lead by the end of the fifth chukker, but Cochrane struck quickly at the beginning of the sixth, bringing the score to 11-6. At this point, the Calgary *Albertan* reported:

• ⊹ ⟨•⟩●⟨•⟩ ⊹ •

The Fish Creek players suddenly realized that their friends who had bet that they would double the score would be out of pocket unless they got busy, and with only four minutes left they gave the best exhibition of the game and succeeded in scoring two goals before time was called, Macnaghten being the chief factor in each of the scores.

• ⊹ ⟨•⟩●⟨•⟩ ⊹ •

It was a promising debut for the new Calgary Polo Club, but it would be five years or more before the grounds would see another match.

Obviously unimpressed by Cowley's 1913 difficulties (or by its own previous experience of failed expectations), Fort Macleod pressed full-steam ahead with preparations for its 1914 tournament. The *Macleod Spectator* could barely contain its enthusiasm:

This tournament will continue for a week and will be the big event of the year in Western Canada polo circles.... Tournament week should be a very lively time in Macleod. At least fifty players will be present from outside points ...[and] there will also be quite a number of visitors here to see the games. Macleod will give [them] a warm welcome.

The host club had spent a good deal of time and effort to bring the field into top-flight condition and even erected a new clubhouse. The eight teams expected would be playing for two trophies: the old Macleod Cup and a new cup presented by Colonel Evans of Montreal (probably local regular Harry Evans' father).

Then, as had so often been the case in previous years, the following news appeared in the *Macleod Spectator* on July 9th:

The people of Macleod will be disappointed to learn that the polo tournament which it was expected to have played here next week, under the auspices of the Western Canada Polo Association, is not to take place owing to the fact that the teams of Cochrane, Fish Creek and Millarville have backed out at the eleventh hour, notwithstanding the fact that when the tournament was arranged, they gave their promise to attend.

The paper grudgingly announced a smaller tournament with teams from Pekisko and Cowley playing the hosts for the two cups, but did not try to hide its disdain for the no-shows:

The members of the Macleod club deeply regret the unsportsmanlike conduct of the teams who have backed out, but it is through no fault of the local club.

In anticipation of this tournament, the Macleod Club have gone to considerable expense in fitting up the grounds. They have had an attractive club house erected and made other improvements.

In the end, even Pekisko failed to appear and Macleod won its own cup in a single match with a team from Cowley. There is no record of what happened to Colonel Evans' new silverware. It may never have been contested.

Fort Macleod's frustration at the failure of teams to appear as promised certainly seems justified. It is tempting to look toward August and see an excuse, but if the coming war had been the reason for the no-shows, the papers would certainly have said so. Rather, the problem again seemed to lie with a weak association which had, for the past few years, begun each season by making promises that it simply did not keep. Only the Cochrane tournament of 1913 came close to meeting expectations. Certainly, after their experiences of 1913 and 1914, neither Macleod nor Cowley would have had much reason to continue supporting the organization.

If the Western Canada Polo Association was weak, it was because its member teams were also weak. Or, at least, they were not as strong as their optimistic springtime promises. At the start of the 1914 season, playing memberships at Pekisko, High River and Millarville were perhaps slightly higher than in the past two seasons, but still not close to their levels of 1909 or 1910. Cochrane had a strong core of sound regulars, but there was little evidence they were attracting a substantial number of new players. Even with a new home, Calgary continued to be what it had been for several seasons: a shadow of its former self. It would be well after the war before Calgary re-emerged as the pre-eminent centre for polo not just in the West, but in all of Canada.

There was little polo reported in Winnipeg during 1914 and only one tournament caught the eye of the local press. During the third week of July, two teams from St. Charles went to Regina to play a pair of teams from that city's Wascana Country Club. Despite its hit-and-miss history in the province of Saskatchewan, polo seems to have found a home at one of Regina's most prestigious social institutions. It would have been encouraging to see the game finally take hold and add another strong presence to the network of western Canadian teams.

There seemed hope, too, that Regina could reverse its province's dismal tournament record as one of the Wascana teams actually won its opening match against a Winnipeg team that featured a visiting Oswald Critchley (Frank McHugh was in town, too, and played a few chukkers for Regina). In the end, though, Winnipeg won the tournament, easily taking both games on the final day.

Within a week, Canada was at war and it would be eight years before Winnipeg's St. Charles Country Club again took to the field. As for Regina, polo was finished once and for all.

It remained only for the High River tournament to close the 1914 season and, as would become obvious in the years that followed, to close the first era of polo in the Canadian West.

How things had changed since the first announcements were published back in the spring. Indeed, it is surprising to learn that the High River tournament was not cancelled long before its scheduled start at the beginning of September.

The tournament was eventually cancelled, but not as a result of the outbreak of war. Rather, it was the weather that proved the great enemy. The ten or twelve teams promised in the spring had been reduced to just three as the tournament opened. It is no surprise, after the events of July, that Macleod and the other southern teams chose not to appear. Cochrane and Calgary also stayed home, the *High River Times* putting their absence down to the clubs having already lost several players to service in Europe.

Pekisko and Millarville opened play on Monday afternoon and, on Monday night, the rain began to fall. By Tuesday afternoon, the field was under water and

A young Bill Holmes at the High River club, c. 1913.

the balance of the tournament was called off. By the time the annual polo social was held later in the week, attendance was small and there were no visitors left in town to join their hosts for the dance.

Still, the *Times* could report that it was "a pleasant affair."

NECK

Polo match in the
Okanagan, c. 1912.

CHAPTER 5

OR NOTHING

BRITISH COLUMBIA
1896–1914

AT THE 1896 TOURNAMENT that had represented both the high and low water marks for early polo on Vancouver Island, the three local teams were joined by a foursome from the Nicola Valley, deep in the British Columbia Interior.

While Victoria and Esquimalt were immediate neighbours and Cowichan Bay only thirty miles up the coast, the Nicola team had invested a tremendous effort to reach the tournament. From the valley, trailing nine ponies, they had followed the rough course of the Nicola River north and west, a distance of some fifty miles, to meet the Canadian Pacific's transcontinental line at Spence's Bridge. From there it was a long train ride down the Fraser River Canyon and across the lower mainland to Vancouver, all capped by a ferry crossing to Victoria.

The club played well enough — beating Victoria and Cowichan while losing only to the Navy — and the press was taken by their tenacity and their planning:

The visitors profited by the forethought and enterprise which had led them to come equipped with nine ponies, enabling them to finish the match with fresh mounts all 'round, while the home team had but one pony in reserve.

For the Nicola team, the tournament seems to have been a "one-off" event. For three of the players — team organizer Captain H.R. Cholmondeley, Captain A.C. Bald and Mr. Broadbent — these would be their only recorded Canadian matches. A fourth, Captain John Nash, would appear again with various Interior teams until his death in the first war.

The brief early history of the Island game notwithstanding, the seeds of a strong, distinct and long-lived tradition of polo in the British Columbia Interior were sown in Victoria.

The sons of William Curtis Ward,
c. 1895 – (left to right) William
Arthur, George Desborough,
Francis Bulkley and Cecil.

It is easy to see, in the development of parts of the Interior, strong parallels with the southern Alberta foothills a few hundred miles to the east over the Continental Divide. Today, the Nicola Valley's dry, rolling grasslands are populated mostly by large herds of Hereford-cross cattle, raised, managed and marketed by a few huge ranches. Like Alberta, these ranches were founded in the last third of the nineteenth century by men and money that flowed into the country in anticipation of booming markets brought about by the building of the Canadian Pacific Railway.

On the face, the connections seem obvious, but under those surface similarities, the two really share little in the way of a common heritage. The men and the money that started and sustained British Columbia's interior ranching boom did not come from the east, either from Alberta or directly from Britain. Rather they came from the south and the west, especially from the substantial pool of homegrown capital that had accumulated in Victoria.

Before the railway arrived, Victoria and the Interior had little or nothing to do with the rest of Canada. Britain was thousands of nautical miles away around Cape Horn and the colony was administered as a private fiefdom of the Hudson's Bay Company. Then, in 1857, gold was discovered in the canyons of the lower Fraser River and Victoria became home base for the flood of prospectors that poured in from all over the world. Those prospectors (including a large number from California who had not struck it rich in the rush of '49) needed provisions and picks, a place to register their claims and banks to handle their nuggets and dust. Victoria and a few small mainland settlements boomed.

What made the Interior largely inaccessible from east or west were the north-south mountain ranges that stretched almost continuously from the Divide to the coast. As the prospectors pushed north up the inter-mountain valleys into the Cariboo country, the first ranchers came behind them. Bringing herds in from Washington and Oregon, they were hoping to sell their cattle and sheep in the flourishing mine settlements and to supply the horses and mules needed to pack supplies up the new Cariboo Road.

As the rush began to pale in the mid-1860s, Victoria found itself the capital of a newly prosperous colony. Many of the boomers drifted away, but many stayed and, in 1871, with the promise of a transcontinental railway link to the rest of Canada, British Columbia's 12,000 white residents agreed to join Confederation. As a measure of the scale of the gold fever that had hit the province, those 12,000 souls amounted to less than half the total population of a single Cariboo boom town of only a few years earlier.

In the years between provincehood and the building of the railway, the British Columbia Interior grew slowly, restrained by the difficulty of moving agricultural products toward the markets that were available. But as the C.P.R. began construction from the East and the West, the demand for livestock to feed the burgeoning work crews drew some of Victoria's gold rush profits toward grassland valleys like the Nicola.

In the late 1870s and early 1880s, anticipating the impact of the railway, a small group of Victoria businessmen began to acquire large blocks of grazing land just east of the Nicola Valley. They also tried to buy options on every cow then grazing in the Interior in order to control the price of beef for the C.P.R. crews. The group's foray into the cattle business resulted in substantial profits from the railway's provisioners and, more important, the birth of the Douglas Lake Cattle Company. To this day, it remains the largest cattle ranch in Canada.

The syndicate member who eventually became sole owner of the Douglas Lake Ranch was William Curtis Ward, a self-made capitalist who had come to Victoria in 1864 as an accountant in the local branch of the English-owned Bank of British Columbia. Rising quickly to manage all of the bank's B.C. operations, he became a central player in the city's financial and business community. And two of his sons would emerge as central players in the history of polo in British Columbia.

When the Royal Navy first challenged the gentlemen of Victoria in 1889, W.C. Ward's son, Cecil, was one of those who picked up the gauntlet. W.C.'s brother-in-law, Mortimer G. Drummond, was another. Cecil played against the Warspite team in 1891 and was on the field again when Calgary came to town in 1892.

Cecil did not play in that last tournament in 1896 and his place was taken by his twenty-two-year-old brother, F.B. Ward. This was the beginning of Frank's lifelong passion for a game he would play until he was past sixty-five years of age.

Another Ward was on the field that day, playing for the Royal Navy team. George Desborough Ward was Cecil and Frank's younger brother and a later biography of William Curtis states that he had a son with "a command in the British Channel Squadron." Clearly, George went on to make a career of the Royal Navy.

Though the game died in Victoria after 1896, several of the players involved appeared again within a year or two, fronting teams of their own in the B.C. Interior.

Cecil Ward left Victoria in 1897 and established a law practice in the thriving Thompson River town of Kamloops. One of his first actions in his new home was to start a polo club.

However, it was not the first time that the people of Kamloops had seen the game played.

In July, 1890, under the small headline "The Polo Match," the *Kamloops Inland Sentinel* reported the following in its account of a Dominion Day horse race meeting:

———— ❖══❖◦❍◦❖══❖ ❖ ————

This event was something new in sports at Kamloops and was looked for eagerly by an expectant crowd. The players took their positions on the field, four on a side, captained by L. Victor and L. Campbell respectively. The ball was tossed in by Mr. J.S. Bennett, and the game commenced.

Very little can be said regarding the merits of the game as evidenced by the play of either side, this being their initial effort. As an exhibition of horsemanship the game had attractive features, the revolutions of the animals, and the rapid and almost human-like manner in which they responded to the touch of the rein, showing the high stage of training reached on the ranges.

Play was continued for about twenty minutes without either side appearing to gain any advantage when time was called and the game was declared a draw.

———— ❖══❖◦❍◦❖══❖ ❖ ————

Nothing more was heard of the game until June 4th of 1897 when this notice appeared in the *Inland Sentinel:*

It is proposed to start a polo club in town and a meeting with that object in view will be held on Monday evening next at 8 o'clock at Fulton and Ward's offices. Arrangements have already been made for the use of George Loney's pasture for a polo ground in the event of the club being formed. If polo should flourish anywhere it ought to be in Kamloops, and the proposed club should prove a success from the start.

In the 1890s, the booming town of Kamloops may have resembled Calgary or any of the other western ranching centres given life by the C.P.R., but it had a history that was far deeper than anything on the southern Prairies. Kamloops was not born as a cowtown or a Mounted Police fort, but as a fur trade post, first for American Jacob Astor's Pacific Fur Company and then for the North West Company and the Hudson's Bay. It was the site of a continuous white presence since the first trading post was built in 1811 and was accessible from the south via a series of waterways, great and small, that connected it to the Columbia River. Its links to the eastern Canadian trading companies were via Fort Edmonton and Jasper House across the Divide to the northeast and the post's position at the confluence of the North and South Thompson rivers made it an obvious centre for the fur trade in the Interior.

Kamloops retained its central importance throughout the fur trade era and then, as that enterprise declined, saw its fortunes rise again as an important commercial hub during the brief, chaotic Cariboo gold rush fever of the late 1850s.

The area was quiet through the 1870s, though the promise of the transcontinental railway (and the appearance of the first Canadian Pacific surveyors at the beginning of the decade) sustained the hopes of both the Hudson's Bay Company and the few cattle ranchers who remained after the collapse of the gold rush.

With construction east from Yale underway in 1880 and the assurance that the railway would, in fact, be going through Kamloops, the town began to boom again. The construction crews soon moved east toward Craigellachie where the last spike in the transcontinental track was driven, but when the first train rolled into Kamloops on July 11th, 1885, the town's future was secured. Although still boasting a population of less than five hundred, Kamloops was incorporated in 1893, already possessed of a small telephone exchange and an electric light company.

(left to right) Arthur Winterbottom,
"Worty" Wood, Bill Fernie and
W.F. Richardson, Kamloops' Watson
Cup winners, 1902.

When the Kamloops Polo Club held its inaugural meeting in mid-June of 1897, its membership reflected the mix of town professionals and surrounding ranchers that would characterize the nature of the game in the district. According to the *Inland Sentinel:*

The organization of the Kamloops Polo Club has been completed. It starts with a good membership and promises to be a great success. Officers were elected as follows: President – James Ogden Grahame; Secretary – C.W. Ward; Executive Committee – A. Winterbottom, E.W. Praeger, C.W. Sarel, F. Parkes and F.J. Deane.

Two good practices have already been held on Loney's field, which makes an excellent ground. Anyone desirous of joining the club should communicate at once with the secretary.

President Grahame ran the Hudson's Bay Company in town and represented the "new" Kamloops. Appointed in 1882 to run a modern general store, he was the first non-fur trader to head the company's operations.

Born in 1863, committee member Arthur Winterbottom had left his native England and settled near Calgary in 1884, eventually selling out and moving to Kamloops in 1896. While there is no record of his participation with the Calgary Polo Club in those years, he was almost certainly a player, at least at the practice level. He is generally credited with taking the first polo ponies across the Divide, but, again, that event is not recorded.

Winterbottom, with his wife and five children, lived in the district for nearly fifty years, operating the Noble Ranch on the North Thompson until he joined the British Columbia Department of Fisheries, retiring in 1935. He served variously as the polo club secretary and team captain for many years and was the man who brought W.J. Roper's new Polo Challenge Cup back with him after a trip home to England in about 1900. Winterbottom died in 1943, just past his eightieth birthday.

E.W. Praeger, employed by the Bank of British Columbia, was only in Kamloops briefly before being transferred to the bank's branch in the Kootenay mining town of Sandon. Wentworth Sarel dabbled in real estate and served as editor of a new Kamloops newspaper, the *Kamloops Standard,* first published in 1897. He remained in town until 1902 when he left for Vancouver.

Francis J. Deane was also a newspaper man, the editor and eventual owner of the *Inland Sentinel.* He remained in the city until after the turn of the century and served one term in the provincial legislature. Perhaps his most notable achievement came as secretary to the Commission of Inquiry into Chinese immigration, the body responsible for imposing British Columbia's now-notorious $500 head tax, specifically aimed at choking off any further Chinese immigration.

Frank Parkes came to Kamloops from England in 1894. He served with the Strathcona's in the Boer War, then homesteaded with his brother at Monte Creek just east of town. He went overseas again in World War I, then moved about the province in a variety of farming enterprises. In 1923 he took his family to Washington's Olympic Peninsula where he worked until his retirement in 1953. He died in 1956 after falling a hundred and seventy-five feet down a cliff while prospecting for uranium west of Port Angeles. He was eighty-four years old at the time.

From the outset, the club was clearly intended to be a serious, well-organized operation. One of its first acts was the publication of a small pamphlet — "The Rules and Regulations of the Kamloops Polo Club" — that required members to play according to the Hurlingham Rules, including the 14-2 limit on the height of their ponies. The publication also defined the club's colours: a pale blue jersey with sleeves and collar of primrose yellow.

During that first year, the club began holding regular Tuesday and Thursday practices and playing pick-up games among the members. The first reported match pitted an "East Side" team of Parkes, Praeger, Deane and J. Beattie against a "West Side" squad of Winterbottom and Sarel, one D. Maclean and a C. Winterbottom whose one-time appearance suggests he was a visiting relative of Arthur's. The game was a dusty 1-goal draw.

Equipping the players proved difficult. Although sticks and balls could be ordered directly from India (as they were by most western clubs), saddles were a problem. With all the Englishmen settling in the district, it is hard to imagine that English riding saddles were hard to find, but apparently they were. Most riders had quickly adopted the sturdier, more practical western saddle. Cecil Ward made saddles one of his priorities and, whenever he came across one in his travels around the district, he would buy it and then resell it at a reasonable price to one of the other club members.

Another problem for Kamloops in its first few years of existence was finding regular outside competition. With only a couple of uncertain exceptions, the nearest serious polo clubs were more than three hundred and fifty miles away, across the Divide in southern Alberta. But there were other polo players in the B.C. Interior.

On October 15, 1897, the *Inland Sentinel* covered a match in Kamloops between the club and a team from "Chilcotin." It was clearly not the first to be played between them since the newspaper called it "another one-sided game, resulting in a win for the home team by 4 to o." That the visitors from the Chilcotin district should have remained in town for some time is not a surprise. The area is some one hundred and fifty miles to the northwest of Kamloops.

The Chilcotin team actually featured only two players from that district, the foursome filled out by two Kamloops regulars, N.J. Hopkins and C.W. Sarel. Both visiting players, however, had solid connections with Cecil Ward and with the beginning of polo in British Columbia. M.G. Drummond and H.F. Newton had played with Ward in that first 1889 Victoria match against the Royal Navy.

On their ranches at Alexis Creek and Riske Creek, Drummond and Newton were often joined by

Kamloops Museum & Archives, 1754

(left to right) W.U. Homfray, George Harding, George Butler, Charles Johnson, Grande Prairie's Roper Cup champions, 1902.

their neighbours — the Armstrongs, T.E. Young and H.P. Bayliff, H. Davis, Charles Moore and R.C. Cotton — for a few rough chukkers of polo, their hardest task usually being to find eight players.

According to Daphne Lodwick, Chilcotin polo began as early as 1890 and lasted for about five years (including one game played during a big thaw between Christmas and New Year) but there was at least a vestige surviving as late as 1897. Lodwick suggests that polo died out as most of the players left the district, a pattern common to many of the earliest teams in the West, but the Bayliff family still ranches in the district and still uses a brand or lumber stamp based on a polo stick and ball.

One man who played with Drummond and then moved on was Lord Edward Seymour, third son of the Marquess of Hertford. While little is known about the eventual fate of most of the players from the Chilcotin,

Seymour does reappear just after the turn of the century, this time as a semi-regular with the club at Millarville, Alberta. By then he was nursing wounds received during the Boer War.

While no other games were reported during the Kamloops club's inaugural season of 1897, it did sponsor the first of what would become a long and successful series of gymkhanas and "paper chases." Indeed, these events, together with horse racing, usually received more attention from the press than the polo matches.

Practice polo and gymkhanas were held in 1898, too, until late September when a new team made its appearance on the record. Grande Prairie was a few miles southeast of Kamloops in the Salmon River Valley. Although its name was later changed to Westwold, the area remains today what it has always been: a small, close-knit community of farmers and ranchers.

From the outset, the team became a thorn in the side of the much larger Kamloops club and of every other team they faced. The first recorded match between Kamloops and Grande Prairie took place at the Grande Prairie racetrack and featured Gibb, Moberly, George Harding and A.E. Nash. Hamilton Gibb (sometimes styled "Gibbs") is largely unknown but has been credited with organizing the team. A.E. Nash, who appeared on occasion with both Grande Prairie and Kamloops (and was no relation to Nicola's John Nash), had come into the country a few years earlier from the Prairies where he and his brothers had been involved in the Northwest Rebellion.

The low-scoring game — 2-1 in favour of Grande Prairie — was attributed to the inexperience of the ponies, but the players were probably just learning the game and what must have been a terribly rough field played its part. The teams played a return match

in Kamloops a few days later, with the home team posting a 4-1 win. This game saw the appearance for Grande Prairie of W.U. Homfray.

Born in England in 1866, Homfray came into the valley with his brother in 1885 and soon turned from farming to a number of commercial ventures. Within a decade, he had built a large hotel named the "Adelphi," together with a store, a smithy and a post office, and clearly intended to build his own village carrying that name. He also owned the highly successful racetrack which sported a grandstand and a number of his own horses. When the venture failed to prosper sufficiently, he sold out in about 1911 and took up the real estate business in Kamloops.

A born speculator, Walter Homfray was probably flat broke as often as he was rich and he died penniless in Kamloops in 1951.

The year 1899 began with Kamloops' now-usual organizational meeting in mid-April. The club scheduled its gymkhanas and accepted Grande Prairie's challenge for a pair of polo games on the long weekends in May and July. Cecil Ward was still the club secretary and E.A. Nash (confusingly, A.E. Nash's brother) was elected president.

The May 24th polo match was 4-0 in favour of Kamloops, but the *Inland Sentinel* suggested that, with more practice, Grande Prairie could become a strong team. Although Kamloops also won the second game in Grande Prairie on the Dominion Day weekend by five goals to one, such victories would come less and less often in the following years.

Decent playing grounds were hard to find around Kamloops during the first few years of the club's life. They began play on the north side of the South Thompson River in a meadow owned by George Loney. Since there was no bridge at that time, it was Loney's ferry that transported players and ponies across the river. The meadow was anything but ideal for polo and, on at least one occasion, the ferry broke loose and carried the Kamloops polo club downstream on the strong Thompson current until a safe landing could be made at the Mission Flats, back on the south side of the river west of town.

A second field was briefly established at Mission Flats, but it, too, was unsuitable (although at least it didn't require a ferry ride). The club tried again on the east side of town, but the area was dry, dusty and very uneven.

The players were not being unnecessarily finicky. In Kamloops and its immediate environs, flat land is hard to find. The city lies along the narrow valley of the Thompson. Just a few hundred yards back from the river, the valley flats give way to dry hills rising precipitously to several hundred feet. Today, the downtown area is surrounded on all sides by terraces of new houses and condominiums that stretch up the hillsides. Most of the available land along the river is either premium, irrigated farmland or covered by tracts of houses and very permanent-looking mobile home parks.

The club eventually settled on land leased from the Kamloops Indian reserve, and, with one brief interruption, used the field continuously until 1939 when it played its last chukkers.

The 1900 and 1901 seasons continued the pattern of inter-club play in Kamloops and Grande Prairie, with the two teams meeting each other once or twice a year. Then, in late 1901, play began for the Roper Cup, a polo challenge trophy which was intended to symbolize polo supremacy in British Columbia.

William James Roper had first come into the country with his brother in 1871 to take charge of the Hudson's Bay Company horses and, the next year, pre-empted land along Cherry Creek just west of Kamloops. Over the years, he developed one of the finest ranching operations in the Interior and is said to have been largely responsible for the introduction of Hereford cattle, still the dominant breed in the area. He was an early patron of many of Kamloops' social institutions, including its hospital, agricultural association and, of course, its polo club.

Two of his nephews came to work for him at Cherry Creek in 1873 and later forged one of the earliest connections between southern Alberta and the B.C. Interior. In 1882, John and William Roper Hull drove a herd of horses across the Divide to Calgary where they fetched a handsome price. With William remaining in Calgary and John based in Kamloops, the brothers developed a chain of retail butcher shops from Calgary to Vancouver and William became one of the first of the

Kelowna Museum

Calgary area's great cattle barons. He is remembered by the polo fraternity for his donation of a trophy to the Calgary club; one that is still being played for today.

The first match for the Roper Cup was played in Kamloops and, by three goals to one, the red-shirted foursome from Grande Prairie became the first to put their names on the new trophy. Engraved beside Homfray, Harding and Butler, is the name F.G. Gordon.

English-born Frank Gordon was well-known in the Grande Prairie area, managing the ranch and hotel operations of an absentee English owner. A short, stocky man, Gordon's great handlebar moustache is immediately recognizable in even the most faded of the old Grande Prairie polo photographs. He played the game until well into the 1920s, putting his name on the Roper Cup at least six times. He died in 1949.

The 1901 Roper Cup match also saw the first report on the fine play of Kamloops' Alfred W. Johnson, who scored the team's only goal. An early member of the club, Johnson was widely known in the area as a Dominion land surveyor. He later set up his own surveying business in the town. He served in the Boer War, leading Kamloops' first contingent of volunteers in joining the Lord Strathcona's Horse, and then enlisted again in 1915. A lieutenant with the Argyll and Sutherland Highlanders and later captain with the Royal Engineers, he was gassed in France in April, 1918 and died a fortnight later.

The 1901 season ended with a banquet at the Cosmopolitan Hotel when Roper presented his cup to Walter Homfray, the Grande Prairie captain.

In 1902, the Roper Cup competition took a new turn as another Interior club began play. Although still a long way from being a tournament of the kind played in southern Alberta, possession of the cup would be determined by a playoff between any contending teams, with the winner to play the current holder for the title. So it was that, on the afternoon of June 13th, 1902, Kamloops travelled to the town of Kelowna to play against its new polo club.

Today, Kelowna and the nearby town of Vernon are the thriving business and agricultural centres of the Okanagan Valley. Located perhaps a hundred miles southeast of Kamloops on a major north-south route between the United States and the northern Interior, the area had long been settled by various Native bands and Christian missions before the first townsites were laid out in the mid-1890s.

Like the operations at Kamloops' B.C. Fruitlands and at Walhachin, the Kelowna area drew large amounts of English investment capital at the turn of the century. Unlike southern Alberta, however, where the attraction was cattle and ranching, this money was directed toward the development of small farming operations and, especially, to orchards. The colonization companies that sprang up in many places in the Interior, including Kelowna and Vernon, were usually the brainchildren of members of the English aristocracy. They provided the capital to acquire the land and build the huge irrigation systems that were crucial in the semi-arid country, hoping to sell improved parcels to other English settlers. The largest landowner in the Okanagan was Lord Aberdeen, who sank vast amounts of money into the area and attracted a militantly English following to his cause. The names of those settling in the area were riddled with hyphens, military titles and strong connections to the squirearchy back home. Polo was a natural sport for these gentlemen, and, before the First World War, teams had been established in Kelowna, Vernon and Coldstream. Even Lady Aberdeen's father, Lord Tweedsmouth, spent some of his time in North America playing the game. He was in a team that toured California and met an Alberta foursome at the Coronado club in 1912.

Typical of the settlers in the Okanagan Valley was Captain Edmund Wilmot, late of Canada's first polo club at Pincher Creek and fresh from service in the Boer War. When, in 1905, Wilmot was induced to return to Canada, he did not come back to Alberta and the cattle business. Rather, he went to Coldstream, the most English of the Okanagan settlements, and took up developing orchards.

Although not much is known about many of those who rode out for Kelowna, Vernon or Coldstream, what biographical data has survived provides a clear picture of the kind of clubs they were.

Walter Pooley was English-born and Cambridge-educated. He came to Kelowna at the beginning of the land boom in the early 1900s, went into the fruit business and, subsequently, into real estate development. Extremely successful and one of the area's leading business figures, he died suddenly in 1915 at the age of only thirty-five.

Robert Lambly was from Quebec and walked into the Okanagan Valley in the mid-1870s, married the daughter of a local rancher and ended up owning vast tracts of land in several places around the district. His first love was horses and he passed that love on to his son, Robert, who also played polo with Kelowna.

Both Lamblys lived in the district until their deaths in the early 1940s.

Many of the Lamblys' fellow players were not so fortunate. H.H. Stillingfleet, the son of an English bishop, went into the real estate business, married Robert Lambly's daughter and was killed in the Great War. The Honorable Michael Howard left the valley to return to England in 1914 and was killed while serving with the 10th Hussars. And there were many, many more fathers and sons from across the B.C. Interior who suffered the same fate. At the Marquess of Anglesey's Walhachin settlement, for example, from a total male population of a hundred and seven, ninety-seven went off to war.

With the men away, the dreams of promoters like Lord Aberdeen collapsed along with the irrigation systems and the neglected, blighted orchards. Some of the English settlers came back after 1918, but most did not (or could not). It would be later generations, from many different countries, that would finally establish the Okanagan Valley as one of Canada's major farm and fruit growing centres.

The Kelowna Polo Club was never revived after the war. Wilmot's Coldstream club and the Vernon club begun in 1914 by his son, Tommy, merged operations and managed to continue into the 1930s, but they never became a strong presence in the provincial game.

The *Inland Sentinel* was apologizing for its team even before the 1902 game with Kelowna had begun, suggesting that the club had enjoyed little opportunity for serious practice so far that year. While the reasons are not clear, the club had seemed quiet and there was none of the usual publicity that had accompanied the opening of their previous seasons. The *Inland Sentinel's* fears were obviously well-grounded as Kelowna rode to a 4-0 win:

The result was fully anticipated here as the home team have had very little practise this year and were badly handicapped in the way of mounts, whilst their opponents were more fortunate all around.

One bright spot for Kamloops was the play of another newcomer to the team, W. Wentworth ("Worty") Wood, the son of a well-known Kamloops prospector and mining promoter. Like Johnson, Wood was a surveyor. He worked for the Grand Trunk Pacific, a constituent of Canada's second transcontinental railway, on its proposed North Thompson River route. He served overseas with the B.C. Horse in the first war and was promoted to captain. After the war, he remained in the Interior, eventually becoming an inspector with the Soldier Settlement Board in Vernon.

Also on the field for Kamloops was F.E. Young, yet another newspaperman. Young bought the *Standard* in 1901 and it flourished under his direction until 1914 when he accidentally shot himself while cleaning his rifle.

The new Kelowna club travelled to Grande Prairie at the beginning of October to challenge for the Roper Cup, but Stillingfleet, Barnaby, Carruthers and Wallis fell one goal short, losing by 3-2 to another Homfray-led team.

The *Inland Sentinel's* coverage of the Kamloops club's activities for 1903 is woefully thin. Other than the season-opening announcement of forthcoming gymkhanas, the paper says nothing further for the rest of the year. The only thing known for certain is that Grande Prairie continued its stranglehold on the Roper Cup, winning it for the third straight year. Whom they played is not known.

It is a matter of local lore that the rules for the Roper Cup stated that the trophy would become the permanent possession of any club that could win it three years in succession. Having accomplished the feat, the Grande Prairie players promptly put the cup back into competition with the stipulation that it could never again be won outright. It was a fine gesture, although it did not prevent the team from continuing to treat the trophy as if it were their personal property. They won seven of the subsequent eleven Roper Cup competitions.

The lack of information about the 1903 season makes the reports on 1904 frustrating in their own right. A new Kamloops trophy was in play — the Watson Cup — but whether it was first contested in 1904 or in the previous year cannot be established.

Also in 1904, the *Inland Sentinel* reports indicate that the Interior teams had abandoned the old four-period matches in favour of the newer six-period standard. The word "chukker" was still apparently unknown to the reporter as he wrote in one article that there was no scoring in the "fifth or final quarters." Whether the change was made in 1903 or 1904 is unknown.

Whatever problems the Kamloops club may have been experiencing, the *Inland Sentinel* seemed to believe they were things of the past. In August, 1904, it reported that the club held a practice on a ground seven miles up the North Thompson:

———◆◆◆◆◆———

...despite the 14 mile ride, no less than ten members turned out and a rattling good game resulted. There is some good material in the club and they will no doubt make a good bid for the Watson Cup. Polo is a game requiring quickness of hand and eye, good horsemanship and plenty of nerve and the experience gained on the polo field will always stand a man in good stead.

———◆◆◆◆◆———

The Watson Cup was played for during the annual Kamloops exhibition in late September and it pitted the home side against its Roper Cup nemesis from Grande Prairie. For once, Kamloops was able to conjure a win, whitewashing the favoured visitors by 4-0.

Kamloops' team captain Winterbottom came in for the usual praise for his careful ball control and W.W. Wood continued as the team's leading scorer, accounting for three of the four goals. It was a new player, however, who added the fourth marker: William Lewis Fernie.

Then thirty-four years old, Fernie was soon to become the city's most famous citizen; a principal player in an event that, to this day, counts as one of the district's most celebrated. Bill Fernie was born in Cheshire, England and came to Canada in about 1887. He spent two years on a Manitoba homestead before coming west to the Chilcotin where he worked as a cowboy on some of the early ranches. He finally pre-empted a half-section in the North Thompson Valley a few miles above Kamloops. Like so many of the area's young men, he responded to the Strathcona's call for volunteers and served with the regiment in South Africa until 1901. On his return, he joined the British Columbia police force.

It was as a provincial constable in 1906 that he arrested Bill Miner, the infamous "Grey Fox." Miner was, by then, well-advanced in years and had already spent more than half his life in a succession of American jails for a series of stagecoach holdups and other crimes, both serious and petty. He had settled near Aspen Grove, posing as a prospector, when he and two local accomplices held up a Canadian Pacific train just east of Kamloops.

True to form, Miner botched the robbery, missing a large sum of cash that had been raised for the victims of the San Francisco earthquake and settling for $15.50 and a box of catarrh pills. Tracked and captured by Fernie and his posse, the gang was convicted after a widely publicized trial in Kamloops and sent off to the penitentiary at New Westminster. Again, true to his usual form, Miner soon escaped and returned to the United States, but his brief, unfortunate foray into Canada was already becoming the stuff of legend.

Fernie continued his association with the B.C. provincial police (retiring in 1934 with the rank of inspector) and with local militia regiments. He had served overseas during the Great War with the 172nd Rocky Mountain Rangers. He died in Kamloops in July, 1943.

Another young man played with the Kamloops club in 1904. His name never appeared in the newspaper reports and he remained in the city for only a few months, but he remembered that summer fondly in his 1945 autobiography.

Robert W. Service was a clerk with the Bank of Commerce when he was transferred to Kamloops from Victoria. Although he initially regretted leaving Victoria, he soon took to his new posting: "It was even more agreeable — a town in the heart of the cattle country, with a river running alongside and cattle ranges all around." Among his first purchases were a pony and a polo outfit and if, by his own admission, he was a terrible player, he nevertheless took to the camaraderie and the excitement of the game.

About the country, he later waxed poetic:

———◆◆◆◆◆———

Life was pleasant, and work light. At four o'clock we were on our horses, riding over the rolling ridges, or into spectral gulches that rose to ghostlier mountains. It was like the scenery of Mexico, weirdly desolate and aridly morose. A discouraged land, forbidding in its weariness and resigned to ruin. I loved to ride alone.

———◆◆◆◆◆———

Polo match at Kelowna,
c. 1910.

the stick, though they rode well and put up a plucky fight"), but, once again, the hosts were frustrated in the final on September 28th:

This morning the match between the local team and the Grande Prairie team again proved the invincibility of the latter, at least as far as Kamloops is concerned. There was plenty of hard playing and the game was exciting, but at the finish the score stood five to one in favour of the visitors.

By the end of the year he was gone, transferred again by the bank, this time to Whitehorse in the Yukon Territory. Three years later, he published the collection that made him one of Canada's most famous poets: *Songs of a Sourdough.*

Kamloops' 1904 Watson Cup victory was one of only a handful of wins over Grande Prairie. The 1904 Roper Cup went to the ranchers, as it did again in 1905 by a one-sided 6-0.

The year 1906 saw what may have been the first multi-team tournament to be held at Kamloops. On the Dominion Day holiday, Kelowna and Grande Prairie came to town to try for the Roper Cup. In the first match, Kamloops defeated Kelowna by 3-0 and thereby won the dubious distinction of facing Grande Prairie yet again. The result was a predictable five goals to one. By now, the home team must have wished that Grande Prairie had just retired the trophy when they had the chance.

In late September, Kamloops hosted another tournament as a team from the Nicola Valley came to meet their hosts and Grande Prairie for the Watson Cup. The games were held at the fairgrounds which had lately become the regular home of the Kamloops club. This relationship would continue until 1911 when the fair association went broke and polo went back to the Indian reserve.

Nicola was no match for Kamloops in the opening game ("...the visitors being weak with

While the club continued to sponsor gymkhanas and paper chases, there was little in the way of polo reported in the papers for the years 1907 through 1909. It may have been some relief to Kamloops when, for reasons unknown, the Roper Cup was not played for in 1907 or 1908. There was a Watson Cup match in late September of 1907 with Kamloops recording a rare win over Grande Prairie, but there was no sign of the teams from Kelowna or from Nicola, which seemed to have slipped back into one of its frequent periods of inactivity.

September, 1907 also marked the end of Grande Prairie's greatest polo years, and it had been a remarkable run.

The team was never more than an informal affair, with a core of serious devotees like Homfray and Gordon supported by a steadily changing cast of players who obviously relished the wide-open Interior's "cowboy polo." Although they mostly played at Homfray's racetrack, over the years the team could be found stick-and-balling on almost any patch of open ground in the valley. In barely ten years, without benefit of executive elections, minute books, a clubhouse or even a permanent field, they had engraved their names on the Watson Cup and won the Roper in every one of the six

years it had been up for play. "Neck or Nothing" was the Grande Prairie motto and they lived by it to the letter. No British Columbia polo team of the first, or any, era better represented the game in its purest form.

The team made one or two uncharacteristically poor appearances in 1912, but nearly a decade would pass before the red shirts were seen again on a polo field. Then, as they had in the early days, they would go back about the serious business of beating Kamloops for the Roper Cup, making the trophy their own every time they tried.

Kelowna took the Roper from Kamloops in 1909 and the cup was back in play in July, 1910. With no sign of Grande Prairie, it was Kamloops versus the defending champions at the reserve grounds.

In the past few years, the roll of playing members at Kamloops changed significantly. Cecil Ward had left his law partnership with Frederick Fulton and moved to Nelson, although he continued to be a significant force in land development around Kamloops and in the running of his family's Douglas Lake Ranch down in the Nicola country. With the exception of Captain Nash, all the other founding names had gone, replaced by a new cast that would see the club through to the war and ensure its eventual rebirth.

Kamloops' 1910 Roper Cup team was captained by Walter Homfray, who had by then probably sold out his interests in Grande Prairie and given up his dreams for Adelphi. He was joined by the George brothers and by a young semi-regular named Walter J. Pearse.

The only son of E.T. Pearse, an early settler in Grande Prairie and later Kamloops' Gold Commissioner, Walter had distinguished himself in both academics and athletics and had left Kamloops a year or two earlier to take his degree at Montreal's McGill University. In 1911, he was awarded a Rhodes Scholarship and was studying at Oxford when the war broke out. He was commissioned in the Royal Horse Artillery and, according to the *Inland Sentinel* of April 20th, 1917, "He was several times wounded and last February was gassed. He had apparently just got back to the scene of action before being fatally wounded." He was twenty-five years old.

Riding out for Kelowna were team captain Benson, Pyman, Smith and Richards and they gave a good account of themselves, retaining possession of the cup for the second year in succession by a score of 8-3. Again in 1911, Kamloops met Kelowna for the Roper, this time on the holder's home field. Again, the result was the same with Kelowna taking a 7-1 win. For all its obvious enthusiasm, dedication and new players, Kamloops' tournament record remained dismal. Even without Grande Prairie, Kamloops just could not win when it mattered.

A new vitality was present in the Kamloops Polo Club at the start of its 1912 season. There was a new slate of officers and the announcement that the club intended to host its first major tournament to coincide with the city's centenary celebrations in September. They were expecting five teams, including Kelowna and Grande Prairie, to compete for the Roper Cup.

Before the tournament, Grande Prairie made a trip to Kamloops for a "friendly" match. They should have stayed in retirement as the home team of G.B. Rimington, the Georges and A.C. Longbourne walloped them 14-0.

The 1912 Kamloops Centenary Tournament was held in mid-September, but only the final match between the hosts and Kelowna rated the press' attention. Kamloops finally won the Roper Cup by 8-5 and that evening a banquet was held in the teams' honour. At the dinner, a B.C. Polo Association was formed with the intention of encouraging new clubs and coordinating province-wide tournaments. It was also announced that as many as eight teams would be in Kamloops for the 1913 Roper Cup Tournament, including aggregations from Vancouver, Victoria, Nicola and Walhachin.

Flushed with its first ever Roper Cup victory (after ten years of ritual frustration), the Kamloops polo team departed on its first extended trip, travelling with Kelowna to Vancouver Island for a number of exhibition matches in late September.

Polo had not been seen in the provincial capital since 1896, although regular rumours of its imminent revival continued throughout the first decade of the new century. The 1912 visit of Kelowna and Kamloops seemed intended to build up public interest in the sport even though there was not yet a local team. The same tactic had worked for Winnipeg in 1905 and would work again for Spokane in 1913.

The *Inland Sentinel* was full of praise for Kamloops (which won at least two games during the visit) and offered patronizing encouragement to the people of Victoria:

Of course, at present, Victoria cannot appreciate the tactics of the game, but they enjoyed the match and should take an increased interest in the doings of their own club for the future.

That 1913 British Columbia season opened with tremendous promise. In hindsight, it is easy to temper the great optimism of Kamloops — and indeed, of every club in the province — with the sobering knowledge of what was then sitting just over the horizon, but polo, in that last year before the Great War, was healthier and more popular than it had ever been in British Columbia.

The *Inland Sentinel* began its 1913 coverage with little but good news. Although the promised eight-team Roper Cup Tournament never materialized, there was renewed activity in the Nicola Valley and Vancouver Island polo was alive again in Victoria, Duncan and Cowichan. In the biggest news of the spring, the paper announced that a polo club had finally been founded in Vancouver.

On the local front, the teams in Kamloops and Fruitlands had announced their formal union (or was it "reunion"?), a move that would allow the formation of at least three teams, pushing up the level of intra-club play. The Fruitlands team was an offshoot of the main club at Kamloops, but had never really developed its own identity. What it had done was draw some Kamloops regulars away without really increasing the overall player pool.

In addition to an invitation to return to Victoria for another tournament (which the club accepted), there was another offer on the table. Spokane, Washington had invited the club to play in its inaugural polo tournament, to be held in conjunction with the Interstate Fair in mid-September.

The invitation (which included Spokane covering all costs) had also gone to every team in southern Alberta and to Vancouver. The Kamloops club deferred its decision and, in the end, only four of the Alberta teams would travel to the tournament.

The *Inland Sentinel* had clearly hired a frustrated poet to cover its sporting news and he travelled with the team as they headed down to the small Nicola Valley town of Quilchena on May 25th, 1913 for the first of a two-game series for the Roper Cup:

* ⋅⋅⋅ ⋅⋅⋅ *

Quilchena was en fete on Sunday, for an air of gaiety graced the sports which the Quilchenans for the first time assayed. Truly, the organizers were in luck as the weather was propitious, the assembly sportive and the entrants skilful.

The outstanding feature of the day's programme was the polo contest between Quilchena and Kamloops, and assuredly the horsemen from the City of Destiny met their match. Each team displayed the greatest enthusiasm; each played and played hard to win. Every point was stubbornly contested and every attack encountered a defence difficult to overcome. Neither side could claim any distinct advantage for the strenuous efforts of both maintained an evenly adjusted balance throughout the game.

* ⋅⋅⋅ ⋅⋅⋅ *

The reporter may have thought the "Quilchenans" were seeing their first gymkhana and polo match, but the game had been played there before. Nicola had come in and out of the Interior polo picture at least twice and their team was hardly new to the game. The Kamloops foursome of Donald George, the Hepburn brothers and Leicester Rimington were down by 3-2 for much of the match and were lucky to escape with an overtime victory. One of the Quilchena men — long-time rancher Joe Guichon — had played in the valley for years and, on this occasion, he was joined by one of the finest players in the west: Frank Ward.

Ward was a polo veteran with a history that went back to the Victoria tournament of 1896. It included a stint in the Chilcotin with his uncle, M.G. Drummond, and a few years with one of Canada's perennial polo champions, Alberta's High River. After running his own operation in Alberta for five or six years, Ward had been installed as the manager of his family's Douglas Lake Ranch in 1909 and from this base he became the dominant personality in British Columbia polo for the next three decades.

The same reporter was obviously present for the Kamloops club's annual gymkhana on June 3rd:

* ⋅⋅⋅ ⋅⋅⋅ *

Ideal weather conditions graced the gymkhana at the Polo Grounds yesterday, for while the peaks of Peter and Paul stood sentinel in the quivering heat, a refreshing zephyr brought grateful coolness to the riverside plain. The arena, indeed, with its verdant fringe of leafage and the pleasant green of its sward, looked the prettiest spot in the vicinity of Kamloops, and the gaily dressed throng of spectators there presented a scene full of charm and animation.

* ⋅⋅⋅ ⋅⋅⋅ *

Whatever the weather at the gymkhana on the 3rd, the polo grounds were under water by the 19th, flooded by the South Thompson, and Leicester Rimington was looking for somewhere else to practice before their trip to Victoria in early August. He was also hoping the reservation field would be dry before Quilchena paid a return visit for the Roper Cup match at the end of the month.

Frank Ward brought his Nicola Valley club to town for the second game in the series on July 29th and the effect of trailing his ponies sixty miles in two days was clearly evident as Kamloops went out to a 9-1 lead by the end of the third chukker and then hung on for a 10-7 win.

Following the game, the players retired to the Leland Hotel for champagne and the endless ritual toasts. The cup was presented to Kamloops by one of its long-time supporters, W.U. Homfray, and, before the celebration broke up, Nicola invited Kamloops to come back down the valley in August to play for their new trophy.

The Thorpe Cup, known properly as the Quilchena Polo Cup, was presented by Thorpe and Co., a Vancouver manufacturer of soda water, and it was clearly intended to become the resident challenge trophy for the clubs of the lower Nicola Valley at what were expected to be their annual tournaments. There is no indication that the August, 1913 match ever took place, or indeed that the cup was ever played for at all. Neither Quilchena nor Nicola ever hosted another visiting team and competitive polo in the valley ended with the First World War. Today, the Thorpe Cup, with no names engraved upon it, sits on display in the bar of the historic Quilchena Hotel.

The new clubs in Vancouver and on the Island began play in 1913 with the kind of overly high expectations familiar to the early days of Alberta polo. The *Inland Sentinel* of June 17th announced that the home team would soon be travelling to the coast to participate in Vancouver's coming-out party:

———— ·‖⁙◆➤◗◆‖· ————

The British Columbia Thoroughbred Association has completed arrangements for a monster polo tournament at Minoru Park early in August, when all the best teams will be here for the big tournament.... The Association is now in touch with the clubs in Coronado, San Mateo, Burlingame, Portland, Vernon, Calgary, Pincher Creek, Kamloops, Winnipeg, Kelowna, Victoria and Cowichan and arrangements are being made to have them represented in the tournament here.

———— ·‖⁙◆➤◗◆‖· ————

In short, invitations had gone out to nearly every polo team then active west of the Mississippi. It was boosterism on a scale that dwarfed even the headiest dreams of prairie polo promoters. It was certainly too much, too soon and the "monster polo tournament" came down to just a single match, played on August 2nd, 1913:

———— ·‖⁙◆➤◗◆‖· ————

The first polo match ever played in the district of Vancouver took place on Saturday last when the Vancouver Polo Club played the strong team from the Kamloops Club. It resulted in a runaway victory for Vancouver who won by 14 goals to 2.

———— ·‖⁙◆➤◗◆‖· ————

In fact, the closest that the West Coast would come to a grand tournament before the Great War took place in Victoria just a few days after Vancouver's inaugural match. Four teams — Kamloops, Vancouver, Victoria and Cowichan — met at the Willows racetrack and driving park.

Newspaper coverage was sketchy, but apparently the crowds were very good and the games were very fast. Kamloops proved itself by far the weakest of the four teams (losing all three of its games by a combined score of 24-10), even though its opponents were all "new" to the game. Or were they?

Two names stand out from among those involved in the Island's new interest in polo, and their presence alone indicates that there was considerable experience in play. One of Kamloops' original patrons, William Roper himself, had sold his Cherry Creek properties in about 1910 and relocated to Victoria. He had continued his strong support for local sports and, along with a polo cup, he had added a second trophy to be presented to the champions of a gymkhana held in conjunction with the polo tournament. Kamloops' victory in that gymkhana was clearly the one bright spot in their western tour.

The second name, leading the new team from Cowichan, was familiar to any Alberta polo player from the first era: Allan Kennington. The man who founded the great North Fork Polo Club had not been seen on a field since he dropped from sight after the 1906 Calgary tournament. He had sold his Alberta ranch a year or two later and retired to the British enclave at Duncan, just north of Victoria.

Kennington went on to fight in the Great War with the Cheshire Regiment and even served with the Pacific Coast Rangers during World War II. He lived in the Cowichan district until his death in 1954 at the age of eighty-four.

The success of the 1913 tournament must have given the fledgling B.C. Polo Association cause for some optimism as it held its second annual meeting after the matches. New President William Roper, his executive and delegates from the four teams

were certainly looking forward to bigger and better things as they formally adopted the Hurlingham Rules (but without any restriction on the size of the ponies) and, probably, talked about the site for the 1914 provincial championship.

In its formation and its makeup, the new organization in Vancouver bore a much closer resemblance to clubs in eastern North America (and even England) than it did to the more rough-and-ready aggregations from Alberta or the B.C. Interior. The names of the founders read like a who's who of the city's social, military and business communities.

While these social groups were firmly established by the end of the new century's first decade, they had not been there long. Unlike Victoria, which had a long history as the legislative, commercial and cultural centre of the province, Vancouver was still almost brand new.

Although today the population of the greater Vancouver area is perhaps two million,

the city owes everything, including its very location, to the Canadian Pacific Railway. Before 1882, when the C.P.R. decided to make Burrard Inlet the west coast terminus of its transcontinental line, the area was home only to a few logging operations and very few permanent inhabitants. But with the railway came the wharves and warehouses needed to connect Canada to the Pacific Rim and the tiny city exploded in a sustained boom that saw its population rise from a mere 15,000 in 1892 to nearly 50,000 in the next decade. A city lot purchased for $8 a foot in 1884 was sold in 1911 for $4,000 a foot and a $750 building site in 1887 changed hands for $100,000 only twenty-five years later.

A good deal of investment capital flowed into the new city from Britain, the United States and Eastern Canada, and that money multiplied a hundred-fold or more. It bred a succession of instant millionaires and established the three great foundations of Vancouver's wealth: lumber, shipping and real estate development. The huge profits from all three were represented in the Vancouver Polo Club.

In 1913, under the leadership of Captain John Isaac, the sixteen or so playing members

had contracted with Calgary's H.K. Snowden to deliver a number of trained Alberta ponies. Snowden himself arrived with the horses and served as the club's manager until the war took him permanently back to England. The club also had playable grounds. Located at Brighouse Park in Richmond just six miles south of the city, the fields were laid out mostly at the expense of Clarence Marpole (whose family fortune came from coal, southern Alberta oil and a fleet of tugboats that plied the Puget Sound) and leased to the club by the Brighouse Estate. Brighouse served as the home of Vancouver polo until the Second World War.

The club also had its own challenge cup. Intended to become symbolic of provincial polo supremacy, the B.C. Challenge Cup was donated in September, 1913 by a large group of individual businessmen, most of whom would have been known to every Vancouverite.

With all the pieces quickly in place, the Vancouver polo club played host to Kamloops in August, 1913 and announced its new place on the polo map by trouncing the more experienced visitors. Vancouver was represented later that month at the tournament in Victoria and, although they lost to the host team, their strong play was a sure sign of things to come. The club did not accept Spokane's invitation to play for the new Thaddeus Lane Cup in either 1913 or 1914, but, in that latter year, they did establish their first contacts in the Pacific Northwest with a trip to Portland, Oregon.

The war stopped play in Vancouver as surely and as suddenly as it did everywhere else in Western Canada, but the team was one of the first to come back onto the field after the armistice.

The front page of the *Inland Sentinel* for June 17th, 1914 was almost exclusively devoted to polo. Two large headlines ran the entire width of the page below the masthead. One announced "The British Team Wins World's Polo Championship" and was followed by extensive coverage of the recently concluded tournament on the U.S. east coast. But the top headline would have been of much more interest to the people of Kamloops: The Governor General, H.R.H. The Duke of Connaught, would be coming to town for the final match of the annual polo tournament.

The accompanying article, which ran two columns wide down the front page and continued onto page four, featured an encouraging editorial and reproduced a series of letters between the president of the polo club and the committee organizing the Governor General's tour of Western Canada.

According to the *Inland Sentinel,* the royal party's train would be stopping in town long enough to allow the duke to attend the final match and present the new Kamloops Challenge Cup to the winners. The trophy, purchased with public subscriptions totalling some $200, was to inaugurate a new era of top-flight competitive polo in the Interior. Invitations had gone out to the six other B.C. teams and probably to Alberta and the U.S. Pacific Northwest, too.

On July 20th, the first of a series of advertisements appeared in the *Inland Sentinel,* announcing the polo tournament, a big gymkhana and a public dance. Vancouver, Kelowna and Nicola all signified their intention to compete for the new cup and everything

seemed in readiness. Only in retrospect do the announced dates cast a cloud over the grand event. The tournament was scheduled for August 13th, 14th and 15th.

Victoria was planning a major event, too. Through the month of July, 1914, the *Victoria Daily Colonist* promised a series of games featuring teams from the Island and, perhaps, Vancouver. On August 6th, just two days before the scheduled opening match, the following notice appeared:

Official notification has been received of the postponement of the polo match and gymkhana arranged for the coming Saturday. The postponement was necessitated by the fact that so many of the club members are on duty with their various regiments. The date of the event will be announced later.

It would be nearly a decade before the new Kamloops Challenge Cup was finally put into play and more than twenty years before another polo match was seen in Victoria.

HURLINGHAM
IN A
HAYFIELD

THE STATE OF PLAY IN THE FIRST ERA

Glenbow archives, NA-2788-85

IN THE LATE SPRING OF 1889, then-Lieutenant George Warrender and three of his Royal Navy ship-mates from the Pacific Station at Esquimalt, British Columbia, challenged the gentlemen of Victoria to a polo match.

In the late spring of 1914, now-Vice Admiral Sir George Warrender's Second Battle Squadron, comprising four of His Majesty's newest dreadnoughts, lay at anchor in the harbour at Kiel, Germany. On the afternoon of Sunday, June 28th, he was watching the kaiser race his yacht, Meteor, in the grand regatta when news of the assassination of Archduke Ferdinand was received. Two days later, as his fleet weighed anchor, Warrender sent a final message to his German hosts: "Friends in the past and friends forever."

In the twenty-five years that passed between those two events, the game of polo emerged as one of the premier sporting and social activities across the Canadian West. From its beginnings on raw patches of fresh-mowed prairie grass to the carefully manicured sod of the finest country clubs, the game flourished and faltered and flourished again, reflecting the changing fortunes of a rapidly emerging society.

How many men actually played polo will never be known to any certainty, but from the few surviving minute books and fragmentary club records, it is clear that for every name that appeared in the tournament

Gymkhana at Fish Creek, 1912.

reports there were a half-dozen more who paid their $5 annual subscriptions and turned out faithfully for the Sunday afternoon practices and mid-week pick-up games. It is probably safe to say that nearly every rancher and cowboy in southern Alberta or the B.C. Interior tried putting mallet to ball at least once.

Some players became fixtures, appearing on the record in every year from beginning to end; playing long enough to see their native-born sons join them on the field. Others were listed only once; perhaps a club player taking his chance to fill in for an injured regular. Where a man's name was found regularly in the tournament reports for a few years, his abrupt absence from those reports could be taken as a sure sign he had left the country.

Not counting the one-time American style aggregations, the all-star travelling foursomes or teams that remained little more than rumour and expectation, the first era of western Canadian polo produced a dozen serious clubs in southern Alberta. In Saskatchewan, there were at least five, with three or four more in Manitoba. The B.C. Interior could boast of a half-dozen, with Victoria, Duncan and Cowichan supporting semi-regular teams on Vancouver Island and the city of Vancouver itself finally came into the picture in the last months before the war.

Polo has always been seen as a game of the English and Anglo-Irish sporting classes and it was certainly those gentlemen who were first to play it in the Canadian West. While it is unquestionably true that the game's survival was ultimately due to its enduring popularity among the cowboys and farmers and feed store clerks who learned it from the remittance men, the importance of the founding squirearchy cannot be underestimated. This is made clear not so much by where they played polo in southern Alberta, but rather by where they did not.

All twelve of southern Alberta's polo teams were established in the narrow, east slope foothills belt that was also the destination for the British investment capital that flooded in from the early 1880s. Wherever that capital settled, the men who came into the country with it played polo.

North of Calgary, where the shortgrass plains quickly give way to aspen parkland, polo was only rarely and briefly seen. In southeastern Alberta, Medicine Hat certainly had a cowtown heritage, but it never had polo. The great ranches that stretched up to the town from the 49th Parallel were decidedly American in character and ownership. They started later and their presence was a consequence of the overcrowded ranges of northern Montana. When the lands were finally opened to farming, the great majority of those who fenced their new half-sections came not from England but from the American Midwest.

Any doubts about the seminal importance of the remittance men to the game of polo in Alberta can be put to rest in the scant forty miles between the southwestern towns of Fort Macleod and Lethbridge.

Fort Macleod had its Mounted Police garrison, retired Mounties-turned-cowmen and a wealth of British money to support its claim as the centre of early ranching in Alberta. It hosted the first polo tournament ever played in the province and, with one hiatus, continued to support a strong team until the start of the Great War.

Just down the road, the town of Lethbridge soon displaced Fort Macleod as the market centre for the region, but Lethbridge was built on coal mining and on the first flood of Mormon settlers from Utah and Idaho. They were farmers and irrigation engineers, not cattlemen, and Lethbridge never saw so much as an exhibition polo match.

Where there were no British ranches and no young British men to run them, there was no polo.

So, what was the state of play in the first era? What was the quality of the facilities and how good were these mostly self-taught remittance men and their protégés? How well did they stack up against the rest of the polo world?

The playing fields were always a problem, but it was certainly not for want of grass. Across the Prairies and the B.C. Interior, there were thousands of square miles of precious little else. But it was not the thick, verdant carpet of Eastern Canada or England. In the semi-arid Canadian West, the native grasses came up in mounded clumps through a gravelly, paper-thin topsoil. In the short Prairie growing season, it sprouted quickly in the late spring, only to go to seed and wither to pale gold by mid-August. Even an especially wet summer would not extend its annual cycle by more than a fortnight or so. Still, grass was the rule and there is no evidence of Alberta polo being played on the rolled, oiled dirt that was a feature of many early fields in the American West.

Though the plains may look flat from a distance, at close hand the land rolls in an unbroken series of irregular, low waves. Any polo field that even approached regulation size was anything but level. Where possible, the temporary fields were laid out along river or creek-bottom flats where the natural undulations were at a minimum and the silts from spring runoffs covered and softened the stony hardpan. The groundwater helped to keep the grasses comparatively thick and green. In short, the early players pegged out their fields in their hay meadows and any contract to mow them before a tournament invariably included the stipulation that the hay be raked off and stacked. It would not be wasted.

Where more permanent fields were established (in Fort Macleod and Cochrane, for example), they often occupied the infield of the local racetrack. Flat racing had been enormously popular from the earliest days of western settlement and the tracks that existed in every community (often at the centre of the local fairgrounds) were levelled, graded and manicured to a degree unseen in most other public facilities. Even these fields, though, were often undersized or oddly shaped.

The second grounds at High River were probably the finest in Alberta for a number of years. Specifically chosen for its flat, level base and its proximity to the Highwood River, the field could even be irrigated if necessary. Level it may have been, but it was drainage rather than irrigation that presented the greatest problem. On more than one occasion, matches were cancelled because of a drowned field. Nevertheless, just before the war George Ross approached the town council with the suggestion that, for a reasonable annual expenditure on its polo field, High River could become the permanent home for the Alberta provincial championships.

Whatever the type of field — creek-bottom or racetrack — maintenance was a substantial expense for every club. While the annual fair committee might have helped put the field in order for a feature tournament, there is no other evidence of formal civic involvement. Where records survive, they show a steady outflow of cash toward rolling, mowing and boarding (but never for seeding). Where the club could afford it, such work was usually contracted to a local farmer who had the necessary equipment, but, as was the case with Pekisko, falling memberships and red ink on the balance sheet meant that the players themselves had to undertake their own maintenance.

But no matter what were the other groundskeeping problems, none likely compared to those posed by *Spermophilus richardsonii,* the ubiquitous Richardson's ground squirrel. Known locally as "gophers," the little rodents could rapidly riddle any patch of prairie with a network of burrows just large enough to swallow a polo ball or a pony's leg.

Poison was a standard item on the expense side of the ledger and even a small club like Pekisko seems to have ordered an inordinately large number of balls on a regular basis. The animals' quick work also meant that the tedious business of filling holes before a match could not be undertaken more than a day or so before the start of play. Adding real insult to potential injury, any attempt to improve the field with a softer soil base and thicker sod would simply have made it that much more desirable to the gophers.

If the tradition of replacing the divots was a feature of games in more civilized climes, half-time in southern Alberta should have seen players and spectators spreading out over the field armed with shovels and buckets of earth.

Questions about the quality of the players and the tenor of the game they played are more difficult to address since the sport existed largely in isolation from other major polo centres. The huge scale of Western Canada made travel both expensive and complicated, especially when a railcar full of ponies was involved. As a result, contact with teams outside each of the four regional centres was at best irregular.

Informed, objective reports on the state of play in the West are difficult to find. The local press was invariably thrilled by the skill of the players and the excitement of the game. Superlatives abounded and nearly every match was some variation on the "best ever seen in the country." In many cases, the reporters were probably watching their first polo game.

Although substantial histories of the game had been published in England and the eastern United States by 1914, Canadian polo barely rated a mention. Chroniclers like T.F. Dale wrote extensively about the origins of the game in Australia, South Africa, Argentina and even in such far-flung Imperial outposts as Brunei and Singapore, but the word "Canada" does not appear in the index. Even when writer T.B. Drybrough, a top-flight player and regular buyer of American ponies, published a revised edition of his early book on polo in 1906 following a trip to California, he makes no reference to the Canadian game.

Polo magazine and such English sporting journals as *Land and Water* did publish occasional accounts of western Canadian polo when local players sent them in, but they must have been perceived more as an interesting curiosity than as evidence of a vital, well-established game.

The reason is probably that there was no significant formal contact between England and Western Canada. Where diplomats and military personnel travelled regularly between London and its colonial holdings, such men were not a feature of life in the Canadian West. There was no ambassador or consul just back from Calgary to play a season at Hurlingham and report on the fine polo he had been enjoying "over there." Neither were there cavalry regiments returning home after a tour of duty on the Prairie frontier. While visiting teams from the United States, Argentina and even Australia soon became a regular feature of the English season, in the final analysis, "out of sight, out of mind" seems to have characterized the larger polo world's attitude to the Canadian game.

While the western game was isolated from the rest of the world, it was not entirely out of touch. The local press regularly took note of who had just returned from a holiday or business trip to England. Sticks and balls and team jerseys were ordered from suppliers in India and England and many an English rancher was a regular subscriber to magazines and newspapers from home.

Magazines and visits kept players abreast of developments in English polo. At several early tournaments, pick-up teams bore names like "Freebooters," a clear indication that someone had been keeping up with polo news from "across the pond." If anything, the American game flourishing on the East Coast was even farther away than England or Ireland. Western Canadian polo retained its English character and remained true to Hurlingham's rules, adopting the height restriction for ponies in 1907 and even keeping offside until 1911. Though the duration of play was probably flexible according to local conditions, the standard four-period matches gave way to six chukkers in 1904, a change that may have come as a result of Alberta's first contact with eastern teams — Canadian and American — the year before.

Alberta and B.C. players continued to stay current with the larger polo world throughout the next two eras. The sports pages of the local newspapers provided detailed coverage of the international matches that drew huge crowds to New York's Polo Grounds during the 1920s and several men kept scrapbooks of clippings about the careers of top players from the United States and Britain. Most players' bookshelves would have held books and magazines dedicated to the game, especially Louis Mountbatten's standard textbook, *An Introduction to Polo*. In the late 1930s, they would certainly have watched as Mountbatten and the Hurlingham Polo Association attempted to draw up a standard set of international rules, but their interest would have remained largely academic. While a few western players eventually were able to spend a season in Europe or at such eastern American bastions as Meadowbrook, it would be 1973 before a true Canadian foursome finally made it across the Atlantic.

Although local histories speak of "cowboy polo" or "hockey on horseback," giving the impression that the sport was a wide-open rollick, the truth probably has less to do with whirlwind enthusiasm than with the formal strictures imposed by a game learned, quite literally, "by the book."

George Ross was, by every account, a man obsessed with team discipline. His players were expected to know their place and to stay there. It is not hard to imagine that some of his practices with a rough, young High River team would have looked more like a chess match than a midway bumper-car ride. He may even have forced his backs to learn

defence by playing without a mallet, as had often been the case in early English matches.

As the Alberta teams began to travel, first east to Toronto and Montreal and later to Winnipeg, Spokane and California, they invariably came in as the underdog. The eastern press, especially, succumbed to the temptations of "cowboy polo," often acting as if the westerners had arrived in town as part of a "Wild West" show. They also liked to belittle the Alberta ponies, remarking on their shaggy coats and wiry frames.

Their turf may have been greener and their horses sleeker, but eastern polo teams and the press corps alike were quickly taught that underestimating a George Ross-led foursome was almost certain to get them on the wrong side of 14-4 or 12-2. And as for the ugly little Alberta ponies, they would soon become one of the preferred mounts for teams all over eastern North America.

The Alberta foursomes, with only a couple of embarrassing exceptions, seem to have had little difficulty with the outside competition they did face. While it is true that both Toronto and Montreal were new to the game, the U.S. teams from Buffalo, Rochester and Syracuse were more experienced and still had considerable trouble with the westerners. Accounts of the games almost invariably put Alberta's wins down to team discipline. The competition may have showed brilliant individual efforts, but, in the final analysis, it was precise positioning and solid defence that carried the day.

Although Alberta players were not often exposed to the best in outside competition, their game did not exist entirely in a vacuum. Their early, severely disciplined style began to give way to the modern hit-and-run game at about the same time as it did in England. This change can be seen most clearly in the difference between two of the first era's greatest players: George Ross and Justin Deane-Freeman. Where Ross stressed position and precision, Deane-Freeman was renowned for his end-to-end rushes and long, smooth stroke. It is said that he could accurately strike a ball the whole length of a two-hundred-yard field.

Ross obviously recognized Deane-Freeman's huge talent. He took him under his wing at the Fish Creek club for a couple of years and then arranged for him to move to Coronado on what was supposed to be a permanent basis. However, the lack of regular top-drawer competition for most of Alberta's teams and players makes it difficult to rate their talent in the larger polo world. Even at home, making comparisons now among the players is speculative, based on what were not very sophisticated news reports.

If the Western Association had developed into a strong organization or if the hoped-for western championships had materialized, it would likely have led to the creation of an American-style handicapping system. While such was not a usual feature of the English polo on which the Canadian game was clearly based, many players would have encountered handicapping on their frequent trips to Coronado. In fact, there is a unique piece of evidence to suggest it was very much in the minds of Alberta's players.

Early in 1911, one of the Hones (probably "Nim") put up a new cup for competition at Fish Creek. It was intended to be a players' trophy and the rules were simple:

The winners of the first match hold the cup for two weeks, when any team not a club team can challenge the holders. Any four players can challenge the holders, but two weeks at least must elapse between the games.

Such a cup would make a handicap list almost a necessity to guard against the kind of "all-star" domination that the *High River Times* had warned about as early as 1908.

Of play for the Hone Cup itself, there is only one brief reference. On July 9th, 1914, a Calgary paper reported that Fish Creek had played host to a successful "American style" tournament where each team played every other and the winner was determined by total goals. The honours went to the foursome captained by Addie Hone. Since the Hone Cup is never heard of again, it is reasonable to think that Addie took it home when he returned to Ireland just after the war. But while the Hone Cup itself may not have survived, something much more important did: a handicap list.

The single, handwritten sheet was prepared by long-time club secretary H.G. Wooley and sent to Millarville secretary Montie Fraser. Dated May 22nd, 1914, it contains the names of forty players with each assigned a handicap number from one to seven. Its pre-season date suggests it was intended to serve for the rest of the year.

The list is far from comprehensive and how players "registered" or were assigned a handicap number is not known. There are few names from High River and none at all from Pekisko or the Pincher Creek district, but Cochrane, Fish Creek and Millarville are well-represented.

Even with its limitations, the list is remarkably instructive for any historian of the Alberta game.

Number one on the list for 1914 was Addie Hone, sporting the only seven handicap. He is followed by perennials O.A. Critchley and Condie Landale with sixes and young Dick Brown with a five.

That Addie Hone should be highly rated is not unexpected; that he should be considered the best then playing the game in the district is something of a surprise. While his play is always mentioned in the newspaper reports, it was rarely the cause for superlatives. There is some evidence that he may have played the game in Ireland before coming to Alberta and already had a leg up on his peers. He certainly had their respect.

There are ten players rated at four goals, including two of Addie's cousins, Joe and Mick. The Deane-Freeman brothers, Willie and Brudenell, are both at four, as are Millarville regulars Douglass, Freeman and Fraser. Critchley's son, Jack, is given a four handicap. He must have assumed he would be in the area for at least a part of the season and it is interesting to speculate about his later ranking had he returned to the Strathcona's after the war.

Calgary original Frank Macnaghten rates a four. From his long record of play, it is a surprisingly low number, especially when compared to his only contemporary on the list, Oswald Critchley. Perhaps he was beginning to feel his age; perhaps his strength had always been his passion for the game rather than his skill.

With senior players at the peak of their game (or just past it), the list records younger men who will come into their own in the next decade. Two Kerfoots are on the list — Pat with a three and Duncan with a one — along with 3-goaler Gordon Hinde. They will come to represent the heart of Cochrane's post-war revival. Frank McHugh is rated only three, but his substantial impact on the second era of Alberta polo will not be measured solely by his skill as a player.

How accurate were the ratings? It is possible to conjure with the numbers and apply them to teams from the end of the first era where all the players appear on the Hone Cup handicap list. In the 1913 Cochrane tournament, for example, the two finalists for the Van Wart Cup would have lined up as follows: Cochrane – Oswald Critchley (6); Condie Landale (6); Gilbert Rhodes (4) and Chester de la Vergne (3). Total goals: 19. Fish Creek – Addie Hone (7); Dick Brown (5); Frank Macnaghten (4) and Mick Hone (4). Total goals: 20.

Despite only a supposed 1-goal difference in the teams, Fish Creek managed a 9-4 win.

In 1914, the result was even more lopsided as the same eight players met to open the new Calgary grounds at Chinook Park. Fish Creek won by 13-6.

If the list was not the most objective measure of the players' talent for the game, it is those names which do not appear that cause the greatest frustration. How would Gunn, Connelly and Milvain of the great North Fork aggregations been rated against their northern opponents? How good was Harry Robertson compared to his peers in Alberta? During his wartime service with the Portland Polo Club, he had been rated at five goals, one of the highest west of the Mississippi. Had Justin Deane-Freeman remained in the province, how good would he have become by 1914? During his brief, sad time at Coronado in 1910, he was already being touted as a 7-goaler.

In the final analysis, it was distance that kept western Canadian polo teams from testing themselves not only against the wider world, but against other Canadian teams as well. Early trips to Toronto and Montreal required a journey of over 2,000 miles and, even with a rapidly improving transcontinental rail service, ponies could be in transit for ten days or more. The sale of those ponies was the prime reason for the trips and the tournaments were a showcase for their quality. Without that motivation, it is unlikely Alberta teams would have been seen in the East at all. The same thing can probably be said for the first visits to Coronado as well.

But even with the money generated by the sale of polo ponies (they commanded far higher prices in Ontario and Quebec than they did in the West), men such as George Ross and Oswald Critchley must have provided a substantial level of personal financial support. The Prairie game may have been strengthened by the presence of its cowboys and homesteaders, but most of these could not have afforded a fortnight in Toronto, much less a month or more in California.

The players who did travel, then, were a mix of the most highly skilled and those who could afford the ticket. At no time did a regular club team face competition in the East or at Coronado and no western Canadian club from the first (or even the second) era ever rode out against the best in the world from Hurlingham or Meadowbrook. It was just too far to go.

At home, the first era of western polo was remarkable for its balance. In the twenty-five years of play before the Great War, no single club became a "dynasty." In fact, the names on the trophies offer clear evidence that, at one time or another, every club had seasons when it was at the top of the heap.

In the first ten years of play, Calgary and High River traded honours about equally, with an occasional interruption from Fort Macleod, but in the first few seasons of the new century, it was High River, under the stern tutelage of George Ross, that emerged as the top team. With Ross' move to Fish Creek, High River declined and never again achieved its accustomed dominance. Fish Creek rose at High River's expense while Calgary, hampered by the lack of its own field

and the loss of several founding players, sank into near-obscurity. As had High River, so did Fish Creek peak in the years before Ross left for California. Oswald Critchley brought fledgling Cochrane into prominence during the last five years of the first era and sowed the seeds of what would be one of the few clubs to survive the war.

Throughout the last decade or so of the era, the North Fork team, with its admixture of the best from the other Pincher Creek district clubs, always seemed able to mount a dangerous foursome. Though they were willing and able to travel regularly to Winnipeg and Spokane, their presence at Calgary-area tournaments was hit-and-miss. But, when they did meet the northern teams (usually on their home turf), only Cochrane seemed able to give them real trouble.

Even as the fortunes of most Alberta teams waxed and waned over those first twenty-five years, one club remained consistently strong throughout its existence. Though they never enjoyed the patronage of a wealthy sportsman like Critchley or Ross and, as a consequence, rarely travelled outside their immediate area, teams from the Millarville Polo Club were always a serious threat to take any tournament they entered.

Anchored by the consistent leadership of Condie Landale and buoyed by the brilliance of the young Justin Deane-Freeman, the club was able to choose teams from its strong roster of playing members and never came to rely too heavily on any small group. Even the loss of Justin did not seem to set them back as his brother Willie proved a more-than-adequate replacement.

It is hard to say how long the Millarville club could have sustained its high level of play had the war not intervened. Already it had begun to lose key players to retirement or relocation and many others were beginning to show their age. But the war did intervene, and Millarville lost its fair share to the trenches. When the old teams began to reorganize in the post-war years, Millarville was not among them and, but for one brief flicker, it would not be heard from again. The club's inability to survive the profound changes brought by the post-war world in no way diminishes its almost two decades of fine accomplishments on the polo field.

While its efforts did not garner the glowing press coverage and, with one or two exceptions, its players were not widely known outside the district, if any single club can be said to epitomize the essence of western Canadian polo during the first era, that club would be Millarville.

In British Columbia, the game's origins were different. The men of the Warspite were hardly a rough-and-tumble gang of amateurs. But the careful, disciplined game they taught to the young men of Victoria changed quickly when those men took it with them to the less civilized climes of the Interior. In the Cariboo and in Kamloops, the game was thrown wide open and a new generation of players developed its own particular brand of cowboy polo.

Nowhere was that more evident than in the tiny community of Grande Prairie. Disdaining protective helmets, carefully mowed grounds and country club formalities, the ranchers of Grande Prairie were the dominant force in the pre-war years. Like Millarville, the players never enjoyed the support of a prosperous patron or the discipline of an experienced teacher. They simply saddled up and swept through nearly every team that rode against them.

The game of polo rose to prominence at a time when the Canadian West was beginning to develop its unique identity and each town's club became an early expression of emerging civic pride. Early tournaments were front-page news not only in the host town, but in every paper in southern Alberta and the annual polo club balls were the highlight of the social season wherever they were held. Even where there was no town, in remote ranch districts like the North Fork, polo was the community centrepiece, drawing isolated families together for Sunday-after-church matches, gymkhanas and picnics. So significant were these gatherings that they are mentioned in nearly every surviving journal or reminiscence of the period.

The Great War changed all that, though change had already been in the wind for a decade before August, 1914. Economics and the disastrous winter of 1906 had all but finished the great English ranches and the homesteaders who flooded in to fence the great open ranges were neither remittance men nor cowboys and polo was not their game. Calgary's population had exploded ten-fold and, by the time the war broke out, oil gushers had replaced cattle at the centre of the city's visions for its future. Where there had once been rows of saddle horses and democrats in front of the downtown stores and hotels, now there were electric trolleys and gasoline-powered automobiles. Even out in the foothills ranges, the car and the tractor were beginning to replace the horse.

As polo was pushed off front pages onto the newspapers' new sports columns, it was forced to compete for the public's attention against the growing popularity of North America's indigenous pastimes — baseball and football — and against the myriad other attractions a large city had to offer. While city editors still felt it worthwhile to cover most of the major tournaments, news of regular club matches was reduced, at best, to a brief note or a final score. And, out on the ranges, the fast-growing sport of rodeo was attracting young cowboys who might once have taken to the mallet and ball.

Still, polo will survive the war and the profound changes that followed it. The 1920s will see fewer teams on the field, but new generations of players and patrons will lift their game to levels of sophistication and excitement rarely seen in the first era. ▧

CHAPTER 7

BLUEBIRDS, CANARIES AND GREEN DRAGONS

THE PRAIRIE WEST
1919–1929

Dr. J.G. Cunningham (left) and Bert Connelly, Spokane, 1916 – Connelly was one of several southern Alberta players who spent the war with polo clubs in the American Pacific Northwest.

IN EARLY 1919, Oswald A. Critchley came back to the Alberta town of Cochrane after five years of active service in Europe. He stayed just long enough to sell his share of the old Bell-Irving Ranch and play one last polo match before returning to England where he remained for the rest of his life.

He was, by then, fifty-seven years old. He had watched Calgary grow from a raw railway town to a city of 50,000, witnessed the birth and death of the great English ranches and seen the first of the oil strikes that would become the new source of the city's wealth.

He had been a founding member of the Calgary Polo Club, played in the first Alberta tournament at Fort Macleod in 1892 and then led a long series of Calgary and Cochrane teams to national and international prominence. He had imbued his sons with his passion for the game and then buried one of them in France.

When O.A. Critchley sold out and went back home for the last time, the old Bell-Irving was shabby from years of neglect and the stick and ball game he had loved so much was in shambles.

The year 1914 had been a year of both frustration and promise. Though the hoped-for definitive western championship series had again failed to

materialize, there was a good deal of top-quality polo being played. Calgary finally had its permanent grounds and there was a new, well-financed club in Vancouver. Winnipeg's St. Charles Country Club, buoyed by the presence of a young, strong officer corps with the Lord Strathcona's Horse, finally seemed ready to fulfill the larger role in the Canadian game that it always assumed it would have. Halfway between the western and eastern teams and close to several clubs in the U.S. Midwest, Winnipeg was entertaining grand dreams of a true national championship.

Four Alberta teams had travelled to Spokane, Washington for an inaugural tournament in 1913 and their rough, entertaining brand of polo had done much to ensure that the game would take hold in the Pacific Northwest. Within a few years, there were fine teams in Portland, Boise and Spokane and it was assumed that a strong Canadian presence would continue to be a feature of their annual Lane Cup matches.

On July 30th, 1914, less than a week before the declaration of war, the *Macleod Spectator* was promoting the second Spokane tournament:

<hr />

Seven polo teams, three American and four Canadian, will compete in the northwest championship meet which will be held in Spokane during the Interstate Fair, September 12 to 20.

Entries from Vancouver, Spokane and Boise will furnish the new blood in the tournament this year, while fours from Portland, Cochrane, Cowley and Macleod have also been named to compete. Entries for the meet have closed and the only remaining detail before the opening of the tourney is the drawing of places.

<hr />

The matter of the draw ultimately proved to be far from the only remaining detail.

The Spokane organizers announced that the war would not affect their plans, but it certainly affected the plans of the northern teams. When the tournament opened, no Canadian teams had made the trip.

The first era of western Canadian polo may have ended abruptly on the drowned field of the High River Polo Club, but while every team suspended play — beginning a long hiatus from which most would never recover — a small group of individuals donned new colours and carried on.

Whatever their reasons for not joining up (there was no conscription in Canada), Harry Robertson, Bert Connelly, Hugh Pettit, Harry Gunn, Jack Graham and Jimmy Milvain were all south of the border, playing competitive polo in Portland and Spokane.

While no Canadian teams contested the Lane Cup in 1914, there were Canadians on the field. Harry Robertson was a playing coach for Portland and Hugh Pettit filled the same role for Spokane. The least familiar of the North Fork players, Pettit spent much of the war in the United States, marrying the sister of one of the Spokane players. He came back to Alberta in 1918, but fell victim to the great influenza epidemic the next year.

"Cowley" (as the team was often called in the American press) was reported at various tournaments in Spokane and Boise in the first three years of the war, although often there was at least one American player with the team. The Lane Cup itself shows no winner

Boise versus Spokane, c. 1918 –
Albertans Harry Robertson and
Hugh Pettit are second and third
from the left.

Polo match at Boise, Idaho,
c. 1918 – Harry Robertson, far left.

Trapper Harry Robertson at his cabin north of Fort St. John in northern British Columbia, 1921 – Two years earlier, with Portland, he had been one of the highest rated polo players in the American West.

for 1915, but there was a tournament, including a Cowley team, and it was probably won by Boise, Idaho. The name North Fork is engraved on the Lane Cup for 1916 and the scattered newspaper reports for that year suggest the team was made up of Connelly, Gunn and Robertson supported by a Spokane player named Mitchell. They won the final match from a Spokane foursome that featured Hugh Pettit. The local papers were impressed by their extremely fast play and somewhat concerned about their disdain for any sort of protective headgear.

Bert Connelly was certainly the best player in Spokane at the time. According to a match report from July, 1915:

Yesterday's shining star was Bert Connelly, the Canadians' youthful, light-haired forward, who seemed to be everywhere at once and anywhere he was needed. He scored five of his team's eight goals, a feat unequalled by any individual player during the previous games of the tourney....

His reputation was matched only by that of Harry Robertson who played for Portland, Connelly himself writing that Robertson, with his five-goal handicap, was the best all-around player he had ever seen.

The Great War finally caught up with the United States and there is no evidence of polo being played in the Pacific Northwest for 1917

or 1918. Whether the Canadians came home to Alberta or remained in the United States for the duration is not known, but, when the game was revived in Spokane, North Fork was there.

Rather than being a post-war comeback, North Fork's appearance at the 1919 Lane Cup Tournament can best be described as unfinished business. With Jack Graham joining long-time regulars Jimmy Milvain, Bert Connelly and Rollo Burn (Harry Gunn could not make the trip), the fabled team (with no American help) finally took the only major piece of silverware that had so far eluded them.

With personal replicas of the cup in hand, the North Fork's great players came back home and hung up their mallets. They retired to their ranches and never again played tournament polo.

The first sign that the Great War had not destroyed the game of polo elsewhere in Alberta appeared in the Calgary press in mid-1920. The *Albertan* of August 6th reported:

Calgary and Cochrane polo teams will play a game at the grounds south of the Country Club at 3 o'clock Saturday afternoon. The teams will be: Calgary: Brown, F. McHugh, A. McHugh, Wolley-Dod Cochrane: Landale, A. Clarkson, Rhodes and Trevenen.

It is tempting to see, in this brief announcement, a sign that it would soon be business as usual on the polo fields of southern Alberta after its six-year hiatus. But the report proved to be more a brief flicker than the start of a bright new flame. The papers failed to report the result of the match and no further references to the game can be found for nearly a year. And, in retrospect, while the teams and the players announced in 1920 had a familiar ring, it is the names not heard which truly tell the tale.

There are no reports from High River, from Pekisko, Millarville or Fish Creek. Fort Macleod is silent, and so are Pincher Creek, Cowley and North Fork. There is no news from the venerable Frank Macnaghten, from the Critchleys, the Deane-Freemans or any of the five Hones. De la Vergne, Limoges and Montie Fraser are missing, and so are Robertson, Evans, Shakerley, Carlé, Snowden, Harper and Pike.

Some eventually came back onto the field; most did not. High River would re-emerge in 1927, even stronger than it had been at the close of the first era. Millarville would try to rebuild its great reputation, but the brief effort would come to naught. In the southwestern corner of the province where Edmund Wilmot had started it all more than thirty years before, competitive polo was finished for good.

Willie Deane-Freeman would be back, leading the High River revival, and O.A. Critchley's son, Walter, would make an occasional appearance for Cochrane. But

Macnaghten was finished and so were the Hones. Addie had returned to his native Ireland and his brother, George, retired to the West Coast. Of their cousins, Mick, Nim and Joe, nothing more would be heard. The great Harry Robertson retired to the Peace River country and Pike went back to raising his Percherons. Shakerley, Carlé and Harper were dead. So too were Lipsett, Shaw and Jack Critchley, with perhaps a dozen others killed, badly wounded or gassed.

Still, the August, 1920 notice did mean that the game would go on. The teams show a blend of seasoned veterans from before 1914 and new players with familiar surnames who would soon become the soul of the game's revival.

Dick Brown was a second-generation Calgary player, the son of O.E. Brown, a charter member of the Calgary club. Born about 1895, Dick's name began to appear on the tournament lists in the years just before the war. On the 1914 Hone Cup handicap roster, Brown was already rated as a 5-goaler, putting him ahead of nearly every other player on the list. During the war, he served in France, rising from private to captain by the time he left the service in April, 1919. In the years immediately after the war, he was a major in the second reserve regiment of the 15th Canadian Light Horse.

Following his post-war years in Calgary, Brown moved to the central Alberta town of Sundre where he managed the Sundre Stampede for many years before his death in 1942 at the age of only forty-seven. He had outlived his pioneer father by less than a year.

Frank McHugh, too, had been a regular for both Calgary and High River in the years before the war. Born in 1885, he was the son of the assistant superintendent of Indian affairs for the Treaty #7 nations. After five years at Montreal's Mount St. Louis School, he settled on the family's H2 Ranch along the Bow River east of Calgary and, from 1903 on, operated a prosperous teamster and construction business.

From his first recorded appearance in 1908, McHugh became a steady and spirited regular (the 1914 Hone Cup list rates him as a 3-goaler) whose huge presence on the field was invariably noted by the press. Nicknamed "Bull," he weighed nearly two hundred fifty pounds yet was always able to find ponies that managed to be light and quick on their feet while carrying his considerable weight. The "A. McHugh" listed in the *Albertan's* 1920 report was Bull's cousin, Alex, beginning a solid, lengthy polo career in southern Alberta and, eventually, on the West Coast.

The name Wolley Dod had been familiar in Calgary area polo for more than two decades. On the 1920 roster, it refers to William, carrying on a tradition begun by his father, Arthur, when he first appeared in a Ladies' Cup match at the Calgary tournament of 1896.

When William R. Wolley-Dod (he was the first to hyphenate the name) appeared for Calgary in 1920, he joined Dick Brown, Chappie Clarkson and many others in the second generation of southern Alberta players. He had just returned from active service in Europe as a captain in the 31st Battalion.

While Bill Wolley-Dod lived most of his life in Calgary, he came to be most closely associated with the Cochrane teams of the 1920s, rising to assume their captaincy toward the end of the decade. His close connection with Cochrane came as a result of his marriage, in 1927, to Valentine Kerfoot. Her four brothers were at the heart of Cochrane's post-war polo revival.

Bill spent his professional life as a surveyor and right-of-way engineer with the Calgary Power Company, spending months at a time out in the front range of the Rocky Mountains preparing the way for the hydroelectric projects then being developed to feed Calgary's growing appetite for electricity. He died in 1974.

H.K. Clarkson carried his father's nickname and his appreciation of polo. Born in the Pincher Creek district, he grew up in the midst of the polo matches and gymkhanas that were a feature of life on the old Roodie Ranch. Chappie Jr. owned a place just west of Cochrane and he appeared occasionally for that team after 1920. Married to the sister of Laurie Johnson, another of the great post-war Cochrane players, he left the district to work in the booming oil fields of Turner Valley south of Calgary.

The name Trevenen is another that spans the first and second eras of Alberta polo. In 1920, it was probably William riding out for Cochrane, but his father had been an occasional presence with several of the Calgary-area clubs in the years before the Great War. The elder Trevenen had been a mange inspector, riding the district north and east of Calgary and, when William was born, the family was living in the town of Alix. This may connect the father to the polo team that existed there around 1908.

"Billy" Trevenen worked as a cowboy and a jockey and he was on the membership list for the Millarville Polo Club from 1910 to 1912 and again in 1914, paying the $5 "playing member" surcharge and appearing for the team in at least one tournament during the period. In about 1913, the family settled in Cochrane and remained there until after the war when they moved to Calgary.

During the war, Billy saw overseas service with the 12th Canadian Mounted Rifles. His brother, John, lost his life in France. After the armistice, he returned to cowboying in the district, branching out into the breeding and showing of jumpers and thoroughbred racehorses. He moved to Winnipeg in 1941 and began to work with racehorses full-time. When he finally retired in 1977, he was one of the best-known and most highly respected trainers in Canada. He died in 1986.

Landale and Rhodes provide the connection to the great days of Cochrane polo when they had teamed with Critchley and de la Vergne to win most of the trophies up for play in the years before the war. Condie Landale would stay on for another decade, laying out a polo field at his Bearspaw Ranch and bringing his son into the game. Eventually, like so many before him, he retired to the West Coast.

Which of the English Rhodes brothers took the field in August, 1920 is not clear. It was either "Dusty" (Gilbert) or "Bumpy" (Bernard). Dusty had been in the country since about 1909, partnered with O.A. Critchley in the old Bell-Irving. Bumpy arrived just after the war and bought out Critchley's share of the Grand Valley Ranch in 1919. He, too, raised a few polo ponies and played a little in the following decade.

Obviously well-heeled, the Rhodes brothers were almost a throwback to the early days of the remittance men; they were every inch the English sporting gentlemen. Dusty was more interested in polo than in the operation of the ranch and spent most of his time at a second home on Vancouver Island. Bumpy eventually joined him there in 1930, but died soon after. Dusty and his family returned to Britain, leaving his share in the ranch to Bumpy's widow who kept it until just after the second war.

Such was the cast of characters that came out on a Saturday afternoon in August, 1920 to begin a new era of polo in the Prairie West. They were probably rusty after the long interregnum, but it must have felt good to be back on the field. The grounds were probably not at their best either. It had been six years since their brief christening in June, 1914.

The significance of the field, regardless of its condition, cannot be overstated. With the tenuous state of the game in the years immediately following the war, having a ready-made place to play must have been enormously encouraging. For that, the players had O.E. Brown and the fourteen other initial investors in The Polo Club Limited to thank.

The years of being without a permanent polo ground had taken their toll on the Calgary club. Membership was down and tournament wins were fewer and farther between. The "serious" players — men like Frank Macnaghten and George Ross — had joined the Hones and A.G. Wolley Dod down at Fish Creek and, for a couple of seasons at least, the name "Calgary" was missing from the rolls. It speaks volumes that when the new grounds finally opened in 1914, it was Fish Creek, not Calgary, matched against Cochrane.

The Polo Club Limited was registered as a joint stock company on September 27th, 1911 with a capital of $10,000. Among the fifteen investors were names both familiar and unknown. Most, but certainly not all, were polo players. A.E. Cross is there, along with A.G. Wolley Dod and the requisite complement of Hones (in this case, Addie, George and Joe). Long-time Calgary real estate partners William Toole and George Peet were both signatories, as were H.G. Wooley and the Calgary club's founding president, H.B. Alexander. Another subscriber, rancher Ross Hett, had played only a little in Alberta, but he would become a fixture of polo in Kamloops when he settled there after the war.

The prime mover in forming the company was Osborne Edward Brown. Although he rarely appeared at tournament level, he was a strong, supportive presence with the club from its inception. He was one of the first log cabin homesteaders in the area, settling along the Elbow River southwest of the city near what would become the club's grounds. He

remained there for most of his life. Many players from Calgary and elsewhere regularly put their faith in polo ponies raised and trained by O.E. Brown.

Unlike some of his contemporaries, Brown's life was not spent much in the public eye, but he was a well-known and widely respected presence in the city. When he died in 1941 at the age of seventy-four, his obituary would remember him as "...one of the very fine type of Englishmen who constituted the vanguard of young ranchers in Alberta. He was a kindly, cultured, fine type of man."

The Polo Club Limited was not the Calgary Polo Club. It was (and still is) a private company, established to acquire and hold the polo grounds. The club itself leased the land for a nominal charge and was responsible for its upkeep and maintenance. This arrangement secured a permanent facility for the club while sparing it the complications of legal ownership and the exigencies of changing and fluctuating memberships. The High River club grounds had been secured by much the same kind of legal agreement in 1904.

Whatever the legal niceties, when the players were ready to resume their game, there was a field waiting. It may have been the one thing that kept the game alive.

The August, 1920 match between Calgary and Cochrane may have suggested that polo was still alive in southern Alberta, but, compared to the state of play just six years earlier, it was hardly thriving. Although Cochrane enjoyed a potential abundance of talent, both old and new, Calgary was hard-pressed to field enough skilled players to hold a decent practice match and the August scrimmage between the two teams represented the sum total of southern Alberta's 1920 season.

Recognizing the tenuous state of the game, or perhaps feeling the need to recapture some of the excitement of pre-war tournaments, the Calgary Polo Club opened its 1921

season with a bold stroke. At the beginning of July, four players packed their sticks and tack, loaded their ponies into a Canadian Pacific livestock car and headed for Vancouver. It was the first time Albertans had crossed the Great Divide for a polo match since the young Calgary club's visit to Victoria nearly thirty years earlier.

The Calgary foursome was led by newly elected club president Frank McHugh and included his cousin, Alex, Dick Brown and something of a surprise: Marston SexSmith.

SexSmith had not been heard from for years, dropping from sight after his professional seasons in Montreal. He had not been much in evidence with his old High River club during its fitful seasons just before the war. There is no evidence of his having served in the war, though he had been a corporal with George Ross' 15th Light Horse in the first decade of the century. He probably retired to his ranch until taking up the post of southern Alberta livestock inspector in about 1915. The 1921 season would mark his last recorded appearances on a polo field but he continued to take a behind-the-scenes interest in his game. He died at his home in Calgary in 1933 following a lengthy illness.

The *Calgary Herald* gave the Vancouver match some solid chukker-by-chukker coverage as Calgary counted seven goals in the first two periods and cruised to a 10-6 win. Alex McHugh led the Calgary scoring, but, according to the *Calgary Herald*, "The Calgary team played a brilliant game. Their shots were hard and straight...there was little to choose between them as a team."

Ironically, the newspaper also reported that Vancouver had the best ponies. One can only assume that Snowden's Alberta horses had taken well to the milder climate and greener grass of the West Coast. The game was watched by five hundred spectators, including Lieutenant Governor W.C. Nichol who presented the Calgary team with the cup. Although Calgary came home with the B.C. Challenge trophy (or, at least, with four miniatures of the real thing), the trip did not immediately result in regular play between the provinces. However, as the years between the wars went by, both Kamloops and Vancouver became semi-regular visitors to Calgary and return trips, though not as frequent, always proved attractive to southern Alberta's players.

Almost immediately upon their return from the coast, three members of the Calgary team travelled west to Grand Valley to face a strong quartet from the Cochrane district. Though most of the men who had brought the area into prominence after 1910 had left, the district emerged from the war years with a string of young players that would have been the envy of any club. With the support of veteran Condie Landale and

Alex McHugh, c. 1919.

Alison Emde/Planet Photography

The Hull Cup – This trophy was first played for in 1923 and was symbolic of Calgary's intra-club championship. It was presented by Calgary ranching legend William Roper Hull (the nephew of British Columbia polo patron, W.J. Roper) and remains in play today.

the enthusiasm of the four Kerfoot brothers, a variety of Cochrane teams was beginning a decade in which they would win more than their share of tournaments.

Marston SexSmith did not make the short ride to Grand Valley and his place was taken by Cochrane regular Bill Wolley-Dod. Facing the McHughs, Dick Brown and Wolley-Dod were the two eldest Kerfoot brothers, Duncan and Pat, Chappie Clarkson and Gordon Hinde.

Born in England in 1885, Hinde had appeared occasionally with Cochrane before the war and had done well at the town's 1913 tournament. The Hone Cup list rated him at three goals. It was probably after settling in as manager of O.A. Critchley's Grand Valley Ranch in about 1912 that he was drawn to polo. As with so many others, Critchley would probably have insisted on it.

The play was close, but the real star of the match was the Kerfoots' Grand Valley polo grounds. The teams spent nearly a quarter of the match either retrieving errant balls from the surrounding rough or digging them out of the scores of gopher and badger holes that riddled the field. Amazingly, no injuries were sustained by man nor beast.

The 1921 season was surprisingly active (considering how few players and how few clubs there were) and the obvious enthusiasm that had taken Calgary to the West Coast in July was an indication that there was still a healthy interest in the game.

There was no long-distance travel in 1922, but Calgary again rode west to Cochrane for a match in early July. Whether playing conditions on the Kerfoot's hay meadow had improved is not recorded, but the Grand Valley team of Chappie Clarkson and three Kerfoots had little trouble with their visitors, posting a 5-0 win.

The Calgary squad included both McHughs, club secretary Bill Adams and another second-generation player making his first foray into competitive polo. His name was Clem Gardner and, although he was a newcomer to polo, the son of Captain Meopham Gardner was already a legend in Alberta and everywhere else that the cowboy was king.

Clem Gardner was a world-champion bronc rider, calf roper and chuckwagon racer and if, at nearly forty, he was getting too old to climb into the chute at the Calgary Stampede, he was anything but too old to take up polo. Unaccustomed to doing anything by half measures, Gardner soon emerged as a central figure in the southern Alberta game and enjoyed a long and successful playing career while his Pirmez Creek Ranch became the social centre for visiting teams from across the West. With men like him coming out to play, Calgary's efforts to attract and school the new members they so desperately needed were beginning to bear fruit.

If there was a year in which serious tournament polo again became an integral part of the Prairie game, that year was 1923.

While it was not like the old days with players and their ponies trailing in from five or six different clubs, life had come back into the game. Both of Calgary's newspapers carried club news regularly and promoted every practice and pick-up match as if it were the western championship. The people of the city responded and crowds at the Chinook Park grounds were said to be both large and enthusiastic.

With the Cochrane district showing real strength, another team had joined the list: Lord Strathcona's Horse (Royal Canadians), late of Winnipeg and the battlefields of France. With their strong tradition in the game, they would add much-needed depth to the southern Alberta polo scene.

In Canada, where military polo was far from the officially approved, well-organized activity typical in Britain and the United States, the Strathcona's would write a unique chapter in the history of the game.

Created in 1899 for service in the Boer War, the regiment was raised and funded by Donald Smith, whose title, 1st Baron Strathcona and Mount Royal, had been his reward for pushing the Canadian Pacific Railway across the West.

The mounted regiment proved enormously attractive to the young cowboys and ranchers of Western Canada and they enlisted in droves. The Strathcona's Horse, as it was originally known, arrived in Cape Town, South Africa in April, 1900, their colonel being the legendary Mounted Police superintendent Sam Steele. They acquitted themselves with distinction, and their Sergeant A.H.L. Richardson became the first Canadian serving with a Canadian regiment to be awarded the Victoria Cross.

Renamed Lord Strathcona's Horse (Royal Canadians) and based at Winnipeg, the regiment fought both mounted as cavalry and dismounted in the trenches during the Great War. They returned to Winnipeg after the war but one of their squadrons was stationed in Calgary. As part of Canada's small permanent force, they were the only regular cavalry regiment in Western Canada.

In the Second World War, the Strath's were converted to tanks and served with the 5th Canadian Armoured Division in Italy and northwestern Europe before returning to Calgary in 1945. Subsequently, the regiment saw service in Korea and, most recently, as part of United Nations peacekeeping forces. In 1996, after nearly eighty years in Calgary, the regiment was moved to Edmonton.

Although never officially sanctioned, polo was integral to the life of the regiment from before the first war until 1939. Under a succession of polo-playing commanding officers like Archie Macdonell and Fred Harvey, nearly every member of the Strathcona's small officer corps seems to have taken to the field at one time or another. In the early years, several young officers had arrived in camp with their own strings of polo ponies and the money to keep them, but after the first war, horses became the team's greatest weakness. Although it was possible for a sympathetic commanding officer like Harvey to sneak a few polo ponies past the Remount Selection Board, that practice had been severely curtailed by the 1930s.

Even with the problems presented by unsuitable horses, the regular transfer of officers and a full program of military duties, the Strathcona's polo team would remain one of the strongest in Western Canada for nearly three decades.

Calgary's first practice of the 1923 season was scheduled for early May and the club took an unprecedented step: "Any person wishing to play can rent ponies on the grounds at a reasonable rate." In a further announcement, club secretary Bill Adams sought the support of the Boy Scouts and the Y.M.C.A. for a plan to offer honorary memberships to boys under seventeen years of age. They would be allowed to play at no cost, though they would have to supply their own ponies and sticks.

Such announcements became a regular feature of the local papers' polo coverage, an indication that enthusiasm alone was not enough to sustain the game in the post-war era.

At the same time that the club was soliciting new players, it was announcing grand plans for the summer season. The club secretary was reported to have contacted teams in the United States, Winnipeg, Vancouver, Alix and High River, inviting them to a grand polo tournament and gymkhana to be held over the long Dominion Day weekend at the beginning of July.

The great tournament did not materialize, but throughout the spring and summer months, the club managed to stage a regular series of Saturday intra-squad matches. Although there were more than twenty-five members (including several from the Strathcona's), it seems that a lack of ponies was proving a real difficulty. The club's response was to play three matches simultaneously.

Two matches of three chukkers each were played between the periods of the main, six-chukker game. This arrangement allowed up to twenty-four players to take the field for a least a portion of the day but, more important, the extended eight-minute break between periods gave the ponies a good rest. It meant that a player with only one mount could play a full three-chukker match.

Thursday, September 20th, 1923, finally saw the opening of the first significant post-war tournament at the Chinook Park grounds. For a gate admission of fifty cents, Calgarians were promised "interesting games daily" among five teams: four from the Calgary club and, for the first time, the Strathcona's. Play opened with two simultaneous matches. Calgary team numbers 2 and 4 would meet, alternating their three chukkers with a game between teams number 1 and 3. The two winners would meet the next day with the victor to play the Strathcona's.

The first two matches went off as planned, but scheduling any outdoor event in Calgary on the first day of autumn is tempting fate and Friday's games were cancelled in the face of a blanket of early-season snow.

A revised schedule was finally played on the following Monday with Calgary 3 defeating the Strathcona's by 2-1 and then, almost immediately, riding out to face Calgary 2. The three-chukker final was a foregone conclusion, though the result was perhaps closer than it should have been. Even with exhausted ponies, the number 3 team lost by only 3-2.

For their win, Calgary number 2 became the first recipients of the new William Roper Hull Challenge trophy. That trophy, still played for today, was presented by the long-time Calgary-area rancher as symbolic of the club championship.

The players at the tournament continued the balance of old and new established in the first post-war years. "Bull" McHugh and his cousin, Alex, the perennial Condie Landale and his son, Alec, all gave good accounts of themselves and they were joined by another name from the club's pre-war days, Major C.E. Amphlett. In 1908, Amphlett had seen his name engraved on the American Day Polo trophy, but appeared again only rarely, spending much of his time in his native England. His last appearance with the club was in 1923.

Calgary lawyer Henry Chadwick would continue to play through the rest of the decade while Jack Jephson, the son of Calgary's most eminent solicitor, was just visiting from his orchards in British Columbia. About J. Duff Robertson, little is known except that he was no relation to the great Harry, nor to High River's Joe Robertson who would emerge as an important influence in that club's revival.

John Hugill was an English-born Calgary lawyer who served with the 15th Light Horse in the Great War and, on his return, opened his own practice, eventually becoming a senior solicitor for the C.P.R. He was elected to the Alberta legislature in 1935 as a Social Credit member and served as attorney general until his resignation from the party in 1937, sitting as an independent until 1940. Hugill is also said to have been a writer, publishing under the pen name "John Harker." He achieved the rank of major with the reserve battalion of the Calgary Highlanders and served on the Mobilization Board during the second war before retiring to Vancouver Island.

Most interesting of the players, however, was a quartet from Cochrane's Virginia Ranch. While each man played individually with the Calgary teams in the Hull trophy portion of the tournament, the ranch team assembled to take on a select Calgary squad in a special match on the Saturday afternoon.

Although the field was still soaked from the melting snow and a biting wind kept the spectators bundled in their wraps, the six-chukker match was, to the newspapers, a game that harked back to the great pre-war days. At the end, it was Virginia Ranch on top by 5-3, a win largely credited to the quality of the ranchers' ponies. According to the *Calgary Herald* reporter:

The polo ponies that performed in Saturday's game showed an uncanny sense of polo knowledge and carried their riders after the ball like a hound in pursuit of a rabbit. They were up on the bit all the time and despite the trying test of constant stopping and starting, turning and dodging, they showed the full worth of their breeding and stayed with each chukker, responding instantly to the rein and knee.

And well they should have since the Virginia Ranch existed for only one purpose: to raise and train the finest polo ponies.

Located on Dog Pound Creek, north of the town of Cochrane, the ranch was founded in the 1880s and had already passed through several owners when it was acquired by Barton French in 1914. French named it the Virginia after his American birthplace and he made several improvements to the property, including the installation of a water system and a self-contained electric power plant, a rarity in the area at the time. In 1919, the ranch was purchased by Captain T. B. Jenkinson and it was then that its polo history began.

Before the war, the English-born Jenkinson was a familiar, if infrequent, member of the southern Alberta polo fraternity. He travelled to Winnipeg in 1905 and again in 1912, first with North Fork and then with High River. At that time, he was raising fine horses at a ranch in the Cypress Hills south of Medicine Hat. The trips to Winnipeg were certainly a mix of business and pleasure. When he sold his Cypress Hills operation and moved onto the Virginia, he focused on raising polo ponies, most of which were sold in the eastern United States and California. He must also have had some business connections in the Spokane area since he appeared there during the 1920 Northwestern International Tournament.

he met Jenkinson and, in 1919, began his nine-year association with the Virginia Ranch.

He was a first-class rider and trainer and played a fine game of polo, too. In the 1923 tournament, he scored all five goals in one game for Calgary 3. With Jenkinson and his Virginia Ranch ponies, Jappy travelled to Vancouver, Toronto and Wyoming and spent a winter season at Alberta's second polo home on Coronado Island.

He left the Virginia in 1928 to take up his own place where he continued to raise and train fine horses. Jappy Rodgers died in 1978 following a riding accident at the age of eighty-two and his descendants still live in the district.

When the Calgary season of 1923 closed with an annual meeting just before Christmas, the club's executives seemed pleased with their progress and, in particular, with the success of the September tournament. In addition to extending an invitation to Edward, the Prince of Wales to become a patron of the club, the executive restated its intention of establishing closer contact with teams in Manitoba and British Columbia.

By 1923, Vancouver and Kamloops were back on the field and southern Alberta polo was recovering strength. It seemed that the long-cherished dream of a true western championship needed only the return of Winnipeg to become a reality. And, in Winnipeg, polo was once more very much alive.

When the game was formally revived at the St. Charles club is not certain, but by the fall of 1922, the club had already held its first major post-war tournament. In early September, 1922, three teams from Minneapolis, Minnesota had come north to face the St. Charles club for a new prize: the Sifton Cup. Presented by a long-time club patron, it was known officially as the International Challenge Trophy and was intended to encourage regular competition between Manitoba and teams from the U.S. Midwest in much the same way as the Lane Cup brought Canadian and American teams

Jenkinson held the Virginia Ranch until 1931 when he sold it and disappeared from the record. In the intervening years, the ranch's players regularly appeared at Calgary tournaments, always a threat to the larger teams. Together with Jenkinson himself, the team comprised a succession of ranch employees, partners and visitors (mostly Irish). Peter Dewhurst was an accomplished gentleman rider who rode three times in the Grand National. About Captain P. Kelly who played in 1923, nothing is known, but Captain John Martin (who later was joined at the ranch and on the polo field by his brother, Cecil) was recognized as one of the finest horsemen in the district. After he returned to Ireland, he continued to ride with the Mead Hunt at least until the end of the 1950s.

The best known member of the Virginia Ranch teams was William Jasper ("Jappy") Rodgers, another of southern Alberta's second-generation players with roots that went back to the beginning of the cattle kingdom. Jappy was the son of James "Dublin" Rodgers and was only six years old when Dublin suffered his fatal accident on the polo field. Jappy grew up in the Okotoks district and when the war began he enlisted in the Strathcona's and spent the next five years handling their remounts. When the war ended, he was in Vancouver, but soon returned to Calgary with his new wife and began work at the stockyards. There

together on the Pacific coast. Like the Lane Cup, which invariably matched Vancouver and an army team from Camp Lewis, Washington, the Sifton Cup usually devolved into a contest between St. Charles and the 3rd Infantry from Fort Snelling near Minneapolis.

Winnipeg polo had grown from two distinct but closely related roots. Before the war, Fort Osborne had been the home to strong teams from the resident militias and the Lord Strathcona's. English officers like Lipsett, "on loan" to the Canadian Armed Forces, and the Alberta-raised officers of the Strathcona's dominated play from 1911 to 1914. "Civilian" polo had always been based at the St. Charles Country Club and it bore a stronger resemblance to Vancouver or to the eastern clubs than it did to the more open and accessible games of southern Alberta and the B.C. Interior.

Membership in the St. Charles club itself seems to have been a prerequisite for playing polo. As a result, Winnipeg teams showed a preponderance of players from the highest echelons of the city's society. The Bawlfs — Chauncy and Eddie — were major Prairie grain dealers while the Siftons and the Oslers were branches of families whose nationwide impact on Canadian political and professional life stretched back for many decades. Players like W.A. Smith and Ralph Moore were regular visitors to England and the Continent and their observations on polo at such places as

Ranelagh were a regular part of the local newspapers' game reports. In the late 1920s, Moore's sons, Dick, Jack and Bob, all joined him on the polo field at the St. Charles.

The club also showed strong military connections outside of the Strathcona's. One Captain Cope was a member of the very first St. Charles teams, while Captain Hugh Osler of the 79th Cameron Highlanders and Colonel Morrell Miller of the Royal Horse Artillery both played a season or two. The Montague brothers, Ray and Price, who led the strong Winnipeg teams of the 1920s had both served overseas and Price remained in the Armed Forces. He commanded Winnipeg's Fort Garry Horse between the wars and, with his legal training, served as judge advocate-general of the Canadian Army overseas and chief of staff for Canadian Military Headquarters in London during the second war.

The U.S. army sent two teams to Winnipeg in 1922, together with four players from the Minneapolis Polo Club, to face three teams from the St. Charles. Fielding twelve players was clearly a strain for Winnipeg as there was some duplication on the second and third squads during the tournament.

Fort Snelling's "A" team was the class of the tournament, beating St. Charles "A" in the two-game Sifton Cup series, but the results of the other games during the week revealed that, while there were more than twenty men taking part, there was a substantial range in their abilities. The player pool may have been wide, but it was anything but deep.

In 1923, Winnipeg sent two teams to Minneapolis. The "A" side would attempt to capture the Sifton while the "B" team would face three American squads for a junior trophy.

The "B" team acquitted itself well, beating Fort Snelling's second side and the Minneapolis Red Jackets on its way to a win in the final over the Green Dragons from the U.S. cavalry post at Fort Des Moines, Iowa.

The "A" team, however, again proved no match for Fort Snelling, losing the Sifton Cup for the second time by a two-game total of 15-8.

The Alberta season of 1924 did not deliver the sustained level of activity promised by the 1923 tournament. Frank McHugh seemed to take a couple of years off and

although the Strathcona's were still at nearby Sarcee Camp, their participation on the polo field was a matter of individual choice. With one exception — 1925 — the regiment did not field another official team in Calgary until 1928. This may have been a consequence of the departure, in 1924, of its commanding officer, Lieutenant-Colonel D.J. Macdonald, a member of the 1923 tournament squad.

But if the Strathcona's were not playing in Calgary, they were in Winnipeg. On August 20th, 1924, a short piece appeared in the sports pages of the *Albertan* under the heading "International Polo":

WINNIPEG: In the first game of three for the Sifton Challenge Trophy, the Fort Snelling "Blacks" defeated the St. Charles "Blues" of Winnipeg, eight goals to five at the international polo tournament Tuesday afternoon.

The Strathcona's first post-war
polo team, Calgary, 1923 –
(left to right) Captain N.A. Gianelli,
Colonel L.F. Page, Lieutenant-Colonel
D.J. MacDonald, Sergeant Major
Roberts and R.S.M. R.R. Richmond.

The Strathcona's Senior N.C.O. team, Winnipeg, 1924 –
(left to right) sergeants Henry, Jacobs, Atkinson and Richmond.
The Strathcona's part in Winnipeg polo after the Great War was
limited to only two seasons, but this, the regiment's only N.C.O.
team, acquitted itself well at the 1924 City Championships.

The 1924 Winnipeg tournament, the largest ever held in Canada, involved nine teams and a week of two games a day. Only Fort Snelling's Blacks and St. Charles' Blues played for the Sifton Cup and, rare for a Canadian tournament of this era, several teams were handicapped.

There was a second team from Fort Snelling and a combined Twin Cities team from clubs at Minneapolis and St. Paul. St. Charles also mounted Red and Yellow teams and the Strathcona's, making a rare post-war appearance in Winnipeg, fielded an officers' "A" team and a "B" team of N.C.O.s. The officers — Rebitt, Powell, Morton and Griffin — would all become familiar to southern Albertans over the next fifteen years.

Also joining in was a foursome from Omaha, Nebraska with the curious name of "Ak-Sar-Ben." Although it sounded more like a Shriners' club than a polo team, the name was actually just "Nebraska" spelled backwards. Although the team was predominantly civilian, it was connected to Fort Snelling through its leader, Captain J.A. Boyers, a top army polo player and teacher.

The tournament, widely reported and well-attended, saw Fort Snelling retain its hold on the Sifton Cup but, more important, it allowed Winnipeg to strengthen its claim as the centre of Canadian polo, a role it believed it could (and should) play. Unfortunately, in the years before the war, the club was rarely able to fulfill those aspirations. The Western Canada Polo Association remained weak throughout its pre-war life, apparently unable to coordinate the timing of various tournaments or to deliver the teams it promised. While the St. Charles club continued to host what it termed the Western Canadian Championship for several years, its own promises to go to Alberta for meetings or to send teams to other major matches were never met. It would be 1927 before a Winnipeg team finally went west to play in a tournament.

Still, there were good reasons for Winnipeg to entertain dreams of becoming a centre for polo, not only in the West but for the rest of the country as well.

The city's self-styled status as the "Gateway to the West" was well-founded. The area had been familiar to fur traders from the mid-eighteenth century and its first rude buildings dated from about 1812. The city itself grew up around a Hudson's Bay Company post that had been established in 1821-22 and was incorporated by 1873 although its population numbered fewer than 4,000 souls. Winnipeg's strategic position, about sixty miles north of the 49th Parallel at almost the exact point where the great Canadian Shield gives way to the Prairies, made it the focus of westward expansion and, with the arrival of the Canadian Pacific and, later, the Canadian National railways, the city boomed. It was almost exactly halfway between the old established cities to the east and the rapidly growing centres to the west while affording the easiest access to such American midwestern cities as Minneapolis and Chicago. Everything (and everyone) moving east or west across the country had to go through Winnipeg.

By 1914, the capital of Manitoba had grown into the third largest city in Canada (and the largest west of Toronto) and saw itself as the wholesale, administrative and financial centre of the Prairie West.

Polo enthusiasts in Winnipeg believed it was the natural location for the major polo tournaments that might eventually develop into truly national — or even international — championships.

But Calgary had its own sound reasons for seeing itself as the logical centre for western polo. If Winnipeg was halfway between Toronto and Calgary, then Calgary was halfway between Winnipeg and Vancouver and the Albertans had long ago lost any interest in meeting teams from the East. Although they had not yet played each other, Alberta's clubs were well aware of the strength of the game around Kamloops in the B.C. Interior and were certainly interested to hear that a new Vancouver club was buying Alberta ponies in considerable numbers immediately before the war. Further, Alberta's American contacts were on the West Coast, in sunny California, where their New Year's visits had become almost a tradition.

If the large 1924 tournament had announced the rebirth of Winnipeg as a serious centre for polo, its early hopes of becoming a focal point for the Canadian game would have to be abandoned. Polo was again going strong in Eastern Canada, but Toronto and Montreal, when not playing each other, were engaged once more with the teams in the northeastern United States that had always seemed their natural opponents. No eastern team had ever travelled out onto the Prairies and no team from the West had gone east in nearly twenty years. Those tenuous, early bonds had been broken too long to be reforged and Canadian polo would never see a true national championship.

In the Rocky Mountain foothills, Calgary and Cochrane had come back on form by the mid-1920s and most of the Strathcona's polo-playing officers found themselves posted to Calgary when the regiment was divided after the war between there and Winnipeg. Another Winnipeg-based mounted regiment — the Royal Canadian Horse Artillery — would also spend its summers at Sarcee Camp, fielding polo teams on the Calgary club's grounds for several seasons. And, within only a couple of years, the old field at High River would be mowed, the gopher holes filled and the legendary scarlet jerseys taken out of mothballs.

To the west, Kamloops again had a strong team and the first order of business for a post-war Vancouver club had been to reconnect British Columbia's polo links with the U.S. Pacific Northwest. First established in 1913 by Cochrane and North Fork and sustained during the war by players like Harry Robertson and Bert Connelly, the competition for Thaddeus Lane's Northwest Challenge Cup always proved more attractive to Alberta and British Columbia than the prospect of meeting teams from Duluth or Minneapolis. It is unlikely that Kamloops and Vancouver had ever thought much about Winnipeg polo, an indifference that was matched by the "Gateway City" itself as far as British Columbia was concerned.

The issue of the true home for western Canadian polo was settled in 1925 as Calgary prepared to host the first post-war Western Canada Championship (with neither British Columbia nor Manitoba represented). From that date forward, C.C. Chipman's trophy would take up permanent residence at the Calgary Polo Club. The trophy itself had probably been brought to Calgary by the Strathcona's when they moved to the city after the war.

The guest list for the competition was in some confusion right up to the first day of play on Thursday, August 27th. As late as the 25th, the papers were reporting a five-team field with Calgary and the LdSH facing three Cochrane district teams, including Cochrane, the Bearspaw Ranch and the Minnehaha Ranch. These last two were pick-up collections of "extra" Cochrane players (another indication of the strength of the area). Bearspaw was Condie Landale's ranch, half-way between Cochrane and Calgary, and he would be supported by his son, Alec, Peter Dewhurst and an unknown named Pearce. The Minnehaha was Bumpy Rhodes' new name for the old Bell-Irving, but, by the time play commenced, the team failed to appear.

The revised draw had Calgary versus the Strath's on Thursday and Cochrane versus Bearspaw on Friday, with the winners to meet in a Saturday final.

Newspaper reports are sketchy, but Calgary bested a Strathcona's foursome of captains Griffin, Bradbrooke, Brown and Powell by 4-1, while Cochrane beat Bearspaw 5-3. In a closely played final, Calgary's Lang, Trevenen, Duff Robertson and Adams bested three Kerfoots and Bill Wolley-Dod to take the Chipman Cup for the first time in the post-war era.

At almost the same time, a pair of St. Charles teams were in Minneapolis for another round of Sifton Cup matches against Fort Snelling, the St. Paul Polo Club, Ak-Sar-Ben and a team of ranchers from Pierre, South Dakota. While Fort Snelling was retaining its stranglehold on the main cup, Winnipeg's "B" side managed to lose possession of the junior trophy to the team from St. Paul.

The 1926 Western Canada Championship was another confusion of players and ad hoc teams from Cochrane and Calgary. Seven teams competed for the Chipman with three from Calgary (the "Magpies," "Robins" and "Bluebirds"), three from the Cochrane area (the "Mossbanks," the "Hayseeds" and Grand Valley) and a foursome from Winnipeg's Royal Canadian Horse Artillery that was spending the summer on manoeuvres at Sarcee Camp.

The tournament opened on Tuesday, July 20th with a game between the Robins and the Bluebirds. Although the score was anything but close — the Bluebirds rode to an easy 10-2 win — the game was nevertheless of considerable interest since it marked the return to competitive polo of one of Alberta's finest pre-war players. Acting as if he had never been away (and scoring three goals in the process) was Willie Deane-Freeman. Deane-Freeman obviously had lost none of his skill and while his old Millarville club would never be successfully revived, his passion for the game would find a permanent home one year later with a reborn High River team.

The six local teams that competed in the 1926 Western Canada Championship show something of the quickly developing strength of the Alberta game. From the rough, halting recovery of 1919 and 1920, the greater Calgary area could now boast a rich variety of talent, both old and new.

Grand Valley fielded Bill Wolley-Dod with three Kerfoots — Pat, Archie and Percy — while the Mossbanks were Cochrane standout Laurie Johnson, Peter Dewhurst of the Virginia Ranch, Duncan Kerfoot and one Ted Mezen about whom nothing else is known. The third Cochrane team — the Hayseeds — should have been stronger than it proved with its lineup of Condie Landale, his son, Alec, and two of the Virginia Ranch's best, John Martin and Jappy Rodgers.

Calgary's Robins, too, should have done better with Dick Brown and H.A. Chadwick, steady newcomer John Hugill and Captain G. Bradbrooke from the Strathcona's. For the Bluebirds, Willie Deane-Freeman was supported by his old friend Billy Trevenen and important post-war recruits Llew Chambers and J. Duff Robertson. The champion Magpies, however, demonstrated once again the value of sound experience as Frank and Alex McHugh resumed their effective partnership with the support of Strathcona's Captain Frank Powell and the highly regarded Kay Lang.

An otherwise highly successful tournament was coloured by a nasty accident. As reported in the *Albertan*, the incident was a fine piece of tragicomic bravado:

The final game was marred at the end of the fifth chukker when C. Lang, of Calgary, who had been playing a fine consistent game for the Magpies, sustained a double fracture of his left leg near the ankle.

The accident happened under the most peculiar circumstances. Lang was riding off Pat Kerfoot near the eastern boards when his mount stumbled and somersaulted. Lang was under his mount when it rolled, but he miraculously escaped serious injury. He remounted, but found that his pony was going short, so he cantered over to the western sidelines, calling for a new pony. As he reached the board he made a flying dismount, but in jumping his left heel caught on the board, throwing him heavily to the ground. As he fell a sharp crack was heard, and when picked up Lang's foot was dangling in his boot.

An ambulance was called and Lang was removed to the Holy Cross hospital, where it was found that he had sustained a double fracture. Lang displayed rare gameness after the accident. He asked to be allowed to lie by the boards to see the finish of the game, but when the doctor insisted upon him going to the hospital, Lang left the field calling upon his teammates to do their best. He was given three hearty cheers by the players and spectators when the ambulance rolled out of the field.

Following the western championship, Condie Landale took a Cochrane team out to the West Coast to join in the Lane Cup Tournament in Vancouver. Although the result was unfortunate for them (the team finished a distant fourth in a four-team field), the trip did re-establish the link between Alberta and British Columbia initiated by Calgary in 1921. It was a bond that would continue to strengthen the game in both provinces until the close of the second era.

The years 1925 and 1926 had seen two consecutive seasons of steady growth in southern Alberta polo and, unlike the alternating years of feast and famine that had dogged the game since the war, 1927 would prove even stronger. There would be a major new team, important new players (not all of them men), more travel and a Western Canada Championship that, for once, came tantalizingly close to being just that: a true championship among all the top teams in the West.

Although hampered by a very wet summer, intra-club play was particularly active. A three-game program scheduled for early July was washed out and the first day of the western championship suffered a similar fate. Still, there were regular games for a "fortnightly challenge cup" and the announced revival of the Ladies Challenge Cup matches. But the most striking feature of the season was the presence of women on the Chinook Park field.

The Royal Canadian Horse Artillery was back at Sarcee Camp and playing regularly through the month of July. Unfortunately, the regiment returned to Winnipeg before the western championship began in late August. In their final appearance of the season on the last Saturday in July, they managed to score a rare win over the Magpies. The regiment's contribution to southern Alberta polo over the previous two seasons was recognized at the end of the match with the presentation of a keepsake trophy to the regiment's commander (both on and off the polo field), Lieutenant-Colonel C.V. Stockwell, D.S.O.

The team rosters for the intra-club matches showed the results of Calgary's efforts to increase the playing membership. Several new names were in evidence — Bruce Taylor, U.S. Pilkington and R.S. McKay — but the most significant addition to the club in 1927 was James Braehead Cross.

Jim was A.E. Cross' eldest son and he had just returned from a brewing course in England to assume the position of secretary with Calgary Brewing and Malting. For the next forty years, Jim Cross would not only prove himself a fierce polo player but also carry on his father's role as the club's most important patron. His support and generous financial backing would prove instrumental in the survival of the western game through the Depression and into the difficult, uncertain years of the post-war revival.

On August 4th, 1927, under a front-page headline that read "The King of Sports," the *High River Times* announced the rebirth of the High River Polo Club:

We learn with much interest that polo is to be revived in High River. A meeting was recently held here and club officers and committees elected.

The club will have the use of the well located polo grounds north of the town on the Calgary road which is now being put in condition for playing. The first practice will be held on Saturday, August 6 and it is hoped to have one or more games about the 16th of August with Calgary and other outside teams participating.

Among the club officers "elected" was an honorary president: H.R.H. The Prince of Wales. He was expected to be visiting his EP Ranch at Pekisko later in the month and the club members believed there was a chance he might attend a local tournament if it could be arranged. Thus, the August 16th date mentioned in the newspaper.

Assuming a simple love of the game would not prove sufficient to sustain the new High River effort, the *Times* went on to offer hope for the revival of another traditional feature of southern Alberta polo:

One of the thoughts in the minds of those who are endeavoring to revive this popular game is that a market may be created for the light type of horses used in this game. There are many of these in the district which are little value under present conditions, but if of the right temperament and properly trained might develope into very valuable polo ponies.

For any other new polo club to try to schedule a tournament within two weeks of its organizational meeting would be unthinkable, but this was no ordinary club. Not only did it have a tradition of fine polo stretching back to the earliest days of the Alberta game and a sound, well-established playing field, it began its new era with a team that would have been the envy of any Canadian club.

Frank McHugh, who had lived in High River for several years, was encouraged by the executive of the Calgary club to bring the town back onto the polo scene. Along with his cousin, Bull would be able to call on the playing and organizational talents of such pre-war stalwarts as Pastro Limoges, Bill Holmes, Frank Watt and Marston SexSmith. He would also benefit greatly from the enthusiasm and practical assistance of Ellison Capers, resident manager of the Round T Ranch. But, easily as important as any other factor, he would have Willie Deane-Freeman as his playing captain.

Not only were High River planning to host a modest tournament before the month was out, they had promised to field a team in the upcoming Western Canadian Championship. To this end, the inaugural meeting closed with the following: "Decided: To practice on Saturday, 6th August, and as often as possible."

In mid-August, Calgary followed Cochrane's 1926 lead and travelled to Vancouver for the Northwestern International Tournament. Again under the leadership of Condie Landale, the team suffered the same depressing fate that befell Cochrane the year before: a distant fourth in a four-team draw.

Still, the team's Vancouver experience did little to dampen spirits as Calgary began its buildup toward the 1927 western championship. It seemed that all the necessary pieces were falling neatly into place and the *Albertan* fuelled the high expectations in a lengthy article that appeared on August 26th:

The big polo tournament to be held at the Calgary Polo Grounds all next week is the first move to make this the Mecca of polo for western Canada. Members of the executive of the Western Canadian Polo Association are satisfied that if the proper support is given the tourney by the citizens of Calgary and the district that the association will decide to make Calgary its permanent headquarters.

On the subject of the grounds, the *Albertan* was equally effusive:

The beautiful Calgary polo grounds which adjoin the Chinook racetrack are considered possibly the best in Canada. Certainly, the experts say, they are the best that can be obtained in the west. The opportunity of meeting under such conditions will weigh strongly with the association when the suggestion [is made] to make the Calgary tournament the annual Western Canadian tournament.

The polo grounds has good accommodation for the large crowd which will probably attend to see the thrilling game which has so many adherents in all parts of the world.

And, the paper saw another compelling reason for Calgary to become the permanent home for the Chipman Cup:

Western Canadian bred polo ponies, raised in the Calgary district, are in great demand throughout the United States and Canada. The best light horses on the continent are raised here in the west. This was amply proved before the war when Alberta players mounted on the best of the Alberta ponies swept through all competitions in the western United States and Canada. The visitors are particularly anxious to stage the tournament here so that they will have an opportunity to replenish their strings of ponies.

The papers were promising a full slate of teams, including the Virginia Ranch, Cochrane, High River and two from the host club. Until the last moment, it was hoped that the Strathcona's, too, would join the list. Although the regiment's driving polo enthusiast, Captain Fred Harvey, had been posted back to Calgary in June, he simply did not have enough time to organize and train a team that could give a respectable account of itself. Calgary would substitute a third team for the absent regiment; there would be other years for Strathcona's polo.

Through the 1920s and 1930s, Fred Harvey was the heart and soul of Strathcona's polo. A fine leader and player, he was a career officer with the regiment and enjoyed a remarkable thirty-one years of service.

Born at County Meath, Ireland in 1888, he came to Canada in 1908 following graduation from Dublin's École du Science. In 1915, he married Lillian Patterson, the daughter of a Mounted Police officer from Fort Macleod. Their only son was killed in the second war.

In 1915, Harvey enlisted at Fort Macleod and went overseas with the Canadian Mounted Rifles. Promoted to lieutenant in 1916, he was posted to the Strathcona's. In March, 1917, as a troop leader of C Squadron at Guyencourt, France he was awarded the regiment's second Victoria Cross. Harvey remained with the Strath's for the duration of the war and, in a series of fierce actions, he also won the Military Cross and the French Croix de Guerre.

Promoted to captain, he returned to Calgary after the war and was later appointed physical education officer at Canada's Royal Military College in Kingston, Ontario. He came back to Calgary in 1927 where he remained until 1935 when he took command of A Squadron in Winnipeg. In 1938, Harvey was promoted to lieutenant-colonel and assumed command of the regiment.

In his polo, as in his military career and his personal life, Harvey was a fearless and inspirational leader. Rarely penalized on the field, he was a stickler for staying within the rules. Nevertheless, he was willing to push those rules to their limit and was always a player that both his opponents and his teammates needed to keep a careful eye on.

After turning over command of the Strathcona's to fellow polo player Norman Gianelli in 1940, Harvey, with the rank of brigadier, commanded Alberta's Military District 13, a position he held until his retirement in 1946. Brigadier F.M.W. Harvey, VC, MC, died in Calgary on August 24, 1980.

The year 1927 also saw the mention of a team from Okotoks. That town lies just south of Calgary on the road to High River and, while it had never appeared on the southern Alberta polo map, it had been home to several outstanding players who made their name before the war with either Fish Creek or Millarville, not far to the west. If polo was indeed being played in Okotoks in 1927, it would be a sign that renewed interest in the game at High River had sparked an attempt to bring the area back into the picture. But when the tournament opened, Okotoks was not present.

The biggest news of all, however, was that Winnipeg's St. Charles Country Club and the Vancouver Polo Club were both coming to play. The *Albertan* quickly made them odds-on favourites:

The two probable finalists in the tourney next week, according to the experts, are Winnipeg and Vancouver. Both teams are bringing practically the same lineups that have previously won games in other tourneys. Vancouver will be handicapped by the absence of J.G. Fordham, who sprained both his wrists in a fall playing at the coast last week. Otherwise the teams will be intact.

Not only would the tournament be the first in which Winnipeg and Vancouver had faced each other on the polo field, it would mark the first time either club had come to Calgary. Only the absence of a team from Kamloops kept Calgary's 1927 tournament from being the true western championship of so many dreams.

Monday, August 29th dawned grey and wet, washing out the entire first day of competition and forcing a tight four-game schedule to be played on Tuesday, albeit under brilliant sunshine.

In the full week of polo that followed, the teams resolved themselves into three series, playing for the Chipman, the Sheep Creek trophy (in play for the first time since the Pekisko Gee-Bungs won it in 1911) and the A.E. Cross Prize. There was also a three-chukker match featuring Calgary's women players.

Vancouver, High River, Cochrane and the Virginia Ranch were clearly the strength of the field, with Winnipeg disappointingly off form. The three Calgary teams ranged from middling to awful, as the club had obviously stretched itself too thinly in trying to balance the draw after the Strathcona's bowed out.

The 1927 Calgary tournament closed on Saturday, September 3rd with three final matches. High River marked its return to competitive polo with a remarkably successful run. After losing its opening match to Vancouver,

Glenbow archives, NA-2268-27

the team did not falter and capped their performance by beating Cochrane in the tournament's only overtime match, capturing the Sheep Creek trophy. Although it was not announced as such, the Sheep Creek trophy match was accepted at the tournament to represent the Alberta provincial polo championship. It was one that High River would fight to keep in 1928.

In the match to settle the "best of the rest," Winnipeg faced Calgary's No. 1 team. The St. Charles side must have felt more than a little frustration after their consecutive losses to Virginia Ranch and Cochrane and they took it out on the best that Calgary had to offer. Scoring almost at will, Winnipeg crushed their hosts by 11-0 to claim the A.E. Cross Prize.

The largest and most enthusiastic crowds of the week turned out to watch as Vancouver completed the week undefeated with a 5-3 victory over the Virginia Ranch and claimed the Chipman Cup. Starring for Vancouver were two names that were familiar to every old-time Alberta player: Frank Ward and Tommy Wilmot. Much more would be heard from them as the second era unfolded.

The condition of the field and the size of the crowds at the 1927 tournament must have impressed the members of the Western Canadian Polo Association since Calgary was assured that again in 1928 (and probably for the foreseeable future) it would play host to the western championship. The Association further

decided that the 1928 Alberta Provincial Tournament and a Manitoba Championship to be held in Winnipeg would both be sanctioned as "warm-ups" for the main event.

Except that its polo teams had finished at the bottom of an eight-team tournament, the Calgary Polo Club had every reason to consider 1927 a thoroughly successful year.

The year 1928 proved to be another time of steady growth across the West as seasons got underway in Winnipeg, Calgary, Cochrane, High River, the B.C. Interior and Vancouver.

After a hurried (though ultimately successful) inaugural year, the new High River Polo Club got down to business early in 1928. At their organizational meeting on April 11th, the members elected officers, set practice times, contracted for the repair of the clubhouse and arranged for the regular filling of the dozens of gopher and badger holes. The club was also looking into procuring a piece of land adjoining their grounds to improve pasturage for members' ponies. Club memberships were set at $10, with any members' children — boys and girls — able to play for free. Individual members under the age of twenty-one would pay $5.

While the season would see a good crop of new players coming out for High River, the club's executive closed its 1928 meeting with expressions of sympathy for the loss of one of its fine long-time players. Pastro Limoges had died the previous October, just weeks after playing in the Calgary tournament.

The re-election of E.H. Capers to the position of vice-president was an acknowledgement of his importance to the revival of polo in High River. Capers was manager of the Round T Ranch just west of the town and, although the name might not be familiar, its connections to the game of polo went back to its earliest days. The Round T was, in fact, the old High River Horse Ranch, home to Herbert Eckford, a founding member of the High River club and long one of its major supporters.

After Eckford sold the ranch to an American syndicate in 1914, it was managed by New York native F.V. Bennis, the new owners' chosen man, and he remained on the property until Capers was appointed in 1925 or 1926. Ellison Capers was originally from Kentucky and, some time in the early 1920s, he and his wife had settled on a small ranch along Pekisko Creek about eighteen miles west of High River.

The Eckford Ranch had always served as the social centre of polo in High River and the Capers moved quickly to re-establish that tradition at the Round T. They entertained visiting teams and hosted the big parties that invariably followed the club championship matches. Owner Hiram Sibley was in full support of the Round T's commitment, even serving as scorekeeper for several matches when he was in residence. But Ellison Capers made another substantial contribution to the success of the reborn High River Polo Club when he offered to keep Willie Deane-Freeman's ponies at the Round T, saving them a regular fifty-mile round trip from Millarville. Without such an arrangement, Deane-Freeman would never have been able to join the High River team.

Capers' and Frank McHugh's evangelical zeal brought a number of young players into the club in the first years after its revival and it was not uncommon to see the Bull out at the grounds running clinics and practices several times a week. Their protégés, including Charlie Arnold, Joe Robertson, Reg Pollard and the de Foras brothers, Jack and Barlow, would become the strength of the team from the late Twenties to the outbreak of the second war. Capers himself was more than simply a patron of High River polo. He and his son, Ellison Jr., both engraved their names on a succession of cups and trophies in the 1930s.

Following a season-opening ball at the Palliser hotel, the Calgary club started play at the end of May with a series of matches for the Hull Cup, symbolic of the club championship. There were three "civilian" teams in the hunt (showing the club's propensity for naming its teams after birds — Canaries, Robins, Bluebirds and, occasionally, Magpies) and the presence of a foursome from the Strathcona's was a clear sign that Fred Harvey thought them ready to play a full season of high-level polo.

The final day of the Hull Cup matches also featured a match between two of the "girls' teams" (usually styled the "Chickadees" and "Bobolinks"), indicating that women's polo was thriving at the club for a second season.

The women's teams were back on the field in early July during a club tournament involving three Calgary squads and the R.C.H.A., who were back again in their summer home. This tournament also added a new twist. Joining the Canaries and the Whites was a team called the "Colors," featuring three men and women's standout Ina ("Bun") Dewdney. Mrs. Violet May was listed as a spare. It was no joke as the Colors beat the Canaries 4-1 over three chukkers and, according to the *Albertan*, "...showed much better form throughout the whole game than their opponents."

Bun Dewdney was the daughter of Archdeacon Arthur Dewdney. The Calgary branch of the remarkable Dewdney family had lived at their ranch in Calgary's Glenmore district since 1909 where Bun developed into an expert horsewoman. She was a well-known participant in every form of Calgary horse show and, clearly, a fine polo player.

The Dewdney Ranch was sold to the City in 1930 and now lies under the Glenmore Reservoir, a major source of Calgary's drinking water. About this time, Bun married an Englishman and moved to his home in Essex.

English-born Violet Bode May was the wife of legendary Canadian bush pilot "Wop" May. A passionate horsewoman, she was a fixture at local horse shows during the brief time she lived in Calgary. She remained in Alberta even after Wop's death in 1952 and died in Edmonton in 1988 at the age of 87.

The club matches (including at least one more which included both men and women) continued through early July with the R.C.H.A. and the Strathcona's joining in regularly. All the teams had their eyes on the 1928 Alberta Provincial Championship set for July 19th, 20th and 21st.

High River would defend its 1927 title against the Lord Strathcona's, the R.C.H.A., Calgary "A" (the Canaries) and Calgary "B" (the Bluebirds), with "A" already picked to travel on to Winnipeg at the end of the month. The teams would vie for a new provincial championship trophy. Presented by the Hudson's Bay Company, the large sterling silver cup would remain in play until 1939.

The opening game between High River and the LdSH was probably the highlight of the entire weekend, matching, with the clarity of hindsight, what may well have been the two best teams at the tournament. The *Albertan* was positively poetic in its enthusiasm:

The picturesque home of the Calgary club, one of the real beauty spots of the city, never looked better, the striking red and green uniforms of the players added colour to a match that will go down in history for a display of riding that seldom has been equalled in the West.

It took three overtime periods before Willie Deane-Freeman counted the winner for High River:

Just as it appeared as though the ball was going out of bounds, Freeman hoisted it 15 feet in the air and it sailed right through the centre of the posts for one of the best goals ever scored at the local grounds.

The rest of the games were somewhat tamer with the Canaries playing well enough to confirm the club's decision that they should go to Winnipeg for the Manitoba Championship.

The Canaries and High River gave the large crowd value for their money in the provincial final, playing what the *Albertan* described as "...an exhibition of very fast and open polo, being just a series of dashes from one end of the field to the other. Both ponies and players were all out during the entire game." In the end, High River retained its title by 4-3.

High River must have been well-pleased by their second straight provincial championship, for it demonstrated that the "new" club was already remarkably deep in talent. Willie Deane-Freeman was the only member of the 1927 team to play in 1928 but his new teammates had acquitted themselves brilliantly. Even substituting an inexperienced Art Holmes for Robertson in the second game and sitting Charlie Arnold out for the final did not affect their performance. The club was obviously close to fielding two very good polo teams.

By the time the Monday morning papers declared the tournament an all-out success, the Canaries' ponies were on their way to the Manitoba Championship.

The Winnipeg meeting was a four-team affair with Calgary playing two St. Charles club teams and a foursome named the Green Dragons, privately organized, led and funded by Prairie grain magnate E.J. Bawlf.

The Green Dragons were the defending club champions, but no team dominated the competition. Rather, the terrible weather and a litany of injuries caused by the sodden grounds kept the matches close. Calgary went through to the final, but lost to the St. Charles Blues by 7-3.

While one southern Alberta team was playing in Winnipeg, another was preparing to travel to Vancouver for the Northwestern International Championship in mid-August. The press called it "Calgary," but the team's connections to the city were tenuous at best. Laurie Johnson and Archie Kerfoot were from Cochrane, as was Condie Landale (despite his frequent appearances at Chinook Park). The fourth was Willie Deane-Freeman. Southern Alberta's two previous forays to the coast had been unmitigated disasters, but this combination managed to make it to the final before losing to Vancouver "A" by a respectable 8-4.

In the meantime, as preparations for the 1928 Western Canada Championship proceeded, regular play continued on the home grounds at Calgary, High River and Cochrane and, at Calgary, many of the matches involved either the women's teams or a mix of men and women. The women even issued an invitation

Violet Bode May, c. 1923 –
The striking and confident Mrs. May,
shown here at an Alberta horse show,
was the darling of the New York
press during the visit of the Calgary
women's polo team in 1928.

Calgary's women polo players in
the Stampede Parade, 1927.

Cochrane's Laurie Johnson with "Mayflower," c. 1925.

to any and all women players in the West to come to Chinook Park for a championship tournament of their own.

With everyone prepared, the 1928 Western Canada Championship Tournament was to begin on Saturday, August 25th.

There were the usual no-show disappointments. It had been hoped that Frank Ward would bring his Douglas Lake team from the B.C. Interior, but he came with Vancouver instead. As recently as the 18th, Winnipeg's St. Charles team was expected, but they also reneged.

Kamloops did not make the trip either, although they were certainly asked. Invitations had also gone out to Portland, Oregon and Fort Lewis, Washington, but their appearance was never considered a serious possibility.

Nevertheless, fully nine teams were in town and ready to begin play on Saturday. Vancouver sent most of its 1927 championship foursome to defend the Chipman Cup against the host club's Canaries and Blacks, the Virginia Ranch, Cochrane and the Strathcona's. High River felt confident enough to send both its "A" and "B" teams. While St. Charles was not coming, Winnipeg would be represented by its Green Dragons.

There would be parking for two hundred cars, special taxis from the downtown hotels, a caterer to provide ample soft drinks, teas and ice cream and the crowds would be serenaded by the band of Princess Patricia's Canadian Light Infantry.

And then, continuing a tradition established at the 1927 tournament, it began to rain.

Heavy downpours on Friday continued through the night, drowning the field and making play impossible. With Sunday matches out of the question, Saturday's two games were pushed forward to Monday in an attempt to put the already-tight schedule back on track.

Monday's three games featured a repeat of the 1927 final with Vancouver drawn against the Virginia Ranch, High River "A" against the Blacks and the Strathcona's, making their first Chipman Cup appearance in fifteen years, facing the Green Dragons.

The newspapers were much taken with the Winnipeg squad from the moment it was announced that they would be coming to the tournament. Bawlf, one of the leading sports patrons in the country, had sent a skating team to Calgary and Banff the winter before and was well-known in the city. As for his Green Dragons, the *Albertan* wrote the following:

A couple of years ago, Mr. Bawlf selected three young men, also members of the St. Charles Country Club, Winnipeg, and formed them into a polo team with himself as coach and captain. These lads, under his direction, have progressed so rapidly and so well that they now are capable of giving any team a run for its money. Mr. Bawlf keeps a string of 13 polo ponies of his own and he supplies nearly all the mounts for his own team.

Bawlf's "lads" were Jack Moore ("one of the most promising young players in Western Canada"), Art Burrows ("a dashing player and a splendid horseman") and Cliff Hargreaves ("a remarkable long hitter"). Bawlf himself is described as "a thoroughly reliable back and an absolute sure hit" who can be counted on to make one or two spectacular end-to-end rushes if not closely checked.

But the paper saved its most eloquent prose for the Dragons' kit:

⁘⊶⬦⊷⁘

When [they] come on the field they are a very pretty and dashing sight. Their colours are green and yellow. They wear green and yellow checkered polo shirts, green helmets, green belts and green bandages on their ponies' legs — and they play as well as they look.

⁘⊶⬦⊷⁘

Two of the Strathcona's — Lieutenant Harry Foster and Captain Jeffrey Griffin — would have known the Dragons since they were from the Winnipeg Squadron. With their teammates Powell and Rebitt, they certainly seemed unimpressed by the Dragons' reputation or their sartorial splendour and rode to a convincing 6-3 win.

Vancouver was clearly the team to beat as they breezed through to the Chipman final, beating High River in the semifinals. For the second year in a row, they would face a Cochrane-area team that had surprised both the Strathcona's and High River "B."

In the consolation series, a closely matched group of strong teams played a series of tight games, with only Calgary apparently unable to win a match. At least six of the nine teams entered in the tournament had shown the potential to win the Chipman Cup. It was an exhibition of strength and depth that demonstrated the post-war game at its finest.

As an added attraction at the tournament, the Calgary women's team of Bun Dewdney, May Atkins, Violet May and Condie Landale's daughter, Lucy, played an exhibition match against tournament referee Tommy Wilmot, Winnipeg's Dickson, High River's

Frank Watt and Billy Trevenen. The old-timers may have won by 3-2, but the newspapers were clearly impressed by Violet May's two goals and her "remarkable knowledge of the game."

The western championship final was played on the afternoon of Saturday, September 1st before the largest crowd of the week. Cochrane, though down 2-1 at the end of the first chukker, dominated the first half of the match and went into the fourth chukker with a 3-2 lead. By the end of the fifth, however, they were down by two and the Vancouver defence managed to blank the final chukker, successfully defending the Chipman Cup by five goals to three.

In a season that was marked by the number of western teams that took to the road, Calgary's women made their only out-of-town trip. In mid-September, five women, together with coaches, chaperons and sixteen ponies from Kamloops and Calgary, left for the Westchester Biltmore Country Club in Rye, New York to play in the first international women's polo tournament.

The meeting was the brainchild of New York millionaire, Albert Fulle, and his son who had seen the women play during a recent visit to Calgary. According to the *Albertan:* "He was so amazed by their brilliant play that he decided that a match or two in New York would go over big." In addition to the tournament in Rye, where five teams were expected to appear, the team was scheduled to play games in Montauk and at the storied Meadowbrook club. Most of the cost of sending the team was covered by Fulle and a group of Calgary "enthusiasts" (including meat packing magnate Pat Burns).

With Tommy Wilmot and Condie Landale along as coaches, Dorothy Hunt-Hogan, Bun Dewdney, May Atkins, Violet May and Lucy Landale played a two-game, total-goal series against a Greenwich women's team. The other promised teams do not seem to have appeared.

Although their ponies were late in arriving and out of sorts after a fifteen-day trip, the team's skill on the field impressed the New York newspapers. They were especially taken by Violet May who played several chukkers on a pure white pony and scored all three of Calgary goals.

Calgary's 1925 Chipman Cup champions – (left to right) J. Duff Robertson, Bill Adams, Kay Lang, Billy Trevenen.

The four-year period from 1925 to 1928 had seen the steady, almost spectacular, development of polo not only in southern Alberta but across all of the West from Winnipeg to Vancouver. While 1929 would be anything but a "down" year, the growth experienced in the past years simply could not continue. Another "new" club would make its appearance on the Alberta tournament scene and there would be a full card of eight teams at the western championship, but every one would be from southern Alberta.

High River did not rest on its laurels of the past two years. The club closed its successful 1928 season with a series of early-October clinics for novice players taught by several members of the "A" and "B" tournament teams and made an early start to 1929 with a mid-April organizational meeting. Along with such routine matters as paying the feed bill incurred at the 1928 Western Canada tournament and setting the non-playing club membership at $5 per year, the club voted to formalize what had been a matter of fact for the past two seasons by electing Willie Deane-Freeman as club captain. It was a position he would hold until well after his great playing days were behind him.

The Calgary club started even earlier, holding its first meeting on March 5th. The year 1929 is the earliest for which minutes survive, recording the day-to-day life of the Calgary Polo Club and painting a much broader, more detailed picture of the state of the game than the tournament-centred reports of the local newspapers. Together with the minutes of the Provincial and Western Canadian polo associations (which also exist only from 1929 to 1939), they are an invaluable resource. Credit for their survival should probably go to long-time club secretary-treasurer Mike Francis.

It is only through the minutes, for example, that one can see that the previous generation of players were

The Calgary women lost the matches by a combined score of 12-3 and there are no reports about whether they went on to play any other games during their visit.

Despite the papers' optimism (they were certain that the New York teams would pay a return visit to Calgary in 1929), women's polo never became a regular feature of the western tournament scene and there is no record of any outside women's team ever coming to Calgary.

Perhaps the most remarkable story from a memorable 1928 season was not the record of a particular team or the success of a tournament, but the accomplishments of a single man: Condie Landale.

By 1928, he was past fifty years old and had been on the field in nearly every year polo was played since he first appeared for Millarville in about 1905, but Landale's passion for the game had obviously not diminished. In a six-week period between the middle of July and the end of August, Landale played in the Alberta Provincial tournament, travelled to Winnipeg to play in the Manitoba at the end of the month (where he badly injured his hand), left immediately to join the Alberta team at the Northwest International in Vancouver on August 13th and then returned to Calgary in time for the western Canadian championship.

still an active presence in the club. A.E. Cross was the president and the selection committee was a who's who of pre-war southern Alberta polo: Marston SexSmith, Cecil Douglass, Vance Gravely, Osborne Brown and A.G. Wolley-Dod. It is also interesting to note that the Calgary women's teams were more than just a curiosity or exhibition distraction between more serious matches. Three female members of the club attended the 1929 meetings and took an active part in the proceedings, with Bun Dewdney serving as a member of the Grounds Committee.

It is frustrating that the club's detailed financial records for this period appear not to have survived. Although club subscriptions were at their highest level since the war (with seventeen playing members and one hundred forty non-playing individual and family memberships), there were clearly some financial difficulties since there were several discussions during the year regarding special assessments and the need to bring in more members. Indeed, members who could not raise their $60 annual subscription might cover the cost by signing up new members whose subscriptions totalled at least the amount they owed the club.

At a meeting attended by representatives from all the Calgary-area clubs, the dates for the provincial and Western Canada championships were fixed, but the members declined an invitation to travel to Vancouver for the annual International at the end of June. No reasons were given. There was an invitation from Winnipeg, too, for the first week in July. Although no Calgary team would be able to attend, the matter was left in the hands of Archie Kerfoot and Laurie Johnson to see if they could cobble together a composite team willing to make the trip. Interestingly, while Vancouver was prepared to keep both grooms and ponies for the duration of their meet, Winnipeg

was offering to feed and house both grooms and ponies and to pay the freight on the horses both ways.

The meeting took up the thorny issue of the cost of the Western Canada tournament. Having placed a $400 limit on costs and deciding to hire a manager for the duration of the tournament, members agreed that additional profits, up to $200, from the tournament should be given to out-of-province teams to help to defray their costs. With provincial teams paying their own expenses and guaranteeing the tournament expenses, any further profits were to be put aside to defray future western tournament expenses.

If polo in Alberta really was "the game of kings," this talk of money would be unseemly, but a look at the clubs' playing rosters shows little evidence of the pre-war squirearchy that could spend so freely on its favourite game. While the revolving door at the Virginia Ranch was clearly bringing in a number of moneyed Anglo-Irish, players like Jappy Rodgers were anything but well-heeled. The Kerfoots, Laurie Johnson and Bill Wolley-Dod were not rich and the High River club, with the possible exception of Frank McHugh or Ellison Capers, lacked anyone who could be described as a "patron." Outside Calgary, polo remained very much a cowboy game and money problems would become more pressing as the Depression deepened through the next decade.

The "new" club on the scene in 1929 was Millarville, on the field again after a fifteen-year absence. High

Calgary women's polo team, 1928 – (left to right) Violet May, May Atkins, Bun Dewdney and Lucy Landale.

Glenbow archives, NA-2924-25

Ken Woo

Silver pitcher presented to Winnipeg's Royal Canadian Horse Artillery by the Calgary Polo Club, July 30th, 1927 – According to the Calgary Albertan: "The trophy was awarded for the successful play and fine sportsmanship displayed by the Manitobans during their games here this season."

River went there to play for the Sheep Creek trophy in early July, bringing both its "A" and "B" sides. Most of the players for Millarville "A" and "B" were unknowns, but the name Nelson had a long association with High River and the old Pekisko club. It seems that Jappy Rodgers' brother, Paddy, was part of the attempted comeback. Of course, the most famous of Millarville's polo names was Deane-Freeman, and Willie must have felt mixed emotions about riding out again onto his old field, this time wearing High River scarlet. Not surprisingly, the games were not really close, with the visitors posting 7-4 and 6-1 wins.

Eight teams had entered the 1929 provincial championship scheduled for July 31st and the newspapers thought they had seen, in the pre-tournament play of the Calgary Blacks, some hope for a reversal of the club's generally disappointing performance at the major tournament level.

In the first draw, however, Calgary reverted to form and both its teams were eliminated. No one expected the Whites to be a match for Cochrane, but the shocker of the tournament was the Blacks' loss to Millarville by 4-3.

While the Strathcona's won their first match against always-dangerous High River "A," the R.C.H.A. again showed a team that was always willing, but rarely skilled as they lost to High River "B" by 13-1.

The Artillery's lack of punch came down to a simple matter of available manpower and time to practice. The R.C.H.A. had been formed in 1905 and it was "C"

Battery, based in Winnipeg, that came to Calgary for the summer. The regiment had been modelled on Britain's Royal Horse Artillery and was equipped with lighter, more mobile field pieces, pulled by horses fast enough to accompany cavalry in battle.

Their C.O., Lieutenant-Colonel Stockwell, had a strong reputation as a player, but his choice of teammates was usually limited to whoever was available to play and how many suitable mounts he could assemble. The team's roster changed often throughout their seasons in Calgary, but the most notable of its players was a young Lieutenant G.G. Simonds. A graduate of the Royal Military College, Guy Simonds went overseas in 1939 and quickly rose through the ranks to become brigadier, general staff of the 1st Canadian Corps. Having commanded the 1st Division in the invasion of Sicily and the 5th Armoured Division in Italy, he was given command of the 2nd Canadian Corps for the D-Day landings, a position he held until the end of the war. Following the war, Simonds served five years as Canada's chief of general staff.

On the surface, it seems odd that a mounted regiment would have trouble finding horses but, fast as they were at pulling gun carriages, the R.C.H.A. mounts were fundamentally ill-suited to the stop-and-start, fast-turning game of polo. Few of the regiment's officers had the means to keep their own ponies. The same problem proved a significant limiting factor to the success of the Strathcona's throughout the 1920s and 1930s.

In the second round, Millarville showed that their earlier victory over the Calgary Blacks had clearly been a case of a team playing well over its head as High River "B" quickly brought them back to reality with an 11-1 drubbing. Strathcona's, playing a tight-checking style, managed a 5-4 victory over Cochrane in a match that was, due to a timekeeper's error, only five chukkers long.

The Calgary Blacks and Whites' losses in the consolation round would not have surprised many, but it is unlikely that anyone in the Saturday afternoon crowd would have predicted the result in the tournament final. The game was played in a light rain that turned briefly into a hailstorm, although the Strathcona's did not seem to mind (or even notice) as they put on a clinic for High River "B" and claimed their first provincial championship with a whopping 15-0 whitewash.

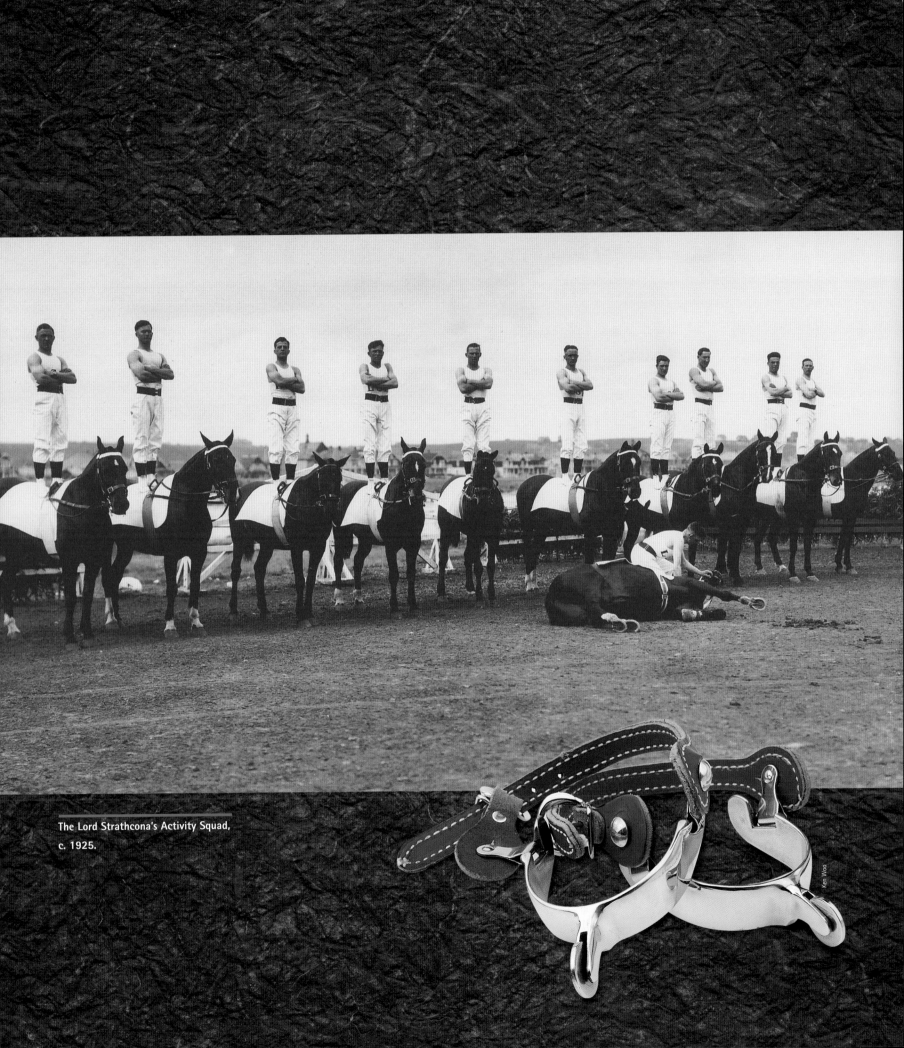

The Lord Strathcona's Activity Squad,
c. 1925.

Ken Woo

It is hard to judge the state of play in Winnipeg in the late 1920s. While there was some regular intra-club play at the St. Charles grounds, the local newspaper coverage was inconsistent, featuring only one major tournament each year. There was barely a word about the game in 1926 and 1927. Matches for the Sifton Cup could be counted on to receive the full period-by-period treatment, as did the 1928 Manitoba tournament, but the Green Dragons' subsequent visit to Calgary did not warrant a mention.

In 1929, as Alberta teams were playing their provincial tournament and getting ready for the Western Canada Championship, the *Manitoba Free Press* announced that Winnipeg was heading east in mid-August for a tournament in Toronto.

For the papers, the old dreams for Winnipeg polo were still alive:

The move of Winnipeg poloists in visiting the eastern city should do a great deal for the game in Canada. It is bound to create a wider interest between provinces and may possibly be the stepping stone to the promoting of a Dominion polo tournament or a series of games with eastern teams in Winnipeg.

Winnipeg might have helped its chances by playing well at the Toronto tournament, but they lost their first match to the host team by 10-6 and were then routed 20-10 by Buffalo, New York, despite being handed an 8-goal handicap.

The *Free Press* predicted that the team would be back in Winnipeg in time for its annual tournament at the end of the month, but there is no evidence the matches were held.

The slate for Calgary's 1929 Western Canadian Championship, with only one exception, was the same as Alberta's provincial tournament. The R.C.H.A. had returned to Winnipeg and their place was taken by the Virginia Ranch. It would be an all-Alberta affair.

In the absence of Vancouver and Winnipeg, the Virginia Ranch was immediately touted as one of the favourites. The *Albertan* based its opinion not only on the ranch's strong previous performances, but also on the fact that they had spent the winter playing in California. Who went and where they played is not known (Alberta's traditional second-season home field at Coronado had been buried under the fairways of a golf course), but Jenkinson's pony business was obviously the motivation for the trip.

The Monday draw was to pit High River "A" against the "Terriers." Formerly the Calgary Whites, the team was hoping to reverse its fortunes with a new name and new jerseys. Also scheduled were Cochrane against Millarville, followed by Virginia Ranch versus the Calgary Blacks. High River "B" would close the round against the LdSH on Tuesday.

Then, once again, the first day of play was rained out.

The rescheduling of the opening matches was further complicated by Millarville. Although as late as Saturday they were expected to appear, they had not submitted a player roster and had asked tournament organizers to move their opening round game ahead to Tuesday. When the tournament did open on the Tuesday, Millarville had still not appeared and Cochrane was through to the semifinals on a bye.

Calgary's performance on the opening day of the tournament was like the weather — dismally true to form. The Blacks had the closest match, but lost 6-4 to a Virginia Ranch foursome that featured a surprise addition to the team's always-changing roster: Frank Ward. His Vancouver team could not make the trip, but he was never one to pass up a chance to play polo. The Terriers, new name and new look notwithstanding, were shut out 5-0 by High River "A." In the third game of the day, the Strathcona's rode to an easy 8-0 win over High River "B."

In the first semifinal, High River "A" eliminated the Strathcona's by 12-5 but the second semifinal matched what were probably the two best teams in the tournament. The Virginia Ranch clearly had the best overall talent, while Cochrane, with its bye, had well-rested ponies. It was for this game that the newspapers

Virginia Ranch, 1929 Western Canadian champions – (left to right) Frank Ward, Jappy Rodgers, Cecil and John Martin.

Glenbow archives, NA-5554-17

trotted out their annual pronouncement about "the finest exhibition of polo ever seen in Calgary." Despite Cochrane's opening score, the Ranch held the lead at halftime and, at the end, it was Virginia Ranch eight, Cochrane six.

In the "junior" round, the Blacks faced the Terriers, assuring the host club of at least one trophy. Even then, it took the Blacks two overtime chukkers to beat their clubmates by 5-4. In the consolation final, Cochrane looked anything but the team that had given the Virginia Ranch such a tough match and the Strathcona's carried an early lead to a 5-3 win.

The tournament ended on Saturday with the Virginia Ranch and High River "A" playing for the Chipman Cup. After two days of sunshine, it was drizzling again, but the crowd was by far the largest of the week. The game was close throughout with each team taking, then losing, the lead. Scoring was balanced and no individual player took a starring role as both teams rode flat-out for the entire match. Overtime looked to be a certainty when Frank Ward scored the winner moments before the final whistle sounded. That goal would engrave his name on the Chipman for the third straight year and he had yet to bring his "home" teams of Kamloops or Douglas Lake to town.

The West had always been prone to economic ups and downs as the price of its principal commodities —

then cattle and grain — boomed and crashed. Times had been good in the 1880s, bad in the 1890s and good again in the years leading up to the Great War. There was another near-crash in 1918 and, by the mid-1920s, much of southern Alberta had been locked in what seemed a perennial drought. But nothing compared with the "Dirty Thirties." Although the 1929 season began with apparent prosperity on the horizon, by late autumn all that had changed and polo's reputation as a rich man's dalliance would not be enough to protect the game, and those who played it, from the economic pressures grinding down on every part of life in the Canadian West. ▨

141

PERSONALITIES IN POLO TOURNEY

CHAPTER 8

MUCH SPORT
AND
MANLY EXERCISE

BRITISH COLUMBIA
1919–1929

IF SPOKANE'S LANE CUP MATCHES of 1919 closed the final chapter on the great polo traditions of North Fork and the rest of southwestern Alberta, they also signalled the game's renaissance in Canada's westernmost province.

The Vancouver Polo Club had enjoyed barely two years of life before Canada went to war. Not founded until 1913, the club had nonetheless quickly established itself as a serious operation, feasting early and often on the long-established club from Kamloops and on teams from Vancouver Island. Early in its life, too, the Vancouver club had shown itself willing to travel freely — to Spokane, Portland and to the Island — in pursuit of a strong opponent.

Caricatures of Vancouver and Kamloops players, probably from the Vancouver Province, mid-1920s.

The war had stopped play in Vancouver as surely and as suddenly as it did everywhere else in Western Canada, but the team was one of the first back on the field after the armistice.

With no one to give them a game anywhere else in the Canadian West, Vancouver headed south to Spokane in September, 1919 to play in the revival of the Northwestern International Tournament for the Lane Cup. There, they faced two Spokane club teams and a foursome from North Fork, Alberta that had spent most of the war south of the border.

Although it did not win, Vancouver acquitted itself well, losing only to the eventual champions from North Fork. On the team were pre-war members J.P. Fell, J.G. Fordham and Bertie Cator. Their fourth, however, was playing the final games in a polo career that stretched back to the first Alberta tournament in 1892. Oswald Critchley had returned to Canada after the war to sell his ranching interests before going back to England and into business with his son. His trip to Spokane must have been his way of saying goodbye to some old friends.

Obviously submitted by a member of the club, the piece is fulsome in its praise both of the facilities and the general quality of life on Canada's West Coast:

* ❦ *

The Vancouver Polo Club has its own clubhouse, two first-rate polo grounds (full size), and its own stabling at the Brighouse racecourse.... The view from the clubhouse of the mountains and surrounding country is unexcelled in any part of the world. It is earnestly hoped that this may catch the eye of certain polo enthusiasts and sportsmen in the Old Country who may care to come out and play next season or possibly settle here. It should appeal to those who cannot really afford to hunt or play polo at home, owing to the high cost of horses, ponies and their keep, to say nothing of the ordinary cost of living and high taxation. Polo in Western Canada is not such an expensive amusement; good playing ponies can easily be bought, mostly in Alberta, from people with ranches who have taken great trouble in breeding and training the right class of pony. Prices range from $250 and upwards, but seldom exceed $600. The club charges each playing member $50 a month during the polo season for the keep of each pony, and this includes grooms, feed, exercise, use of clubhouse, stabling, etc.... Apart from the polo, Vancouver offers advantages to sportsmen generally, particularly to those of limited means....

* ❦ *

Although Captain John Isaac is generally credited with being the driving force behind the creation of the Vancouver club in 1913, he lost his life in the war and the club's rapid reorganization in 1919 was largely due to the efforts of James Pemberton Fell.

In many ways, Fell typified the membership of the Vancouver club, and it was anything but "cowboy polo." Born in 1873, Fell had come to Vancouver in 1897 as manager of the huge Lonsdale Estate on the North Shore. In that capacity he was largely responsible for the layout and development of much of what is today the city of North Vancouver. In 1911, he organized and then commanded a field company of the Canadian Engineers, rising to the rank of lieutenant-colonel with the First Division during the Great War. Following war service, he was a founder and trustee of the B.C. Corps of Commissionaires, serving as its chairman until 1954. Fell died in Vancouver in 1960 at the age of eighty-seven.

Major J.G. Fordham was cut from the same cloth. A rugby "Blue" at Cambridge, he had come to Vancouver just before the turn of the century and remained deeply involved in public life until his death in 1940. His particular interest was in the welfare of returning veterans and he also served for several years as director of unemployment relief for the Province.

Vancouver went back to Spokane in 1920 and, at an Interstate Fair that also featured "A Thrilling Display of Auto Polo!", they played Spokane and nearby Fort Wright in a total-goal affair. Vancouver engraved its name on the Lane Cup for the first of what would become eight victories over the next decade. Indeed, after 1920, the Lane Cup took up permanent residence at the Vancouver Polo Club and every subsequent Northwestern International tournament would be held there until 1931.

Two members of the club also spent part of the winter of 1920 playing at George Ross' Coronado Club in San Diego. They were joined there by Douglas Lake's Frank Ward and by another visiting Critchley: Oswald's son, A.C., by then a brigadier-general.

The high hopes for the post-war future of Vancouver polo were evident in a lengthy report on the club's activities that appeared in the March, 1921 edition of England's *Polo Monthly & Racing Review.*

It is a piece worthy of any Chamber of Commerce, but $50 per pony, per month during a season that stretched from May through September would hardly have seemed a bargain to Vancouver's fellow poloists from Kamloops or Calgary. "Limited means" clearly meant something altogether different to an English sporting gentleman.

The year 1921 saw the return of regular tournament play at Brighouse. In June, there was a series of handicap matches that featured at least one Kamloops player — Ross Hett — who apparently couldn't wait for his own club to get back onto its field. In July, the B.C. Challenge Cup was up for grabs and a reborn Calgary club made its first post-war trip across the Divide for the event.

The Kamloops Polo Club had begun to show new signs of life as early as 1919. The *Kamloops Standard-Sentinel* of August 19th carried an appeal for players young and old, experienced or not, to come to an organizational meeting during "Fair Week" in September. The paper hoped that play could recommence with the 1920 season, provided that satisfactory arrangements could be made for a field.

Not content to see the club return to its old, dry ground on the reserve, the paper suggested it was time Kamloops had "something in the nature of a country club," including a full-size polo ground, surrounded by a racetrack, clubhouse, tennis courts and a golf course. By way of encouraging support, the *Standard-Sentinel* went on to observe that:

Polo is not necessarily a rich man's sport alone. Much sport and manly exercise may be derived quite cheaply, especially by ranchers and others who always have a saddle horse or two for their own use.

It is justly claimed that this is the principal horse-raising country in the whole of Canada. Surely, therefore, this district ought to set an example in the way of those forms of sport dear to lovers of horses.

Whether there was sufficient interest to warrant holding the meeting was not reported and the Kamloops Polo Club did not play in 1920. But, by the spring of 1921 they were ready.

On February 22nd, the *Standard-Sentinel* reported that the club had elected its new officers and, with twenty members on the rolls ("and many more expected"), was intending to hold its first match on April 3rd. There would be no new country club field and the game was scheduled for the old reserve ground.

The club's first post-war executive had Frank Ward as its vice-president, a sign that even after more than two decades of polo, the manager of the Douglas Lake Ranch had not lost his love for the game. The committee members, too, were "old-timers," including such pre-war stalwarts as Harper, Longridge and Dr. George. The president, however, was a newcomer: H.F. Mytton, the man generally credited as the impetus behind the game's revival.

Mytton was the resident manager of the B.C. Fruitlands, a huge development across from the city on the north side of the Thompson that stretched west for miles along the river. The B.C. Fruitlands had been incorporated in 1909 with some 6,000 acres, a holding that had expanded to more than 20,000 by 1920. Fully irrigated, the land was intended to produce fruit and vegetables, but the company also ran 2,500 head of cattle and raised substantial forage crops to feed them. B.C. Fruitlands was also a form of "colonization company" and, over the years, it brought in hundreds of would-be farmers and orchardmen from England, Germany and eastern Europe and leased small plots to a large number of Chinese and East Indian truck farmers.

Mytton was sent out from England as resident manager for the British owners in 1915 and remained at Fruitlands until 1923 when the corporation was reorganized. In those eight years, Mytton continued to lend his patronage to the polo club, including, one suspects, at least some financial assistance for travel and grounds maintenance. It is easy to imagine the players looking enviously west across the North Thompson from their dusty, unwatered field to the broad, irrigated pastures of the Fruitlands, but they would remain on the reserve.

The only game recorded during that first year took place in early September between two teams styled the "President's" and Vice-President's." The players' names give an indication that, while the Kamloops club was back, the same could not yet be said for Nicola-Quilchena or Grande Prairie.

For the President's, it was pre-war Kamloops regulars R.B. Longridge and Bill Fernie (by then past fifty years old), joined by Ross Hett and Nicola's Geoff Lodwick.

The Vice-President's team was Frank Ward of Nicola, Douglas Lake, Kamloops (and anywhere else polo was being played), Joe Guichon from Nicola and Grande Prairie perennials Tottie Clemitson and Frank Gordon.

The game wasn't close — Ward's team had by far the better of the play in a 7-0 victory — but the crowd was good, the weather was fine and polo was back in the B.C. Interior.

But the pleasures of that Labour Day Sunday afternoon were short-lived. Just after midnight, the Winterbottom barn caught fire and burned to the ground. It was the overnight home for some of the visiting ponies and the losses were severe. Frank Gordon lost two of his best, while Clemitson and Alex Pringle, who had brought some of his string up from Grande Prairie, lost one each. Frank Ward was lucky. He had three top-flight ponies in town for the day, but had sent them south towards Douglas Lake at the end of the match. Good polo ponies were scarce

KAMLOOPS POLO CHALLENGE CUP.
WON BY VANCOUVER POLO CLUB, AT KAMLOOPS B.C. AUG 25TH 1923.

Vancouver with the Kamloops
Challenge Cup, 1923 – (left to right)
Martin Griffin, Tommy Wilmot,
umpire J.G. Fordham, J.P. Fell,
Senator Bostock, "Bimbo" Sweeny.

enough in the country after the war and the death of four well-trained mounts was felt deeply in the Salmon River Valley.

While play in 1922 was limited to a series of Sunday afternoon intra-club matches, the membership seemed to be growing. A few more pre-war members were back on the roll and several of the new names that would become familiar in the second era had begun to appear.

The year 1922 also saw the publication, in the *Standard-Sentinel,* of an irregular series of articles variously titled "Kamloops Polo Club Notes," "With the Polo Ponies" and "Musings of a Polo Groom." The columns (submitted by a number of authors, some identifiable, others anonymous) would run for the next few years and offer a nice insight into the workings of the club that even the minutes (had they survived) would not have provided.

One of the first columns appeared on October 10th, and it conveyed some very interesting news: T.B. Jenkinson and his daughter were in town from their Virginia Ranch near Cochrane, Alberta. They were staying with Ross Hett out at Heffley Creek and looking to buy "a carload of blood ponies for the New York market."

Ross Hett had quickly become a significant presence with the Kamloops Polo Club, not only as a fine player, but also because of his continuing strong connections to southern Alberta.

Hett's life before he came to Kamloops had been one of changing circumstance and cowboy dreams. His mother was born to a prosperous English family that had moved to Barrie, Ontario in 1836. His father was a young English lawyer who had arrived at their home with a letter of introduction on his way to British Columbia in 1871. They were married in about 1875 and moved to Victoria where he had established a legal practice. Ross was born there in about 1884. His father, who had become attorney general for the province in the late 1870s, died suddenly before his fiftieth birthday and Ross, his mother and seven other children went back to Ontario.

Although his brothers all went into the professions, Hett had always dreamed of owning cattle in the Prairie West and, at age eighteen or nineteen, rode a colonist car to Calgary. After working at a series of odd jobs for area ranchers, Hett took his own homestead near Fish Creek where he raised hay, kept a few cattle and took to playing polo with the Fish Creek club.

When the Great War broke out, like nearly every other young man in the district, he enlisted immediately and soon found himself back in Victoria with the 2nd Canadian Mounted Rifles. It was there that he met his future wife (they were finally married in England in 1918 where she had been serving as a voluntary aid worker). Hett served overseas and, with the Armistice, came back to Canada with his new wife. They stopped in Calgary long enough to arrange for the sale of the Fish Creek homestead and ship some of his best horses to the new ranch at Heffley Creek near Kamloops. He soon became widely known and respected, both on the field and in the sales ring, for the quality of his polo ponies.

When the Kamloops Polo Club re-formed after the war, Hett took to the field and remained a strong, consistent presence with the team until it ceased play in 1939. T.B. Jenkinson would not have been the only visitor as his home was always a favoured stopping place for many of the ranchers he had met (and played polo with) before the war.

The Hetts remained on the ranch until about 1949 when they retired to Victoria, buying twenty acres of land that Ross would discover had once been owned by his father some seventy years before. Roslin Martyn Hett died at Victoria on August 17th, 1968.

Vancouver, well-recovered from the wartime hiatus, came back into the Interior polo picture in 1923 as the coast club played a home-and-home series with Kamloops. The teams had met only twice before, in Vancouver's first two years of existence, but this series, once re-established, soon became one of the main features of the Kamloops polo season.

Kamloops sent two teams to Vancouver in mid-June to play for the B.C. Challenge Cup. Given the humiliating scores from the pre-war games, Kamloops' 5-2 loss looked almost respectable and the *Standard-Sentinel* reported that both ponies and players were quite evenly matched. Still, the Vancouver club was proving that its early years were no fluke and its teams would remain by far the strongest in the province through the first decade of the second era. Their economic situation would always ensure that there was plenty of time for regular practice and the money to buy and keep the best ponies.

Vancouver's return visit to the Interior was set for Saturday, August 25th and, in the town of Kamloops, the game was being treated as a major event. Club patron (and senior local political power), Senator Hewitt Bostock presented a cheque to the team to help cover the entertainment expenses, including a post-game banquet and a public dance. And, the game would be watched by Lord Lovat, chairman of the Empire Foresters Convention. In the midst of a western Canadian tour, Lovat's train would be hurried and the start of the game delayed in order to make his attendance possible.

In an interesting note in its report of the team's final practice before the game, the *Standard-Sentinel* pointed out that films of the Kamloops-Vancouver game from mid-June would be a part of the program at the Empress Theatre during the week. Those newsreel films have, unfortunately, never resurfaced.

Vancouver's foursome of Martin Griffin, Tommy Wilmot, J.P. Fell and "Bimbo" Sweeny was clearly their "A" team and had already shown that it was considerably stronger than anything Kamloops could send out against them. Although the papers had been gently suggesting that the result should be the same as it had been in Vancouver, Kamloops certainly made its presence felt, in the early stages of the game at least. Ralph Chetwynd, Frank Gordon, Ross Hett and R.B. Longridge started quickly and finished the first chukker with a 2-1 lead. As the game progressed, however, the Vancouver ponies began to show their strength — in both quality and number — and the final score was 12-3.

Courtesy of Diana Hett Palmer

Long-time Kamloops regular Ross Hett, c.1920.

At the banquet, Vancouver was presented with the B.C. Challenge Cup (finally up for play for the first time since the war had cancelled Kamloops' 1914 tournament) and the compliments flowed freely during the speeches and toasts. Colonel Fell seemed particularly impressed by the Kamloops club:

You have twenty-five playing members, while in Vancouver we have to be satisfied with eight or nine. You have a wonderful natural ground, which only requires cutting, rolling and levelling here and there to make it the very best on the Pacific coast.

Two things in his remarks are surprising. The Vancouver club was still much smaller than one would have assumed for a city of its size, boasting fewer than half the members it had enjoyed in its brief pre-war life.

Fell's observations about the Kamloops grounds are harder to understand, unless he was simply being overly polite. Without an irrigation system, the reserve field was often more dust bowl than green carpet and its generally poor condition was the cause for regular complaint from both the press and the players. Although the reserve field cannot have compared to Vancouver's Brighouse Park, Fell's excessively positive comments would be repeated whenever Kamloops matches were advertised in the local paper.

The Kamloops polo season extended well into October (something the Alberta teams could only dream about) and play for the club championship continued through the fall. The club had three teams, the "Country," the "City" and the "B.C. Horse." This latter team was made up of players who had an association with the locally based militia regiment, but it was not an established military team as was the case with the Strathcona's or the R.C.H.A. in Calgary. The tournament was played "American style" over the course of several weeks with each team playing the others in short Sunday round-robins. The winner of the Watson Cup was determined on total goals scored.

Kamloops (left) and Vancouver
after the 1924 Kamloops
Challenge Cup matches.

"With the Polo Ponies" appeared three times in the October, 1923, issues of the *Standard-Sentinel.* Authored by "R.C." (almost certainly Ralph Chetwynd), the columns offered advice and encouragement (mostly about the number and quality of the ponies), but their principal concern was manners, specifically tardiness. The habit of certain players turning up late for matches and practices is something that would become a recurrent theme with the club for years to come. While it could be put down to the distance that some players had to travel into town, such was obviously not the case. It was the Country team that took the club championship in 1923, aided in the total-goal format by the regular failure of some City team members to show up, resulting in at least one forfeit.

Kamloops again sent two teams to the coast in June, 1924, with the "A" squad set to play for the B.C. Challenge Cup. In preparation for the match, Vancouver held a series of warm-up games at Brighouse at the beginning of the month. Clearly, the club had been busy with a winter membership drive and the "eight or nine" players to which Fell had referred the previous autumn had grown sufficiently to allow for three club teams — "A," "B" and "Novice" — and a team from the Vancouver detachment of the R.C.M.P. to take part.

This was another brief appearance by the Mounties in a game that should have been second nature to them. Over the years, there had been occasional reports of R.C.M.P. teams at places such as Fort Macleod and Regina where the police presence was a major feature of town life. In garrison towns like Fort Macleod, teams would often be called "The Mounties" or "The Police," but were usually made up of two or three members of the force, supported by a civilian or two, and created for intra-club matches. The constables were clearly playing on their own time.

Cavalry regiments in Britain and the United States had long encouraged polo as a natural adjunct to formal military training and, in Canada, the Strathcona's and the Royal Canadian Horse Artillery enjoyed near-official blessing for their polo teams. Yet, through all the decades that horsemanship was a

Courtesy of Penny Wilmot

Camp Lewis versus Vancouver at the Northwestern International Tournament, Brighouse Park, 1924.

B.C. Lieutenant Governor Nichol presents the Lane trophy to Vancouver captain J.G. Fordham, Vancouver, 1923.

fundamental part of a Mountie's training and daily life, there is no evidence that polo ever had official support in Canada's national police force.

The B.C. Challenge Cup final was a repeat of 1923, with Vancouver riding to an easy 6-0 win over Kamloops "A" and the Vancouver-Kamloops polo axis was settling into a predictable pattern. The B.C. Challenge Cup Tournament would be held at Brighouse in early June, while the Kamloops Cup would be up for play at the beginning of September. Between those two events, Vancouver would host the Northwestern International for the Lane Cup around the beginning of August. That tournament would usually feature the host club and a number of American teams from Washington and Oregon. Participation by other Canadian teams was, at best, irregular.

The 1924 Lane Cup matches were delayed by a week as the result of a quarantine problem with Camp Lewis' horses and the officers were forced to apply to change their leave, something which the newspapers assumed

they would accomplish with little trouble. When Camp Lewis finally got to town, they arrived in style. According to the *Vancouver Province,* "The Camp Lewis team came up fresh from their recent victory over the crack Boise team, bringing twenty horses and a battery of attendants and officers, including General Alexander, the Commandant." It was a clear indication that polo enjoyed the approval of the U.S. army.

Although their ponies compared well with the cavalry's, defending champion Vancouver was beaten by Camp Lewis' more accurate shooting and, by seven goals to four, the Americans took the Lane Cup home.

Vancouver went east to defend the Kamloops Challenge Cup in early September. They sent seven players and eighteen ponies, enough to field an "A" team and provide some informal competition for a Kamloops "B" squad to fill out the week's play. For Kamloops, there was good news and bad news: Grande Prairie had also sent a team. After a decade-long break which saw a few of its core players appear occasionally with Kamloops club teams, Grande Prairie had reorganized (as much as Grande Prairie could

ever have been said to be "organized") and come back into tournament polo.

On Saturday, September 7th, Grande Prairie and Kamloops "A" would play to determine who would face Vancouver for the cup. On Monday, Kamloops "B" would play Vancouver "B" in a non-cup match, with the Challenge Cup final set for Wednesday.

Grande Prairie had two of its old-time regulars — Frank Gordon and Tottie Clemitson — together with Frank Ward and Alex Pringle, a fine player whose family connections to the Salmon Valley stretched back as far as the late 1860s, and whose descendants still live there today. It was Pringle's hayfield that served as the Grande Prairie grounds through the 1920s.

After blowing a 6-3 lead at the end of the fifth chukker, it took Kamloops' Chetwynd, Fernie, Gordon and Longridge a few minutes of overtime finally to secure a 7-6 win and earn the right to face Vancouver for the Challenge Cup.

The championship match went to overtime, too, with Vancouver's Drysdale scoring

Tommy Wilmot (left) at Coronado, 1924 – The Coronado club had been a regular winter home for many western Canadian players since well before the Great War, but this was probably the last season of play on the Island.

the winner with a broken mallet. Kamloops, despite its large membership, regular practice and permanent field, seemed to have slipped back into its pre-war pattern of performing well in the preliminaries, only to lose the final.

The 1925 Interior season opened in early April with the news of a three-game, season-long series for the Roper Cup, commencing before the month was over. Kamloops was out for practice early, playing a seven-chukker pick-up match that featured fifteen members, including old-timers Walter Homfray and Donald George.

The game, again matching Pringle, Gordon, Clemitson and Ward against Kamloops' Longridge, Hughes, Chetwynd and Lunn, was an added feature of the annual Kamloops bull sale, and the crowds were predictably good. The result, too, was predictable: 6-4 for Grande Prairie. As the *Standard-Sentinel* put it: "...it was a popular victory for experience, practice and teamwork, all three of which are always winners."

The newspaper did not report on the other games in the series. If they were played, the end result was no different since it is Grande Prairie's name engraved on the Roper Cup for 1925.

Kamloops did not send a team to the coast for the Challenge Cup matches in 1925. Rather, their place was taken by an all-star foursome of Frank Ward, Tommy Wilmot, Frank Gordon and Ross Hett. The Vancouver papers called the team "Douglas Lake (Grande Prairie)" but they could just as easily have referred to it as "Kamloops (Nicola)" or any other combination of Interior names.

The difficulty of identifying the welter of Interior polo teams in the years between the wars has led a number of historians to believe that the game was far more widely played than it was. The simple change

Tommy Wilmot (centre, facing camera) at Coronado, 1924.

from the word "team" to the word "club" left many writers with the mistaken impression that Douglas Lake, Falkland, Nicola, Quilchena, Ashcroft and many others were actually greater than they ever managed to be. If by "club," one means an organization with a permanent field and schedule of intra-club matches or an annual tournament, then none of these places would qualify. Kamloops, Kelowna and Vernon-Coldstream were certainly "real" clubs, and Grande Prairie was close to meeting a loose definition, but there never was a Douglas Lake polo "club," nor were there ones at Falkland, Quilchena or Nicola. Rather, there were two men — Frank Ward and Tommy Wilmot — who had both the passion and money to travel widely in search of a good polo game and it was they who appeared on the rosters of nearly all the so-called clubs in the Interior. The titles they gave their teams were, in effect, "flags of convenience" rather than an accurate reflection of their origin.

Whatever they chose to call themselves in 1925, Ward's men were better than anything Vancouver could send out against them and the host team lost its permanent grip on the B.C. Challenge Cup by 5-4. Ward's team won the match despite the presence for Vancouver of Major Rob Houstoun, a 4-goal "ringer" from a British regiment based at Aldershot. Another member of his family, Major Andy Houstoun, was an outstanding regular with the Vancouver club.

August saw Camp Lewis back in town to defend the Lane Cup. This time they were joined by the Portland Hunt Club, but the Oregon team was not nearly so strong as the Harry Robertson-led foursomes that had dominated Northwest polo before the war. Camp Lewis and Vancouver, however, were evenly matched, and the trophy came back to Canada by 8-7 on the strength of Fordham's overtime goal.

Shipping twenty ponies ahead on the Canadian National Railway, Vancouver arrived in Kamloops at the end of August to defend the Kamloops Challenge Cup. The teams and most of the players were the same as 1924, as was the format, with Kamloops and Grande Prairie playing to see who would face Vancouver.

The 1925 result differed slightly from the previous year as Grande Prairie knocked out the home side by 5-4, but the final remained true to form as Vancouver won its third successive Kamloops tournament by 7-3. The game was much closer than the score indicated as Grande Prairie made Vancouver work hard through the whole match and held an advantage in overall play. The difference in the game came down to three Vancouver goals scored on penalty shots, awarded, according to the paper, "for minor offences."

The year 1926 opened in Kamloops with the customary early-April games at the reserve grounds and the usual comments about the lateness of players. There was also a complaint from the Indian Agent about polo spectators bringing liquor to the matches. Since the reserve was officially "dry," club officials were nervous about losing their lease if the practice continued. The club sent off its annual Roper Cup challenge to Grande Prairie and there was continued speculation about when polo might finally make another comeback in Victoria. There were also rumours about a revitalized Nicola Valley club at Quilchena.

Polo was indeed being played south of the city again, and it is no surprise to find Frank Ward behind it. He brought his new team to Kamloops on May 16th and, although the papers referred to them as "Douglas Lake" it was a familiar foursome: Ward, Geoff Lodwick, Joe Guichon and Frank Gordon. It was a friendly match, with Kamloops taking the opportunity to play as many members as possible, sending out different teams for each half.

Ponies were again the key as Douglas Lake rode to a 6-2 victory while the Kamloops players — especially in the second half — spent too much time trying to control their unruly mounts.

Waiting out the rain, Brighouse
Park (Tommy Wilmot in foreground),
c. 1925.

In the main event, Vancouver was too much for Douglas Lake. Tommy Wilmot was playing with an injured shoulder and had to leave the game when a blow to the same shoulder unhorsed him. Only Ross Hett's steady defence prevented the score from being worse than 10-5.

The players returned to Kamloops in time to begin intra-club play for the Watson Cup. Again played as a three-team round-robin, the four chukker matches were scheduled for the first Sunday in July, August and September. The club also played a game as a successful fundraiser for the local hospital and, at the end of July, saw a visiting chief of Canada's general staff, Major-General J.H. MacBrien, ride out for three chukkers during a regular practice game.

Vancouver's 1926 Lane Cup Tournament saw the appearance of a team from Cochrane, Alberta. Led by Condie Landale and featuring two of the British "imports" from the Virginia Ranch, the team joined Portland and Camp Lewis in trying to wrest the trophy from the host team.

With four teams in the draw, the tournament was a round-robin affair with each team playing three games, the trophy winner to be determined on games won and goals scored.

Camp Lewis and Vancouver again proved to be the class of the field, with the host team retaining possession of the cup, but Cochrane provided the biggest surprise of the week. With some of the strongest players in Alberta, the team was overwhelmed in every one of its games, finishing the tournament having scored only three goals while allowing thirty-five. Whether Cochrane's experience was a true reflection of the state of play in both provinces would be shown more clearly in the next few seasons as teams began regularly to criss-cross the Great Divide.

With the members expressing continuing hopes for the return of Grande Prairie and Quilchena, the *Standard-Sentinel* report closed with some suggestions for the local players:

1. *Practice in hitting the ball*
   while galloping is essential.
2. *Marking your opponent is one*
   of the main features.
3. *Don't crowd your own side, but keep your place.*
4. *Assume the ball is going to be hit and*
   place yourself accordingly.

While Kamloops continued with its Sunday club matches, Frank Ward was planning a trip to Vancouver to defend the B.C. Challenge trophy. He would take with him the same teammates as in 1925 — Hett, Gordon and Wilmot — and with the tournament being moved back to the week of June 20th, Kamloops might also be able to take part.

In the end, Kamloops did send a team, but not to compete for the cup. Rather, a foursome of Rupert Duck, Bill Fernie, Joe Guichon and R.B. Longridge played a friendly match against a Vancouver "B" side during the week.

In September, Vancouver came back to the Interior for the Kamloops Challenge Cup, but the three-time champions were off their game and lost to Frank Ward's "all-star" Douglas Lake team, this time featuring Kamloops' Ralph Chetwynd. Vancouver "B" could do no better, losing to Kamloops "B" by 8-1.

The 1926 season concluded with another traditional Kamloops ritual: losing the Roper Cup to Grande Prairie.

The next year proved comparatively quiet. Kamloops did not go to Vancouver, nor did Vancouver make its annual trip to the Interior. Kamloops' opening-day chukkers featured some new faces, including Kay Lang (a recent arrival from Calgary and a fine, experienced player), and some of the regular members again delayed the start of the game by showing up late.

Frank Ward took another aggregation to Vancouver in mid-June, attempting to recapture the B.C. Challenge Cup, but his hand-picked team of Kamloops' Chetwynd and Longridge together with Grande Prairie's Alex Pringle was no match for the hosts and were thoroughly beaten by ten goals to two.

Longridge and Chetwynd were typical of many Interior players of the second era. They may have had English money behind them, but they were largely self-made in their new country.

Robert Begbie Longridge had come to the Kamloops district just before the war. He had farmed in his native Cheshire and found work at one of Walter Homfray's properties in the area. At the same time, he took out a homestead and began to build a post office and general store just south of town on the Nicola Valley road. He named the post office Knutsford after his English birthplace and it soon became the centre of the growing farm and ranch community in the area.

Longridge returned to England when war broke out and rejoined his old regiment, the 16th Lancers. Upon returning to Knutsford after the war he sold the store but continued to live in the district and play for the Kamloops Polo Club until the late 1920s. He later retired to the West Coast and died in Victoria at the end of 1970.

Ralph Chetwynd was also born in England, the son of a baronet in Staffordshire. He arrived in British Columbia in about 1908 and settled in the Ashcroft area but, by 1912, he was managing the Marquess of Anglesey's ill-fated colonization efforts at Walhachin and operating a freighting business for the Canadian Northern Railway, then under construction.

Chetwynd served in the war with the Royal Field Artillery, was wounded at the Somme and received the Military Cross for his actions. When he returned to the Interior, with Walhachin in ruins, he began to work for the Douglas Lake Ranch and became a prime breeder and trainer of both his own and Frank Ward's strings of top-quality polo ponies. He was a fine player

Courtesy of Penny Wilmot

In the final, Ralph Chetwynd scored three times for Douglas Lake and they retained the cup with a solid 6-3 performance against the red shirts.

The *Standard-Sentinel* continued to look for reasons for Kamloops' depressingly consistent performances at its own tournament:

Kamloops team did not show up very well, but the main reason was very obvious, viz. ponies. The Grande Prairie and Douglas Lake teams have far greater opportunities to get hold of good ponies and have the work for them which is the best training for polo, namely cow work.

Kamloops at least can boast the best ground in the Interior and in time will get better ponies and learn how to play better combination.

---

for a number of Interior teams and travelled widely with Ward and Wilmot through the 1920s.

After holding a number of agriculture marketing positions, he was elected to the B.C. legislature in 1952 and was immediately appointed minister of railways, trade and industry in the new Social Credit government. The town of Little Prairie in the Peace River country was renamed Chetwynd in honour of his work to extend the railway into that area. He remained in the legislature for the rest of his life and had just been appointed minister of agriculture when he died of a heart attack in April, 1957. He was sixty-seven years of age.

Undaunted by the 1926 debacle, Condie Landale brought another Alberta team to Vancouver for the 1927 Lane Cup. This time, he was accompanied by Calgary regulars Jim Cross, Dennis Yorath and Llew Chambers, but the result was no different from the previous years. Indeed, it may have been even worse as Portland, Camp Lewis and Vancouver ran roughshod over the Alberta team by scores of 14-1, 16-3 and 17-1.

The other entries proved perfectly matched, trading games so evenly that, at the end of the draw, all three teams were tied both in wins and goals. A series of three-chukker playoffs was scheduled for the Monday afternoon, but it was never played. Perhaps the officers from Camp Lewis could not extend their leaves indefinitely. The tournament was declared a draw and the names Vancouver, Portland and Camp Lewis were all engraved on the Lane Cup for 1927.

Again held in early September, the 1927 Kamloops Challenge Cup Tournament was an all-Interior affair. Vancouver (including Frank Ward and Tommy Wilmot) had opted to go to Calgary for the Western Canada Championship at the end of August. That left the home team matched against Grande Prairie for the right to challenge the holders from Douglas Lake.

The Clemitsons (father and son, Tottie and Robert), Alex Pringle and newcomer H.E. Talbot won decisively over their hosts, the papers putting their 8-2 win down to the quality of their ponies.

The paper was probably right about the ponies. Kamloops was like any other sizeable town in the 1920s: moving quickly toward full motorization. There was no longer a horse or two in every backyard and, although some of the town players did live on surrounding ranches and acreages, most were town professionals for whom ponies were rapidly becoming a luxury, increasingly difficult and expensive to board.

There was another reason, as well. Douglas Lake, with Frank Ward as a patron, regularly drew off some of Kamloops' best players. Ross Hett, who was raising fine ponies at the time, shared his time between the teams. Ralph Chetwynd, probably Kamloops' best, became fully involved with Douglas Lake, playing regularly and, with Tommy Wilmot, taking responsibility for training the long string of ponies that Ward always had ready to play (or sell).

As if it were needed, the 1927 Roper Cup match was another confirmation of Kamloops' continuing problems. Predictably, Grande Prairie won the cup again, but this time it was almost a new team. Alex Pringle engraved his name for the fourth time, but H.E. Talbot was back for only his second attempt. The other two, J. Allan and R.G. Woods, were rookies. In the B.C. Interior, much as was the case in southern Alberta, "cowboy polo" was proving itself more resilient in the face of dramatic social change than was its city-centred opposition.

It was Ward who took the Interior team back to Vancouver for the Challenge Cup in 1928. The games were to be held during "Polo Week," an event that received extensive coverage in the local press. Wives of the Vancouver members seemed to be trying to outdo each other in providing lunches, teas and dinner dances for the visiting players and the highlight of the week would be a grand ball held at the new Grill Room of the Hotel Vancouver. Planning for the event and a detailed description of the lavish polo-theme decorations dominated the front page of the *Province's* Sunday magazine section on June 10th.

Playing with Wilmot, Chetwynd and Hett, Ward seemed determined not to miss an opportunity for a good match. Although already past fifty, he was travelling more than ever, playing against Vancouver in June and then for them in Calgary in September. His pace was matched only by a younger Tommy Wilmot and, perhaps, by Alberta's Condie Landale. Under Ward's management, the Douglas Lake Ranch was highly profitable and he was prepared to use at least a portion of those profits to indulge his great passion for polo.

Still, his record playing for Vancouver was better than his record playing against them and Douglas Lake went down almost without a fight in the Challenge Cup match, losing to their hosts by 13-4.

For the first time since the Lane Cup came back into play after the war, Camp Lewis did not come to Vancouver in 1928. With visitors from "Calgary" (actually players from three southern Alberta clubs) and Portland, the host club fielded two squads to round out a four-team draw.

It may have been the absence of the traditionally strong Camp Lewis team, the fact that Vancouver had divided its forces or just the luck of the draw, but southern Alberta's representatives did far better than in the previous two tournaments. They managed to edge past Vancouver "B" by 8-7 and advanced to the final against a Vancouver "A" side which had trounced Portland 19-2 on the strength of twelve goals by Norman Drysdale.

Drysdale contributed six more goals in the final, but Calgary managed to keep the score respectable, losing by only eight goals to four.

It was in 1928 that the two great anchors of the Vancouver Polo Club appeared on the field together. As Eric Werge Hamber had been the strongest supporter of the club from its first years until the hiatus of the early 1930s, so Clarence Wallace would bring the game back to Vancouver and lead the club through its final seasons before the second war.

Hamber's family came to Canada after a reversal of fortune in their native England. Eric was born and educated in Manitoba, excelling at every sport he played (and he played them all). While working in England for the Dominion Bank, Hamber met and married the daughter of John Hendry, a New Brunswick lumberman who had come early to the West Coast and built a sizeable business (and personal fortune) in timber and sawmills.

Hamber joined his father-in-law's firm and soon, after Hendry's premature death in 1917, found himself running the entire operation. Under Hamber's guidance, what had already been hugely profitable enterprises continued to grow and prosper and he soon emerged as one of Vancouver's leading business and social leaders.

Hamber first appeared with the polo club just before the Great War and was a perennial feature

throughout the team's great years in the 1920s and early 1930s. Although he did not often travel with the team, he maintained a fine and extensive string of first-class ponies and one suspects his cheque book was often opened to ensure that the club remained competitive.

Hamber served as the club's president from the early 1920s to 1931 and, in 1936, he was appointed British Columbia's fifteenth lieutenant governor, a post he filled until 1941. Following a long battle with cancer, he died in Vancouver in 1960.

Clarence Wallace first appeared with the club in 1928 as a member of the "B" side and, in Calgary, was a spare for the team during the Western Canada Championship. He was one of the first of the second generation of Vancouver players to move up to a regular place on the "A" side.

Like Hamber, Wallace had the money to indulge his love of horses and polo. His father had founded the huge and influential Burrard Dry Dock Company and Wallace, after serving in the first war and achieving the rank of colonel, eventually took over as owner and president. Like his friend Hamber, Clarence Wallace was later appointed lieutenant governor of British Columbia, serving from 1950 to 1955.

Calgary's 1928 Western Canada Championship was held in the third week in August, a week or so earlier than usual, allowing Frank Ward to win his second consecutive Chipman Cup for Vancouver and still be back in the Interior in time for the Kamloops tournament at the beginning of September. His usually daunting presence notwithstanding, the Kamloops Polo Club finally accomplished something it had never managed to do before. It won the Kamloops Challenge Cup.

The 8-7 result was a surprise, probably even to the club itself. Three of the players — Carr, Bostock and Kinloch — had never been in a tournament match before and the captain, H. Willes, was far from Kamloops' most experienced. They were facing a Douglas Lake squad of Woods, Wilmot, Chetwynd and Ward that, on any other day, would have been one of the strongest in Western Canada.

Douglas Lake's horses were late in arriving and the team played the first half on borrowed ponies, but after the match Ward dismissed its effect on the game, giving the locals full marks for their team play. When their ponies arrived, Douglas Lake tried to draw Kamloops into a wide-open match, but the hosts, whose mounts made up in agility what they lacked in speed, stayed close to their checks and took quick advantage of any opportunity that presented itself. Kamloops held the lead until the end of the third chukker and scored the eventual winner with just seconds to play.

On a cold, blustery September 29th, the same young Kamloops team travelled to Grande Prairie to try for the Roper Cup. They faced Alex Pringle, Tottie Clemitson, et al. on a less than ideal field. It must have been a good year for Pringle's hay crop since the paper reported grass so thick that it "permitted no rolling of the ball." If the Kamloops team had any illusions of putting their name on the cup for the first time in sixteen years, they were short-lived as Grande Prairie rode to a comfortable 8-1 win.

Sadly, the city had lost its final chance as this was the last year in which the Roper Cup was put up for play. It had been contested fourteen times since 1901 and, but for Kelowna's three-year hold between 1909 and 1911 and Kamloops' single triumph of 1912, it had been Grande Prairie property. Following the 1928 match, the cup was retired to a place of honour on Alex Pringle's mantelpiece.

The year 1929 saw the resumption of the Kamloops-Vancouver home-and-home series with Kamloops heading west for the B.C. Challenge Cup in June and Vancouver coming to town in September to try for the Kamloops trophy.

While four players from the Interior made the trip to the coast — Ward, Hett, Carr and Talbot — only three managed to play in the tournament. Ellis Talbot broke his collarbone in a warm-up match and they filled out the team with Vancouver's Norman Drysdale. With

The B.C. Challenge Cup – This trophy was created in September, 1913 by a group of twelve Vancouver businessmen. Usually played for in Vancouver, the cup was generally considered to represent the B.C. provincial championship although Alberta teams occasionally appeared at the tournament.

(left to right) Vancouver's Chuck Wills and Reggie Chaplin with Prince Henry, Duke of Gloucester, Brighouse Park, 1929.

Kamloops' Bostock, Kinloch, Willes and Carr with the Kamloops Challenge Cup, 1929.

such a lineup, the team should have done better than their 10-4 loss, but the host team's ponies (many originally from the Kamloops district) were the difference.

The trophy was presented to the Vancouver team by Prince Henry, Duke of Gloucester, still recovering from his own fractured shoulder recently sustained on the same Brighouse polo field.

Following the "main event," the club held a handicap tournament which involved members of the Kamloops team and a pair of host squads, named the "Canadians" and the "Old Country." Such American-style games were a regular feature of the Challenge Cup tournament, used to fill out a week of polo where the cup final was usually a one-game affair.

It is interesting to note that the B.C. Challenge Cup games (and most major tournament matches for the past few years both on the coast and in Kamloops) comprised seven chukkers of eight minutes each. This timing was also used during at least some of the Lane Cup matches, but whether it was in regular use elsewhere in the American Pacific Northwest is not known.

Neither the Interior nor Alberta sent a team to the Northwestern Championship at the end of July (and

Vancouver missed the 1929 Western Canada in Calgary), but Camp Lewis was back, along with a team from Seattle's Olympic Riding and Driving Club. Vancouver again fielded two squads to fill out the draw.

According to the *Province,* the Seattle team was making its first visit to Vancouver for an outdoor match, but had been north twice before to play indoor polo. How common or popular the indoor game was in Vancouver simply cannot be determined from the local papers. The matches, probably played in the late winter or early spring, received no coverage at all. Even the location of the games cannot be established, but there was an arena at Brighouse large enough to accommodate the game. With only one brief reference to indoor polo in the Alberta newspapers, too, one can only assume that, while the game was certainly played in the Canadian West, it never achieved anything like the popularity of the outdoor version.

The Lane Cup matches reverted to their old format for 1929 with a round-robin series, the cup winner to be decided on the basis of number of wins and, if necessary, total goals. Unlike 1927, the tie-breakers were not needed as Vancouver "A" showed itself the top of the field, finishing with a 3-0 record and taking its seventh Lane Cup of the second era.

Ignoring the Western Canada tournament, Vancouver arrived in Kamloops at the end of August to join Grande Prairie in trying to wrest the Challenge Cup away from the host team. For once, as the holders, Kamloops had a bye into the final.

Grande Prairie sent the same team which had captured the Roper Cup in the previous year and the foursome continued on form with an 8-6 win over Vancouver. In this match, as so often, it was the horses that made the difference. While Grande Prairie's were as fast as usual, the Vancouver ponies were dead tired even before the match began. They had been loaded in Vancouver on Monday morning and did not leave the car until it arrived in Kamloops at 4 a.m. on Wednesday. By mid-afternoon, they were on the field.

Frank Ward and Ross Hett, joined by Willes and Kinloch, defended the cup for Kamloops, but it seemed not to matter who took on Grande Prairie over the years, the home side very rarely got the better of it. So it was in 1929 as Grande Prairie claimed the Kamloops Challenge Cup by 7-5.

The first post-war decade of western Canadian polo ended on a plateau. After three or four years of sustained growth in the mid-1920s, the game settled into a consistent, year-by-year pattern, consolidating the gains that had already been made.

In the pre-war era, polo was characterized by its freshness; by the newness of the sport and the enthusiasm with which it was embraced by players and audiences alike. Small town clubs often represented a genuine source of civic pride, especially when their teams rode off to such major centres as Toronto, Montreal or Winnipeg and proved themselves the best in the nation. At what other game or enterprise could High River or Pincher Creek, Alberta have justifiably laid claim to being a national champion? The players, too, were exciting; young men in a young land who, away from the field, were deeply involved in building a new society.

For these, and other somewhat more romantic reasons, that first era has been called "the golden age of Canadian polo." But was it? Certainly, polo was more at the centre of social life in those early days. In nearly every centre, including Calgary, the annual polo club ball was the highlight of the social season and, on the club rosters, one could find the same names as appeared on the communities' first hospital board or newly organized town council.

By the end of the 1920s in most centres, polo was far from the only sport. In some, it had ceased to be played at all or simply become worthy of just another column in the local paper's sports pages. Perhaps the men who played the game were not so influential in their communities as they had been when those communities were newer and smaller.

Nevertheless, on a game-for-game, tournament-for-tournament basis, there was probably more good

From the Vancouver Province, c. 1930.

Vancouver City Archives, CVA703-5.19

polo played in the 1920s than in most of the pre-war era. Easier travel, combined with enthusiastic new players and financially secure veterans, meant that the first post-war decade came closer to seeing a true western championship than had ever been the case before. With top-quality players like Frank Ward, Tommy Wilmot and Ralph Chetwynd from the Interior, Condie Landale, Willie Deane-Freeman and Laurie Johnson from Alberta and their peers in Winnipeg and Vancouver, the games were fast, wide-open and, for the crowds, incredibly exciting. If the first era represented the golden age of polo as a social phenomenon in the Canadian West, the Twenties were the game's golden age on the field. ▓

CHAPTER 9

HORSE-TRADING

FOR MORE THAN A CENTURY, vast stretches of southern Alberta and the British Columbia Interior have been cattle country. The brief era of the open range, the rise and fall of the great syndicate ranch and the evolution of the smaller, family-owned operation have all been studied in encyclopedic detail and the published histories of the cattle industry would easily fill a tall bookcase.

Sadly, the same cannot be said for the horse. With only a few exceptions (like George Lane and his legendary Bar-U Percherons), the horse business remains almost a footnote in the saga of western Canadian ranching. And yet, at its turn-of-the-century peak, the raising, training and selling of horses probably rivalled the cattle business in total dollar value.

There were strong parallels between the two businesses as well. As the early influence of Texas cowboys on the ranching business has often been overstated, so has their contribution to the breeding and raising of horses. While the rough cayuses ridden into the country with the early cattle drives were much in demand for the new ranches, it was not long before the English proprietors and managers began intensive programs of breed improvement. Along with the purebred Hereford and Shorthorn cattle brought in to upgrade their herds, they began to import substantial numbers of thoroughbred mares and stallions from Eastern Canada, the United States, England and Ireland. Ads extolling the bloodlines and breeding prowess of these new acquisitions began appearing in southern Alberta newspapers as early as the mid-1880s.

The great Alberta-bred pony, "Bendigo," photographed in England, c. 1898.

163

Several of the early ranches were dedicated almost exclusively to the production of horses. Although the animals required more specialized care than cattle, smaller operators found the higher value of horses (usually three to five times as much per head) could realize them a substantial, and more predictable, income.

As the long string of new Prairie towns grew and flourished along the route of the Canadian Pacific Railway, the most substantial of them established a fairgrounds, invariably assembled around a half-mile racetrack. The racing season at these tracks quickly became the social centre of life in the small towns. From well before the turn of the century, Calgary, Fort Macleod and High River and others were hosting juried horse shows that offered prizes for a wide variety of breeds and purposes.

For those who could afford it, there were bigger prizes than the local fairs could provide. The annual meetings at Regina and Winnipeg both offered substantial money and southern Albertans were prominent on the winners' lists almost from the start.

The same winners also appeared on the playing rosters of southern Alberta's polo clubs. Alexander, Critchley, Samson, Eckford, Holland and many others maintained stables of thoroughbred horses and it was from their breeding programs that they began to build their strings of polo ponies. No doubt many of the early horses that were trained for polo were rough-looking local stock. When they weren't on the playing fields, they were fine working cow ponies. Only a few southern Alberta or Interior players could afford Sunday polo ponies that did not earn their keep out with the herds during the week. By the close of the first era, however, the cayuses were all but gone, replaced by a mix of thoroughbreds, half- and quarter-breds. They may have been taller and sleeker, but most would still have known their way around a cattle pen.

Before the turn of the century, the polo pony "business" was largely a local affair, with each man acquiring and training his own mounts. That is not to say there was not an active market among the players. From the outset, tournaments offered the opportunity to show off one's ponies and many players brought more mounts to the gatherings than they needed for the games.

Evidence for this lively trade in trained ponies can be found in the entry and prize lists for the gymkhanas which were a feature of nearly every major polo tournament in the Canadian West during the game's first fifty years.

Newspaper coverage of the gymkhanas was generally more extensive than that afforded the polo matches themselves and spectators were often far more numerous. Held on a day on which there were no games scheduled, the gymkhanas offered more than a dozen tests of rider and horse. Events ranged from straightforward quarter- or three-eighths-mile dashes (with some over hurdles) to such cavalry traditions as tent-pegging. These were supplemented by a series of bizarre and humorous games with names like "Oolta-Poolta," "Brandy and Soda," "Ladies' Nomination" and "Balaclava Melee."

While reports of polo matches rarely mentioned the names of the ponies involved, coverage of the gymkhanas often did and one can follow a specific horse as it passed through a succession of owners. Herbert Samson's 1895 race-winning "Kaffir" won again in 1896, but this time under O.A. Critchley. Other ponies such as "Hell" and "Vice" seem to have had a succession of owners over the years.

Such reports also make it possible to track the career of "Bendigo," the most famous polo pony ever raised in Western Canada.

Raised in southern Alberta, he ended his days running on the fields of Hurlingham under one of the greatest players of the age. His story tells much about the state of polo in the Canadian West before the turn of the century.

Bendigo's precise origins are unknown but he was almost certainly born in Alberta in the mid- to late-1880s. He may have been foaled by Michael Oxarart, a French Basque who brought several herds of horses into southern Alberta early in the decade. Although the Mounted Police had questions about exactly how he had acquired them, he was never convicted of theft. Oxarart finally went straight and settled in the Cypress Hills where he raised large numbers of workhorses and kept a stable of thoroughbreds which he raced successfully everywhere across Western Canada. In 1891 and 1892, Oxarart had several wins with a horse called "Bengo." Given the habitually inconsistent spelling in the newspapers of the day, it is possible that the horse was in fact Bendigo. There is no indication, however, that Oxarart ever played polo or was at all interested in training ponies.

Another (and more likely) account has Bendigo raised by Michael Holland at his Beaver Creek Ranch in the Porcupine Hills north of Pincher Creek. Holland was an original member of the Pincher Creek Polo Club and was widely known for the quality of his thoroughbred horses and his half-bred polo ponies. Beaver Creek was an important early social centre for southwestern polo and its attendant gymkhanas so Bendigo's appearance, in 1892, as a well-trained pony at the first tournament in Fort Macleod would not be a surprise.

The horse next appeared at a Calgary polo tournament and gymkhana in 1893, owned by club president Harry Alexander. Already he had acquired a considerable reputation (he is said to have won twenty-three races) since two different polo team photographs taken in the early 1890s identify not only the players in the picture, but Bendigo as well.

Alexander played him again in 1894 and then sold him to Oswald Critchley for the 1895 season. His last appearance on a Canadian polo field was under Oswald's brother, Harry, at the 1896 Calgary tournament.

Within a year, Bendigo had left the rough fields of the Prairie West for the beautiful turf of Hurlingham. Impeccably groomed and carefully posed with a young stable boy, Bendigo's photograph appears in T.B. Drybrough's *Polo*, published in England in 1898. Although the solidly built, half-bred gelding looks completely at home in his new surroundings, no amount of brushing can completely hide the old Alberta brand burned into his left shoulder.

Drybrough writes:

I am pleased to be able to add to my list of illustrations a photograph of Mr. Buckmaster's Canadian pony Bendigo, which he tells me is, with the exception of the English pony Sunshine, the best polo pony he has ever owned. Bendigo won twenty-three races in Canada.

Such high praise must have been warranted since his owner was one of the best-known players in the world. A member of such legendary teams as the "Freebooters" and the "Old Cantabs," Walter Buckmaster was, according to T.F. Dale: "The greatest polo captain in England [and] the best player of our time."

Since Bendigo could not have been in England for more than one season when Drybrough included him in his book, he must have come to Buckmaster fully trained. That speaks well for the overall quality of western mounts during the first era, and for the skills of Holland, Alexander and the Critchleys as trainers.

Bendigo's travels indicate the existence of at least a limited pony trade between the Canadian West and Britain before the turn of the century, a trade that certainly involved the Critchley brothers.

They owned Bendigo when he was sent to England in late 1896 or early 1897 and it is not likely he travelled there alone. It was also not the brothers' only such venture. In September, 1899, the *Calgary Herald* had announced that "H.D. Critchley purchased a bunch of polo ponies in the Pincher Creek District last week for shipment to England." The date corresponds closely with the Critchleys' return to England. Clearly, when the brothers pulled up stakes, they took another shipment of polo ponies with them.

The appearance of Bendigo in the mecca of the polo world is remarkable enough on its face, but it is all the more unusual because he was the product of a game that was less than ten years old in the West. When he was born in southern Alberta, no one had yet played a polo match.

Bendigo's prowess did not result in an English stampede to acquire western Canadian ponies. The transatlantic trade before the turn of the century was primarily based in Chicago, Illinois, and on the American east coast. Players from these centres built their strings with raw stock from Texas, Wyoming, Montana and the Indian territory of Oklahoma. After training, the Americans regularly took substantial numbers of these "made" ponies to Britain and the Continent where they were in great demand. T.B. Drybrough puts the attractions of the U.S. ponies down to a combination of their speed and agility, their comparatively reasonable price and, especially, to their height. Finding 14-2 horses among Britain's native thoroughbreds, hunters and cavalry chargers was apparently no easy matter.

With very few exceptions, the pony trade in the Canadian West remained a local business until after 1900 when the teams themselves began to travel. And when they did travel, it was not to Hurlingham or Meadowbrook.

The broadening of Alberta's polo pony trade after the turn of the century took place within the larger context of a huge growth in the province's horse business in general. Through the period 1900 to 1914, newspapers like the *High River Times* and the *Pincher Creek Echo* were filled with column-length accounts of the various agents who were sweeping across southern Alberta buying horses of every variety and purpose. From Percherons to good, steady wagon plodders; from carriage and saddle horses to military remounts, everything was in high demand both for shipment out of the province and to supply the needs of the booming homestead movement. At least once, agents for the German cavalry were reported to be in the High River area looking for suitable mounts.

Despite all the press jokes about their scruffy appearance, Calgary and High River polo ponies were highly regarded from the moment they ran circles around the eastern mounts at tournaments in Toronto and Montreal. The game was new there and players were likely suffering the same shortage of suitable homegrown stock that faced their counterparts in England. When George Ross first shipped his long strings of ponies to Eastern Canada, he was pleased by the prices they commanded. Western breeders could expect three or four times more than their horses would have been worth at home and the eastern buyers were paying a third to a half of the going rate in Toronto. Everyone was happy.

California, with its abundance of horses and long-established polo history, was probably not much of a market when Albertans began to visit in 1908, but at least some of the boxcar-loads of ponies that went south for those winter seasons changed hands.

Both High River and Pincher Creek took more ponies than they could play when they visited the new club in Winnipeg between 1905 and the outbreak of the Great War. The members of the St. Charles Country Club began to play on horses from Alberta and when they faced the Strathcona's, they faced Alberta-trained players mounted not on their outsized regimental chargers, but on their own Alberta-bred polo ponies.

Vancouver became the next serious customer when the club started in 1913. The new members bought their first ponies in a single lot, gathered and delivered from southern Alberta by an agent with strong connections to the Prairie game (and a new job in Vancouver as the club manager).

The post-war era opened with a major change to the pony business. T.B. Jenkinson's purchase of the Virginia Ranch near Cochrane in 1919 gave Western Canada its first professional facility dedicated to the raising and training of first-class polo ponies.

Before the Virginia Ranch, ponies largely changed hands at tournaments or moved around according to personal friendships among the players. That "personal" trade continued throughout the history of the game, as witnessed by the late 1920s travels of "Redskin." Raised and trained in Kamloops, he was first brought to Alberta by Millarville's J. Spooner who sold him to Dick Brown. Brown then sold him to Frank McHugh who played him for a while before selling him to Colonel J.P. Fell of Vancouver. However, it was the Virginia Ranch that first made western ponies regularly available to areas of North America outside the established touring venues of the Canadian clubs.

Jenkinson gained access to these lucrative new markets through an association with a major American operation located at Bighorn near Sheridan in northeastern Wyoming.

In the birth and boom of their ranching industries, Wyoming and Alberta share a strikingly similar historic pattern. Both saw enormous investments of British capital and both benefited (and suffered) from the presence of substantial numbers of remittance men. As in Alberta, Wyoming's rough range cattle were subject to early and intensive programs of improvement through the importation of purebreds from Britain and the eastern U.S. and the raising of horses was a huge and still underappreciated business. Indeed, the area around Sheridan was, from the outset, more dedicated to the horse than to the cow.

And, in both places, at about the same time, the British ranchers began to play polo. While Alberta had its Edmund Wilmot and George Ross, the Bighorn country had Malcolm Moncrieffe and the Honourable Oliver W. Wallop (later Earl of Portsmouth).

While Bendigo was the prize example of what was a limited Alberta pony trade with England, Moncrieffe and Wallop seem to have carried on a much livelier

"Tangle Toes," one of the Virginia Ranch's prized polo ponies, 1927.

Glenbow archives, NA-1943-3

business with their home country. Both imported substantial numbers of English thoroughbred stallions and both shipped their half-bred progeny back to Hurlingham, Ranelagh and Cirencester. T.B. Drybrough was enthusiastic in his praise for the Wyoming ponies, as he was for the products of the smaller, shorter-lived operations in eastern Montana.

Although both southern Alberta and the Sheridan area were hotbeds of polo from the turn of the century on, their players never met each other on the field. Even between the wars, when western Canadian teams began regular visits to such American venues as Spokane and Minneapolis, Bighorn teams were never a part of the draw. It is not that Calgary would have been unaware of the Wyoming game (A.E. Cross' brother operated a substantial spread in the area and the two families were in regular contact). Rather, it was probably the difficult rail links between the two places that kept them apart.

How T.B. Jenkinson formed his association with Bighorn's Circle V Ranch is not clear, but he had always travelled widely on his buying and selling trips and could have encountered Circle V manager W.M. McCoy almost anywhere polo was being played in the American west. If Moncrieffe and Wallop's business with England had declined, Bighorn's connections to the eastern states had flourished. This was especially true where the annual winter polo season at Aiken, South Carolina was concerned.

The 1920s were the glory days for polo in both Canada and the United States. Crowds of 30,000 were not uncommon when a visiting team from England played a hand-picked American foursome in New York and the free-spending era that led up to the Great Depression saw more polo teams and players than any time before or since. Years before Florida became the eastern centre for the winter polo season, players from all over North America (including Toronto and Montreal) flocked to Aiken for what was a veritable polo festival. At one time or another, every major figure in the world of top-flight polo spent the season at Aiken, playing against his peers and adding to his stables with the best ponies the country had to offer. The Circle V's horses were always in evidence; always in high demand. Many of those ponies had originally come from southern Alberta.

In the spring, Jenkinson and his mostly Irish staff would gather, select and begin training the two or three dozen ponies that were bound for the Circle V. Most had been raised on the Virginia, but Jenkinson also purchased additional mounts from such local breeders as Clem Gardner. In August, the semi-trained ponies were sent off on the long trip to Wyoming where their schooling was completed. By the end of December, the Alberta horses were loaded into boxcars along with the products of the Circle V to make the five-day rail journey to Aiken in time for the start of the winter season.

It was a strong, profitable relationship that lasted throughout the decade, ending only when the Circle V dropped out of the business in about 1929. The Virginia itself was gone by 1932, an early victim of the Depression. What happened to T.B. Jenkinson after he left Alberta is not recorded.

While the Virginia Ranch was probably the largest commercial pony operation in the West, it was certainly not the only one.

Every western Canadian polo club had suspended play during the Great War and, in the 1920s, as the game was once again showing signs of life, local newspapers were quick to grasp the commercial potential of the game. Alberta's *High River Times* was only one of the boosters, reporting in 1927:

One of the thoughts in the minds of those who are endeavoring to revive this popular game is that a market may be created for the light type of horses used in this game. There are many of these in the district which are of little value under present conditions, but if of the right temperament and properly trained might develope into very valuable polo ponies.

The *Kamloops Inland Sentinel* of October, 1922 had been even more straightforward:

The right pony for polo is worth almost anything you like to ask when broken to the game, and this is something worth knowing when you consider there is practically otherwise no sale for the light horse. [It] is quite possible we have quite a few ponies in this district which would command a big price.

In British Columbia, long-time Kamloops player Ross Hett raised ponies and they were a steady income supplement for his small cattle operation. Tommy Wilmot made the better part of his living from breeding and training polo ponies and Douglas Lake's Frank Ward always had a few for sale (though he never had to worry much about the economics of the business). Around Calgary, Osborne Brown, Clem Gardner and, for a few years at least, Cochrane's Archie Kerfoot could be counted on to produce a steady supply of reliable ponies.

In addition to the Virginia Ranch, there was at least one other substantial, fully professional operation in southern Alberta.

Born in Wales, Llewellyn Owen Chambers came to Alberta in 1912 and settled on two and a half sections at Balzac just north of Calgary. His father had run a substantial cattle and horse operation in Northampton and Chambers had accompanied several loads of his father's thoroughbreds and Hackneys to Toronto in the early years of the century. Before he settled permanently in the West, he was already a skilled show rider, light horse judge and a fair hand with a polo mallet.

Llew Chambers first appeared with the Calgary Polo Club in the early 1920s, one of a number of new players who would lead the club through the second era. Combining business and his love of the game, he was a regular out-of-town player at a time when only a few of the members could afford to be on the road. He had already established a strong reputation as a top breeder, importer and trainer of light horses when he began to concentrate on the polo pony business. Those animals he did not breed himself were generally acquired in the Pincher Creek district. Chambers always found his top prospects in that area. They were, he thought, strong on stamina, generally well-trained and took to polo easily. Chambers and Jenkinson often cooperated to fill an order when either man was short of stock.

While T.B. Jenkinson concentrated on shipping through Wyoming, Chambers built a direct relationship with William and Frederick Post of Long Island, New York, the largest dealers on the east coast. Beginning in 1922, Chambers shipped several hundred head of partially trained ponies to the Posts. Prices averaged about $1,300 per head, but horses that might be worth $300 in Alberta could command up to $3,000 by the time they were sold to an eastern American player. The profitable relationship continued for at least eight years and ended at about the same time as Jenkinson's arrangements with the Circle V. The huge trade in polo ponies was a casualty of the growing Depression and, once severed, Alberta's links to the eastern American markets were never substantially reforged.

Chambers continued to ship horses — mostly hunters — to Long Island throughout the 1930s, getting out of the business only when, according to Chambers, there were almost no more suitable horses available in Alberta.

Approaching sixty years of age, he sold his Balzac operation during the second war and moved to a smaller place near the Calgary Polo Club. Although he gave up polo soon after the war, Chambers continued to train and ride for many years. He died in Calgary in 1972.

The highly specialized commercial trade in western Canadian ponies fell victim to the same changing times that affected the state of the game itself. The tough years of the 1930s that saw the end of polo in Vancouver, Winnipeg and Cochrane (and almost finished it everywhere else) also dramatically reduced demand across the continent. The business returned to what it had been before the Great War: a smaller, local trade principally carried out amongst the players themselves. That local market, too, was severely curtailed as clubs like Calgary saw their number of playing memberships fall into the single digits.

With the failure of the post-war boom of the 1950s to produce a substantial market for trained polo ponies, hopes for a return to the halcyon days of large-scale horse-trading had finally ended. ✖

Clem Gardner on "High Tower" at the 1919 Calgary Stampede. Gardner was a world-champion bronc rider and chuckwagon driver before he took to the game of polo in 1922.

CHAPTER 10

BY THE SKIN OF THEIR TEETH

1930–1939

THE THIRTIES opened with the huge fact of the Depression. Although its full weight would not be felt for a year or two, it was already beginning to affect people's thinking, their planning and their dreams. For the polo clubs and players in Western Canada, any hope of growth for their sport would be replaced by a steady, constant fight even to maintain the strong base they had built in the previous years. Some clubs would stay the course; others would barely manage to survive. There would be one or two new clubs founded, but others would be early (and permanent) casualties.

The Calgary club's overarching concern at its 1930 organizational meetings in April and May was the condition of Chinook Park. The question of the playing fields — a main, tournament field and a practice ground — had been a central issue in the previous year and it seems that little had been resolved. The practice ground was so rough and uneven that it led to overuse of the main field and concerns were then raised about its suitability for major tournament play.

The problem was money. A proper reconditioning of the practice ground had been priced at $2,500 and the club simply did not have it. The membership drive of 1929 had been a solid success, but most of that money had gone toward paying down the club's debt. President A.E. Cross made a personal contribution of $500 toward repairing the practice ground and it was used to undertake the levelling of the field. There had also been improvements made to the pavilion and an enlargement of the kitchen was accomplished by removing the unused ladies' locker room (a clear sign that women's polo in Calgary was finished). The club secretary also reported that "the sanitary arrangement previously in the pavilion, and which was so objectionable, has been removed."

These were all stop-gap measures. Problems with the pavilion, the privies and, especially, the playing fields can all be traced to the fact that the polo club was still without a regular supply of water. During the dry years to come, the issue of water and the condition of the grounds would continue to plague the executive.

At the 1930 High River spring meeting, the club went about the usual business of electing officers, setting practice days and appointing its representatives to the Western Canada association. They also wrote to the Calgary club to say they could not afford to help defray the costs of renovating the Calgary grounds, but would consider waiving its share of any profits from the provincial and western tournaments.

The High River club could count on the return of most of its playing members, but one name in particular was missing: McHugh.

After years of regular play for Calgary and, lately, for High River where they were largely responsible for bringing the scarlet jerseys back onto the field, the McHughs had finally given up the game for good. Alex's final appearance was at the 1928 Western Canada tournament and his cousin, Frank, last played at about the same time, although he continued to attend meetings at the Calgary club until 1931. Alex eventually moved out to the West Coast where he died in 1952, while Frank continued to live on his ranch and manage his various business interests.

In his final year, Bull McHugh had this to say: "Now I live an obscure life, but I've had many a high-old-time in my day — and I still love horses and polo." He died in 1957 at the age of seventy-two.

The 1930 Alberta Provincial Championship opened on Wednesday, July 23rd with six teams: the defending champions from the Strathcona's, Calgary's "Terriers" and "Blacks," the R.C.H.A., Cochrane and High River. Millarville had been included in the draw, but failed to make an appearance.

The preliminary rounds played out as expected with Calgary and the Artillery again showing they were no serious threat to Cochrane, High River or the Strath's. High River finally took the cup from the Strathcona's but the wide disparity between first and second rank clubs seemed set to continue into the new decade.

The St. Charles Country Club opened play for the Sifton trophy at the beginning of August but only two teams came up from Minneapolis. The Fort Snelling Blacks were there to defend the trophy against St. Charles' Blues, while the local Reds would play the "Twin Cities Civilians" for the "B" trophy. It was a long way from the six to nine teams that competed on the country club grounds in the Twenties and a sure sign that the Depression was beginning to take its toll both in Manitoba and south of the border.

In the Midwest, too, there was a clear division between the top clubs and the rest. Winnipeg's "B" side could usually handle its American competition in the junior rounds, but only Winnipeg "A" and Fort Snelling's Blacks were really top-rank, with the Fort always showing itself the best by a goal or two. The U.S. army never lost the Sifton Cup.

In Western Canada's other international series, four teams contested the Lane Cup tournament in mid-August. Vancouver's "A" and "B" squads faced Camp Lewis and a four-some from the Seattle National Guard. The first day's games were both terrible mismatches with Vancouver "A" and Camp Lewis winning by a combined score of 33-1.

(left to right) Muriel Farmer, Betty Ward, Daphne Fernie, Mary Fernie, Phyllis Willes, Kamloops, c. 1932 – Betty Ward is shown holding the stick in her left hand. Although it caused some difficulty on the field, she was always allowed to play left-handed. Women's polo flourished briefly in Kamloops, Calgary and Winnipeg in the late 1920s and early 1930s but the teams never had the opportunity to play each other.

These two teams were undoubtedly head-and-shoulders above any others in the area and, while Vancouver could obviously mount one serious tournament team, it was not deep enough to manage two. The final match was close — Camp Lewis took the trophy by 8-4 — but Vancouver's "B" side beat the National Guard by 10-2 in the consolation, further emphasizing the widely different levels of talent at the tournament.

The R.C.H.A. was again back in its Winnipeg barracks before the start of the 1930 western championship at Calgary and St. Charles sent a telegram withdrawing their entry due to an injury to a key player. Millarville, although expected, simply could not raise a team. Efforts to restart the game there were clearly not going to bear fruit. Willie Deane-Freeman might have been able to provide the catalyst, but he continued to feel a strong allegiance to Capers and the High River club who had gone out of their way to bring him back into the game. He was also nearing the end of his second decade of competitive polo and, after working so hard on the High River revival, was probably enjoying the winning seasons and just not feeling up to starting another reclamation project.

Once again, Calgary failed to get a team into the main show as both the Blacks and the Terriers lost their first round matches. To be fair, though, the draw seemed always to pit Calgary against one top team or another in the first round. There is no doubt that the host club could have done much better at these affairs had it not always felt the obligation to send out two (and sometimes even three) teams to ensure a full draw.

Although the tournament avoided its traditional rain-out, the 1930 Chipman Cup final was played in a cold sleet. The weather kept the crowds away, but did not seem to hamper the game and High River's Willie Deane-Freeman, Charlie Arnold, Ellison Capers and Jack de Foras simply outplayed a better-mounted Cochrane foursome of veterans Archie Kerfoot, Bill Wolley-Dod and Laurie Johnson and newcomer Bill Bagley. The final score was 5-2.

Kamloops closed the 1930 B.C. season with its annual Challenge Cup matches at the end of August.

Clem Gardner playing a backhand for the Calgary Blacks against High River, 1930.

It was scheduled as a three-team round robin among themselves, Vancouver and Grande Prairie. Surprisingly (given their usual performance), Kamloops beat a good Vancouver team by 8-6 in the opening match but, for some reason, Vancouver had to cut their trip short and only played one more match (against Grande Prairie) before they left for home.

That left the defending champions to face Kamloops for the cup and the home team quickly returned to its traditional form, losing by a 7-3 score that did not really reflect Grande Prairie's domination of the game.

In his 1930 year-end financial report, Calgary secretary-treasurer Mike Francis presented a picture of a club that was barely holding its own. Playing memberships had declined by three to fourteen, but non-playing subscriptions had plummeted from one hundred forty to only thirty-seven. The club had discussed holding a membership drive during the year,

but it seemed the executive was too preoccupied with other problems to mount the campaign. While the provincial tournament had shown a small profit, the Western Canadian had produced a deficit and the vagaries of the Prairie weather were to blame. The field had been so dry at the beginning of the week, the club hauled in water to soften the turf. By the final day, cold rain and snow had cut deeply into the gate receipts.

The club had spent nearly $600 on the grounds (including rent to the Polo Club Limited and repairs to the two playing fields), a figure that was barely covered by the subscriptions. Without a substantial donation from A.E. Cross, the club would have faced a considerable loss. It was going to be a difficult decade.

Despite the troubles of the previous season, 1931 saw more non-tournament polo reported in the Calgary papers than had been the case for two or three years. With very few matches having been played outside the two annual main events in the past years, the club announced its intention to schedule at least some form of a game on every Saturday during the summer.

The club began its season by playing a series of matches for the Hull Cup. Symbolic of the club championship, the cup had not been played for since 1928. Four teams entered the American style, four-chukker matches with the cup to be awarded on total goals. Joining the Strathcona's were three club teams, representing almost all of Calgary's playing membership. The names would have been well-known by 1931. Most had been playing for several seasons and there were no new faces. Whatever growth there was in the late 1920s would not be sustained in the new decade.

Responding to members' complaints about Calgary's terrible tournament record over the past few years, the club decided to appoint a selection committee to ensure that its "A" team was just that: the best the

The Calgary "Pirates," surprise winners of the 1931 Alberta Provincial Championship – (left to right) Henry Chadwick, Archie Kerfoot, Bill Wolley-Dod, Mike Francis.

club could field. The powers of the committee were sweeping. Its decisions on the makeup of the two or three teams would be absolute, it would appoint the captains and move players around as it saw fit. This authority would be vested in three men: one player (who would also be captain of the "A" team) and two non-playing members.

A four-chukker match in mid-July was the first test of a new club policy. The game featured two Calgary squads named the "Possibles" and the "Probables," selected by the new committee. If the committee thought its work would be easy, it was a brief hope as their first selections played to a scoreless draw.

High River, too, was playing regular polo, looking forward to defending its two championships. The club was on the field before the end of May and, on June 20th, Jim Cross brought his Terriers to town for a friendly match. The result probably contributed to the complaints from Calgary that led to the creation of a selection committee. The Terriers lost again.

By July 20th, with just over a week to go before the provincial championship, the selection committee announced its final decision. Calgary's number one team would be Dennis Yorath, Clem Gardner, Alec Landale and his father. Number two would be Trevor Willans, Llew Chambers, Jim Cross and Fred Pardee.

Held in reserve were Hugill, Adams, Chadwick and Francis. The committee further announced that, should a member of the first team be injured, his place would be taken by his like number from the second team and the appropriate reserve elevated to fill the gap.

The committee had broken up Cross' Terriers, but after all the warm-up games and what was probably a certain degree of acrimony, the number one team was three-quarters of the Hull Cup-winning Canaries from back at the end of May.

The provincial tournament opened on Wednesday, July 29th with five teams: High River, the Strathcona's, Calgary's "A" and "B" and a "dark horse" entry hurriedly thrown together to fill the draw in Cochrane's absence. Called the "Pirates," the team was made up of two Calgary reserves — Chadwick and Francis — and two Cochrane regulars — Archie Kerfoot and Bill Wolley-Dod.

The 1931 Provincial Championship was anything but a resounding success for the new Calgary selection committee. In the opening match, the Pirates (sporting white jerseys with a skull and crossbones emblazoned on the front) promptly dispatched Calgary "A" by 7-6. They then went through to the finals with a 7-5 win over Calgary "B."

The Strathcona's again drew the defending champions from High River in the first round. Again, it was a tiring string of LdSH ponies that let High River pull away in the final chukkers for a 5-1 victory.

In the consolation rounds, it was the turn of Calgary "B" to confound the committee, overwhelming the club's best foursome by an easy 9-3 and then, to the surprise of nearly everyone, beating the Strathcona's in the consolation final.

On Saturday, August 1st, High River defended its title against a team that did not even exist a week before the start of play. Led by Deane-Freeman, High River went out to a 3-0 lead in the second chukker but, by halftime,

the Pirates had closed to within one at 4-3. By the end of the fourth period, Wolley-Dod had equalized for the Pirates and they held the champions scoreless through the last two chukkers.

From the throw-in at the start of overtime, Calgary's Chadwick headed straight down the field and scored the winner, making the Pirates the 1931 Alberta provincial champions.

At a meeting of the Calgary Polo Club on August 4th, the selection committee was reorganized.

On a motion by Hugill and Chadwick, the playing member of the committee was dropped and the two remaining members — C.J. Yorath and Lieutenant-Colonel L.F. Page — were authorized to add to their number only from amongst the club's non-playing members.

The playing member of the committee (and captain of the ill-fated "A" team) had been Condie Landale and, whether it was coincidence or the sign of deeper trouble, the old man had played his last game for the Calgary Polo Club.

The 1931 Western Canada Championship Tournament was set for August 22nd, and, for the first time since 1928, there would be a B.C. team in the draw. Earlier in the month, Calgary had decided it was essential for the success of the tournament that an "outside" team be present. A letter to Kamloops acquit itself well in the supporting handicap tournament, winning the total-goal series.

Kamloops' biggest problem, as it had been in the earliest days of the club, was finding anyone else to play. Kelowna had never come back after the war, and Vernon rarely left home. Grande Prairie had stopped mounting even its once-a-year challenge and the Nicola Valley had fallen quiet, without even the rumour of a new polo team. On the coast, Vancouver was still very active but, despite annual predictions of their imminent revival, Vancouver Island's polo teams had yet to resurface. With Frank Ward and Tommy Wilmot now playing most of their polo in Kamloops, the invitation from Calgary would have been an enormously attractive one. Without Ward and Wilmot, it is unlikely that Kamloops would have even been able to consider it.

On Saturday, August 22nd, play began for the 1931 Western Canada Championship, opening with Kamloops versus the Calgary "Blues." This would be followed by Cochrane versus the Strathcona's on Monday and defending champions High River versus Calgary's "Whites" on Tuesday. The pace would pick up to two-a-day matches on Wednesday, the 26th with the Chipman Cup final set for Saturday.

Calgary's revamped selection committee had dropped its "A" and "B" levels and shuffled the deck again for the tournament. The Blues were Yorath, Willans, Cross and Pardee, while Francis, Adams, Gardner and Alec Landale made up the Whites. As a reward for winning the provincial title, Francis had been elevated from the reserve squad all the way to team captain.

When Kamloops and the Blues met, it should have been a match between two clubs that had never been able to win when it mattered. But this was not a typical Kamloops team. Under the leadership of Frank Ward, the foursome featured Tommy Wilmot, one of the finest players the province ever produced. Kay Lang, a strong all-rounder, was making his first appearance in Calgary since he had left the city in 1927 and Grande Prairie's Ellis Talbot had emerged as a strong, steady player who could be counted on to take advantage of any scoring opportunity.

The *Albertan* put it succinctly:

The visitors played their positions ably; hit well and accurately and co-operated as a team, whereas it appeared to be every man for himself as far as the locals were concerned. Individually, the Blues did well, but collectively they were below form.

offering to pay the freight on their ponies had been positively received and the Interior club put its name into the draw. Any hope for another outside team was quashed by the *Albertan* on August 5th:

It is hardly likely that Winnipeg will be represented as polo has been a dead issue in the Manitoba metropolis this summer.

What had been a strong and vital polo club for nearly two and a half decades simply disappeared from the scene. The field at the St. Charles club would eventually be covered by the golf course and the game would not reappear in Manitoba until the 1970s.

While Calgary was struggling with declining memberships and ongoing financial problems associated with the quality of its playing fields, Kamloops had begun its 1931 season on an optimistic note.

The *Kamloops Inland Sentinel* reported a "particularly good number of playing and non-playing members" at the organizational meeting in mid-March. Under president Bill Fernie, the club was still dealing with the chronic problem of tardiness (deciding this year to levy a small fine against any member who showed up late), but the winter had been mild and the club's reserve field was deemed ready for the first match, scheduled for Easter Sunday.

In mid-June, Kamloops made its annual trip to Vancouver for the B.C. Challenge Cup matches. Although they again failed to win the prize, losing to Vancouver by 10-5, the team did

The result was 10-4 for Kamloops, a score perfectly indicative of the play.

Again, the Strathcona's had a difficult first round draw, but at least it wasn't High River. Campbell, Rebitt, Powell and Harvey were a good team, but Cochrane, with Wolley-Dod, Johnson, Archie Kerfoot and Condie Landale, was favoured to move through, perhaps as far as the finals. But it was the Strathcona's who were out to a 6-0 lead by the end of the second chukker and, despite a fierce Cochrane charge in the final period, the regiment held on for an 8-6 win.

High River's Deane-Freeman, Arnold, Capers and Robertson closed the first round with an easy 10-4 win over the Whites, earning a bye into the Chipman Cup final. But finding out whom they would face would have to wait as heavy rains washed out both Wednesday matches. The *Albertan* thought it a blessing: "the rain...will lay the dust at the grounds, freshen up the turf and give the ponies an extra day of rest."

When play was resumed on Thursday, the Strathcona's were again underdogs, this time to Kamloops. Again, they played a close team game in a match that was marked by a number of penalties and by Rebitt being knocked to the turf twice. He also scored four

goals as the Strathcona's won a very close 6-5 semifinal.

In the second series, Calgary's woes continued as the Whites and Blues both lost again, to Kamloops and Cochrane respectively. In the consolation final, Kamloops won a strong 11-5 victory, despite being down 3-0 after the first four minutes.

A large crowd was out for Saturday's final between the Strathcona's and High River and the game lived up to their expectations. By now the Strath's were probably tired of being the underdogs, but they were again cast in that role and again they beat the odds. On the strength of Harvey's defence (and his four goals), the Strathcona's won the 1931 Western Canadian Championship by 6-5, claiming their first Chipman Cup since 1913.

Everywhere but on the field, the Calgary club had a successful year in 1931 as both tournaments ended in the black. The profits were not large, but did cover the cost of shipping Kamloops' ponies and paid off the loss incurred by the 1930 Western Canada Championship.

The trip to Calgary meant that the Kamloops Challenge Cup would not be contested in 1931 and Ward and the team returned to the Interior to close out their 1931 season with a one-day handicap tournament amongst the club members. The afternoon was notable for the presence on the field of Bill Fernie's daughter, Daphne. According to the *Sentinel,* "her remarkably good shots...brought forth much enthusiastic applause from the spectators." And, she scored a goal.

A few years earlier, Calgary's women players had issued a challenge to other western women to establish a tournament. Unfortunately for the future of the women's game, Kamloops' women players did not appear until long after Calgary's effort had folded, and female players were never really much of a feature at any other B.C. or Alberta club. But the Interior's women players did

go on to make a solid contribution to the Kamloops club in the few years they were on the field.

Vancouver's 1931 season looked, on the surface, much as it had for several years. The B.C. Challenge Cup had gone off as scheduled in June and Camp Lewis had again come up for the Northwestern International, bringing with them another badly overmatched foursome from Seattle's Olympic Riding and Driving Club.

The year 1931 marked the last Canadian appearance of the U.S. army team from Camp Lewis. They had always fielded a strong team and won the Lane Cup in four of the ten years they had contested it.

Vancouver managed to take the Lane trophy back from Camp Lewis in 1931, but had not even tried to form a second squad to provide a balanced draw. The Hambers hosted their usual round of dinners and dances for the visiting players and their wives, but there was the uncomfortable feeling that, somehow, the life was going out of the game in Vancouver. Other than Hamber and Bimbo Sweeny, the original members had all hung up their sticks and, with the great exception of Clarence Wallace, the newcomers had not emerged as players strong enough to take their place on the "A" team.

The club that travelled so widely in its early years had become a largely stay-at-home organization, with Kamloops its only regular out-of-town date. In the two years that Vancouver went east to Calgary, the names that stood out on the Vancouver roster were Frank Ward and Tommy Wilmot, neither of them regular club members. It may have been that the growing Depression was creating a division between the "haves" and "have-nots" of the Vancouver Polo Club in much the same way that it had among the clubs of the Interior and southern Alberta.

In 1932, the weight of the Great Depression began seriously to affect the fortunes of polo in the Canadian West. Winnipeg had already given up, southern Alberta would lose one of its traditional powers and, in British Columbia, the Vancouver Polo Club went suddenly quiet.

Exactly why the apparently lively West Coast club ceased play is not clear. There was no formal announcement, but such regular tournaments as the B.C. Challenge and Northwestern International were simply not held. Certainly the Depression had taken its toll, and many of the early club stalwarts were moving well into middle age, but the departure of Eric Hamber must have had a chilling effect on the club.

It was about this time that Hamber retired as president of B.C. Mills, Timber and Trading and moved up the Fraser Valley to a new residence near Coquitlam. "Minnekhada" was a sprawling farming and ranching operation that also boasted fine shooting marshes and, in fact, all the comforts of a fine country estate. The Hambers expanded their holdings to nearly 3,000 acres and built extensive stabling and other wonderfully spacious accommodations for their racehorses and, especially, for their polo ponies.

Polo was a regular feature of weekends at Minnekhada but it remained only a passionate pastime. Hamber was never again seen on a tournament field after he left Vancouver. The Hambers lived at Minnekhada until 1958 when Eric's failing health dictated a return to Vancouver. In that year, the estate was sold to Hamber's old polo club teammate, Clarence Wallace.

The 1932 annual meeting of the Calgary Polo Club convened on May 9th with the news that two of its most important patrons had died earlier that year.

Club vice-president C.J. Yorath was the influential head of Canadian Western Natural Gas, Calgary and southern Alberta's major supplier. Although never active as a player, Yorath had lent crucial support to the club in a number of administrative areas.

The other name that would be missing from the 1932 season was club president, A.E. Cross. He had died in Montreal on March 10th following major surgery.

With the club already beginning to feel the effects of the Depression, the loss of its two major patrons was a blow that could well have proved fatal. However, both men had left a legacy to the club that would assure its survival: their sons.

Dennis Yorath and Jim Cross both joined the club in 1927 and, by the time of their fathers' deaths, they were already playing first-rate polo. Dennis worked with his father and then took over as head of the company, staying in the natural gas business until well after the Second World War. He was one of the men who reactivated the club in 1945 and continued to play until the end of the 1948 season. At that time, changes in the nature of the gas business necessitated his moving to the provincial capital of Edmonton.

Jim Cross took over his father's extensive business interests and continued to provide substantial support to the polo club. He also emerged as the club's leading player and remained a fierce presence on the field for another thirty years.

It is also worthy of notice that the 1932 season would go on without another of southern Alberta's great players and field generals. Condie Landale's appearance with Cochrane at the 1931 western championship turned out to be his farewell both to that team and to competitive polo. After his tournament tour-de-force of 1928, he had continued to play regularly in Calgary, but was not a major presence. The 1931 selection committee mess probably told him it was time to retire from the field.

He left his Bearspaw ranch soon after and retired to the West Coast, taking his son, Alec, with him. He died in March, 1948, in the town of New Westminster.

For 1932, Calgary simply could not sustain the high level of intra-club play established the year before. The number of paid subscriptions from playing members had dropped to six, an all-time low, and that decline was reflected in the non-playing memberships, too. The club secretary reported these facts with the terse, obvious comment that the situation "...appears to be due to the general financial condition." The executive did not even bother to discuss means to remedy the problem.

In Kamloops, the club was back on its field at the beginning of April for five chukkers of all-in polo. The muddy country roads kept many of the out-of-town players and their ponies away, but their place was taken by at least five women — Daphne and Mary Fernie, Ruth and Muriel Farmer and Kathleen Lang, all determined to play with their fathers. These family connections, which were characteristic of women's polo in the Interior, had not been the case with the Calgary club in the late 1920s.

In response to declining memberships and, especially, to the growing difficulty of finding and keeping decent ponies, Kamloops introduced a new system to its regular practices and club matches. Before play commenced, each player was asked how many chukkers he (or she) intended to play and a quick schedule was drawn up. It was hoped that the schedule would reduce wasted time between chukkers, put as many players as possible on the field in the course of an afternoon and avoid wearing out the few ponies available. The club also

ensured that at least two chukkers were set aside for junior play, with a senior member assigned to each team as a playing coach.

Unlike 1931, southern Alberta did not have much to report before the provincial championship at the end of July, but the Strathcona's did manage to get down to High River for a tournament warm-up. With relaxed substitution rules, the two teams played a full six chukkers, High River taking a 4-3 win.

The 1932 provincial tournament opened with only four teams: High River, the Strathcona's and Calgary's Whites and Blues. Cochrane could not mount a team and there was no surplus of players to allow for another band of Pirates.

The names of the players, and results of the opening round matches were both familiar and predictable. High River beat the Whites; the Strath's beat the Blues. In the consolation and cup finals, played before about three hundred fifty spectators, the Whites beat the Blues by a resounding 10-1 while High River regained its provincial title from the LdSH by a much closer 5-3.

A small column appeared in the Calgary *Albertan* around the time of the provincial championships. "Polo Notes," under the by-line "Player," was similar in tone and style to Ralph Chetwynd's contributions to the *Kamloops Inland Sentinel* of a few years earlier. The identity of the "Player" is not known, but his column was full of club news. Any chronicler of the game can only wish that such reports had been a more regular occurrence in the press.

The Player announced that Kamloops would again be in town for the western championship and that, as a consequence of the home club's performance at the provincials, the Calgary selection committee had again been revamped and the players reshuffled. Selection to the two teams would now be accomplished by a vote among the playing members.

The new teams were tried out at the Strathcona's Sarcee grounds on the second weekend in August and at least once again before the championship. In his column of August 13th, the Player seemed impressed by the "new" Blues and Whites, although he did not report the scores.

On August 22nd, the Player had some good news: Cochrane would be sending a team to the western tournament. The issue of Cochrane's participation had been on the minds of the Calgary executive at every meeting in 1932. The team missed the provincials and Archie Kerfoot had already informed the Calgary executive that their presence at the Western Canada Tournament was highly unlikely due to the club's dire financial circumstances. If some sort of monetary incentive had been offered to Cochrane, it was not reported in the Calgary minutes but, given that the club had authorized another $200 to bring in Kamloops, such an offer would not have been out of the question.

It was not simply the sad matter of seeing a strong, competitive team fall away after more than two decades. The tournament needed a six-team draw to ensure that play could be held on two consecutive Saturdays. The gate receipts from those two days would mean the difference between red ink and black on the balance sheet and Calgary could not afford to cover any sort of a loss.

Some heavy rains during the preceding days gave the club a chance to roll its beleaguered field at Chinook Park and, on Saturday, August 27th, play began for the 1932 Western Canada Championship.

Opening day's games saw the revamped Whites facing High River and Kamloops versus the Blues. At least the Whites kept their match close. Cross and Gardner had the Whites out to an early lead and managed to hold it through most of the game, keeping Capers and Deane-Freeman under control until the last chukker. Then, in the final minutes they each got loose for a goal and High River advanced by a narrow 6-5.

The Blues ran into serious trouble against a Kamloops team that had brought a surprise with them. Three of the players from 1931 — Ward, Wilmot and Talbot — were back and their fourth had previously been announced as Ross Hett. At the last minute, Hett was replaced by A.J. Bullock.

How Bullock came to be with Kamloops is not clear (he never appeared with the team again), but he had probably been visiting Tommy Wilmot. Like Wilmot, Bullock was a travelling professional. English by birth, he had played a good deal with various teams in California and with the Big Horn club in Wyoming. The *Albertan* reported that he spent the 1931 season at Hurlingham and had played some matches in central Europe. Bullock and Wilmot must have remained friends for several years afterwards since, in 1938, Bullock became godfather to Wilmot's only child.

In the 1931 western tournament, Kamloops had come up only one goal short of playing for the championship and Frank Ward, never one to let an opportunity pass, had obviously seen that one goal (and more) in Alex Bullock. From the moment the team beat the Blues by 10-1, Kamloops became the overwhelming favourite to win the Chipman Cup.

With both Calgary teams again relegated to the second series, High River was scheduled to complete the first round against the Strathcona's on Monday, the 29th. After four chukkers, with High River holding a 5-1 lead, heavy rain, mixed with hail, brought the game to a halt. It would be completed on Tuesday before the scheduled match between Kamloops and Cochrane, which had held the first-round bye.

High River and the Strathcona's finished their game under clear skies with two scoreless chukkers, ending the Strath's hopes to repeat as champions. In the second match, all four Kamloops players scored, apparently at will, and rode to an 11-1 win. Cochrane, clearly patched together at short notice for the tournament, had regulars Archie Kerfoot and Bill Wolley-Dod, joined by the soon-to-be-defunct Virginia Ranch's Cecil Martin and Calgary's Trevor Willans. They were simply outclassed.

Patched together or not, Cochrane had no trouble with the hapless Calgary Blues on Wednesday, winning an easy 10-2 match. In the second game of the day, the Whites surprised everyone with a 7-3 win over the Strathcona's. Not to take anything away from their victory, the Whites were playing an LdSH team that was not nearly as strong as the championship foursome of 1931. The greatest blow had come with Rebitt's departure from the service at the end of the 1931 season. His replacement, Captain Freddie Vokes, while steady enough, lacked Rebitt's experience and his scoring ability. Another new player, Lieutenant C.H. ("Eke") Campbell, had replaced the veteran Gianelli.

For the first (and only) time, the Chipman Cup final would be a two-game, total-goal affair with the first match played on Thursday, September 1st. With Bullock, Ward and Wilmot all on their game for Kamloops, High River simply could not keep up and dropped the first match seven goals to four.

The second game on Saturday afternoon was a repeat of the first, only more so. Despite High River's fast ponies and solid hitting, Kamloops' position play was reported to be the finest example of the game of

Jappy Rodgers – The legendary Alberta horseman was a stalwart with the fine Virginia Ranch polo teams of the late 1920s and early 1930s.

polo ever seen in Alberta. For once, the papers' hyperbole may have had some substance as Wilmot and Bullock combined for eleven Kamloops goals in a 13-3 rout. Their two-game total was 20-7, and this against what was certainly the best team in Alberta at the time.

There was another game on Saturday: Cochrane versus the Calgary Whites. The score was not important — 4-3 for Cochrane — except that it sent Cochrane out on a winning note. The 1932 Western Canada Tournament marked the last time a team from the Cochrane district was seen on the polo field.

From its organization under Oswald Critchley in 1909, the collection of players and teams called Cochrane, Glenbow, Grand Valley or the Virginia Ranch had always been more than competitive and amassed a tournament record of which any western Canadian club would be proud. In the end, money was too tight, new players were too hard to find and the core of veterans either moved away or grew too old for the game. Time and the Great Depression just proved too much for Cochrane polo.

Frank Ward took the Chipman Cup back to Kamloops and its arrival was greeted by front-page headlines in the *Sentinel*. The cup was put on display in the front window of W.J. Kerr's jewellery store and the team was feted by the Board of Trade. In response to their generosity and pride in their polo team's accomplishment, Frank Ward sent them a letter. In part, it read:

Should the Board of Trade be disposed to help the Kamloops polo club in finding a more suitable ground, it would be greatly appreciated. We play on the Indian Reserve. Unfortunately there isn't a water system for the ground [and] with continuous playing and Indian ponies using it for a rolling ground, it becomes dusty and worn, making it difficult and disagreeable to play.

Two grounds are needed, one for practices, another for matches. The size of a boarded field is 300 by 200 yards.

The letter was received and filed.

The Calgary Polo Club would have sympathized with Ward's complaints. "Difficult and disagreeable" almost perfectly sums up the club's attitude toward both its grounds and their owners, the Polo Club Limited. The combination of chronically dry weather, a deeply troubled economy and the lack of a watering system had taken its toll on both the principal field and the practice ground. By the end of 1932, both were all but unplayable. Despite the fact that at least one day of the western tournament was traditionally lost to rain, sleet or hail, such downpours were no substitute for regular soaking and rolling. To preserve the turf for the two annual tournaments, the club had accepted the Strathcona's offer to practice and play all non-tournament games on their field at the Sarcee military reserve to the west of Chinook Park. But even resting the fields was not solving the main problem. The ground was hard, the grass was thin and the divots were like small craters. And, the water problems were not restricted to the playing surface. The ladies who served the teas were used to finding all sorts of things floating in the water barrels from which they filled their kettles.

The Calgary club had been spending piecemeal on the grounds for several years. Studies were commissioned, soils were tested and recommendations received, but every one of the proposed solutions had been far beyond the club's means, even in better days. Although the Polo Club Limited owned the land, the Calgary Polo Club, which paid an annual rental fee of $10, was responsible for its upkeep, insurance and taxes. In October, 1932, the Polo Club Limited sent a letter to the club. In it was the following resolution:

That no polo be played on the grounds next year unless the grounds committee to be appointed [by the Polo Club Limited] approve of having the Provincial Tournament or the Western Canada Tournament or both played on the grounds.

The resolution also said that the Polo Club Limited was not prepared to rent either of the playing fields (or the stables and pasture) to the club for 1933.

The polo club had an offer from the adjoining Chinook Jockey Club to play their games on the infield of the racetrack. The rent would be a nominal one dollar per year for five years. The deal looked promising and the secretary was directed to accept it.

By the time of the April, 1933 annual meeting, however, there was no deal with the jockey club and the polo club had reopened negotiations with the Polo Club Limited. It may have been that the cost of putting the racetrack infield into playable condition was simply too great. The club's new offer to the Polo Club Limited was for a five-year lease agreement at $50 per year with the guarantee that the club would spend at least $200 per year on maintaining and improving the grounds.

It would take another year for the matter to be resolved, but until it was, the Calgary Polo Club held all of its practices and games, including the 1933 Provincial and Western Canada championships, at the Strathcona's Sarcee grounds.

The provincial tournament opened on Thursday, July 27th with only four teams in the draw. With Cochrane gone and Calgary unable to field more than one team, the opening games featured High River versus Calgary and the Strathcona's against the "Magpies." This latter team was a variation on the Pirates, featuring Trevor Willans from Calgary and three Strath's: Vokes, Roberts and Richmond.

The Strathcona's, having clearly reserved the best of its players for the number one team, had little trouble with the Magpies. Their 4-1 victory was, in the words of the *Albertan,* "not particularly brilliant, the Strathcona's no doubt were saving themselves for the final."

High River and Calgary played a much closer match. Deane-Freeman, Capers, Robertson and Watt were hard pressed to come away with a 5-4 win over the single Calgary

foursome of Cross, Francis, Adams and Gardner. Clem Gardner was the star of a game that saw the lead change several times before High River managed to score the winner in the last moments.

The two-day tournament concluded on Saturday with Calgary posting an impressive 8-0 win over the Magpies. With the win and a close game with High River, it must have seemed to the home club that it had finally hit upon a combination that could play with any team. They must have wondered, too, how things might have differed in past tournaments had they not felt obliged to field two competitive foursomes for the sake of the draw.

The final went to the defending champions from High River by 8-2, but it was a win against a Strathcona's team that was severely handicapped by the loss of Major Harvey who had been badly injured during Thursday's game.

There was no chance that the 1933 Western Canada Championship could give the Calgary club its two Saturdays of play. Only four teams registered for the draw, but, nevertheless, this would be a true championship. Calgary, High River, the Strathcona's and Kamloops were the only surviving polo clubs in the Canadian West.

Kamloops had again accepted the offer of paid transportation for their ponies and would be in town to defend their title. With decidedly mixed feelings, the newspapers reported that A.J. Bullock would not be returning as a member of the team. Two games would be held on Friday, September 1st, with the finals on Saturday and a pair of exhibition matches on Labour Day Monday.

The Strathcona's were still without Harvey when they rode out against High River and by the end of the second chukker, they were down by 4-0. High River was better mounted and outriding the Strath's at every turn, but the cavalry slowly pulled even to tie the score at six before full time. It took two

overtime periods until a goal by Campbell finally put the Strath's into the final.

Without Alex Bullock, Kamloops was just another good polo team. Ward, Wilmot, et al had by far the best of the first-half play against Calgary but led by only 3-2 at the break. The fourth chukker was played in a brief hailstorm with Wilmot putting Kamloops up by two, but the final two periods belonged to Calgary. After they had tied the score in the fifth, Trevor Willans put Calgary into the final with the only goal of a fast sixth chukker.

In Saturday's consolation game, High River lost its second game in a row for the first time in years as Kamloops took a steady 4-1 win, leaving Calgary and the Strathcona's to settle the final.

The Strathcona's kept the game close but never managed to take the lead. With two goals each from Cross and Willans and singles from Gardner and Cross' pony, Calgary captured its first Chipman Cup since 1925.

Kamloops went home (probably to considerably less fanfare than in 1932) and closed its season in early September with an intra-club handicap tournament. The prize was the Ward Cup, first presented by Frank's wife, "Kenny," a year or two before. The three teams — the "Town," "North River" and "Douglas Lake" — played a nine-chukker round-robin that featured not only club regulars Talbot, Ward, Willes and Hett, but also Daphne Fernie and Ward's daughter, Betty.

The 1934 Strathcona's – (left to right) Captain F.C. Powell, Lieutenant F.E. White, Captain R.E.G. Morton, Lieutenant C.H. Campbell, Major F.M.W. Harvey. The year 1934 was the regiment's finest on the field. The members are posed with their season's haul: the Sheep Creek, Hudson's Bay, Chipman and Calgary Challenge cups.

Also present were two new names: the second generation of the Fulton family to be associated with the club. Fred Fulton, Jr. and his brother Davie were the sons of Frederick Fulton, a long-time Kamloops solicitor and, originally, partner to Cecil Ward in both a legal practice and in forming the original Kamloops Polo Club. Davie Fulton would not appear often for the club, winning a Rhodes Scholarship on his way to continuing the strong political involvement that characterized the family. His father had been a member of parliament and his grandfather was a former provincial premier. Davie himself was a long-time representative in Ottawa and well-regarded federal minister of justice. He served as justice of the B.C. Supreme Court from 1973 to 1981.

At High River, the club returned to its home field and closed the 1933 season with a short series of practice games, designed to get as many players on the field as possible. The *High River Times* had its tongue firmly in its cheek as it reported on a game between "The Wise Old Men" — Ellison Capers, Willie Deane-Freeman, Frank Watt and C.W. Roenisch — and a team of "younger" players, otherwise referred to as "Those who will uphold the gay banner of flaming youth." The sadness of the joke is that the junior players were hardly new to the game. Joe Robertson, Charlie Arnold and the de Foras brothers had all been playing

with the team for several years. They may have been younger than Deane-Freeman and Frank Watt, both of whom began their polo careers well before the war, but, sadly, they were not a sign that High River's youth had suddenly taken up the game.

There was, however, one new player on the field: Clinton W. Roenisch (always known by the nickname "Kink," distinguishing him from his son, Clint, Jr). That September, 1933 pick-up match marked the first mention of a name that would become synonymous not only with the last years of High River polo, but with the Calgary club, too. At this writing, a fine young player named Daniel is the fourth generation to carry the Roenisch name onto the polo field.

Calgary's 1933 Western Canada win came with a cost that was much more than the price of the engraving on the Chipman Cup. Moving play to the comparatively remote Sarcee grounds cost the club several more of its non-playing memberships and total subscriptions for 1933 were just over $100, down from $325 in 1932. The distance to the grounds, the limited draw and the habitually miserable weather made for smaller crowds and the western tournament showed a loss of $85.

With the club already eating steadily into its cash reserve, the new deal with the Polo Club Limited (if and when it was signed) required the club to install a permanent water supply and an irrigation system for the grounds. Even with the City's cooperation, it would be an expensive undertaking.

By the time of the 1934 annual meeting, the club had managed come to an agreement with the Polo Club Limited for the five-year lease of the Chinook grounds. The deal still hinged on the provision of a permanent water supply and since those arrangements had still not been formalized, the season would once again be played at the Sarcee camp.

Kamloops wrote to invite Calgary to play for their Challenge Cup, but the matter

was tabled until the club's plans for the year had been finalized. In the end, Calgary did not travel west. The Interior club began its season with the customary early-April chukkers, although the level of activity (at least as reported by the *Sentinel*) seemed to be diminishing year by year. There was a plan to fence the field and the usual invitations to the public to come and watch the Sunday games but, without a Douglas Lake, a Grande Prairie or a Vancouver to provide the opposition, one suspects that the crowds were small.

Calgary got out on the field with a series of matches for the Hull Cup involving four teams from the club and officers of the LdSH. In High River, the club opened with a June 10th match against the Strathcona's for the Fish Creek Challenge Cup. Substitution rules were relaxed to allow every player to spend at least some time on the field. The Strathcona's won the match by 6-3 in front of a large and enthusiastic crowd, and a visiting Frank Ward played two chukkers in his old scarlet jersey.

One name was significant by its absence. Willie Deane-Freeman was missing his first match since the club's rebirth in 1927. The *High River Times* says that he was "not yet sufficiently recovered from illness to take his place on the field," but it was more serious than that. Willie had been suffering from arthritis and the condition was worsening. The closest he would come to competitive polo in 1934 was as an umpire at the High River club matches and at the Western Canada Tournament. Although he would lead High River again on occasion, his best playing days were well behind him.

The provincial tournament opened at a dry and very dusty Sarcee grounds on August 9th with four teams: Calgary's "Hawks" and "Strollers," the Strathcona's and a team from the Round T Ranch. The ranchers — Roenisch, Capers, Pollard and Fleming — were substituting for High River, which had announced it would not be playing tournament polo in 1934.

Capers had become a strong presence with the High River club, but, without Deane-Freeman and his supporting cast, the Round T lacked experience and dropped their first game to the Hawks by 8-4. Without an injured Harvey, but with the help of Frank White, recently arrived from Montreal, the Strathcona's were an easy winner over the Strollers by 6-1.

A heavy shower just before the finals damped down the dust and improved the conditions immensely. In the consolation final, the Round T managed a 6-5 overtime win in a match marked by a spectacular wreck. Jim Cross' pony tripped over his stick and went down. Two other horses collided behind him and one fell across the prostrate Cross. Although he was shaken up, surprisingly he was not badly hurt.

Having already won the old Fish Creek cup from High River, the Strath's added to their 1934 laurels by taking the Hudson's Bay trophy with a 4-1 win over the Hawks.

Lord Strathcona's Horse was not an aggregation of part-time soldiers. It was regular army with a training regimen that involved much more than parades and polo matches. During Calgary's troubles with its fields at Chinook Park, High River had suggested that it would be pleased to host the Western Canada Tournament. Their offer was declined, not because Calgary was unwilling, but because the Strath's could not be away from their barracks for so long without a better reason than a polo game or two.

Between the provincial and western tournaments, about sixty officers and men of the LdSH headed off across country for their annual manoeuvres. They travelled a long circle through the foothills for ten days, reaching as far south as Pincher Creek, and covering some three hundred miles. As they camped at High River on their return trip, they organized a polo match with the local club (and played a little softball, too). The polo was four-chukkers and the host club managed a 3-2 win, putting at least seven riders on the field in the course of the game. Playing in front of referee Willie Deane-Freeman was his twenty-year-old son Clive, making one of perhaps only two or three appearances in a competitive polo match. In a few years, Clive's younger brother, Desmond, would begin to play regularly, first with High River and then with the Strathcona's.

On Thursday, August 30th, four teams began two days of play for the 1934 Western Canada Championship. Sadly, the Strathcona's, Calgary, High River and Kamloops again represented the sum of the teams available to play for the Chipman Cup. With two games on Thursday, two finals on Saturday and two exhibition matches on Labour Day Monday, the scheduling acknowledged both the need to play as many games as possible and to give the ponies a good deal of rest. No one had a surplus of horses, good or bad.

Reversing its earlier announcement, High River sent a team, although Willie Deane-Freeman was not among the players. Kamloops' shipping expenses were again covered and, even with Frank Ward's legendary free-spending passion for the game, it is unlikely the team would have made the trip without the subsidy. For Calgary, Jim Cross' injuries at the provincial tournament must have been more severe than reported and he would not be playing. Despite their loss to High

River the week before, the Strathcona's, with two trophies already won and Harvey back on the field, were clear favourites to sweep the year's honours.

The cold rain on opening day was more than was needed to keep the dust down, but the games went off before what the papers called "a fair crowd." Kamloops, with four goals from Talbot, beat High River by 8-0, although the score was not really representative of what was reported as a good, fast game despite the wet field. Kamloops' scoring was opened by Peter Lodwick, the son of Nicola and Kamloops regular Geoff. The younger Lodwick and Fred Fulton, Jr. (substituting for an absent Tommy Wilmot) were proof that not all second-generation Interior players were daughters.

Defending champions Calgary, with Francis, Yorath, Adams and Clem Gardner, had nothing for the Strathcona's, who rode to an easy 5-0 win.

In the consolation final, High River lost to Calgary, making 1934 the second year in a row the team had failed to win a game at the tournament. It was another sign of increasingly hard times for the club.

As predicted, the Strath's won the Chipman Cup with victory over Kamloops, but it's unlikely that many of the touts would have predicted such an easy 6-1 win. Showing the results of a good deal of practice, Morton, Campbell, Powell and Harvey shared the scoring and never let Kamloops get organized. However, the press report that the Strath's were "perfectly mounted" would have amused the players. It had been years since they had been able to slip a polo pony or two in with their remounts and were reduced to playing on their chargers, not the most nimble of horses.

The Calgary Polo Club's financial situation continued to deteriorate through 1934 and into 1935. The club had only five playing members and, even though they could not use Chinook Park, they continued to pay the rent, taxes and grounds maintenance. The City managed to provide some horse-drawn water carts (filled from the nearest fire hydrant), allowing the fields to be soaked for over two weeks and the improvement in the turf had been noticeable. The club was beginning to entertain thoughts of playing at least the western championship at Chinook in 1935. Meanwhile, with the cost of watering and a loss on the western tournament, the club's meagre cash reserve continued to shrink.

There was another invitation from Kamloops awaiting the members when they convened their 1935 annual meeting in late April. After electing Jim Cross playing captain (the first the club had named in several years) the matter of Kamloops was left in his hands.

Whether it was a little guilt about the Interior team's four consecutive trips to town without a reciprocal visit or just that they needed to get out on the road for the first time in years, Cross and the other four playing members of the club began to plan an early-June trip across the Divide.

The 1935 Kamloops Challenge Cup Tournament was the first to be held in the Interior for several years and there would be four teams competing. Joining Calgary and their hosts at the beginning of June would be two pick-up teams from the area: the "5th B.C. Horse" and the "Okanagan Black Cats." Their members indicate both were created just for the tournament. The B.C. Horse featured Kamloops' regulars Willes, Fulton and Peter Lodwick, while the Black Cats had Tommy Wilmot and Ellis Talbot.

Calgary's Cross, Gardner, Chambers and Francis proved the strongest at the meeting, though not by much, finally beating Frank Ward and the host team by 6-2 in the final. A couple of days later, Calgary faced a pick-up Interior foursome and was lucky to escape with a 2-1 win.

On the surface at least, High River was in better shape than Calgary at the start of their 1935 season. The club expected to have seventeen members, old and new, on the field for the first practice on May 12th and had already won its first tournament of the year. Earlier in the spring, the club beat Calgary and the Strathcona's at a series of indoor games held in conjunction with the Calgary Horse Show, but the newspapers did not report on the matches and this one brief mention seems to be the sum of indoor polo in southern Alberta. Certainly the indoor game never became a regular feature of the polo season.

Kink Roenisch offered to provide the planks necessary to board the field and the club decided to install a new scoreboard and

Chipman Cup champions, High River, 1936 — (left to right) Fred Scott, Kink Roenisch, Joe Robertson, Jack de Foras.

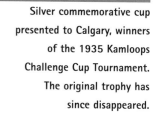

Calgary's Kamloops Challenge Cup winners, 1935 — (left to right) Mike Francis, Jim Cross, Clem Gardner, Llew Chambers.

KAMLOOPS CHALLENGE CUP
L·G·CHAMBERS
CLEM GARDNER
J.B·CROSS
H.W·FRANCIS

Ken Woo

Silver commemorative cup presented to Calgary, winners of the 1935 Kamloops Challenge Cup Tournament. The original trophy has since disappeared.

upgrade the pavilion. Money was still very tight, though, and it would be the players themselves coming out to mow and roll the field. But there would be a return on their investment. The High River Polo Club was to host the 1935 Alberta Provincial Championship.

The event was moved from its traditional mid-July date to allow the Strathcona's to attend and, when the tournament opened on Thursday, August 8th, both High River teams rose to the occasion. The Whites won a close-checking game with Calgary while the Reds had an easier time with the Strathcona's. Harvey had been officially transferred to Winnipeg earlier in the year and his absence from the team's practices and this game was obvious as the LdSH went down by 9-2.

The Saturday finals were drowned out in a day-long heavy rain. The games would have been rescheduled for the Sunday, but the Strathcona's had to be back at their barracks and could not stay to play. The final match

was re-scheduled for August 18th with Calgary and the Strathcona's left to play the consolation game at some future date. There is no evidence to suggest they ever did.

When the provincial final was finally played on August 18th, Charlie Arnold, playing what was probably the game of his career, scored four times for the Whites as they won an exciting 6-4 game over Willie Deane-Freeman and the Reds.

The 1935 Western Canada Championship opened on Saturday, August 31st, with two games scheduled and the finals to be played on Labour Day Monday. Again, Kamloops was in town to face the Strathcona's, High River and Calgary. There was still no one else in the West who could muster a team. There seemed little new in the way of players either. High River had sent Deane-Freeman, Roenisch, Robertson and Arnold, while Calgary was represented by Chambers, Gardner, Cross and Francis. Making the trip from Kamloops were Ward, Talbot, Fulton and Hett. Harvey had managed to be in town from Winnipeg and he would head an LdSH foursome that included Wattsford, Powell and Campbell.

Kamloops, with an aging Frank Ward and no Tommy Wilmot, lost their opening match to the Strath's by a very close 4-3. High River had less trouble with Calgary, winning by 6-2.

The consolation final was the lowest-scoring of all the matches as Calgary held Frank Ward in check and made a pair of goals by Clem Gardner stand up for a 2-1 victory. The Chipman final was close, too, with High River and the Strathcona's going into the sixth chukker tied 2-2 before Charlie Arnold capped his fine tournament play with the winning goal.

While the provincial tournaments made a small profit in 1934 and 1935, the Western Canada Championship was beginning to pile up a serious debt. Nearly $300 worth of red ink had accumulated by the end of 1934 and 1935 added another $40 to the total. These losses, although aggravated by the unpredictable weather, could be accounted for by the continuing $200 annual outlay to bring the Kamloops ponies in for the tournament.

Club secretary Mike Francis summed up the 1935 season in his annual report:

We are slowly but surely eating into our reserves and unless something is done to increase our revenue, either by way of subscriptions or profits from tournaments, the future does not look bright, which when you consider that Alberta was the first district to introduce the game of Polo to the North American Continent, it is indeed sad.

Francis' grasp of the game's history may have been a little shaky, but his appraisal of the club's state at the beginning of 1936 was entirely accurate. And, it was a situation that would only worsen as the season progressed.

Calgary could raise only three playing and seven non-playing memberships during 1936, a number unprecedented since the club was founded in 1890. Although the Chinook Park grounds would again be available for tournament play, there was still no permanent water supply and the bills still had to be paid. Whether Frank Ward had already indicated his Kamloops team would not be coming is not recorded, but there would be no offer to transport their ponies. Ward was not in the chair at the Western Canada Polo Association meeting in 1936 and Kamloops would never again cross the Divide for a polo match.

With no outside competition, the provincial tournament was cancelled in favour of retaining the cachet of the western Canadian championship and its Chipman Cup. Still, only three teams would finally make the draw and Calgary itself would not be among them.

The High River Polo Club did not bother to hold an annual meeting in 1936 and Calgary's minute book shows only one brief meeting on April 21st. At that meeting, along with a vote of thanks to Jim Cross for providing fertilizer over the past two

years, it was suggested that sheep be put onto the grounds to keep that well-fertilized grass under control. Things were faltering.

Outside the western championship, scheduled for the beginning of September, polo seemed to be at a low ebb from High River to Kamloops. The B.C. club did manage a late summer home-and-home series with a team from the town of Ashcroft, about fifty miles to the north. The *Sentinel* was enthusiastic about the game's prospects in that ranch town, but the team, based at the Matier family's old Basque Ranch, would not be heard from again and it was up to Kamloops alone to keep the game alive in the Interior.

Certainly, the biggest event in an otherwise quiet year was the departure of a combined High River-Calgary team to join Kamloops in Spokane, Washington.

The *High River Times* of May 21st covered the news with some enthusiasm:

High River Polo Club will be represented by two players at the North West Polo Tournament to be held in Spokane, starting about June 7. C.R. Arnold and C.W. Roenisch will be joining with Clem Gardner and Jim Cross of Calgary to make up a quartet of players....

This "hands across the line" is the first step in encouraging American teams to visit Calgary and play in the tournaments up here. It will add great interest to provincial tournaments to extend entry to American players, and will also stimulate play.

The *Times* article closed with a clear indication that things were not equally tough for all:

Mr. Roenisch's specially built truck for transporting the mounts was in town the other day, the centre of interest. The truck is equipped to carry six horses comfortably, giving them a pleasant view of the world as they travel.

The *Times* was not entirely correct in suggesting it was the first time an attempt had been made to draw American teams into the Alberta tournaments. Although no Alberta side had gone south for years, Calgary had met some American opposition in Vancouver a few years earlier and a suggestion was made in 1930 that they might be invited to come north to Alberta. The idea was first rejected by the western Canadian teams but, in 1931, the secretary of the Western Canada Polo Association was instructed to write to the American Polo Association "with a view to trying to attract American teams to the tournaments." Now, in 1936, it seemed the U.S. Northwest held the only hope for widening the competition for the pitifully small pool of Canadian clubs.

The Spokane tournament, billed as the Northwestern International, is the first indication in the western Canadian press that the game was again alive and well in Spokane. The club, which had hosted the earliest Lane Cup matches to so much promise, had gone quiet in the early 1920s. Spokane had never appeared at the Northwestern Championship in all the years it was a fixture at the Vancouver club and no Alberta team had played them since North Fork retired from the field in 1919. Indeed, after Vancouver's demise at the end of the 1931 season, no names had been engraved on the Lane Cup.

Although the Canadian papers had taken no notice and no Canadian teams had participated, the Northwestern International had in fact been revived in the mid-1930s with a Pacific Northwest-only flavour and the Spokane "Blues" went into the 1936 tournament as defending champions.

The tournament was scheduled to run for a full twelve days with the Blues defending against five teams: the Spokane "Reds," Calgary, Kamloops, Seattle and Toppenish, Washington. Boise, Idaho had been announced, too, but they failed to appear.

Both Canadian teams played well throughout as Kamloops' Ward, Wilmot, Talbot and Lang managed two victories before bowing to Calgary in the semifinal. Calgary lost its first-round match to Toppenish after two overtime periods but then moved smoothly through to the final where they again faced the ranchers from the Yakima Valley. In the final, it was Toppenish over Calgary again, this time by a more decisive 6-2. Clem Gardner's second injury of the tournament was credited with throwing off their team play and giving Toppenish an easier time of it.

The 1936 Lane Cup Tournament was a great success for Calgary's beleaguered squad but, more important, it reforged Alberta's links with the Pacific Northwest. Those links, first established just before the Great War, would prove invaluable as the second era of western Canadian polo moved toward its conclusion.

Cross and Gardner's extended trip to Spokane and the fact that the Strathcona's were off on manoeuvres in Saskatchewan for the better part of a month meant that there was almost no polo played in Calgary during the 1936 season. The same seems true for High River without Roenisch and Arnold.

The smallest Western Canada tournament in recent memory opened at the Chinook grounds on September 3rd. With only three teams present, the event would be a three-day round robin.

A weakened Strathcona's opened against the Round T. The team was, in fact, a mix of High River and Calgary that included Ellison Capers, Willie Deane-Freeman, Jim Cross and Mike Francis. The Strathcona's, without Harvey, kept the match closer than might have been expected, but lost 6-4 as Cross scored four for the Round T.

The LdSH went back on the field the next day to face High River and again they kept the score close, losing to Roenisch, Robertson, Fred Scott and Jack de Foras by only 4-3. That left the Round T and High River to play for the western championship.

Although the Round T went out to an early lead, High River came back in the third chukker and then simply rode away in the second half to post an 8-4 win and retain possession of the Chipman Cup.

Sadly, the loss to High River was the last game played by the Strathcona's Captain Frank Powell. A regular with the team almost since its post-war revival and certainly its most prolific scorer, Powell was killed in a riding accident on September 30th, 1936.

The 1936 western championship marked the first tournament appearance for lawyer and soldier James Frederick Scott. He would emerge as a skilled regular with both High River and Calgary and became the fourth member of the Alberta team that swept the 1938 Vancouver tournament.

Scott was born in Ontario in 1892 and came west in 1911 to homestead with his brother, Bert, west of Alsask, Alberta. The brothers both joined up in 1914 and Bert was killed at Courcelette in 1916. Fred served for several months with the Royal Flying Corps and then transferred to the 50th Battalion before returning to Calgary at war's end.

Fred Scott with the
Royal Flying Corps, 1916.

He established his law practice in Calgary and joined the 15th Canadian Light Horse as a lieutenant. By 1935, he was in command. When the 15th was amalgamated with other regiments to re-form the 15th Alberta Light Horse, he was again given command. In 1939, he led the Calgary Highlanders overseas and, while he returned to his law practice and to the Calgary Polo Club after the war, he played only a few more years before retiring from the field.

The 1936 tournament showed a small loss and then, adding a final insult to what had been the worst ever season for western Canadian polo, a December storm blew down the fence between the field and the pasture, adding the cost of repairs to an already substantial Calgary deficit.

While Alberta polo was holding on by the skin of its teeth, there was life again on the West Coast. Rumours of a revival in Vancouver and Victoria had been circulating since the early part of the decade, but they had come to nothing until about 1936 when several teams suddenly appeared almost simultaneously.

Clarry Wallace had never lost his great love for the game and was largely responsible for bringing polo back to Vancouver. Almost invariably, he teamed with his four sons, Blake, Philip, Dick and David. At about the same time, several other players gathered under the umbrella of the Lion's Gate Riding and Polo Club. This club was based at the Vancouver Riding Academy, operated by the recently arrived Cripps brothers. Herb Cripps became the manager of the club and players could rent ponies from the academy. The teams played some games at Brighouse, but also at other venues around the area. They also played indoors at Exhibition Place. Only the senior Wallace and one or two other players seem to have had any direct connection to the old Vancouver club.

What caused the rebirth of interest in a game that had enjoyed only sporadic popularity on Vancouver Island since the mid-1890s is not clear, but between 1936 and 1940, there were as many as seven teams active in club and tournament play. The Victoria club called itself "The Centaurs" and was associated with the Victoria Riding Academy. The club could manage to field as many as three teams for intra-club play, including Jack Boorman, Geoff Edgelow, Gerry Aitken and George Tyson, the father of Canadian music legend, Ian. Retired Strathcona's Captain H.R. Rebitt also came out to play on occasion.

The Centaurs' competition came from two Esquimalt teams and another pair from Duncan, including the 62nd Field Artillery Battery which featured a mix of military and civilian players. One of the Esquimalt teams was led by Major A.G. Piddington

while the other was based at a local riding stable operated by Brudenell Deane-Freeman, youngest brother of Millarville greats Justin and Willie.

Victoria sportsman Horace Beer, owner of a popular local eatery called the Poodle Dog Café, put up a trophy and several tournaments were held in the years leading up to the war. There was an Island Championship in 1938 and the new Vancouver club sent teams to try for the Beer trophy, managing to carry it home in both 1938 and 1939.

While there was new life on the coast, the 1937 Kamloops polo season was almost non-existent. The team was out for its first practices and club matches in mid-April, but there was no sign they would be travelling to the coast or that they would be hosting any visitors.

Still, the ageless Frank Ward remained active. In August, he took Kay Lang, Ellis Talbot and his son, Pat, down to Toppenish to try again for the Northwestern International. They faced the defending champions and teams from Spokane and Yakima. Kamloops was 1-1 after the first two games and Ward had been unceremoniously "dumped in a tulle swamp" when "Foxtrot," his twenty-one-year-old pony, jumped the sideboards. The *Sentinel* did not report the final results of the tournament.

The Prairie game could not have survived another year like 1936 and, in fact, 1937 opened on a much more optimistic note. As it was with the nation at large, the worst of the Great Depression was over. With Calgary back at Chinook Park, the Strathcona's could rest their worn-out Sarcee field, using it only for a little stick-and-ball practice. Without doubt, the Sarcee ground could not have continued to support the two clubs that had come to rely on it while the Chinook fields were rehabilitated, but its very existence in those crucial years may have saved the Calgary club from extinction.

The Strathcona's also managed to come up with several new players for 1937. They were present at the Calgary annual meeting at the end of April and their numbers swelled the playing member roster of the club to nine from the three of a year before. Non-playing memberships were up, too, a direct result of the return to Chinook Park.

It had become obvious to the members that the key to saving the game of polo was not only to find new players, but to make sure those beginners had as much time on the field as possible. Given that most of them would be lucky to possess more than a single pony, the club introduced a new sliding scale of membership fees. It remained at $25 for players with three or more ponies, but dropped to $15 and $10 for those with only two or one mounts. This new approach to a simpler, more economical game was also extended to the Western Canada Tournament.

A 1937 polo report in *The Strathconian,* the LdSH's regimental magazine, provided a detailed look into the new approach to the game:

Each Saturday afternoon saw anything from six to nine chukkers, and on most occasions the Calgary Club found two teams and the Regiment one team. These teams in most cases consisted of six players, two of whom stood down as required and a round robin of everybody playing everybody three chukkers was the order of the day.

In the 1937 western tournament, the playing captains all agreed to continue to put as many men in the games as possible. As a result, the usual substitution rules were dropped and the tournament opened as a round-robin with each of the five teams using as many as six players in the games.

The Strathcona's had Gianelli, Fred Vokes and Ronnie Morton back with the club and they were matched with three young lieutenants — Art McKibbin, John Bingham and Gerry Chubb — who had little or no experience with tournament polo.

Calgary's two teams, the "Canaries" and the "Blues," sent out a total of ten players ranging in skill from established members Cross, Yorath, Francis and Gardner, to new faces Doug Forrest, Jim Williams and Glen MacDougall.

Of the new players, only Jim Williams would stay in the game. Brought into the club by his brother-in-law, Dennis Yorath, he played regularly until 1940 when he joined the Calgary Highlanders. Williams was badly wounded overseas and returned to Alberta where he finished out the war as an instructor at Currie Barracks. He was present at the first post-war meetings of the club in 1945 and, until he gave up the game in the early 1960s, he remained a steady performer on the field and a constant presence in any number of administrative positions.

High River managed to send two teams for the first time in a while. The "Whites" included Reg Pollard, Ellison Capers and his son, Ellison Jr., Jack de Foras and Kink Roenisch while the "Pinks" featured Charlie Arnold, Clint Roenisch, Joe Robertson and a Deane-Freeman, but it was not Willie.

Although re-elected team captain for 1937, Willie Deane-Freeman's playing career was over. With his arthritis steadily worsening, his appearance in the 1936 Chipman Cup final had proved to be his last. On his retirement, southern Alberta polo lost its last tenuous connection to the pre-war era.

Willie's place on the High River team was taken by his son, Desmond, a young man just beginning a polo career that would carry the family name well into the second half of the century.

With all the new players and the new round-robin format, the results of the 1937 Chipman Cup matches were confusing at best. Suffice to say that, when the three days of preliminaries were over, the High River Whites rode out on day four to play the Pinks in the final, assuring High River of another western championship.

Calgary's 1938 multiple cup winners – (left to right) C.W. Roenisch, Clem Gardner, Jim Cross and Fred Scott. In one of Calgary's best seasons ever, the team captured the Lane trophy, the B.C. and Kamloops Challenge cups and Chipman Cup.

The game was close as the Pinks went out to a 2-goal lead at the half and then watched as the Whites came back steadily to tie the score in the fifth and score the winner in the final minutes for a 4-3 win.

With its new memberships and a return to Chinook Park for the whole season, the Calgary Polo Club seemed to have stopped its decline. Even the 1937 western tournament did not lose money, actually turning a profit of sixty-one cents. The club was not nearly as strong as it needed to be, but its survival, at least, seemed to be assured.

High River's future, however, was not nearly so certain. The Depression had hit the community hard, robbing its narrow, land-based economy of much of its value and costing many the farms and ranches they had worked so hard to secure for their own, and their children's, future. The High River Polo Club was in serious jeopardy, too.

The land on which the club sat had been acquired in the same manner as had Calgary's Chinook Park. A group of local investors had purchased the one hundred twenty-three shares (at $10 each) of the High River Polo Club Limited in 1904. Like the shareholders in Calgary's Polo Club Limited, the investors were a group of significant local landowners and town professionals. Some, like George Ross, F.R. Pike and Herb Millar were polo payers, too, but many were not.

The capital raised had gone to buy land "for the purpose of playing polo or any other outdoor game or recreation." Even during the nearly thirteen years when polo was not being played on the grounds, the taxes were paid and the field was there when the club resumed activity in 1927.

Over the years, though, many of the original shareholders had moved or died or otherwise disappeared. The company's charter was close to being revoked yet it was nearly impossible to muster a quorum of the shareholders to make any sort of decision on the company's future.

The matter was first raised at the club's annual meeting in 1934. Secretary F.L. Watt was requested to look into the process by which title to the grounds could be acquired by the club itself. The man he wrote to for advice was Herbert Eckford.

The former proprietor of what had become the Round T had not lived in High River since selling out in 1914 but he had obviously retained a paternal interest in the club he had been instrumental in founding forty years earlier. Eckford and his wife had each purchased ten shares in the new limited company back in 1904 and, as the Depression deepened, they had taken responsibility for ensuring the club's survival. In addition to paying the taxes, Eckford had been buying up the company's shares wherever he could find them.

By 1936, he and his wife owned forty-nine shares and sent them to the High River Polo Club to do with as they saw fit. The Eckfords' shares, when taken together with those still held in the town, were enough to allow the club to save its grounds.

In the end, the High River Polo Club Limited surrendered its charter and control of the land was transferred to a group of trustees that included Frank Watt, Jim Cross, C.W. Roenisch and Charlie Arnold. For the time being, at least, the High River Polo Club would have a place to play.

Interestingly, at about the same time Eckford also sent his shares in Calgary's Polo Club Limited to the Calgary polo club, giving them at least a little more clout in what was a sometimes difficult relationship with the owners of their grounds.

Calgary's membership numbers for 1938 showed a small increase, including some new revenue from the officers of the Lord Strathcona's now also playing at Chinook, but there were still only five Calgary players with more than two ponies at their disposal.

Again in 1938, with no prospect of outside teams coming in for the Western Canada Tournament, there would be no Alberta Provincial Championship and, in general, polo news is hard to find. However, there was one event that drew the attention of the press. With Vancouver back on the field again, a combined High River-Calgary team made the long trip out to the coast to play for at least three major pieces of silverware. The team was Jim Cross, Clem Gardner, Fred Scott and Kink Roenisch, with Kink's son, Clint, going along as a spare.

Beginning at the end of August, the tournament would feature five teams, including two from Vancouver and visitors from Seattle, Calgary and Grande Prairie (by then known officially as Westwold, although the area's polo players never acknowledged that unpopular fact). There would also be a gymkhana and a major light and heavy horse show at Hastings Park.

The tournament was the highlight of a "Polo Week" celebration that rivalled the grand social swirls of a decade earlier. Together with visits to the horse show, the visiting players were to be treated to dinners at the Hotel Vancouver and the Jericho Country Club and a cruise up Howe Sound on Clarry Wallace's yacht, Ethelyne.

The matches were to be held at Brighouse Park under the sponsorship of the Lion's Gate Riding and Polo Club. Playing alongside the president of the club, Colonel A.T. MacLean, were Herb Cripps, Charles Wills and John Whittle. They would ride out as "Vancouver B," while the Wallace family was designated as the "A" side.

Seattle put on a much better performance than it had in past visits, beating Grande Prairie on opening day, but the biggest surprise of the week was the dismal performance of both Vancouver teams. The "A" side was drubbed by Calgary 15-1 and the "B" team looked only a little better in losing to Grande Prairie by 7-2. The tournament final matched Grande Prairie and Calgary and, in a game that cost Pat Talbot one of his best ponies, Clint Roenisch scored three goals, leading Calgary to a close 4-3 victory.

Calgary's win garnered them three major pieces of British Columbia silverware. The team was declared winners of both the Lane Cup and the B.C. Challenge Cup and, it seems, the Kamloops Challenge Cup as well.

This last prize was not reported in the Vancouver or Kamloops press, but a miniature of the Kamloops Challenge Cup itself lists the same four Calgary names as the other cups, together with a score of 4-3. There is no evidence that Calgary stopped off for a match in Kamloops on either the outward or homeward leg of their trip (indeed, the timing of this tournament and the start of the Western Canada would have prevented any stopovers). Perhaps Frank Ward, knowing that there would be no Kamloops tournament in 1938, took the cup along to add to the excitement.

Back in Alberta, the 1938 Chipman Cup Tournament drew only four teams: Calgary, High River, the

LdSH and a group called the "Wanderers," a catchall mostly for younger Calgary players and any extra Strathcona's. Eight names were listed on the Wanderers' roster and as many as six of them would appear during each game. Calgary sent out the same team that had won in Vancouver.

The inexperience of the Wanderers showed immediately. Despite the presence of Mike Francis and the Strath's Morton, they went down to Calgary by 11-1 in the opening round. The Strathcona's, with Des Deane-Freeman, Norman Gianelli, John Bingham and Ralph Richmond, did better against High River, but Clint Roenisch, de Foras, Robertson and Arnold had a 4-0 lead going into the second half and, despite being outscored in the final chukkers, managed a 6-3 win.

Play was washed out on day two, pushing the second round back to Friday, September 9th, but the rest did not help either the Wanderers or the Strathcona's as favourites High River and Calgary went into the final with easy wins.

The LdSH took Saturday's consolation final by 11-4, while Calgary, despite an injury to Clem Gardner and at least one serious pileup, defeated High River by 8-4 to break that team's three-year hold on the Chipman Cup.

As it had been twenty-five years before, so it was in 1939 that western Canadian polo seemed poised for a great regeneration at the very moment events in the larger world were conspiring to stop it in its tracks. The game was alive again in Vancouver and on the Island while, in the Interior, Kamloops once again could count on some outside opposition to supplement its meagre diet of intra-club play. In Calgary, membership was holding steady and the Chinook match ground was in good playable condition (though the practice field was still a little rough). While the

Courtesy of the Calgary Sun

Strathcona's had lost many of their most experienced players, the regiment could still field a sound team, as could High River.

Once again, after a three-year hiatus, there would be a provincial championship tournament in 1939 (to be played at High River) and, most important of all, there would be teams from outside Alberta coming to Calgary to play for the Chipman Cup.

At its annual meeting in early May, Calgary was talking about fielding up to three teams for the season. The "A" team would comprise the same players who had gone to the coast in 1938, but they would have the right to borrow from the other two teams either to find replacements or just to try them out, ensuring that the best foursome was always available. The other two teams, each with five or six players (if that number was available), would remain together for the season under their own captains encouraging them to develop a better sense of team play.

The Polo Club Limited was offering a new two-year lease agreement and Jim Williams was proposing a drive to recruit new members. A new publicity committee was created and the grounds and playing committees were instructed to start regular fortnightly meetings. With paid subscriptions pushing the $500 mark, the new feeling of optimism was palpable.

Out in Victoria, the 1939 season got underway at the end of May. Sadly, as it had in 1913-14, the area was showing signs of a

strong resurgence of polo at the very worst moment. The tournament, held at The Willows racetrack (now Carnarvon Park), is commonly said to have been played before a visiting King George VI and Queen Elizabeth, but the royal party had already left the city by the time the first matches were underway.

Two teams from the host club were joined by Island foursomes from Esquimalt, Cowichan and the 62nd Battery of the Royal Canadian Artillery based at Duncan. The Wallace family was there, as was an Interior team from the Falkland Ranch. This latter aggregation was yet another cover for Tommy Wilmot and Frank Ward.

The Wallaces and Falkland soon showed themselves to be the class of the field, leaving the other teams to play for the consolation prize. That second series victory went to the Artillery by 5-0 over an Esquimalt team featuring two names that would have been familiar to every Alberta polo player. Joining Major Piddington and his daughter, Sylvia, were Alec Landale and Brudenell Deane-Freeman.

Clarry Wallace and his sons beat the Falkland Ranch by 6-3 in the final, taking possession of the Horace Beer Trophy and ending the brief renaissance of Vancouver Island polo. But the final game marked more than just the end of the second era of West Coast polo. It was also the last serious tournament for Tommy Wilmot, closing a storied career that stretched back to before the Great War.

It was Frank Ward's last game, too. His great Douglas Lake Ranch would be sold soon after and Ward would retire to the West Coast to live out his remaining years.

Victoria continued play into 1940 and even managed an indoor tournament with two teams from Victoria and two from Vancouver in March of that year, but the war finally caught up with the game and polo disappeared from Vancouver Island until the early 1960s.

Back on the Prairies, the 1939 Alberta Provincial Championship was held at the High River Polo Club on Saturday and Sunday, August 12th and 13th. Showing remarkable depth, the Strathcona's were just one player short of sending two full teams to play against High River and Calgary. Needing Calgary's John Ballachey to fill out their "B" side, the regiment had probably stretched itself a little thin and both teams lost their Saturday matches.

The "A" side of Des Deane-Freeman, McKibbin, Bingham and Chubb drew High River in the opening game and Arnold, Robertson, Kink and Clint Roenisch were simply too strong, posting a 6-2 win. The Strath's "B" side should have done better. Joining Ballachey were veteran players Morton, Campbell and Vokes and the team managed to keep it close against a Calgary foursome of Cross, Scott, Williams and John Ballachey's brother, Alec. Calgary broke open a tight match with two goals by Jim Cross in the fifth chukker to take a 5-3 victory and go through to the final.

The Strathcona's two sides met in the consolation match, with the "A" team scoring a victory for youth over experience by four goals to one. It is interesting to speculate about the tournament result had the regiment simply fielded its best foursome. They obviously opted to fill out the draw rather than try for the title and, while it was the sporting thing to do, it probably cost them their final chance at a provincial championship.

In Sunday's match for the Hudson's Bay trophy and provincial polo supremacy, High River continued its strong team play, coming back from a 2-1 deficit to beat Calgary handily by 7-2.

The *High River Times* was ecstatic about the whole event:

————◦❦❖◦————

Ideal weather favored the success of this provincial event which drew a great gallery of spectators from far and near. Calgarians by the score attended on both days, enjoying the dashing performance of men and mounts, and enjoying also the pleasant social atmosphere which centred round the clubhouse. Pekisko and other parts of the foothills were well represented as well as adjacent towns. Visitors were present from Montreal, Vancouver, Winnipeg and other distant cities.

————◦❦❖◦————

It is good to know that the weekend was such a success, reminiscent of the early days when the people of High River closed their businesses on game days and came out in droves to see what they knew was the best polo team in Canada. The 1939 Provincial Championship was the last major tournament ever played at the High River Polo Club.

Tuesday, September 5th saw the first game in what would be the largest Western Canada championship tournament since 1928. High River was there, along with the Strathcona's and three Calgary teams. Vancouver, with both "A" and "B" sides, was back

in town for the first time since their two straight Chipman Cup wins in 1927 and 1928. The eighth entry was from Toppenish, Washington and they would have been familiar to the Alberta players from their 1936 trip to Spokane. In fact, without the presence of so many out-of-town teams, it is unlikely that the tournament would have been held at all.

Everyone had known for some time that war was imminent and probably inevitable. While the Lord Strathcona's, as part of the Permanent Force, would certainly be involved, every western polo club counted the officers of various militia regiments among its members. Calgary's Lieutenant-Colonel Fred Scott, then commanding the 15th Alberta Light Horse, was one of the first to be "warned for service." During an intra-club match in mid-August, the district officer commanding had walked across the field and told Scott that he was to take command of the Calgary Highlanders. On August 25th, some Calgary militia were called out to guard some vulnerable sites and the public knew that the situation was serious.

Vancouver's David Wallace remembers vividly that he and his brothers were waiting to check in to their Calgary hotel when the radio at the front desk announced that Germany had invaded Poland. The last faint hope for peace was gone. The Calgary Highlanders were mobilized and the officers and men of the 15th Light Horse would be joining them. Nevertheless, Fred Scott managed to take his place with Calgary "A."

Before a small crowd on a slippery, rain-soaked field, Calgary "A" opened play with an easy 13-1 win over Vancouver "B." The second game of the day was pushed ahead to Wednesday due to the dangerous condition of the field.

The weather was much better on day two as Vancouver "A" won its postponed match from Calgary "B" by 12-0 and High River took Calgary "C" by 13-2. Toppenish and the Strathcona's played the only close match of the opening round. Both teams had plenty of scoring chances, but Toppenish took better advantage of theirs and posted a 6-3 win. Once again, the luck of the opening draw more than the quality of their team was dictating the Strathcona's chances for the title. And, it was clear from the first-round games that, while there were plenty of players at the tournament, the level of their experience ranged wildly.

Calgary "A" was three-quarters of the defending Western Canada and Lane Cup championship team, with Jim Williams replacing Kink Roenisch who had elected to play with his son for High River. Joining the Roenisches were Robertson and Arnold, while the Strathcona's fielded what should have been a fine foursome of Deane-Freeman, Bingham, Vokes and Chubb. Calgary's

"B" and "C" squads represented a mix of senior players like Yorath, Francis and the Strath's Bradbrooke, supported by such relative newcomers as Alec Ballachey, Cam Corbet and Geoff Parker.

Vancouver "A," the defending B.C. provincial champions, was a family affair. Clarry Wallace had brought his four sons, ranging in age from sixteen to early twenties. Vancouver "B" were father and son John and Jack Whittle, supported by Jack Patterson and Herb Cripps.

As always, in a now fully motorized age, the horses played a large part in deciding the outcome of the tournament. Running simultaneously with the polo tournament was the Calgary Fall Light Horse Show and several players took the opportunity to enter the competitions. From a total of forty-eight entries in the light and heavy polo pony judging, Toppenish and Vancouver ponies took the first four places in each category. Such quality would tell as the tournament progressed.

With the tournament divided between the very good and the indifferent (with the Strath's caught somewhere in between), the second-round games became much tighter. In the championship series, it took Vancouver "A" two overtime chukkers to beat Calgary "A" by 4-3. The winning goal was scored by young sixteen-year-old David Wallace, substituting for his injured brother, Dick. Toppenish barely got past High River, 6-5, scoring the winner after the bell had rung to end the first overtime chukker.

The consolation series saw Vancouver "B" over Calgary "B" by 5-4, while the LdSH easily beat Calgary "C" by 10-2. In the final, the Strath's had no trouble with Vancouver "B," winning by 7-1 on the strength of Des Deane-Freeman's four goals.

With a solid win in what would be their last match after three decades of top-flight polo, Lord Strathcona's Horse were again left to wonder what might have happened had the first-round draw gone in their favour.

Saturday's championship final was to be a three-trophy affair. In addition to the Chipman Cup, the Thaddeus Lane Cup, symbolic of the Northwestern polo championship, would also be going to the winners. The third prize to be presented was the venerable Calgary Challenge Cup. The cup had not been mentioned in the press or in the Calgary club minutes since well before the First World War, but it had always been in play. In every year from 1927 to 1939, the shields on the trophy show the same names as the winners of the Western Canada Championship.

The Vancouver-Toppenish final was closer than the 9-4 score would indicate. Playing before the first decent-sized crowd of the tournament, the Americans went out to a 3-0 lead in the first chukker and added three unanswered goals in the final period, but the middle periods of the match were closely fought. Vancouver was still without Dick Wallace and their ponies, previously as good as any in the tournament, were tired out by the end of the fifth chukker.

On Sunday, September 10th, 1939, the day after the Strathcona's Lieutenant-Colonel Fred Harvey presented all the silverware, Canada's official declaration of war finally came. ▓

The Hudson's Bay Company Trophy – Symbolic of Alberta provincial polo supremacy, the sterling silver cup was presented nine times between 1928 and 1939. In addition to the Pirates' improbable victory in 1931, High River captured the trophy six times and the Strathcona's twice.

THE
THIRD
ERA

CHAPTER 11

ON THE 29TH DAY of March, 1945, seven members of the Calgary Polo Club sat down for lunch at the old Ranchmen's Club. It was their first meeting in nearly five years and, whether or not they realized it at the time, it was a meeting of the sole surviving polo club in Canada.

In his annual financial report for 1939, Mike Francis had delivered good news and bad news. The blackest depths of the Depression had passed and there was renewed interest in the club. There were some fourteen playing members, with six stabling three or more ponies. Together with subscriptions from the sixteen non-playing members and the Strathcona's, the total take for the year was approaching $500, up nearly $150 from 1938 and more than $200 over 1937's quiet year.

The bad news was that, due to the unfortunate weather and uncertainty surrounding the events in Europe and Ottawa, the Western Canada Championship had lost $285, bringing the tournament's total deficit to over $600. With only $9.82 in the bank and other debts of over $150, Francis saw the need to call a special meeting to deal with the perennial problem of finances. He made his own feelings on the subject known in his report:

It had always been the practice for this club to finance and run the Western Canada Tournament, although strictly speaking there is no reason why we should, except that the tournament is generally held on our grounds.

(left to right) Gordon Sellar, Clint Roenisch, Mike Francis and Jim Williams, Chinook Park, 1949.

Obviously, the tournament which the club had worked so hard to see permanently established in Calgary after the first war had become a mixed blessing. No one could have anticipated the devastating effects of the Depression or that Calgary would become the only city, with the possible exception of Vancouver, that could afford to fund the tournament. Still, the club could look back over the past decade and realize that, without its generosity, the Chipman Cup matches, the western championship and possibly the very game of polo itself, would long since have disappeared from the Canadian West.

When the war broke out in 1939, western Canadian polo did not suffer the sudden collapse of 1914. The first year of "phony war" let Calgary hold its regular organizational meeting on May 1st, 1940 (albeit two months later than usual), but the club clearly understood it would not be an easy year.

While the word "war" does not appear in the minutes (the secretary apparently preferring such euphemisms as "circumstances" or "the European situation"), its reality is everywhere on the page. There was a proposal to fix the annual subscription at $25, regardless of how many ponies a member might have, and the Polo Club Limited was asked to waive its $50 annual rental fee. While a slate of officers, a grounds and a play committee were elected as usual, the secretary was instructed to send a questionnaire to all members in an attempt to determine exactly who might be ready for play.

The results of the questionnaire could not have been encouraging and, on August 23rd, the executive met again to put the club into a holding pattern. There would be a payment to the Polo Club Limited for the year 1940 only and a promise to "consider" paying the taxes on the property for as long as the war lasted. Members would be asked to pay fifty per cent of their normal subscription in return for a share of the club's supply of sticks (presumably to allow some informal practice) and a "committee of one" was struck to "...look into the prospects of Polo next year."

Before adjourning what would prove to be its last meeting for nearly five years, the Calgary Polo Club donated its supply of balls to High River. It was a sign that at least a few players were determined to carry on.

Out on Vancouver Island, after the 1939 tournament, the game moved indoors and held on until the next spring. In March, 1940, there was a three-a-side tournament at The Willows featuring two teams from Vancouver (including the Wallaces) and two from Victoria but a hoped-for summer season never materialized.

The request for Calgary's supply of balls would have come from Kink Roenisch and the remaining members of the High River Polo Club. They, at least, had every intention of continuing with their weekend matches.

While the newspapers clearly had other things on their minds, the *High River Times* did try to keep its readers up to date on happenings at the polo grounds. Throughout the early 1940s, there were brief, but regular accounts of summer Saturday afternoon matches among players whose names had been familiar for years.

Kink Roenisch played on, as did his three sons, Clint, Davis and Harold. Old High River captain Bill Holmes was well into his fourth decade of competitive polo, while Jack de Foras, Joe Robertson and Charlie Arnold had been part of the team since its 1927 revival. Jim Cross, whose Okotoks ranch was as close to High River as it was to Calgary, came down regularly and there were the occasional guests, too. Flying Officer Clive Deane-Freeman rode out once or twice in 1943, taking a break from his pilot training duties at the Vulcan Flying School just east of town.

Despite the fact that Roenisch's barn burned in September, 1942 (it cost him no ponies, but most of his tack, saddles and sticks were lost), High River polo continued until 1944 when it finally disappeared from public notice.

The continuing efforts of High River, Calgary and Victoria notwithstanding, Canada's declaration of war in 1939 effectively closed the second era of polo in the Canadian West. As it had been in 1918, only the clarity of hindsight reveals the irreparable damage the Second World War inflicted on the western game.

In Alberta, Lord Strathcona's Horse (Royal Canadians) had gone off to fight again, but this time, while the regiment would come back to its home at Sarcee, there would never again be a Strathcona's polo team.

High River had tried to keep the game alive, but its decades-long tradition of great cowboy polo had long been living on borrowed time when V-E Day finally came.

In British Columbia, the Kamloops club had folded in 1939, never to be revived, and it would be well into the 1980s before anyone in the Interior would see another polo game. After 1940, polo would not be played again on Vancouver Island for more than twenty years and, although the game came back to Vancouver in 1953, it was at a new grounds with new players and precious few connections to the old club.

The members of the Calgary Polo Club held three organizational meetings in the spring of 1945, taking stock of what they had mothballed in 1940 and methodically appraising their prospects for the new era.

There was less than $100 in the bank and the club's main "asset" was the more than $600 it was owed by the Western Canada Polo Association, a debt it could never expect to recover. The Polo Club Limited was willing to allow the club to use Chinook Park in return for the usual payment of taxes, repairs and maintenance, but the main field was utterly unplayable.

Equipment was also presenting problems. While the club had obtained a supply of new balls from the United States and sticks were said to be in stock at a Calgary sporting goods store, proper helmets and spurs were simply unavailable. One of the members agreed to try to obtain some army surplus headgear while another was sent off to examine the suitability of using miners' helmets.

Subscriptions were set at the sliding pre-war scale of $25 for those with three or more ponies down to $5 for single, non-playing members and there was a determined effort to bring new players into the club.

Gordon Sellar (left) and "Funny" Gregg, Chinook Park, 1949.

Courtesy of Gordon Sellar

As it had been after the Great War, the rebirth of the Calgary Polo Club in 1945 was driven by the surviving members of the previous era. Long-time secretary-treasurer Mike Francis, Jim Williams, Kink Roenisch, Dennis Yorath and Jim Cross were all anxious to see the game revived. Clem Gardner and Llew Chambers turned out to lend their support, too, but at sixty years of age, their playing days were all but over. Further cementing their links to the previous era, the club asked the Strathcona's great leader (on and off the polo field), Brigadier Fred Harvey, to accept the position of honorary president.

By early June, the recruiting drive had brought eighteen paid-up and prospective members to the

third meeting. Six of them were young women, the first to be seen since the late 1920s.

The issue of women players had been discussed at the first organizational meeting, a sure sign that the matter had been raised by some prospective new members. It was agreed that there would be a women's playing membership (set at $5 per year) and that the grounds could be made available for them to play, but "...not necessarily when senior members are playing." When it was decided to put the Hull Cup back into play in early June, the ladies were offered three chukkers worth of time between breaks in the main event, but no further provisions were made for them.

How long women's polo continued in those early post-war years is not certain but, in 1946, the club passed the following resolution:

...it was decided that the ladies should form their own committee and arrange games to be played either after the regular men's games or on a day that would be suitable to them. It was also decided that the regular Saturday afternoon games should not be mixed.

It may well have been that the senior members felt they had enough on their plate just trying to bring the field and the other facilities back up to scratch without the added problem of rebuilding the women's locker room that had been removed in 1930. Whatever the reasons, the 1946 resolution marks the last mention of women's polo in the club minutes for many seasons.

For the next couple of years, life at the Calgary Polo Club was very much a matter of consolidation rather than development. The main field at Chinook Park remained a serious problem and the minutes record a steady stream of annoyances, especially with molehills and gopher burrows. The members were often tapped to flatten the hills and young boys were promised a bounty of five or ten cents for each mole they could capture. For several seasons, the club attempted to find anywhere up to thirty sheep to put out on the grounds in lieu of the cost of mowing. At least twice, the club expressed its thanks to Jim Cross for his donation of sufficient funds to level and seed the main field. They would not be the only instances that Cross' generosity helped pull the club through some very tough times.

Subscriptions for the years 1945-48 had grown slowly, although several of the new members apparently did not take to the game, dropping off the list after only a season or two. Most of the growth in memberships was certainly due to an increasing number of non-playing, or "social," memberships. Nevertheless, by the end of 1948, the club's income and expenses were in balance. Acknowledging the new realities of the third era, the $600 debt from the Western Canada tournaments of the 1930s was finally written off.

In 1949, after four years of consolidation and isolation, Calgary began to hunt for some sign that it was not entirely alone. How far afield the enquiries went is not recorded, but the only response came from eastern Washington state.

When the ranchers from the Yakima Valley community of Toppenish got back onto their field is not known, but the Yakima club joined the United States Polo Association in 1949, followed by Spokane who joined (or, probably, rejoined) in 1950. It may well have been the contact from Calgary that provided the catalyst. Winners of the Chipman, the Lane and the Challenge Cup at the 1939 Calgary tournament, Toppenish agreed to come north in late July to defend their Western Canada title. Calgary, in turn, promised to join in a Northwestern International Tournament in Washington at the end of August.

A fortnight before the tournament, Calgary warmed up with a series of Saturday chukkers for the Hull Cup (the old club championship trophy) and the fact that the club could field four teams, albeit for only a period or two each, spoke well for the state of the game in Calgary at least.

The Hull Cup game was a further demonstration that southern Alberta's tradition of family polo was still healthy. Joining second-generation leader Jim Cross were his son, Donald, and his nephew, David Dover. Barney Willans' grandfather, Norman, had played for Millarville in the early years and his father, Trevor, was a Calgary regular before his death from a riding accident in 1939. Colonel Fred Scott and his two sons, Fred and Jimmy, were there, as were Kink, Clint and Davis Roenisch.

Lieutenant-Colonel Gerry Chubb, late of the great Strathcona's teams of the 1930s, came out to play again while Clem Gardner made what must have been one of his last appearances with the club. Captain Gordon Sellar joined the club after the war, but his association with Calgary polo went back to the mid-1930s. Too young to be a member, he was always eager to exercise horses and help out in other ways. As a reward, he was allowed to play the occasional practice chukker. Early in the war, he went to Royal Military College in Kingston, Ontario, and was commissioned in the Calgary Highlanders with whom he served in northwest Europe.

After the war, he joined the Princess Patricia's Canadian Light Infantry and played with Calgary through 1948 and 1949. Service in the Army then kept him away from the game until he was posted to the British War Office in London in the late 1950s. The position gave him the chance to play with the Ham Club at Richmond and for an English team against Ireland at the Dublin Horse Show. Like Des Deane-Freeman, while serving later with the Canadian Army in Ghana, he joined other Europeans and North Americans at the Accra Polo Club where they played three days a week in a year-round schedule. Following his retirement, Sellar settled in Kingston where he became master of the Frontenac Hunt.

The Hull Cup match also saw another new player making his first appearance and he would come to assume a prominent role in the third era of western Canadian polo. H.T.R. ("Funny") Gregg had first joined the club with the annual meeting of 1948, beginning a long presence with the Calgary Polo Club that would also involve his father and, eventually, his sons.

Toppenish arrived with sixteen ponies and a team that included three players from the 1939 tournament. The two-game, total-goal series (with an added exhibition match against a Calgary "B" side) was witnessed by several hundred spectators who saw the teams split the games with Calgary taking the championship by 11-6. The stars of the week were the three Roenisches who shared seven goals among them in Calgary's 8-0 win in the second game.

With no hope for the emergence of another southern Alberta team and no sign of the game's revival anywhere else in the Canadian West, reforging the thirty-year-old links to eastern Washington and the Pacific Northwest was critical to the continuing health of the game in Calgary. Travel and outside competitions had been an integral part of western polo from its very inception and, while probably not essential to its survival, they had always provided clear focal points for the season and, on a more practical note, served as an important venue for the buying and selling of ponies. Tournament gate receipts certainly had the potential to supplement a club's income from subscriptions even if this potential had rarely been exploited. In a larger sense, too, the tournaments had seen the start of new friendships and non-polo business connections, some of which survived for years after the players had retired from the game.

Following the relative success of the 1949 matches with Toppenish, Calgary worked to maintain its links with the American teams. Spokane came to town in 1951 to play for the Northwestern International Championship and Calgary paid a return visit in 1952 to face Spokane and teams from Yakima and White Swan (another ranch team from the Yakima area). Calgary's first multi-team meeting of the post-war era occurred in 1953, when both Spokane and Boise appeared to play a pair of Calgary squads in another try for the Northwestern Championship.

For a number of reasons, Calgary's on-field performance through the 1920s and 1930s had often been dismal. Rarely able to beat its Alberta competition, it had fared little better against Vancouver, Spokane or Toppenish. After the war, however, the "A" team managed a series of very respectable performances against what was rated as superior American competition.

Calgary had beaten Toppenish in 1949 and, in 1951, retained its Northwestern title after tying a total-goal series with Spokane. This tie was all the more remarkable since Spokane had brought in some heavy artillery to replace a player injured in the first match.

Tom ("Red") Guy was an Idaho native who played with the Boise club when he wasn't travelling around the world as a professional. While he had been at the top of his form in the 1930s and his handicap had dropped in the past two years, he was still rated at six goals, making him one of the finest players in the United States.

The quality of Guy's game was immediately and brilliantly obvious to everyone as he scored four of Spokane's five goals. Nevertheless, Calgary scored four of it own to tie the two-game series.

Western Canadian clubs had rarely concerned themselves with handicaps. Since no team had shown itself widely and consistently superior to any other during the second era, handicapping had remained a largely informal method of trying to balance play in "American style" tournaments or club championships.

Handicapping became a hard, formal reality for Calgary in September, 1952 when the club finally joined the United States Polo Association.

There were probably a number of reasons why Calgary had not joined the USPA many years earlier. In the period prior to the Great War, southern Alberta's contact with the United States had been irregular at best. With the exception of the 1913 Spokane tournament, visits to the States had been a matter of individuals travelling south for the winter season in California. At

Trophy presentation at Southlands, Vancouver, 1953 – (left to right) "Gibby" Gibson, Margot Woolrich, Basil ("Nip") Parker, Tommy Wilmot.

Courtesy of Tony Yonge

that time, even the California teams were not USPA members. During the war, Harry Robertson and the North Fork players were probably assigned handicaps, but nearly all contact between southern Alberta and American teams had ended in 1919.

The question of joining the USPA had been raised in the early 1930s, along with the matter of inviting the Americans to compete for the Chipman Cup, but both issues had been put on the back burner in the face of the then-developing strength of the Western Canada Polo Association. By the mid-1930s, when so many Canadian teams had already fallen by the wayside, Calgary was fighting for its own survival and hardly capable of assuming the additional costs and responsibilities that came with a USPA membership.

As the third era opened, Calgary realized that its only hope for outside play lay south of the border and the need for a more formal connection with the larger polo world became obvious. Calgary's application for membership was accepted and the club was assigned to the Pacific Coast Circuit that already included Spokane, Boise, Portland and Yakima.

The first USPA-member tournament to take place in Western Canada was held at the Calgary Polo Club in late August, 1953 and it featured teams from Spokane and Boise. The Idaho team (without Tom Guy) was rated at four goals while Spokane was set at two. Calgary's "Reds" and "Blues" were both reckoned at zero, a baseline rating reflecting the fact that, to the USPA, Calgary's players were an unknown quantity.

The team ratings seemed accurate enough and, with the exception of one blowout (when Boise beat the Blues by 11-4, all four Calgary goals being granted on handicap), every game was close. Spokane took the tournament honours, but probably only because Boise had to leave town before the final, handing the win to the Washington team by default. It is doubtful they could have beaten them on the field.

Although the game was clearly back on a firm footing in Calgary, two problems continued to nag at the club throughout the 1950s: the condition of the Chinook Park grounds and the chronic shortage of well-trained ponies.

A special meeting of the club in September, 1950 had defined the problems with the grounds and Mike Francis invited the chief groundskeeper from the Calgary Golf and Country Club to make an analysis of the conditions and recommend a treatment. The report was straightforward enough: a heavy application of manure in the fall, followed by a course of weed killer, fertilizer and seed the following spring. The cost for the manure alone was estimated at more than $1,000. As Francis pointed out, the club had only about $600 at hand and that figure included over $350 in uncollected accounts receivable.

In the end, the club did what it could afford. With the help of nearly $700 in donations, over $1,000 was spent on ground expenses in 1950, a figure that would increase steadily every year for the rest of the decade. The costs would be covered by a dramatic increase in the number of non-playing subscriptions and the ongoing generosity of club patrons like Jim Cross and the Gregg family.

Calgary lawyer Funny Gregg was brought into polo in 1948 by his partner, Fred Scott. He had just returned from overseas service with Scott's regiment, the Calgary Highlanders. Within a year or so, he had introduced his father, Hamlet ("Hammy"), to the club. Hammy was born in Ireland and, after a brief, unfortunate stint at Trinity College, his family sent him off to Canada to make his own way. In this, he might almost qualify as one of the last in the great tradition of the remittance men. He settled first at Walsh, near Medicine Hat, and then moved to High River. He brought his family to Calgary in the 1920s and remained in the insurance business with North West Life for the rest of his working years.

Hammy was no rider and had no interest in learning to play the game, but he was a strong supporter of the club and was elected president in 1951. He held the post until his death in 1962, providing leadership through a period that would be among the most difficult in the club's long history.

The pony problems which had plagued the second era were only magnified after the Second World War. "Cowboy polo" had finally died with the last High River teams of the late 1930s.

Where once a rancher or cowboy could have had his pick from a long string of working horses (and even ensured that at least a couple of them were always properly schooled polo ponies), mechanization and the Great Depression had conspired to make the horse a pure luxury for anyone but the serious cattleman.

Where once southern Alberta ranches had built flourishing businesses in the buying, training and selling of polo ponies, the last remnant of the wholesale trade had ended with Llew Chambers' retirement just before the second war.

Any Calgarian who took his polo seriously in the 1950s was facing some serious (and expensive) commitments. In addition to the price of acquiring two or three credible mounts, there were the problems of boarding, grooming, training and transportation to Chinook Park. Even if the man had an acreage on the outskirts of the city, the days of riding in over miles of open grass were gone. While the club sometimes offered some limited boarding and pasturing for the members' mounts during the season, there were years when even that service was unavailable.

Tournament travel presented another set of problems. It was no longer possible simply to add a carload of ponies to a Spokane-bound freight train. Horses now moved by road and that meant long hours behind the wheel of a truck, hauling an expensive trailer. When Spokane came north in 1951, the matches were shortened by a chukker or two to compensate for the lack of horses. The Washington team could not bring enough of its own mounts and Calgary had no surplus to make up the shortfall.

As Calgary continued to grapple with its problems at Chinook Park, the game was once again beginning to show some signs of life on the West Coast. A brief note in the Victoria newspaper in October, 1952 suggested that negotiations were underway to establish a polo field on the infield of a new racetrack being proposed for Saanich, a semi-rural community just north of the city. Twenty-three members of what had been the pre-war Victoria Centaurs Polo Club (including Victoria alderman Geoff Edgelow) were said to be preparing to draft new bylaws and elect officers before the year was out.

While that effort did not bear fruit, the summer of 1953 saw the beginning of the game's revival in Vancouver. At the Southlands Riding and Driving Club, an equestrian complex between the downtown and the University of British Columbia, some young members began to bat a small beach ball around with whisk brooms. The brooms were soon abandoned in favour of regular mallets and three-a-side polo began on a pasture at the south end of the club. The field was a rough two hundred yards long and the players used the much slower ball designed for indoor polo. Ponies were available from a number of local riding stables (at the rate of $1 per chukker) and the game immediately proved immensely popular among the Southlands members.

The revival also brought a number of experienced pre-war players back into the game. Tommy Wilmot, having sold his Falkland Ranch and moved to the coast, operated a nearby stables and even sold a few of his Interior-bred ponies for two or three hundred dollars apiece. Wilmot couldn't resist playing a little on occasion and was the source of some valuable instruction for such new players as Tony Yonge, Basil ("Nip") and Jonty Parker, Bill Powell and New Zealander Pat Samuel.

Another early mainstay (and later president of what would become the new Vancouver Polo Club) was Martin Griffin. His connections to the Vancouver game stretched back to the 1920s and his enthusiasm had never diminished. Cochrane, Alberta's Alec Landale rode out a few times, too, and the matches were often refereed by pre-war Vancouver regular Jock MacLean and Kamloops' Fred Fulton.

For the next few years, polo at the Southlands stayed largely an informal, pick-up affair, mixing men and women and, as always, without a sufficient number of good ponies. The emphasis was on the simple joy of the game and such events as parties and fund-raising dinner dances bred a great camaraderie among the young members.

Vancouver made its first contact with the outside polo world in 1956, inviting Spokane up for a tournament, the first meeting between the two clubs since 1920. The American players were impressed by the quality of the field and the social swirl that accompanied the matches, but the games themselves were hardly close. The lopsided results were a clear indictment of Vancouver's mounts and, over the next few seasons, home-and-away games with Portland, Yakima and Toppenish provided an opportunity for several of the members to begin acquiring higher quality ponies.

New players (many with the means to buy and board proper ponies) certainly improved the standard of play at Southlands, but the progression also raised the cost of staying in the game. By the end of the 1950s, the surrounding riding stables and their cheap rentals were mostly gone and few of the original players remained active.

Through the 1950s, while Calgary and Vancouver both played regularly against teams from the Pacific Northwest, there was no direct contact between the clubs. The travel costs were probably just too much to bear. It is unlikely the level of play on the West Coast would have been sufficiently well-developed to warrant an invitation to Calgary's first USPA-sanctioned tournament in 1955.

That event — officially known as the Pacific Coast 8-Goal Tournament — would prove a frustrating learning experience for the club and speak volumes about the general state of polo in the first decade after the second war.

Secretary Mike Francis had begun the organizational work in September, 1954, soon after the tournament had been awarded. His first letters were a string of simple questions: Were handicaps essential? Who would set the dates, invite the teams and pay the expenses? Who was responsible for any debts (or, who got to keep any profits)?

It was already 1955 before those questions were answered and, in April, invitations were sent out to every club in the Pacific Coast Circuit and to a few other U.S. Midwest teams, too. By early June, only one reply had been received and the August 13th opening date was closing rapidly.

The fact that the Southern California clubs were not coming was probably not a surprise, but the lack of firm responses from the Pacific Northwest must have been frustrating. After a flurry of letter writing and telephone calls over the next six weeks, Mike Francis had a tentative "Yes" from Spokane, but the three teams from the Yakima district had all said "No," as had Boise, Portland, Sheridan in Wyoming and Minot, North Dakota.

New to the USPA, Calgary had run into a problem that was probably old news to long-time members of the association: the

Calgary's Pacific Northwest Tournament winners, Portland, Oregon, September, 1956 – (left to right) Harry Irving, Jim Cross, Barney Willans, Funny Gregg.

politics of handicapping. While the Yakima Valley teams had begged off for a number of non-polo reasons, Francis was told their real reason for not coming was the rumour that Jim Cross was planning to pack his team with paid professionals from California; professionals whose handicaps were widely regarded as much too low.

Since there had been talk of a couple of California players being in Calgary for the summer season, Francis was quick to try to dispel fears that they were 5- or 6-goal ringers brought in specifically for the tournament. It is easy to understand how the rumours had started. Jim Cross was the only Calgary player with any real connection to the Pacific Coast Circuit. He had been wintering at Santa Barbara and would have been well-known to the Southern California players. He, above all others, would have wanted his home club's first USPA-sanctioned event to be a success.

While there may have been something to the rumours and the politics, the real reason for the lack of positive response to Calgary's invitation was probably more basic. The state of the game in the 1950s, particularly in the U.S. Northwest, was far less settled than it seemed.

By 1955, after a brief revival, Sheridan had not seen a polo match for three years and the Minot club had dropped its USPA membership in 1954. While Yakima had what could be seen as a "proper" club, its neighbours from White Swan and Toppenish were more family-oriented teams, closer to the old cowboy polo aggregations from Grande Prairie and North Fork than to the more permanent organizations at Spokane or Calgary. In the mid-1950s, Portland polo was in the doldrums, as was Boise, with both having difficulty sustaining the enthusiasm of the post-war revival. As August approached, it looked increasingly unlikely that any out-of-town teams would make the tournament.

In the end, two American teams appeared at Chinook Park for the 1955 Pacific Northwest Tournament, but each had a cobbled-together look. Only Spokane brought the maximum 8-goal aggregation (including one player from Oregon) while Boise, with its 5-goal rating, was from that Idaho city in name only. Two of its players were Don Cross and Geoff Parker from Calgary while the third was an American 3-goal player named C.R. Colee. Only 2-goaler Don Jacobs actually lived in Boise. Expenses for both Jacobs and Colee were paid by the Calgary club.

Calgary's number one team — the Reds — comprised Jim Cross, Clint Roenisch and Funny Gregg (all rated at a single goal) together with Pat Linfoot, a 2-goal Californian whose father had originally homesteaded in Cochrane, Alberta. Calgary's Blues were Jim and Ed Arnold, Barney Willans (all zero-rated) and Davis Roenisch who carried a one handicap.

On paper, it should have been Spokane well out in front, with Boise and the Reds fighting to see who could make it to the final, but that was not how it came out. Boise may have had two strong players, but its two Calgary pick-ups were clearly playing over their heads. Boise lost all three of its matches while the Reds went through undefeated, including a 12-3 drubbing of Spokane. They then went on to beat the Washington team 9-3 in the final.

Despite the difficulties (and disappointments) in bringing American teams to town, the tournament itself was a sound success with good coverage in the media and a crowd of over 1,000 out to watch a Sunday all-star exhibition match between Calgary and the Americans. Concerns about finances were allayed by a small profit and Calgary had officially become a part of the North American game.

With fifteen players and a social membership that could have been much larger than the maximum of one hundred necessitated by the limited clubhouse facilities, the club had an active executive and, after years of hard, expensive work, two very good fields. The culmination of that work was the installation of a modern irrigation system. Despite ongoing difficulties with obtaining enough quality ponies, intra-club play was well-established and a new series of club dinners had built a solid social framework (and proved to be a money-maker). On the surface, at least, the club seemed strong and vital.

As far as the larger game was concerned, the problems were principally geographical. The club was a long way from the Southern California heart of the Pacific Coast Circuit and, of those northern American clubs that were its closest neighbours, only

Spokane was proving consistently reliable. Boise, Toppenish and White Swan had all gone quiet in the late-50s. Portland and Yakima, while always promising to try, had rarely delivered a team when it mattered.

Despite their low handicaps, Calgary's best foursome had won the 1955 Pacific Coast Tournament and, in 1956, travelled to Oregon and repeated the feat. In September of that year, Jim Cross, Barney Willans, Funny Gregg and Harry Irving met teams from Spokane and Portland on the grounds of the Oswego Hunt Club and came away with the championship of the Pacific Northwest. There seemed a brief hope that the forty-year-old tradition of Lane Cup tournaments between Canada and the United States might be ready for a revival.

Calgary was again awarded a USPA tournament in 1957, but the same difficulties that had plagued the organizers two years earlier proved too much to overcome. With only Spokane having promised to appear, the matches were cancelled.

A charming letter from Portland's John Emery, written in response to Calgary's invitation to the 1957 tournament, gives a humorous (but telling) assessment of the state of play in that city and, but for Spokane, across the Northwest in general:

The news that you will have an eight-goal tournament in Calgary and you have extended an invitation to Portland is a real honour. We certainly would all like to come. However, in making up an eight-goal team, we consolidated every man who had ever played polo in Portland and the highest rating we could attain was 4 3/4. I just dropped a line to an old aunt of mine who used to be pretty highly rated in polo...and if I can get her away from her rocking chair we might be able to qualify. She is the beer garden type, but I don't think she would be too embarrassing on the field, but socially we would have to hide her out between games.

The year 1958 was another of the watershed years that had regularly marked western Canadian polo since its birth and it began on a terribly sad note. On February 19th, the club's longtime secretary-treasurer, Mike Francis, died.

Francis had joined the club in 1922 and played steadily through the next two decades. However, it was his tireless behind-the-scenes work on behalf of the club that was his real contribution. He took over for an absent secretary at a meeting in the late 1920s

Three visiting Yakima, Washington players (on the left in Kelly Oil shirts) at Vancouver's Southlands Riding and Polo Club, 1959.

and, from that day forward, became the only permanent member of the executive. It was Francis, even more than the changing presidents, who took responsibility for arranging the tournaments, coordinating the committee work and, perhaps most important, carrying out the endless and often touchy negotiations with the Polo Club Limited. In all this he was ably assisted by his wife, Ilene, whose association with the club continued even after her husband's death.

His long, steady contribution to the preservation and promotion of western Canadian polo was recognized in 1964 by the dedication of the Mike Francis Memorial Trophy, a prize that is still a major event in the Calgary club's season.

Mike Francis was still corresponding with friends and colleagues right up to the week of his passing and, in one of his last letters, he offered a cogent appraisal of the current state of his game:

It now looks as if those players who are interested have got to get together to decide what the policy of the club should be. It is very sad to think that the oldest club in Alberta might fold up, and we are certainly the oldest polo club in the whole of Canada.... I think everyone realizes that to carry on we have got to have more players and more enthusiasm has got to be shown by the Calgary players if they want to continue.

With quiet resignation, he saw all this as a problem for the younger generation, suggesting he would finally be leaving the province at the end of the year for retirement in Vancouver.

In another letter, responding to a request from a polo magazine for an article, he was even more direct in expressing his frustration:

I am not mailing a polo story or photographs of last season's play as it was very uninteresting. We barely had enough players to get competition within the club and we are all on our own in Canada and cannot draw on any other competition except from the state of Washington or Idaho.

We were allotted the Pacific 8-Goal Handicap last year but, unfortunately, although we expected Spokane and Portland to come up, the thing fell through.... We seem to go down to the United States to play in the Pacific Coast Tournament, but we have great difficulty in getting people to come up here although we probably have two of the finest grounds on the American continent, both boarded.

In these and other letters written in the last weeks of his life, Mike Francis also related another even more pressing problem facing the club: the future of those fine, boarded grounds was in serious jeopardy.

In the years following the Second World War, Calgary experienced another of the sustained periods of dramatic growth that had characterized it from its earliest railroad days. The year 1947 had seen the beginning of a series of huge oil discoveries in central Alberta and Calgary, Canada's energy capital since before the Great War, boomed once again.

At the end of the second war, Calgary's population stood at something less than 100,000; by 1965, it had ballooned to more than 315,000. The huge population increases sparked a residential building frenzy that had pushed the city limits out in all directions. When the Polo Club Limited had acquired the land for the polo grounds in 1911, it was a long five miles south of the city boundary. By the mid-1950s, new houses were already well within sight of Chinook Park.

First to go was the neighbouring racetrack, sold to a developer in 1957. The loss of its infield would severely hamper the Polo Club's efforts to stable and pasture its own ponies and mean the end of such arrangements for any visiting team's mounts. And, for Mike Francis, "It would be very hazardous indeed to carry on our drinking arrangements with a lot of people crowded into small houses, each with a back door." In the bluestocking Alberta of the 1950s, the club had never qualified for a liquor licence.

With the sale of the racetrack, it became obvious to everyone that the polo grounds could not survive much longer. It was not

simply the prospect of the club being surrounded by houses. The forty-acre tract had become far too valuable for private recreation. With expansion of the city boundaries, the land would be zoned for residential use and the taxes would skyrocket. It was the club itself, not the Polo Club Limited, that would be responsible for paying the new assessments and they could not have afforded it.

Francis proposed a two-part strategy: sell part of the grounds as soon as possible and, with the money, buy raw land away from the city to the south. Then, after spending two or three years developing new turf, sell the rest of Chinook Park and, with those proceeds,

build decent stabling and clubhouse facilities at the new grounds.

Mike Francis' sudden death in February cast a pall over the club that lasted through the entire 1958 season. The thin files for the year record one of the lowest levels of activity in the club's long history. Meanwhile, at the Polo Club Limited, plans for the sale of the grounds were being developed.

The year 1959 saw a more active season, although the problems that had so worried Francis were still very much in evidence. The number of truly active players had continued to drop from its mid-decade high and, in 1959, only nine names appeared on the USPA handicap list. Jim Cross, Funny Gregg, Harry Irving, Clint Roenisch and Barney Willans had all been awarded a 1-goal rating; the rest were

at zero. Calgary would have had trouble mounting even a regular series of club matches, let alone hosting a serious tournament.

Calgary's phenomenal development during the 1950s and 1960s was overwhelmingly driven by oil and gas and the growing international nature of that industry fundamentally changed the face of the city. It was during this era that the "Americanization" of Calgary really took place. By 1965, there were about 30,000 Americans living in Calgary (almost 10% of the population) and the city had more in common with Houston and Tulsa than it did with Toronto or Montreal.

The earliest days of southern Alberta polo had been dominated by British players

and they passed their game along to a new generation that was primarily Canadian-born. At the end of the 1950s, with the death of Mike Francis and the fact that several of the pre-war members were approaching the end of their playing days, that English and Canadian pool was drying up. The new life the club needed to sustain the western Canadian game would have to come from the American oilmen that now called Calgary's "oil patch" home.

One of the first to arrive was geologist Warren Hunt. Raised in San Francisco, he had been drawn to Alberta's oil boom in the early 1950s. In his youth, Hunt had cowboyed for a few years and accompanied show horses around Southern California for the ranch owners. He credits Mike Francis for introducing him to polo and he first appeared on the field in 1955. He was also encouraged by his wife's family. Pattie Hunt, who became the club's long-serving timer and scorekeeper in 1956, was the daughter of William McCallum, a breeder and trainer of polo ponies from Lloydminster, Alberta. The ponies had been much in demand at Winnipeg's St. Charles club in the 1920s and McCallum himself had played there several times. Hunt was an active regular with the club for nearly two decades before an accident (unrelated to polo) forced his retirement.

Hunt's polo career closely paralleled that of Calgary businessman Harry Irving. One of the few new players who was neither American nor directly working in the oil business, Irving had been a star athlete at Montreal's McGill University and gone on to quarterback the legendary Calgary Stampeder football teams of the late 1940s. He started playing in 1954 and, through a career that spanned two decades, emerged as a steady defensive presence who could also score handily when the opportunity presented itself. He got the tying and winning goals at the 1956 tournament in Portland and his name appears on most of the major club trophies until the mid-1970s.

Another of the new Americans was Charles R. Hetherington, late of Norman, Oklahoma. He received his first USPA rating with Calgary in January, 1959. Familiar with polo since his early days in Oklahoma, he first learned the game as a part of his reserve officer training at the University of Oklahoma. His brother,

Clark, boasted a 3-goal rating with Tulsa and Norman's Broad Acres clubs by 1960, went on to be a well-known high-goal player and manager at several American clubs and, eventually, served as chief umpire for the USPA.

Hetherington had been in Canada since the late 1940s, building a series of small oil companies into major concerns. But he made his greatest mark on Canada's energy map as president and CEO of Panarctic Oils, a government and industry consortium established to begin the exploration and exploitation of the nation's Arctic oil and gas resources. In 1985, under Hetherington's direction, Panarctic delivered the first commercial tanker-load of Arctic crude to a refinery in Montreal.

From his home base at the Rocky Mountain Ranch near Millarville, Hetherington brought his sons and, eventually, his two granddaughters, Kelly and Cassie, into the game and remained a major force with the Calgary club as it moved from the difficult years of the early 1960s into the boom of the 1980s.

As first president of the new Eldorado club at Indio, California, he was instrumental in its rapid growth toward becoming what was probably the largest polo club on the continent. The close connections between Southern California and Calgary represented a re-forging of the old bonds that had been established by George Ross, Justin Deane-Freeman and a succession of Alberta polo players in the first two decades of the new century.

Always generous with his time (and his ponies), Charles Hetherington served as Canadian governor for the USPA and stayed active on the polo field until he was past his seventieth birthday.

Californian Bill Daniels came to Calgary in 1958 to work for the Williams brothers in the oil business.

David Williams (no relation to long-time Calgary player, Jim) was based in Calgary for a time and had played a good deal of polo at his family plantation in Aiken, South Carolina. Tired of borrowing mounts from fellow club members like Harry Irving, Williams charged Bill Daniels with acquiring some decent ponies. Daniels approached Charles Hetherington about the ponies and, even though Daniels did not know how to ride, Hetherington and Jim Williams convinced him to join the club with the promise that they would teach him the basics.

Although Daniels returned to California in 1964, he was by then a regular (though still raw) player and stayed with the game. Under the tutelage of such top players as Billy Linfoot, he eventually reached a two handicap. He came back to Calgary in 1972 and, in the decade that followed, made a strong and enduring contribution to the survival of the club.

Jake Harp was another American with oil patch connections. Sent to Calgary from his native Louisiana in the early 1950s by H.L. Hunt, Harp lived near the old Chinook Park grounds and his daughters would often hot-walk ponies for the club members. He did not begin to play the game himself until about 1965 when he purchased a spread just south of Calgary. Over the next thirty-five years, Jake Harp continued to develop his game and his string of ponies, becoming a regular traveller with the club and joining Hetherington for the winter season in California.

In 1959, there was early talk of trying for another Pacific Coast Circuit meeting but, with the exception of Spokane, there was really no hope of any outside competition coming to town. Spokane did arrive for a series of games in mid-August to face Calgary's Reds and Blues but the friendly matches were a long way from being a tournament.

The real highlight of the year was the June visit of 10-goaler Bob Skene, at that time one of the best players in the world. Skene represented one of the first real benefits of Calgary's USPA membership since the Pacific Coast Circuit had subsidized his teaching tour of the northern clubs. Calgary players were unanimous in their belief that his week-long workshops had genuinely improved their game but, with the exception of Jim Cross (who was still playing winter polo in Santa Barbara), their enthusiasm must have been tempered by the frustration of being so far from regular contact with men of his calibre.

Hopes for a visit from another world-renowned polo player failed to materialize as the club's efforts to have a visiting Prince Philip play a few chukkers were gently rebuffed.

Although club president Hammy Gregg had offered mounts which, while not up to the Prince's usual standard, could at least be guaranteed not to put on a "bucking exhibition," Buckingham Palace was polite but firm. The prince, said the reply, looked upon polo as "a relaxation and a sport to be enjoyed amongst friends. Any attempt to arrange a quiet game during an official visit is doomed to failure as it is bound to attract a good deal of [media] attention. It then becomes a strain and no fun."

Early in 1960, the news that everyone had been expecting finally came: the Chinook Park polo grounds had been sold.

All three of Calgary's historic polo fields had now been lost to the encroaching city. The problem that faced the members after each loss had been the same: the need to find a large area of flat ground far enough away from Calgary to be affordable but close enough to be accessible to players and spectators alike.

President Hammy Gregg pushed for the club to relocate to the old Fish Creek grounds, first established by George Ross in 1906. Although the land was available, in hindsight it would have been an unfortunate choice. By the mid-1980s, Calgary's sprawling suburbs had already begun to transform the area.

In the end, it was decided to move the club to a new site fifteen miles south of the city limits near the village of De Winton. The land was purchased from Jim Cross.

In mid-September, the clubhouse, the barns and assorted outbuildings were winched onto flatbed trucks and driven south. It was the second move for the clubhouse. It had originally been brought to Chinook Park from the old Elbow Park racetrack and polo field that had briefly hosted the Calgary club before the Great War. At De Winton, the buildings would join the Polo Club's most precious asset (indeed, the only asset that really mattered): the hard-won turf of its playing fields.

First seeded in 1912, the grass had survived the ravages of Depression-era drought, war-time neglect, gophers, moles, weeds and a host of other dangers. Finally, in the mid-1950s, the turf had seen its first reliable supply of water and that had brought it as close to perfection as any field of prairie grass could hope to be. No one was prepared to abandon the results of all that time, frustration and money.

Even as the Sullivan Brothers construction company began to cover the perimeter of the old grounds with the split-level houses of the huge new development, the playing field sod was carefully stripped, strapped onto pallets and sent south to the new grounds.

The fifteen-mile move to De Winton was greeted with a mood of resignation and cautious enthusiasm. There were those who had hoped to stay at the old grounds. Although it would have become an island in a sea of houses, it was close to the city centre and convenient to those players, social members and spectators who lived in Calgary. Some members remembered how both attendance and non-playing subscriptions had plummeted in the years the game was played out at Sarcee, a location much closer to the city centre than De Winton. Those hopes, though, were completely unrealistic. The loss of the pasturing and stabling available from the racetrack and the inevitable huge increase in property taxes left the club no choice.

The new De Winton grounds were substantially larger than Chinook Park (an initial fifty acres; ten more than the old grounds) and the money received for the old property would allow the club to undertake the kind of facilities development that was previously out of the question.

While there was plenty of room for playing fields, pastures and stables, the costs of bringing the

Courtesy of Warren Hunt

new grounds up to scratch would be high. In order to guarantee the steady supply of water that was essential to the quality of the turf, a coulee adjoining the property would have to be dammed and an irrigation system installed. The old clubhouse, hopelessly inadequate at Chinook Park, would be even less acceptable at De Winton and construction costs for even a modest new facility would be substantial.

All this would have to be undertaken at a time when the club's playing membership was at a post-war low and many simply did not have the means to cover any dramatic increase in the annual subscription.

Balancing the inconvenience of a move away from the city and the risk of losing social members and spectators was the fact that the De Winton area had emerged into something of an equestrian centre. Jim Cross' Bar Pipe Farm was nearby, as was the Greggs'

The first western Canadian team to tour Britain at Cowdray Park, 1973 – (left to right) Jonty Parker (Vancouver), Charles Hetherington (Calgary), Tony Yonge (Victoria), Patrick Oswald (Vancouver).

Oldtown. Other members, like Harry Irving, even though they worked in Calgary, had acreages or small ranches in the vicinity. Close to the town of Okotoks and a short drive from the ranching communities of High River and Millarville, the new polo grounds were probably more easily accessible to many of the members than Chinook Park.

It was the pre-war stalwarts, men like Jim Cross, Mike Francis, the Roenisches and Jim Williams, who had invested heavily in the survival of polo in a rapidly changing post-war era. President Hammy Gregg had guided the club through the difficult time after Francis' death and the move to De Winton, but he died in 1962. It would be up to a new group of patrons and players to ensure that the game put strong roots down into its new ground. Such new members had begun to appear at the club in the months before the move, and more would join through the next decade or so.

Although the Calgary club, in its dealings with the USPA, seems to have considered itself the sole survivor of what had been the once-vital western Canadian game, polo was still very much alive on the West Coast.

While many of the young people and Vancouver club veterans who brought the game back after the war had moved on, Southlands continued to host regular polo matches until the end of the 1960s. In 1957, the City absorbed the original field into a golf course but Southlands provided a site two hundred yards by one hundred yards on its property and, after much re-turfing, proper mowing and rolling, a fine boarded field allowed the use of a regulation hard ball and bred a much faster game. A new arena, constructed in 1966, also allowed indoor polo.

Clubs from Washington and Oregon were regular visitors at Southlands and the Vancouver players paid occasional return visits to Portland and Tacoma. Although Vancouver also joined the USPA, the club barely rated a mention in Calgary's attempts to lure outside competition to its Pacific Coast Circuit tournaments.

In 1962, polo also reappeared near the site of those original Royal Navy matches of the early 1890s. Bill and Barbara Powell, together with several other Southlands players who had moved to the Island, began to play polo on a new field in Central Saanich, just ten miles north of Victoria. Styled the Vancouver Island Polo Club, it survived for perhaps six seasons when most of the players moved to a new field and established the Victoria Polo Club in 1968.

The new Victoria club, playing on ten acres of newly seeded farm pasture, promised regular Sunday matches and encouraged new members — especially teenagers — to come out and learn the game. Under president (and Southlands alumnus) Tony Yonge, the club joined the USPA and became a regular host to teams from Vancouver, Tacoma, Portland, Toppenish and Yakima. Whenever possible, the club also paid return visits to the United States. By 1973, however, a lack of regular players caused the club to collapse.

In Vancouver, by the late 1960s, polo had grown increasingly incompatible with the facilities at Southlands. Many of the newer players had begun to acquire short strings of good ponies and, as a result of their regular exposure to other clubs, started to take the game more seriously. The short field was proving a serious disadvantage and polo was coming into conflict with other fast-growing equestrian disciplines at Southlands. The days of leisurely, three-chukker softball polo on rented ponies were long gone and the players moved out.

In 1970, thirty-five acres of land were purchased in Delta, south of the Fraser River about twenty-five miles from the city. With two exceptionally fine fields and an indoor arena, the Vancouver Polo Club began a new era of play. Sadly, it would be short-lived. After a decade, falling membership forced the sale of the property. It would be another decade before another group began play again on leased land in Delta, but this group, too, succumbed to low membership and polo once again (and perhaps for the last time) disappeared from British Columbia's lower mainland.

It was the British who brought polo to Western Canada in the late 1880s and Hurlingham that had set the rules and dictated the style of play. Despite the world-wide reach of the game, Britain remained the mecca for polo in much the same way that St. Andrew's had continued to be the spiritual home of golf. While an occasional player might have spent a season or two in England, in the eighty years that polo had been played in Canada, no western team had ever crossed the Atlantic to play polo and no British team had ever toured the West.

Then, in August of 1973, Victoria's Tony Yonge, a twenty-year veteran of Southlands and Vancouver Island polo who had also played in England, arranged an invitation from the Hurlingham Polo Association for a series of matches with its member clubs. Joining team captain Yonge were his brother-in-law, Jonty Parker, and Patrick Oswald, both of Vancouver, and Calgary's Charles Hetherington.

The team toured Britain for four weeks, playing five formal matches, a practice game and dividing up for numerous extra chukkers with other teams. Although they rode different borrowed ponies for every game and had never played together before, the Canadians acquitted themselves very well. They won a round-robin series (and the Perth Cup) over Scottish teams from Dalmahoy, Dundee and Perthshire before travelling south for matches at Tidworth and the Guards Polo Club. The tour ended with a practice and two games at Cowdray Park. Their final record was 2-3 and, according to Yonge, they were treated royally from start to finish.

In 1974, five players selected from each of the clubs that had hosted the Canadians the year before became the first British team to play in Western Canada. If the Canadians' memories of their tour were built around the elegant lawns of Cowdray and idyllic rides through Windsor Great Park, the Britons' first impressions of Canada would have been quite different. They arrived in Calgary at the start of the riotous annual Stampede and their first weekend was given over not to polo but to watching bull riding, calf roping and chuckwagon races.

The team did manage to squeeze in three games during their week in Calgary, facing a different host foursome each time and winning all three.

Still wearing Calgary's traditional white cowboy hats, the "Hurlingham Rovers" then flew west to the more civilized climes of the Vancouver Polo Club. The three-game series, punctuated by ocean cruises and a trip to the old Douglas Lake Ranch, ended in a draw with each team winning once and one game tied. The Rovers re-captured the Perth Cup on total goals.

Both tours were reckoned to be a complete success and British captain Mervyn Fox-Pitt concluded his recollection of events with "Long may this new dimension to international sport continue." But the series was not repeated and on-field encounters between western players and their British counterparts sadly remain very rare.

It was oil patch connections and personal friendships that brought men like Jake Harp and Bill Daniels out to play Calgary polo in the 1960s and, as long-time constants like Jim Cross, Clint Roenisch and Funny Gregg approached the end of their playing days, their sons (and daughters) were ready to make their mark.

Alison Emde/Planet Photography

The Mike Francis Memorial Trophy –
Created to honour the memory
of the long-time Calgary player and
club secretary following his death
in 1958.

Nevertheless, the club's first years on its new grounds were anything but easy. Jim Williams retired soon after the move and his young son, Dick, who had begun to play in the last few years at Chinook, was also forced to give up. Other players came out for a season or two, but did not continue. Ponies were often cited as the reason. While Cross, Hetherington and Gregg were always generous with their mounts, any player who wished to take the game seriously eventually had to confront the cost of acquiring and keeping his own string. For some, it was an expense they simply could not bear.

It seemed for a while that Cochrane would again become a presence on the southern Alberta polo scene. Rancher Geoff Parker had been a semi-regular player with the Calgary club during the late 1950s, filling in when a visiting Boise team found itself short-handed in 1955, but in the early 1960s he began to hold regular stick-and-ball practices on his ranch with several Cochrane-area players. They played as a team against Calgary on more than one occasion and the prospects for their regular participation at the club looked bright. Unfortunately, a serious illness forced Geoff Parker from the field in the mid-1960s and, without his leadership, the opportunity was lost.

Led by Peter Dix and the Spokane Polo Club, American teams continued to come to Calgary through the 1960s. Sheridan visited in 1966 for the Pacific Northwest Tournament and one of its players, Malcolm Wallop, could boast family connections that stretched back to the late nineteenth century origins of the game in northeastern Wyoming. Several Oregon teams, usually featuring up to three members of the

Emery family, were also regular visitors, capturing the Calgary Challenge Cup in 1970.

Pete Dix had been coming north since the early 1950s and, by 1966, he was leading a Spokane team that was almost a family affair. His son, Pete Jr., had become a fine player in his own right, while Pat was, at that time, the highest rated player in the Northwest and already making his mark in high-goal tournaments across the United States. He would show the strength of his game by scoring eight times against his hosts in a three-chukker outburst during the 1966 tournament. They continued to visit Calgary through to the end of the 1960s, engraving their names on the Calgary Challenge Cup in 1969.

The Dix family still dominates Spokane polo and a third generation now makes regular visits to the Calgary Polo Club.

By the early 1970s, the club was clearly beginning to show the strain of the obligations dictated by its expansive new home. Membership had slumped toward a post-war low and the expense of maintaining the turf and the facilities was taking its toll. The west field, planted soon after the move, was fast becoming unplayable and even the original east field, so carefully brought down from Chinook Park, was deteriorating.

The problems being experienced by Calgary were not unique. The game itself was suffering reversals across much of North America. Many clubs that had enjoyed a renaissance after the war had declined, their fields, like Chinook Park, being sold for housing developments or, in many cases, turned into golf courses. A consequence of the general malaise, Calgary's long-standing relationship with Spokane and the Pacific Northwest had withered by the mid-1970s, again leaving the Canadian club very much by itself at the distant edge of the Pacific Coast Circuit.

Perhaps most important of all, Jim Cross had finally retired from active participation. His strong leadership and fierce competitive spirit had dominated the club since before the war and his departure left a void that would be difficult to fill.

The largest problem was probably the members' tendency, over the years, to rely on men like Cross, Francis, Williams and the Greggs simply to take care of the administrative details. Calgary had always been a

Cup of the Americas champions,
Calgary, 1983 – (left to right)
Steven Cobb, Jake Harp,
Steve Dalton, Fred P. Mannix
and Tim Gregg.

club that ran on strong tradition rather than strong organization, but the expensive complexities of new facilities called for much clearer direction.

By the mid-1970s, Bill Daniels had been back with the club for a couple of years and, at the urging of newer members like Rob Peters, he undertook to create what was certainly the first serious organizational and operational plan for the polo club. It was a plan that came into effect in 1976 as Daniels assumed the club presidency. Under him, a series of vice-presidents would be in charge of such areas as games, facilities, finance and grounds. Daniels' plan still forms the basis of the club's organization to this day.

The club's traditions were not entirely jettisoned in the interest of modern management. Contacts were renewed with Spokane and the Dix family and the new plan also looked back at nearly a century of polo and sought to bring some of the old silverware back onto the field. Over the years, many of southern Alberta's premier trophies had disappeared. Often, they were taken home by a member of the winning team, occasioning a frantic search before the next year's tournament. Several of the cups were kept at Calgary's Ranchmen's Club (it had served as the unofficial club headquarters almost from the founding of both institutions) and at least two had been donated to local museums.

Charles Hetherington, c. 1983.

Courtesy of Fred P. Mannix

Both the Osler Cup (first brought to Alberta from Winnipeg by North Fork before the Great War) and the Chipman Cup (symbolic of the Western Canada Championship) were put back into play, while the venerable Calgary Challenge Cup was repaired and restored. First presented in 1892, the solid silver trophy is almost certainly the oldest polo cup still being played for in North America. Along with the reappearance of the old silverware, names like Millarville and Fish Creek would eventually be resurrected for Calgary club teams.

As the first post-war generation retired from the field, new players and patrons were ready to carry on. Harry Irving brought Calgary stockbroker Rob Peters into the club at the end of the 1960s. Peters took to polo with a passion and has remained a strong, constant presence, both on the field and behind the scenes. Texas-born oilman Morris Palmer had moved his drilling business (and his love of horses) to Alberta in the early 1950s and was brought into the polo club in the late 1970s by his friend and business partner, Charles Hetherington. Palmer was also a major investor in the new Eldorado club.

Harry Irving retired from active play in 1974 and Warren Hunt traded the stick and ball for the chief umpire's jersey at about the same time. Clint Roenisch was ending more than forty years of fine play for High River and Calgary and Funny Gregg gave up the game in about 1973.

Hetherington remained a significant force with the club until his death in 1995, dividing his time between Calgary and the huge new Eldorado club at Indio, California. Although Bill Daniels had retired by the mid-1980s, Jake Harp continued to play until the end of the century.

The 1970s also demonstrated that the old family traditions of western Canadian polo were still strong. As Clint Roenisch and his brothers had followed Kink onto the field, so Clint's sons, Rob and Rich, with their wives, Julie and Jan, became a top-flight presence with the Calgary club. When Rob and Julie's son, Daniel, took to the game, he became the first fourth-generation player in Western Canada. Julie and Jan Roenisch were also the catalyst that brought serious women's polo back to the Calgary Polo Club for the first time in fifty years.

Funny Gregg and his sons, Tony and Tim, carried off the Calgary Challenge Cup in 1968 while Bill and Pratt Hetherington engraved their names next to their father's on the 1972 Chipman Cup. So it was with Morris Palmer's sons, Byron and Scott.

Growing up in western Texas in the 1920s and 1930s, Morris had seen some of the first-class players and clubs for which the area had always been renowned, but he did not take up the game himself until well into the 1970s. Scott began to play in the late 1970s and soon became a strong regular with several teams at the Calgary club. He also made the occasional winter visit to Eldorado. He remains a playing member

Pekisko versus Fish Creek, Calgary, c. 1985 – (left to right)
Rob Roenisch, Bill Turnbull, Fred P. Mannix, Rich Roenisch.
The 1970s and 1980s saw the revival of several
of the old southern Alberta club names, playing
once again for many of the old trophies.

Benson Petroleum, winners of the Bonavista Cup, 1992 – (left to right) Susan Abbiati, Ron Greene, Marcelo Abbiati, Steve Benediktson.

with the Calgary club, regularly making the long trip up from the Palmer family ranch south of Pincher Creek. His brother, Byron, began to join him on the field in the mid-1980s and his Millarville ranch put him within easy reach of the fields at De Winton. He continues to play both in Calgary and at Eldorado and has recently begun actively encouraging the development of the indoor game as an economical way to extend Calgary's short summer season.

Despite serious medical setbacks and an injury to his hands, Funny Gregg had played steadily with the club since the late 1940s. His sons had been introduced to the game at a very young age as they exercised their father's horses and were a constant presence around the old Chinook Park grounds. Although they were too young to begin competitive play, both were exposed to the inspirational presence of Bob Skene during his visits to Calgary. Soon after the club's move to De Winton, their grandfather purchased the Oldtown Ranch in the foothills east of Millarville. The family moved there permanently around the time of Hammy's death and the boys regularly rode across country to the new fields.

Tim played his first full six-chukker match at the age of fourteen. Tony was two years older and their polo careers developed more or less in parallel. Their father gave up the game in the early 1970s, but the brothers continued to grow into fine players as the decade progressed. Tim quit for a while in the late 1970s, but came back in 1981 and played fine polo until his career as a player and trainer were ended by a serious injury suffered during a game in 1989. He still lives in the foothills near the Oldtown, which was sold in about 1975. Tony also played on and off for Calgary through the 1970s and well into the 1980s when he moved to United States. He is currently a top rodeo and polo announcer and divides his time between Cody, Wyoming and Eldorado. Funny Gregg died in 1990.

The new management plan set the Calgary Polo Club on a steady course for the future and gave it a stability which allowed it to exploit the changes that were to sweep the polo world beginning in the late 1970s.

Never again would there be the heyday crowds of 30,000 and 40,000 that came out to watch international matches in the 1920s, but polo (and nearly every other equestrian sport) was transformed by the buoyant economy of the 1980s.

Across North America, new clubs were founded and old clubs came back to life. High-profile corporate sponsors strung their banners around the fields and their names were prominent on the players' jerseys. The small, embroidered image of a polo player frozen in mid-stroke adorned the breast pocket of one of the largest-selling lines of sportswear and Hollywood celebrities once again became a fixture at grand charity tournaments. A few even took the game seriously and played on after the lights and cameras had been packed away.

There was a new vitality in the pony trade as top mounts from North and South America began to command prices that had not been seen in fifty years. Winter season gatherings, like those at Aiken, South Carolina in the 1920s, again became a feature of the game as players from all over the continent descended on Florida and the Southern California desert. The ease of travel meant that professional players, teachers and trainers could divide their time between North America and Argentina and players from New Zealand, Australia and Europe became commonplace with the larger clubs.

Calgary, too, was caught up in the new and expanding world of North American polo. Where, in the 1950s and 1960s, the occasional visit of a top player like Bob Skene was greeted with great anticipation, the club moved to ensure that playing and teaching professionals became an integral part of the season. Not only did the imported talent allow Calgary to schedule high-goal tournaments, but it also gave the club players season-long access to top quality instruction, something no three- or four-day clinic could match.

Alberta-born oilman Steve Benediktson had not played polo before his business took him to Argentina in 1983. At fifty years of age, he was introduced to the game by his business associates and began to play as regularly as possible. Over the course of his four years in the country, Benediktson acquired a substantial string of Argentine ponies and a 1-goal handicap. When he returned to the Cochrane area in 1987, he built a polo field at his ranch and brought eight of his ponies by air to Miami, purchased a truck and trailer and drove them up to Alberta. Accompanying him on that trip was Marcelo Abbiati (later to become his son-in-law). In one stroke, Benediktson had brought the first South American ponies and the first of a succession of Latin professionals to the Calgary Polo Club.

Benediktson's "Benson" teams (featuring Abbiati and such local players as Tim Gregg and Scott Palmer) were a serious presence in Calgary's new high-goal

USPA National President's Cup (8-goal) champions, Eldorado, 1992 – (left to right) Ron Greene, Kimo Huddleston, Marcelo Abbiati, Tyrol Sutherland.

tournaments throughout the late 1980s and he has continued to play with the club into the new century.

The old western Canadian connections to Southern California, broken with the end of polo at Coronado and later re-established at Santa Barbara by Jim Corss in the 1950s, found a new vitality at Eldorado. The early 1980s saw substantial Canadian investment in the expanded facilities and new club-house while a succession of Calgary players, including Tony Gregg, Jake Harp, the Roenisches and Calgary club president John Burns, figured prominently in the tournament record. At Santa Barbara, too, western Canadian teams and players won more than their share of major tournaments in the 1980s and 1990s.

While Calgary had the facilities and the financial backing to support its new high-goal aspirations, most members simply did not have the skills (or even the desire) to play at that level. In this, the Calgary club

was no different from nearly every other club in North America as fully eighty per cent of all USPA-rated players carried a handicap of two goals or less. Ensuring a balance between the weekend stick-and-ballers and the high-goal professionals became the greatest challenge for a succession of Calgary executive committees throughout the 1980s.

It was a challenge that would have been familiar to every significant western Canadian club almost from the beginning of the game. As far back as the mid-1890s, Fort Macleod had expressed its concerns about the difficulty of mounting a respectable team when its few top players were regularly defecting to other clubs in search of a tournament win. High River's unassailable teams from the first decade of the new century had all but collapsed by 1910, a consequence, some said, of losing players to a series of new "all-star" aggregations. At least one High River tournament was held without a

Calgary 4-goal league winners, 1993 – (left to right) Donna Wilson, Rob Peters, Brent Watson, Byron Palmer, John Rooney.

The Earl Mountbatten of Burma Memorial Plate, presented to the Calgary Polo Club by Countess Mountbatten of Burma, August 13, 1989 – The plate was donated by the Earl Mountbatten of Burma Memorial Society of Alberta and is played for annually.

home team as their top foursome had decided to play in Winnipeg instead. Through the lean years of the Depression and the difficult post-war period, bringing new members into the game had not proved nearly as difficult as keeping them.

The Calgary club responded by establishing formal low-goal leagues and increasing the number of low-goal tournaments. The zero-goal tournament for the Kimo Cup soon became one of the most popular events of the season. New members could count on easy access to the fields and the use of some respectable ponies, along with a regular series of instructional clinics. The Thursday night dinners, a feature of the club's social life for more than sixty years, were expanded and charity fundraising matches became an integral part of the tournament schedule.

By the end of the 1980s, the Calgary Polo Club was home to more than forty active players, each able to play regularly at a level at which he or (increasingly) she was comfortable. It was a number that no club in the long history of western Canadian polo had ever come close to achieving.

Building on the strength of the home club's foundation, southern Alberta's high-goal players began to make their mark on North American polo at its most rarefied levels. At Eldorado in the fall of 1992, Calgary-based teams, led by player-patrons Fred P. Mannix and Ron Greene and featuring homegrown professionals

Julie and Rob Roenisch, fought through to the finals of three major USPA tournaments.

More than eighty years after George Ross first led his Alberta ranchers and cowboys against the best that Southern California had to offer, Fred P. Mannix's 26-goal team, wearing the name of Ross' old Fish Creek club, came within a whisker of winning the U.S. Open final. At the same meeting, Ron Greene's foursome won the 8-goal National President's Cup and the Roenisches, following in the footsteps of Alberta-raised professionals like Harry Robertson and the great Justin Deane-Freeman, led a reborn Millarville team to the U.S. Open Handicap title.

But the near-sweep in the California desert was much more than just a coming-out party for Calgary's new high-goal game. It also marked a centennial: it had been exactly one hundred years since Edmund Wilmot, George Ross and the Critchley brothers rode out to play the very first season of tournament polo in the Canadian West.

While Western Canada's original polo grounds have all but disappeared, converted to golf courses or covered by housing developments with names like "Polo Park," the equestrian boom of the 1970s and 1980s saw the game come back to several of its original venues and clubs were also established in places that had never before seen the game. Tony Yonge and a small group of players still keep a steady schedule of matches at the Victoria Polo Club, while the Okanagan club, founded in 1988, draws its members from towns like Kelowna and Vernon that, decades ago, supported their own fine, if short-lived, polo teams. Dr. Ross Fargey brought the game back to Winnipeg in 1974 and his Springfield Polo Club has since re-established the old links with the American Midwest. In the same year, an English physician, Cledwyn Lewis, who had played polo during his army service, moved to Grande Prairie, Alberta and quickly founded a lively, well-supported club in that northern community. Alberta's capital city of Edmonton had no part in polo's first century but now plays host to an active club. In Saskatoon, Mike Sifton has brought the game back to Saskatchewan, continuing a long family tradition that began with Winnipeg's St. Charles club and led Toronto's polo revival in the late 1950s.

Countess Mountbatten of Burma and Fred P. Mannix, Calgary Polo Club, July, 1999.

But only the Calgary Polo Club can truly lay claim to the unique history of the western game. From its beginnings more than a hundred years ago on the rough, shortgrass plains of southern Alberta, part and parcel of a new society only then emerging from an uncertain mix of imported traditions and new realities, the club has seen its fortunes ebb and flow according to the boom and bust uncertainties of life in the Canadian West.

Calgary polo has survived two world wars and a crushing depression. It has seen its playing membership swell from an an original eight to two dozen or more and then, more than once, sink back to fewer than it took to play a four-a-side game. It has fought to save its hard-won grounds from the ravages of drought and wartime neglect only to lose them to an expanding, land-hungry city. Through it all, the game has endured. From its young men with English money and Irish titles to its homegrown ranchers and cowboys, businessmen and oil patch executives, Calgary polo has always been able to find its new generations of passionate players and generous patrons whenever it has needed them most.

Today, the old gopher-riddled hay meadows have given way to one of the largest and finest facilities anywhere. On seven full-sized fields, with clubhouses, arenas and barns that sprawl across two hundred acres of eastern slope foothills, the men and women who play their galloping game at the Calgary Polo Club have already carried the unique heritage of western Canadian polo well into its second century. ▩

EARLY POLO IN ALBERTA
by MRS. R.B. CLARKSON

(from the Pincher Creek Echo *and* Calgary Herald, *1927)*

t an afternoon tea-party the subject of our conversation happened to be polo — that glorious game of science and good horsemanship. Someone casually remarked: "It was fine, Calgary starting polo." At once, I was "on my ear" as the western saying goes and absolutely stuck to it, that it was given its start at the very unimportant village of Pincher Creek in 1889.

In 1888, at a luncheon party at Lionel Brooke's charming ranch, "The Chinook" (the house built of big rough logs on the side of a lovely lake surrounded by splendid trees — the big hall hung all around with great lifelike pictures representing bucking bronchos, bears, wolves, eagles, and so forth, all painted by the owner, most unique but a perfectly delightful hall) we began discussing polo matches lately played in England, someone said "Let's try a game." A great laugh ended in all rushing out to see how it could be done. It wasn't long before they had cut off rake and fork handles and made kind of a ball, ponies were rushed in and they had quite a sporty little match.

In the meantime Colonel and Mrs. Macleod, Mrs. White Fraser, Mrs. Teddy Wilmot, my sister, (now Mrs. George Heaton), Nelly, my daughter and myself, clambered up on a small haystack that was being built in a corral to watch the game. It was really a joke, particularly when Mr. Brooke's housekeeper clambered up with the afternoon tea and the half-finished haystack began sliding. There was a rush to land safely and escape tea-cakes and jam, but it was very successfully done and all enjoyed the joke.

The first polo sticks were brought out in the spring of 1889 by Captain Teddy Wilmot, who had gone on a visit to England. When he came back, the Pincher Creek club was formally started in 1889. Captain Wilmot, now living in Vernon, B.C., was secretary and Louis Garnett

The Pincher Creek polo team, 1892 – (left to right) Billy Humfrey, Louis Garnett, Dr. Herbert Rimington Mead, Jack Garnett. All of these gentlemen were on the field for Western Canada's first polo match in the summer of 1888.

of "The Grange," another rancher who now lives near Victoria, B.C., was president. Captain Wilmot sent accounts of all matches played by the Pincher Creek club to "Land and Water," edited in England. The first organized challenge tournament, with cups, was held at Macleod in 1892, when all clubs were invited to attend. Captain Wilmot also had the names of players and goals scored in "Land and Water" in 1892. At the mayor's residence, Pincher Creek all cups and trophies may be seen.

Glenbow archives, NA-459-3

Polo gathering at the Roodie Ranch near Pincher Creek, May, 1899 – Maria Clarkson is seated second from the left.

Later, polo was started on Sundays at Roodie Ranch, being Billy Humfrey's place, as the regular Wednesday games were played in Pincher Creek.

I remember once when the South Fork of the Old Man River, which bounds our Roodie Ranch, was in flood, Captain White Fraser and his wife started for polo from Pincher Creek. Mrs. Fraser was a good and fearless rider and insisted on fording at our crossing. When half way over the water reached her saddle. She got up on her knees on her side saddle and got across nearly dry. It was a risky business, but in those days we took many chances and came through rippingly. Such crowds used to turn up to see a game on Sunday afternoons, and it made many a one a little brighter for a happy Sunday in the lovely country, where we kept open house for all who came to encourage that splendid game.

The first pick-up polo team was comprised as follows: Mr. Louis Garnett (The Grange); Mr. Jack Garnett (The Grange); Mr. Lionel Brooke (Chinook Ranch); Mr. Billy Humfrey (Roodie Ranch); Captain Teddy Wilmot, John Brown, Dr. Mead (Pincher Creek); Mr. Foster, a friend from England.

The preceding article was written by Maria Clarkson and it is as accurate as it is charming. Many details in her account are confirmed by other reliable sources, leading one to accept that the balance of the story happened just as she reports it.

Maria was born in Dublin, Ireland in 1848 and married into the Humfrey family. One of her children, Billy, was proprietor of the Roodie Ranch near Pincher Creek and she joined him there in 1886. Apparently, she had already been in Canada for three years as lady-in-waiting to Lady Lansdowne, wife of the Governor General.

In 1890, she married a former Mounted Policeman, R.B. Clarkson, and they eventually took over the running of the Roodie. They remained at the ranch until retiring to Victoria, British Columbia in 1915. Following Clarkson's death in 1922, Maria returned to Alberta and lived in Calgary until she died on March 14th, 1939. She was 91 years old.

Her obituary remembers her for her "charm of manner" and for being one of the finest horsewomen in the West. "Her death," it concludes, "removes another link with the far-off and carefree life of the early pioneers when open-hearted hospitality prevailed everywhere."

he stories vary, but in the end they all agree on one central fact: that Captain Edmund Meade Wilmot, late of Derbyshire, England, founded the first polo club in Canada.

The location of that club is known to a certainty. It was on the rolling, foothills grasslands of the Alberta Ranche Company near Pincher Creek in the south-westernmost corner of what was still Canada's North-West Territories.

About the date, however, there has always been confusion (and perhaps more than a little wishful thinking). Many accounts would have that first rough chukker played as early as 1883, making it not only one of the earliest in Canada, but in all of North America. Some put it as late as 1889, while others, hedging their bets, are content to record it as anywhere between those two extremes.

But Edmund Wilmot is not of interest simply by virtue of his having brought an ancient game into a new country. Rather, in his life we can see reflected the lives of hundreds of men and women who built the foundation of a new society that is still a vital part of the Canadian West.

In many ways, Edmund M. Wilmot was the very model of the "Remittance Man," one of those second and third sons of England's landed gentry who came (or were sent) into Canada's Prairie West at the start of the great ranching era. While we know little of the Wilmot family and its circumstances, much can be inferred from Edmund's life in the years before he came to Pincher Creek.

Born in the English midlands county of Derbyshire in 1860, Edmund was one of several children in an untitled, but prosperous, family. He was educated at the storied public school at Rugby and, at the age of nineteen, was commissioned as a second lieutenant in the 1st Volunteer Battalion of the Sherwood Foresters. Service in such a part-time infantry regiment was seen as fulfilling an obligation to be enjoyed by the sons of the landed gentry.

In 1881, Wilmot came to Canada and enrolled at the Agricultural College in Guelph, Ontario. This stop was common among remittance men on their way west. Presumably, their studies were intended to smooth the transition from the green and gentle fields of England to the markedly different circumstances they would face on the Prairies.

In 1883, Edmund Wilmot came west. A sketch of his travels is recorded in his obituary:

With two companions, Lord Boyle and Ernest Hanson, Captain Wilmot crossed from Toronto to Winnipeg. Starting out from Winnipeg, the three young men swam their cart across the Red River and then proceeded on to Calgary.

Captain Wilmot's first taste of life after coming to Western Canada was tending cattle in the Crow's Nest Pass. He stayed there for months at a time without a companion within many miles. At last, however, mountain fever struck him down and he was forced to return to the lower plains.

Edmund Wilmot.

It is a charming story with just the right touch of romance and danger, but it ignores one substantial fact: Wilmot was no young man footloose and fancy free in the wild west. And neither were his travelling companions. They, along with others in their Guelph graduating class, were the sons of well-heeled investors in Alberta's first great ranching enterprises.

The fathers of Wilmot, Boyle and Hanson, along with Sir Francis De Winton (secretary to Canada's Governor General, the Marquess of Lorne), were the principal backers of the Alberta Ranche Company. The company began operations near Calgary in 1882-83 and, in 1884, obtained substantial lands and leases totalling some 28,000 acres near the small town of Pincher Creek at the eastern gateway to the Crow's Nest Pass.

Apparently content with his prospects at the Alberta Ranche, Wilmot returned to Derbyshire in 1885 and brought his new wife, Agatha Jesopp, back with him to Pincher Creek.

As for polo, Wilmot's interest as an athlete and country sportsman would have exposed him to what was becoming a passion among his peers. He would also have had reason to believe the game might catch on in his new foothills home. If blessed with little else in the way of amenities, the Alberta Ranche certainly had a boundless supply of broad, flat meadows, plenty of horses and capable riders. Also, it was said, Wilmot saw the game as a worthwhile distraction and entertainment for his cowboys after their chores were done.

The popular story of those first few games was later retold by *Polo* magazine. The following report on the birth of the game in Canada appeared in its issue of January, 1897:

There is other, more reliable evidence that the "broom handles and cricket balls" were first tried in the summer of 1888, but they proved a popular diversion for, in 1889, Wilmot returned from another trip to England, bringing with him a healthy stock of decent polo sticks and proper balls. The Pincher Creek Polo Club formally came into being shortly thereafter, generally recognized as the first true club in Western Canada.

The combination of enthusiasm, raw talent and decent equipment had an immediate effect on the surrounding ranches and, within five years, there were at least four well-organized clubs playing regularly within only a few miles of Pincher Creek.

Although Wilmot's name does not appear consistently on the roll of any team from the Pincher Creek area, he continued to support (and play) the game he had brought into the country. It is fitting that he will be remembered as one of the 1892 Fort Macleod team that captured the Macleod Cup in Canada's first multi-team tournament.

At some time around 1894, for reasons unknown, Edmund Wilmot left Pincher Creek and moved to the town of Duncan on Vancouver Island. While he retained his financial interests in the local ranching business, he never again lived in southern Alberta. His obituary records that soon after taking up residence in Duncan, he was called back to England following the death of his mother. He was still in England when the Boer War broke out, whereupon he rejoined the Sherwood Foresters. Promoted to captain, he embarked for South Africa on December 11th, 1899.

Wilmot's war would prove to be a brief but adventurous campaign. Captured by the Boers in June, 1900, he was sent to Cape Town and quickly released in August of the same year, rejoining his battalion at Pretoria. By April, 1901, he was back in England and possessed the Queen's South Africa Medal with three clasps.

He remained in Derbyshire until 1905 (the last year in which he appears on the British Army List), when Ernest Hanson, his old friend from his first trip into the West, convinced him to move back to Canada and settle in British Columbia's Okanagan Valley. Wilmot, with his wife and their two sons, bought an orchard in Coldstream, a British enclave on the outskirts of the town of Vernon. In the years following, he built up substantial holdings in farmland and cattle ranches (perhaps with some of the proceeds from the 1902 sale of the Alberta Ranche Company).

Staying true to form, in 1911 Wilmot founded the Coldstream Polo Club. It is said he was still an active player in his seventy-third year. His sons, Edmund Sacheverel (known as "Chev"), born in 1892, and Francis Hurt (always called "Tommy"), both took up their father's game. While Chev was lost to the Great War, Tommy went on to enjoy a long career, emerging as one of the greatest players and trainers in British Columbia history.

Agatha Wilmot died in Vernon in August, 1931. Captain Edmund Meade Wilmot followed her in March, 1935.

Tommy Wilmot was born in England in 1894. Whether it was during one of his family's frequent trips home or after they left Duncan permanently is not known. He was raised and educated in England until 1905 when he got his first real look at the Canadian West. He took to it immediately. Those who remembered his early years in Coldstream recalled a boy who cared for little else but horses.

He learned his polo from his father and, when Edmund founded the Coldstream club, Tommy responded by creating another which he named for the nearby town of Vernon. It was not a "proper" club, but rather a young team he created to play against his father and the other Coldstream members.

Tommy enlisted when the Great War erupted, but his only overseas service was as a member of the Canadian Siberian Expeditionary Force. Sent to Russia after the outbreak of the Revolution, he spent a cold, miserable six months in Vladivostok training anti-Bolshevik forces and guarding western Siberian rail lines. He was home by early 1919 and soon settled in as player-manager of the post-war Vancouver Polo Club.

Courtesy of Penny Wilmot

Tommy's polo skills developed quickly in Vancouver and, by 1923, he was one of the club's leading players, regularly singled out by the press for both his scoring and his defensive skills. He had also come to the attention of patrons and teams outside British Columbia and spent the winter of 1924-25 playing at Coronado.

He remained with the Vancouver club until about 1925 when he began to divide his loyalties between the West Coast and the Kamloops district. He was in Kamloops in April for the express purpose of buying ponies for Vancouver, but finished the season with Frank Ward's Douglas Lake outfit at the 1925 B.C. Challenge Cup Tournament. From 1926 on, he was as much associated with the Interior game as with his former club and worked closely with Ward on developing the fine strings of Douglas Lake ponies.

How Tommy came to be connected with the larger world of high-stakes polo is not clear, but he became probably the only western Canadian player to appear at the great Meadowbrook club in New York, something he did more than once during the late 1920s. He supplied some ponies and went along as a coach when the Calgary women's team played in New York in 1928, but there is some evidence it was not his first trip to the East Coast. And it was Wilmot's eastern U.S. connections that took him to Europe.

In the summer of 1929, he sailed for France in charge of a number of ponies belonging to one of the Lehman Brothers, the New York stockbrokers, and at Deauville, in late August, Tommy led a team to victory in the Prix de Casino Tournament. Two months later, the stock market crash brought the free-spending glory days of international polo to an end.

In 1934, with his international travels behind him, Wilmot settled down on a ranch in Falkland, British Columbia, midway between Kamloops and Vernon and, in the same year, married Dorothy Keith from nearby Enderby. Their only child, Penny, was born in 1938.

There was little in the way of polo in the Interior in the last years of the 1930s and, while he continued to play where he could (usually with Frank Ward), Wilmot continued to work with a wide variety of horses, including polo ponies, hunters, jumpers and thoroughbreds.

The 1939 Royal Visit Tournament in Victoria proved to be Tommy's last significant polo competition. Although he was only in his mid-40s and may not have been contemplating retirement, it would be nearly fifteen years before the game was revived and, by then, it was too late.

He left the Falkland Ranch and moved to Vancouver in 1953, just in time to see polo begin at Southlands. He ran a stable at the facility, taught the finer points of the game to the new players and even joined in their three-a-side matches, but increasingly focused his attention on racehorses, building his reputation as one of the finest trainers in the Canadian West.

Following Dorothy's death in 1958, Penny moved to England and her father joined her there the following summer. Although he had hoped to remain in England, he missed British Columbia and they came home in 1960. When Penny joined the Air Force later that year, Tommy went to stay with old friends at the Alkali Lake Ranch in the Cariboo country and remained there until he moved to Vernon in 1962.

Happily back home, Tommy again began playing golf (a game he had first learned in the 1920s), fly-fishing and hunting. He even obtained permission to shoot on his old ranch at Falkland.

Tommy lived in Vernon until 1970 when, on June 14th, he died suddenly from a post-operative infection.

240

GEORGE ROSS

Colin George Ross was the first great player and patron of western Canadian polo. He was on the field for the first Alberta tournaments in 1892 and his profound influence on the game stretched across the entirety of the first era, continuing even after he left the province for Southern California just before the Great War.

Ross was born in 1866, the third of a prosperous Manchester merchant's five children. The family's fortune, established by George's great-grandfather, had been built on the sugar trade with Jamaica and Guiana, but records indicate that George's father may also have been involved in the East Indies trade.

The Rosses were an altogether remarkable family. Great-grandfather Hercules had left Scotland for Jamaica in 1761 and entered the sugar trade. He served as a purser in the Royal Navy during the American Revolution and, in 1779, opened his Jamaica home to a seriously ill Horatio Nelson who was suffering from yellow fever. This led to a close personal friendship between the two men that continued after Hercules' return to Scotland in 1782. In 1801, Nelson was godfather to Hercules' son, Horatio.

Horatio became a legendary figure in the Scottish Highlands. After an uninspired stint with the 14th Light Dragoons, he retired with the rank of captain and went on to serve one term as a member of parliament before marrying Justine Macrae,

daughter of the Macrae clan chief. Horatio was a phenomenal competition shooter and horseman and, in 1826, riding his prize horse, "Clinker," he won a match race against Lord Kennedy's "Radical." With £1,000 bet on the outcome, the race is generally accepted to be the first steeplechase ever held in Britain. To commemorate his victory, Horatio commissioned a large painting of the event from leading equestrian artist, John Ferneley. That painting sold at a New York auction in 1999 for more than $1 million. In shooting, his nerve and his eye stayed sharp and he continued to win major competitions for Scotland until well past his sixty-fifth birthday.

While living at his Rossie Castle estate in the 1850s, Ross also took an interest in the new medium of photography. A founder of the Photographic Society of Scotland, he made some of the earliest known photographs of the Scottish Highlands. It is for these photographs that Horatio Ross will be remembered. A bound volume of his hunting photographs recently brought more than $150,000 at a London sale.

Horatio died in 1886 and it may have been the proceeds from the earlier sale of his extensive shooting estates that helped to fund his family's foray into the Alberta cattle business.

In 1885, Ross' father, also named Colin George, toured the foothills ranch country around High River to size up the investment prospects. Liking what he saw, he sent his son and a manager out a year later to establish a stock-rearing operation. The Rosses could not have picked a worse time to go into the cattle business. The stock they brought from Ontario in 1886 and settled on the new Ace of Spades Ranch suffered terribly that first winter, by far the worst on record. Whether it was the inability of the eastern cattle to survive the ice and cold or the ranch's unfortunate location wasn't important; they lost almost everything. Abandoning the land, young Ross moved what was left of his stock onto the property of a man named Podger, whom he bought out around 1890.

The new place was located about sixteen miles south of High River on the Little Bow River and it was there, in the late 1880s, that George Ross began to play a little polo.

At about that time, George was joined on the ranch by his youngest brother, Horatio. How long Horatio remained in High River is not known but, by the mid-1890s, he had left for the southeastern Alberta town of Medicine Hat where, true to his nautical name, he became involved in the building of steam-powered sternwheelers. Intended to ply the Saskatchewan River system between Lethbridge and Winnipeg, they proved a brief (and disastrous) experiment. Unlike the Missouri, where such boats had been in use since the 1840s, the South Saskatchewan River was ill-suited to navigation. Swinging wildly between only two extremes, it seemed either in full flood or nearly bone-dry.

After building several vessels, and losing at least one (the Assiniboia in 1906), it was Horatio's ill-fated City of Medicine Hat that closed the steamboat era on the South Saskatchewan. Designed to carry over two hundred passengers and built at a cost of $30,000, she steamed for Winnipeg in May of 1908. The boat made it as far as Saskatoon where a flood-swollen river drove her into the concrete piers of the city's new Victoria Street Bridge. Within moments, the badly crushed hull keeled over and Ross, who was at the wheel, barely escaped with his life.

The wreck of the City of Medicine Hat effectively ended steamboat traffic on the upper Saskatchewan and Ross (or, more likely, his father) had to cover the entire loss. His insurance only protected the boat against fire. Horatio left Medicine Hat soon after and, undaunted, established the Ross Navigation Company, a river freighting service that operated for several years out of The Pas, Manitoba. Horatio Ross died from an accidental gunshot wound in The Pas in February, 1925. He was fifty-six years old and left no family.

By 1903, when the High River Polo Club was established on its own grounds and set on a firm legal foundation, George Ross had built his mix of ranchers, cowboys and townsmen into the strongest teams in southern Alberta. His reputation for fierce discipline and a near-obsession with team play allowed High River to win regularly over teams which might have

A young George Ross at the Ace of Spades Ranch, c. 1888.

Glenbow archives, PD-314

boasted superior individual talent or better ponies. Indeed, polo seems to have been the sole centre of his life. As the *High River Times* reported in 1907:

George Ross is accustomed to calling his players down firmly, but not gently, and in picturesque language.... The effect of this is unanswering obedience — in a word, discipline.

Ross' ranch never counted among the great outfits of the cattle kingdom. Unlike Cross and Samson, his name never appeared among the founders or directors of the new livestock or ranchmen's organizations that were springing up across the district. His name is also conspicuous by its absence from the early membership lists of Calgary's Ranchmen's Club.

If cattle were not particularly interesting to Ross, neither were purebred horses. While his polo-playing friends, Eckford and Alexander, were building reputations for producing large numbers of top-quality working and race horses, the Little Bow outfit remains, at best, a footnote in the story of High River ranching. Indeed, outside of polo and his brief tenure as owner of a High River hotel, there is little mention of Ross in the local histories.

Other than polo, George's only real public presence in High River was as commander of Alberta's 15th Light Horse. Although he held the rank of captain (and then major) in this storied militia regiment, there is no evidence that he had any formal military training. He was only twenty when he came to Alberta and little is known of his teenage years in the English Midlands.

This lack of information about Ross in a town that takes enormous pride in its heritage also extends to his family. Ross' wife, Letitia Clyde, makes only one brief appearance in the pages of the *High River Times* at a time when coverage of social events was both extensive and detailed. Who she was, when they were married and whether they had children cannot be discovered.

If Ross had any serious business interest at all, it was polo ponies. It was Ross who first led southern Alberta's polo players to tournaments in Eastern Canada in the first decade of the new century and, according to the local press, the players were invariably accompanied by a carload of Ross' ponies. The new clubs in Toronto, Kingston and Montreal were first stocked with horses purchased from Ross and a few other local trainers.

Ross' profound influence on the development of polo in southern Alberta was clear by 1906. Three of his locally trained players were beginning to make careers of the game, playing for pay in Toronto, Montreal and even Saratoga, New York, but the most telling evidence of his authority and leadership came with his move from High River to Calgary. With his departure, High River's greatest seasons came to an end. With his arrival in Calgary, his new Fish Creek club quickly produced teams that would dominate the last years of the pre-war era.

In 1908, George Ross forged another new connection between western Canadian polo and serious outside competition. At about the time he gave up on travelling to Eastern Canada, he made his first foray to Southern California. He played his first winter season at Riverside and it was there he was introduced to the Spreckels family.

Whether they met on the polo field or Ross' old family connections to the sugar business meant that he already knew the American sugar king is not known, but Ross never got over his first exposure to high-goal California polo and the rich social swirl that surrounded it. On his return to Alberta, he announced that Spreckels horses would be coming to race at the new High River track and began making plans to take a local team to Spreckels' club on Coronado Island for the 1909 winter season.

Over the next five years, under Ross' patronage, players from High River, Pekisko and Calgary became a regular feature of the Southern California season. Ross himself was offered the opportunity to manage the Coronado club (at a reported $10,000 per year) and 1909 saw the first of several announcements that the coming Alberta season would be his last before a permanent move to California.

Although he continued to play with Fish Creek through to the end of 1911, he did not come back from the 1912 winter season. But for two later visits, George Ross never returned to Alberta.

Through 1913 and early 1914, he continued to host Alberta teams at Coronado and elsewhere on the West Coast tournament circuit, joining them on the field if an injury left them a man short. Even with his new position as manager of the club, he continued to play hard and there is clear proof that the years had not mellowed his fierce temperament. In February, 1913, the *High River Times* picked up and published a story which had originally been reported in the tabloid *New York World* under the headline "Major Ross Hits Mexican":

Major Colin Ross, millionaire Canadian poloist, was at one time the centre of interest in the game of February 4th between a picked Coronado team and three Canadian players. Of the three "Canadians," one was Juan Fuennes, a Mexican, who is a trainer and stablemaster for Walter Dupee, a millionaire.

Fuennes is a splendid horseman, although it is said that as a poloist he has won no medals. He preferred riding rings around Major Ross to chasing the little ball. On one occasion, an interval between two "chukkers," the Major, in a moment of ungentleness, struck Fuennes over the head with his mallet.

Fuennes bit the dust, but he took the Major with him. Automobiles, as emergency ambulances, were pressed into service and rushed to the scene of conflict. There were no fatalities, but the mallet was a total loss.

In June of 1914, Ross reappeared in Calgary for the official opening of the club's new Chinook Park grounds and refereed the game between his old Fish Creek club and Cochrane. He was back again in January, 1915, this time to do his part for the war effort.

He joined the 12th Canadian Mounted Rifles as a major in command of a squadron. In March, he became their second-in-command. His wife, Letitia, was listed on his record of service as his next-of-kin and her address given as the prestigious Hotel Del Coronado. She clearly didn't accompany him on his visit.

And, a "visit" is what it turned out to be. Ross resigned his commission in September of 1915 and returned to California. At forty-eight years of age and with no previous war experience, he was an unlikely candidate for overseas service and his role was probably always intended to be that of helping prepare the regiment to fight.

With the war's end, western Canadians again began to make their annual pilgrimage to Coronado and George Ross was there to ensure they were treated well. Players from Vancouver and Cochrane's Virginia Ranch, together with Tommy Wilmot, Frank Ward and A.C. Critchley, were all guests of the club during the early 1920s. Ross had built a house on Isabella Street in Coronado and seemed to have settled in as a permanent part of the prosperous island community.

But polo was almost finished at Coronado. By 1923, the number of matches being played had decreased dramatically and the field was used as much for horse shows and high school football games as for polo. By about 1924, the polo club was gone and its grounds eventually were turned into a golf course.

With the end of polo on Coronado Island, Colin George Ross disappears from the historical record. Although it is hard to imagine that he gave up the game he had played with such passion for more than thirty years, he does not seem to have settled with any other West Coast club. He certainly did not return to Alberta and, although High River's local history holds that he died in California, no record of his passing, nor that of his wife, has come to light. He might have returned to England, but, again, no record of his presence there can be discovered. In fact, the Ross family itself seems to have vanished from memory.

O f all the polo-playing families of southern Alberta, none has been quite as colourful as the Critchleys. A fixture of the game from its earliest days on the Prairies until the outbreak of the first war, the Critchley family (including a couple of in-laws) produced at least eight serious players, any four of whom together would have been among the favourite teams at any tournament. And, more than that, the Critchleys' story is the story of western polo itself.

The Critchley saga begins with three brothers: T.O. (Tom), Oswald Asheton and Harry. Born at Salwick Hall in Preston, England, Tom was the first to head west, establishing a ranch just north of Calgary in the early 1880s. Oswald came next, finding his way to his brother's ranch by what seems to have been the remittance man's preferred route: via a brief course at the Agricultural College in Guelph, Ontario. He was about eighteen at the time. Harry, the youngest, arrived later and established his own operation near the city.

Other than tournament records, which show endless combinations and permutations of Critchleys playing polo throughout the pre-war period, most of what we know about the family comes from the pen of Oswald's eldest son, Alfred Cecil Critchley. Nearing the end of what had been a long and most remarkable life, A.C. sat down in the late 1950s and wrote his autobiography, *Critch!*

Though the language now seems dated and some of A.C.'s childhood recollections are perhaps a little too authentic, *Critch!* tells an amazing story that is equal parts comedy and tragedy; a charming amalgam of the glorious, the improbable and the downright unbelievable. Much of what follows is drawn from that book.

After spending his first two years in Alberta with his brother, Tom, doing little but hunting and fishing, Oswald had settled in as owner of the Stapleton Ranch,

Group of hunters near Calgary, early 1890s – Oswald Critchley is on the left.

Glenbow archives, NA-18-13

fronting on the north bank of the Bow River about six miles west of what were then the Calgary city limits. He named the ranch after a family estate in Scotland.

Described by A.C. as "...tall and lean; a great horseman, a first-class shot and a tremendously keen fisherman," O.A. shared the ranch with his wife, Maria Cecil Newbolt. She was the daughter of one Colonel Newbolt of the Royal Horse Artillery, a man who had spent most of his military life in India. Maria's uncle was Canon Newbolt, Dean of St. Paul's. It was at the Stapleton Ranch, in 1890, that she was delivered of their first child, A.C. Oswald and Maria's life together ended just over two years later when she died giving birth to their second child, Walter.

Almost immediately, Critchley returned to England and married a childhood friend, Winnifred Holt, of the Holt Shipping Lines family. In November, 1893, O.A.'s third son, Jack, was born.

Despite these upheavals, the Critchleys had already emerged as a major force in Alberta polo. Both Tom and Oswald played for Calgary in the province's first major tournament, the Macleod and Colonel Macleod Cup matches of June, 1892 (with Tom as captain). Tom also played for Calgary in September of that year as the city hosted its inaugural tournament.

Both Oswald and his then-brother-in-law, Bob Newbolt, appear on the 1891 list of the first members of Calgary's prestigious Ranchmen's Club, a clear indication that they were both well-established at the heart of the city's rapidly expanding ranching and business élite. It was from this club in 1893 that O.A. launched his brief political career.

A.C. records that his father's campaign began as the result of a boast (that "any fool could get into politics") and a bet ($1,000 from an unnamed club member that he could not get elected). Oswald decided to run for a seat in the North-West Territories legislative assembly, choosing the riding of Calgary West, a huge, thinly populated area that stretched some seventy miles from north to south and at least half that distance from east to west. One of the candidates who had already declared his intention to contest the seat was A.L. Sifton, a teetotalling Methodist Liberal (three things that could not possibly have endeared him to Critchley). His brother, Sir Clifford Sifton, was Prime Minister Wilfred Laurier's minister of the interior and easily the most influential figure in the Canadian West.

Even taken with more than a grain of salt, A.C.'s account of his father's campaign describes a mad romp, involving, among other things, a skeet-shooting contest for all the votes in a small town at the northern end of the riding and an election day race to get his brother-in-law's handyman to the polls in time to cast his ballot. Apparently, this last rush proved decisive as O.A. was elected (after seven recounts) by that single vote.

Critchley lasted only one term in the legislature at Regina, a five-year tenure that was hardly a great success. Even A.C. does not sound impressed: "...the only legislation put through by my father was to

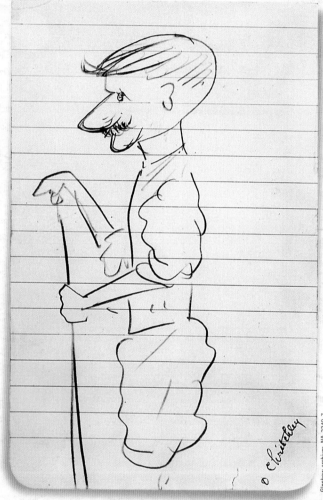

Sketch of O.A. Critchley by Randolph Bruce, c. 1897.

Glenbow archives, NA-2240-7

change certain laws to secure the greater protection of wild life." O.A. wisely decided not to seek re-election in 1898, leaving his seat to be captured by another political neophyte (and teetotalling Methodist), R.B. Bennett, who would go on to become Canada's eleventh prime minister.

Through it all, the Critchleys (together with Newbolt and Winnifred's brother, Tom Holt) managed to sustain their passion for polo, one so deep that A.C. reported the following about his father's captaining the Calgary team:

With little money and no guarantee of a posting after his course, A.C. attended the Army's Musketry School near Ottawa (and, apparently, played for the Rough Riders football team) and waited for a promised commission in the Lord Strathcona's Horse, then stationed in Winnipeg, Manitoba.

With A.C. waiting (and still short of funds), Oswald Asheton Critchley came back to Canada and, almost immediately, returned to southern Alberta.

With his partner, G.H. Rhodes, Critchley purchased a ranch in Grand Valley, a short distance northwest of Calgary near the town of Cochrane. The near-simultaneous arrival of two or three more experienced players meant Critchley was soon in the midst of a polo boom in Cochrane and the team instantly became a force to be reckoned with.

Two of his best players were remittance men — ex-British cavalry officers who had played first-class polo in England, but who had a fondness for the bottle. Whenever Calgary were playing an important match Father would persuade the Chief of Police to lock them up overnight.

A.C. is too much of a gentleman to name names. The Critchley's massed influence on Alberta polo probably peaked during the Calgary tournament of August, 1896 with the appearance of the Stapleton Ranch team comprising Oswald, Tom, Harry and Tom Holt.

A.C. and his brothers lived a wild, idyllic life at the ranch. Without much schooling, they were barely literate, but they knew how to ride herd, becoming expert horsemen and learning to hit a polo ball. Then, in 1899, it all came to an end. Their father pulled up stakes, sold the Stapleton (for nearly four times what he had paid) and took the boys back to England, ostensibly to get them an education. It was ten years before they all returned to Canada.

A.C. was the first to come back, but not to his childhood home. Straightened financial circumstances (precipitated, he says, by the birth of two more brothers) ended hopes of a Sandhurst education and, in 1906, he was sent to work as a clerk in the Bank of Montreal's head office. Transferred to Halifax (and the supervision of his father's friend who had once managed the Calgary branch — and played a little polo), A.C. continued to chafe under the stultifying atmosphere of the bank and set his sights on attending the Royal Military College in Kingston, Ontario. He was enrolled in 1908.

(left to right) Walter, A.C., Oswald and Jack Critchley, 1914.

Meanwhile, A.C. received his posting to the Strathcona's at Fort Osborne Barracks in Winnipeg. In 1911, he was joined by his brother, Jack, who had also received his commission. Oswald's third son, Walter, unable to avoid what was to have been A.C.'s fate, was pushed (reluctantly) into banking.

Like their father, wherever the Critchley brothers went there seemed to be an outbreak of polo and, in short order, the Strathcona's were represented by a first-class foursome comprising A.C. and Jack, Douglas Cameron and A.E. Shaw (another southern Alberta expatriate). With their connections to the Calgary area (and with Cochrane in particular), the Strathcona's were soon travelling to, or hosting, matches across the Prairies.

For two or three years, the Critchleys were at the top of their game, but it all came to a shuddering halt in August, 1914.

Following the outbreak of war, Walter found himself with a commission in the 10th Battalion of the Canadian Expeditionary Force while Jack and A.C. moved with the Strathcona's to Val Cartier, Quebec, a last stop before going overseas. Needing help with the training of new recruits, the Strathcona's colonel, Archie Macdonell, was convinced by A.C. to approach Oswald, then fifty-two years old. Though his military experience had been limited to a brief attachment to the Westmorland and Cumberland Yeomanry, O.A.'s reply was just what one would expect: "Have done almost everything except go to war. Count me in." Before heading overseas, the four Critchleys posed together, in uniform, for a photograph. It was probably their last. Although in May of 1915, a father and his three sons would be briefly reunited at Locon, there would have been no time for picture taking.

Walter survived the war, earning the D.S.O., and served again in World War Two. In March, 1917, Jack, already wearing the Military Cross, died of wounds received while in temporary command of the Strathcona's at Villers-Faucon.

Of the other members of the great Strathcona's polo team, Douglas Cameron survived, winning the Military Cross and the D.S.O., and served again two decades later. Captain A.E. Shaw, the former Mountie whom A.C. had first met at the Royal Military College, was killed in 1916 commanding infantry in the Ypres Salient.

Twice wounded, by November, 1918, A.C. Critchley had risen from captain to brigadier-general and been seconded to the Royal Flying Corps where he was involved in pilot training, a role he would continue, with the rank of air commodore, in the next war. By the time his autobiography was published in 1961, he was A.C. Critchley, C.M.G., C.B.E., D.S.O. He had amassed a sizable fortune, been a member of parliament, introduced greyhound racing to England and served as director general of the British Overseas Airways Corporation (now British Airways). And, he had been blind for nearly a decade. He died at his home in England on February 9th, 1963.

Oswald returned to Alberta after the Great War but soon sold his ranching interests to his partner and returned to England where he went into business with his son, A.C.

In 1935, he visited the Honorable Frank Macnaghten at his estate in Northern Ireland. They had been close friends since their earliest polo-playing days in Calgary. Following a full day of shooting and two or three rubbers of bridge, Oswald Asheton Critchley walked upstairs after tea to change for dinner, sat down on his bed and died.

THE PEKISKO GEE-BUNGS

A Portrait of a Southern Alberta Polo Club

T
he year 1904 saw the tournament debut of a new southern Alberta polo team: Pekisko. Never more than a post office, a trading post and a small Anglican church, Pekisko (from the Blackfoot for "rolling hills") was a loose-knit ranching community set deep in the foothills about forty miles southwest of High River. The area was prime cattle country, dominated by the presence of two of the most storied of the great ranches, George Lane's "Bar-U" and A.E. Cross' "a7."

The Pekisko club was born, and remained, a satellite of the older and larger aggregation at High River. Indeed, the first reference to the club appears in a *Calgary Herald* account of a tournament held at High River in early August, 1904:

The Calgary team was beaten in their draw by the High River quartette, while the cowpunchers team from Pekisko, who all proved excellent sportsmen, was beaten by the High River club's second team.

That match was played just before the club's organizational meeting.

The polo club was founded primarily because the distance between the Bar-U and the High River grounds was too great for players to travel for regular practice or the occasional pick-up game. Also, the opportunity to play regularly with either of High River's two tournament teams was severely limited for anyone who was not a highly skilled player.

The organizational meeting was short and to the point. The minute book records the following in a neat, plain hand:

The Bar-U Ranch, Pekisko, Alberta, late 1890s.

At a meeting held at Pekisko on the 15th of August 1904, at which Messrs. Brown, Shakerley, Millar, Bedingfield & Pike were present, it was decided to organize a Polo club & the following bye laws were passed. That the name of the Club be the "Gee-Bung Polo Club." That the colors shall be black shirts with a gold band running diagonally across the breast.

According to local lore, the club's name (which is prominent on the cover of their minute book) came as the result of a visit to the district by Australian author Rolf Boldrewood. He is said to have remarked that the polo game he witnessed (probably at High River) bore a close resemblance to the riotous affair

Glenbow archives, NA-3627-10

described in the famous Banjo Paterson poem of the same name. Sadly, the club is never again referred to, by itself or by anyone else, as the "Gee-Bung"; it is simply called "Pekisko."

The minute and account books offer a detailed look at the workings of the Gee-Bungs beyond anything provided in the published accounts. And no complete set survives for any other club.

At the club's first meeting, the members also appointed Bar-U owner George Lane as president and, acknowledging their connection to High River, George Ross as vice-president. As was usually the case with southern Alberta teams, these two positions were largely ceremonial, recognizing a patron or supporter of the game. A.C. Shakerley was appointed team captain and F.R. Pike secretary-treasurer. These gentlemen, together with J.H. Brown, were already members at High River,

such joint memberships being common throughout the life of the club. Indeed, many southern Alberta players maintained memberships in at least two clubs.

Pekisko's annual membership subscription was set at $5, with any five members constituting a quorum. An application for membership could be disqualified by three dissenting votes. During the life of the club, however, no one who applied received as much as one dissenting vote, let alone the three needed to keep him out. In that first year, the club could boast seven paid subscriptions.

Total expenses for the year 1904 were itemized as follows in the club's account book:

3 dozen polo balls $9.00
4 dozen bottles of beer $8.50

Next year, at its meeting of May 28th, the members got down to the business of finding a suitable field ("full sized if possible") close to the Pekisko post office. At that time, the post office was located at the homeplace of the Bar-U along Pekisko Creek and the field was eventually laid out on a low bench above the valley immediately to the north. The field was boarded and a pavilion constructed that summer. At the second meeting of the year in September, Messrs. Brown and Millar offered to donate posts and poles to fence the whole grounds to keep the cows off.

The secretary was instructed to write to the Millarville club and invite them down for a game in early October. He was also to write to High River and encourage its members to support Pekisko's efforts by taking out memberships. Eight new members joined the club in 1905.

Expenditures for the year included lumber for the pavilion and stovepipe for goal posts; four silk shirts in club colours (imported from England) and four white practice sweaters. There are bills for mowing the grounds and hauling off the hay and, finally, a fifty per cent increase in beer consumption.

Such was the pattern for dealing with the club's business, but the minutes and accounts are a clipped, cold record of the formalities. They do, however, suggest that more is going on behind the scenes. The land on which the field sat was Bar-U property and its proximity to the homeplace made it a valuable patch. Still, no rent payments were listed in the annual accounts, just a thank-you letter to George Lane. When money was needed to pay the cost of the pavilion, three members immediately donated $25 each to cover the debt. There were offers of posts and wire; an offer to transport materials from High River without charge and no shortage of volunteers to help with fencing the field. In addition, the accounts regularly showed donations from members in excess of their membership and tournament fees.

What we see at Pekisko was probably occurring at every other polo club in southern Alberta: a healthy spirit of voluntarism backed by the continuing generosity of those who could afford to support the club financially.

Matches at Pekisko with outside teams were rare. High River came to play in 1906, winning easily by 8-1. A.C. Shakerley was badly injured in the first period when he was stepped on by his pony after a fall. The newspaper report gives some indication of his skill as a player, suggesting that the score would have been different had he been able to stay in the game. Many spectators came from High River to watch the game, including "Mr. Koch's automobile friends," a sure sign that the times were changing. In the latter part of the decade, membership grew slowly each year. The charter members continued to form the core of the club and their names would have been well-known throughout the district. Herb Millar was the foreman of the Bar-U (and no relation to the Millar for whom Millarville was named). An Illinois farm boy, he had come to the ranch in 1882, driving a herd of twenty-one purebred bulls purchased in Chicago the year before. He would remain at the ranch for more than fifty years.

"7-U" Brown was one of the legendary characters of the High River-Pekisko district. His given names were Joseph Harrison, but he was always known only by his brand. 7-U was born in County Cavan, Ireland in 1856, came to Canada with his family and settled in Peterborough, Ontario. He sailed around the Horn to arrive in British Columbia in 1882 and eventually drifted inland to the BX Ranch in Vernon. When the BX trailed 1,200 head of horses over the Divide to Fort Macleod in 1883, Brown was hired to bring three hundred of them up to the Bar-U. He remained in charge of the ranch's horses for fifteen years.

In 1886, he went into partnership with Frank Bedingfield, keeping his share of the herd on the Bedingfield Ranch until 1910 when he bought a place of his own nearby. Brown never married and lived at the ranch with two of his sisters (and, apparently, prodigious quantities of carefully secreted whisky) until his death in 1936. His sisters carried on the operation and after they died, according to their wishes, it was operated as an "estate" for the benefit of destitute ranchers, cowboys and their families.

Frank Bedingfield came to Alberta with his widowed mother in about 1884. Mrs. Bedingfield had been married to an English army officer stationed in India and, on his death, she brought her son to America, settling briefly in Iowa before coming north. After a brief stint as housekeeper at the Bar-U, she purchased a property immediately to the west and established her own operation. Though she loved her life in the West, she remained aristocratic and high-born in her manner and is said not to have got along well with the cowboys, leaving most of the day-to-day management of the ranch to her son.

When Frank announced, in 1919, that the Bedingfield Ranch was up for sale, George Lane showed the place to a visitor who had expressed an interest in owning land in the district. The sale was made that year and the ranch renamed for its new owner. It became the EP Ranch, property of Edward, Prince of Wales.

Of founding members F.R. Pike, Richard Carlé and Kenneth Snowden little is known other than that they were from England and held smaller homestead ranches in the area, a common feature after the turn of the century when many of the great leases were withdrawn in favour of increased numbers of settlers. Walter FitzHerbert had come from England in about 1902 and worked for most of the major ranches in the district before taking a homestead near his two brothers, Hal and Lionel. Two more brothers and their mother came into the country in 1907. At least four of the five FitzHerbert brothers — Walter, Hal, Lionel and Anthony — became Pekisko members.

W.G. Hanson, back from his adventures in the Klondike, settled on his "Chinook Ranch" along the Highwood River, raising prize Herefords and Shire horses and playing polo for both High River and Pekisko. A.C. Shakerley came out in 1898 and took up the homestead next door.

By 1910, all three of the Robertson brothers — Harry, Hugh and Edgar — held memberships, as they did in the High River club, and the great Harry himself donned the Pekisko black and gold on more than one occasion.

Through to 1909, the club continued with its regimen of regular Sunday afternoon practices, continued discussions about whether to fence the entire field (the final answer, in 1907, was "No"), letting contracts for mowing the grass, filling gopher holes and keeping sufficient sticks and balls on hand. The account book shows a regular income from the members' $5 annual subscriptions and, after expenses, a continuing balance of around $100.

The question of the real cost of playing the game is one which remains difficult to answer, not only for Pekisko, but for other clubs as well. With one exception, neither the Pekisko club minutes nor the account book reflects any concern with expenditure connected with travel to out-of-town tournaments, even those close to home in Calgary, Millarville or Fish Creek. Shakerley, Carlé and Snowden were in Winnipeg, along with William Holmes of High River, to play for the Winterton and Chipman trophies in early September, 1909 but the club's books make no reference to the trip at all. One can only assume that the money to transport the players and their ponies came out of their own pockets.

The exception comes after the jointly sponsored High River-Pekisko Tournament of September, 1909. On October 31st, the club held a special meeting "...for the express purpose of getting the opinion of the members as to the liquidation of the debt incurred by holding the tournament at High River."

Though the minutes are not explicit, there was clearly a problem among the members. Shakerley and Snowden had attended a meeting at High River where they had agreed to share the costs of the tournament. While they had apparently spoken with a majority of the members before the meeting, there had been no formal agreement on the subject. Pekisko's share of the debt was now known: it was nearly $150.

Shakerley proposed that the balance of the club's funds be applied to paying the debt and that those who had played in the tournament should make up any deficit. The motion was carried unanimously and the books show a cheque in the amount of $148.86 being sent to the secretary of the High River club. Ten members then anted up $4.40 each to cover their share of the shortfall in the club's account.

Nothing more was said in 1909 (except to order new team uniforms with a gold waistcoat over a black, short-sleeved shirt), but the 1910 annual meeting opened with the resignation of long-time secretary F.R. Pike ("...he would like someone to take his place...as he did not take the necessary interest in polo now....") and the announcement that the club was in debt to the tune of $21.67. Lacking funds to pay for maintenance of the grounds, the members decided to undertake the work themselves on a rotating basis with everyone agreeing to a "call out" whenever special attention was needed. For reasons unknown, the Pekisko club was conspicuously absent from the 1910 High River tournament.

The difficulties of 1909 are all the more sad and puzzling since that year was certainly the high-water mark for the Gee-Bungs. Pekisko players had comprised three-quarters of the combined team that had captured the Winterton trophy in Winnipeg. Then, just over a month later, those same players had beaten Fish Creek to claim the High River Challenge Cup.

Though the official record is vague, the spirit seems to have gone out of the club and, following the problems of 1909 and 1910, they never again held a joint tournament with High River.

Like Calgary, Millarville, High River and the others, Pekisko did have its own trophy. Donated by George Lane and first contested in 1908, the Lane Cup was intended for annual competition "on the American principle," that is to say by pick-up foursomes assembled from the club players at a tournament in the same manner as Calgary's Ladies' Cup.

It was up for play again in 1909 at the joint tournament and the High River club initially included it in their plans for late July, 1910, together with their own challenge cup. Then, at a meeting of May 30th, High River decided that the tournament would include only their own cup and a new trophy, the Van Wart Cup. The secretary was asked to convey the news to Pekisko while, at the same time "...offering the Pekisko Club the use of our ground at a later date for their tournament, at which it is suggested the Lane Cup be played for, our club cooperating with the Pekisko Club in the best of their ability in order to make their tournament a success as far as this is in our power."

This, and the financial problems of 1909, may explain Pekisko's absence from the 1910 tournament. It also marks the last recorded mention of the Lane Cup.

Pekisko's hopes for a tournament of its own were realized only once. In 1911, High River came out, though Millarville had to beg off at the last minute. The game was one of the few times that Pekisko managed a clear victory over its old rival by six goals to three. The absence of Millarville left room for an "American" game on the second day.

In the 1911 Pekisko club accounts, there is the following expenditure: "November 18: Shields & engraving on Pekisko Cup, $5.25." Presumably, the trophy had been purchased in anticipation of an annual

The Pekisko Gee-Bungs, 1912 – (left to right) Harper, Snowden, Shakerley and Carlé.

tournament on their home ground, but 1911 seems to have been the only year in which it was played for. It may even have been the Lane Cup. Since the trophy has never resurfaced, it is impossible to know.

Both "A" and "B" teams made an appearance at the High River tournament of 1911 and a foursome took part in the Fish Creek matches the same year. "Pekisko" is the name engraved on Millarville's Sheep Creek Challenge Cup for 1910 and 1911. In 1912, the Gee-Bungs won the Fish Creek tournament outright, embarrassing the hosts by 14-2 and then defeating a usually strong Millarville team 8-7.

By 1913, however, the minutes reflect a concern over the shortage of playing members and the club apparently suspended maintenance on the Bar-U field, opting to use a smaller practice ground nearby. The account book shows only ten annual memberships collected, Carlé, Snowden and Shakerley being the only names which have turned up regularly on the tournament lists. At the back of the account book, the annual roll of members documents the decline:

M. Alexander – left the country
J. Kent – left the country
J.R. Anderson – left the country

And so on for a half-dozen more, including original secretary F.R. Pike who disappeared from the register after the 1912 season.

Although there is no record of the team's activity in southern Alberta in 1913, the black and gold did make one significant appearance on a polo field that year.

In the program for the eighth annual tournament of the Coronado Polo Club near San Diego, California, there is a posed photograph of a foursome wearing short-sleeved shirts under a bright waistcoat. Though called "The Canadian Team," three of the players were old Gee-Bungs: Richard Carlé, Kenneth Snowden and Harry Robertson. The fourth is the ubiquitous Oswald Critchley. The High River newspaper suggested they had been at Coronado for most of the winter season, becoming great crowd favourites and playing well at the tournament, losing only to teams from Pasadena and Hawaii. As usual, the money for the trip must have come out of the players' pockets (with help, perhaps, from the Coronado club secretary, former High River captain George Ross). There is no mention of the event in the Pekisko minutes.

The 1914 annual meeting, held on April 26th, opened with what seems a renewed optimism. There were fourteen men at the meeting, including four new members, and the first order of business was to form a committee to fix up the Bar-U field and repair the pavilion in advance of the first practice on May 9th.

Millarville came to Pekisko at the end of July, losing to their hosts by 7-3 in a match marked by Carlé's headlong collision with a goal post, resulting in minor injuries to rider, horse and post. The next day, there was the now-traditional "American" game won by the team under Millarville captain Montie Fraser.

As the last order of business at the 1914 annual meeting, secretary Carlé was instructed to send the usual letter to George Lane expressing the club's gratitude for the use of the field. The remaining pages in the minute book are blank. The end of the 1914 season marked the end of Pekisko's Gee-Bung Polo Club.

Carlé, Harper, Anthony FitzHerbert and Stanley Rigg were killed in the war. So was A.C. Shakerley (together with two of his brothers) and probably others, too, whose fate is not recorded in the local histories. Kenneth Snowden survived, but he did not come back to southern Alberta, preferring to remain in his native England to manage a golf club. F.R. Pike relocated to Bassano, east of Calgary, where he continued to raise his prize-winning Percherons.

Tucked in the back of the minute book is a small sheet of paper titled "Members of the Pekisko Polo Club, Aug. 1925." Below the title is a list of thirteen names, all of them familiar from the years before the war. At the bottom of the sheet it says, "Notices for meeting, Aug. 23, sent August 11." There is no evidence that the meeting was ever held or, if it was, that the black and gold was ever seen at Pekisko again.

Today, the Pekisko area is still cattle country and the descendants of early club members Cartwright, Gardner and Nelson still operate their ranches to the west and south of the old polo grounds. The EP Ranch has become part of the Cartwright spread. The homeplace of the great Bar-U itself is now a national historic site and the old buildings are undergoing major renovation and restoration. There is even talk of rebuilding the polo club pavilion.

he names Ward and Douglas Lake are inexorably linked to the history of ranching not only in British Columbia but across all of the Canadian West. From its formal birth in 1884 until well after the Second World War, the great Douglas Lake Cattle Company had been at least partially owned by the Ward family. For the last forty years of that period, it was an exclusive family holding under the strong, guiding hand of Francis Bulkley Ward.

When founding partner William Curtis Ward bought out his two co-founders in August of 1910, the Douglas Lake operation boasted 100,000 acres of deeded land that was capable of wintering 10,000 head of mixed-breed beef cattle, built from and sustained by purebred herds of Hereford and Shorthorn. While the deeded land supported the commercial herd through the fall grazing period and produced vast quantities of winter feed, spring and summer saw the cattle spread across the southern Interior valleys on a huge patchwork of Crown leases.

Frank Ward had joined the Douglas Lake Ranch in October, 1909, very much over the objections of his father's partners and their old-time managers who did not think he was up to the task. Born in 1875, the sixth of W.C. Ward's ten children, Frank had always wanted a career in the Army and planned to attend the Royal Military College, but a serious illness when he was just sixteen years old derailed any hope of a life in the military and he joined his father at the Bank of British Columbia. When his illness persisted, outdoor work was prescribed as the only possible cure and he was sent out to Douglas Lake to be a cowboy.

He went back briefly to banking at the turn of the century, but decided that ranching was his destiny and, early in 1903, in partnership with his childhood friend, Joseph Pemberton, bought the Two-Dot Ranch near High River, Alberta. There he learned the cattle business and, in High River, developed his lifelong devotion to polo. He had played the game earlier in Victoria, in the Chilcotin and, probably, with his brother Cecil in Kamloops, but it was with the great High River teams of the new century that polo became his abiding passion.

In the five years he lived in Alberta, Ward married Ethel ("Kenny") Kennedy of Fort Macleod, the daughter of pioneer Mounted Police surgeon George Kennedy, and she gave birth to their only child, Betty. He also began to raise and train polo ponies and may have joined other southern Alberta players on their treks to Coronado for the winter season. His growing skill on the polo field was certainly in evidence at the annual Millarville, Calgary and High River tournaments held during his tenure at the Two-Dot.

The growing influx of homesteaders, the perennial absence of his partner and his failure to hold the huge leases essential to his plans for the Two-Dot herd drove Ward to sell out in 1908 and take his new family home to British Columbia and back to Douglas Lake.

Frank Ward (left) with his long-time cow boss, Joe Coutlee, on the Douglas Lake Ranch, 1934.

When the Ward family took full control of the ranch in 1910, Frank became its undisputed manager.

W.C. Ward had returned to live in England and most of his children (including Frank's brother, Cecil) soon joined him there. When he took the manager's job, Frank had believed (indeed, insisted) it would be a temporary appointment, lasting only until the ranch could be sold and he could buy a place of his own. But the good years (and strong profits) leading up to the Great War put the sale plans on hold. W.C. even rejected at least one offer of more than $1 million. In 1914, the old man divided ownership of Douglas Lake among himself and his nine surviving children. Although the ranch remained unofficially "on the block," it would be another forty years before the family directors saw an offer they would all accept.

Realizing he was probably committed to Douglas Lake for a long time, Frank Ward began a program of expansion and consolidation that soon made it into one of the biggest cattle operations in Canada. He purchased many smaller neighbouring properties outright and pushed the ranch toward self-sufficiency in winter feed production. In the early years, based on his experience with the Two-Dot, he led the Nicola Valley ranchers in their fight to keep the dry rangelands from being carved into homesteads. He also worked tirelessly to found and support associations of cattlemen and stock breeders with the intention of promoting the interests of their industry with both the provincial and federal governments.

Through the 1920s and 1930s, Ward worked to rebuild the Douglas Lake herds to their pre-war levels. The once-thriving heavy-horse breeding operation was cut back and their pastures given over to cattle. While the rebuilding effort was generated mostly from within the herds themselves, Ward travelled extensively to acquire top-quality bulls and breeding stock. Changing with the times, he began to eliminate the unfashionable Shorthorn blood from his herds, elevating his prize Herefords to the dominant line.

Through the good years of the 1920s and the depths of the Depression, Douglas Lake remained consistently profitable. Operations were carefully expanded or cut back according to the dictates of the times, but even through the worst of the 1930s, Ward continued to acquire more land as it became available (usually through tax sales) and, by the end of the second war, the Douglas Lake Ranch comprised over 140,000 acres. The herds were back to 10,000 strong and the winter feed meadows could produce 8,000 tons of hay a year.

Through it all, Frank Ward was clearly in charge, but it did not make him a stay-at-home manager. With a number of trusted long-term employees heading the various ranch operations, he was free to travel widely and constantly, whether on ranch business or on behalf of his various associations and organizations. But what the power and the money of Douglas Lake really supported was Ward's obsession with polo.

Almost from the moment he took over at the Douglas Lake, Ward went back to the game he had refined during his years at High River. He brought polo back to the Quilchena field in 1912 and his hopes for the game in the Nicola Valley were only derailed by the Great War. The changes that followed the Armistice stayed Ward's plans for a fully organized,

tournament-hosting club in the valley and, for the next twenty years, while he would be most closely associated with Kamloops, he never really called any club "home."

He bred, bought and built a long string of top-flight ponies, quartered them at the Douglas Lake and had them trained by Tommy Wilmot and Ralph Chetwynd. At a moment's notice, the string could be loaded and on its way to wherever there was a polo tournament. Over the years, Ward played for nearly every club in British Columbia, riding out regularly for Vancouver, Kamloops and Grande Prairie. When those teams were unable to travel or when a foursome was needed to balance a tournament draw, Ward could be counted on to conjure a dangerous aggregation that would invariably become the favourite to capture whatever trophy was on offer.

Usually in the company of Tommy Wilmot, the only other man apparently able to travel as far and as often for a polo match, Ward led the Vancouver club to Calgary in the late 1920s and twice won the Western Canada Championship. In the early 1930s, after the Vancouver club collapsed, it was Ward who took Kamloops east over the Divide and repeated his Chipman Cup wins. When there was no B.C. team to make the Alberta trip, he went by himself and joined Cochrane's Virginia Ranch for yet another cup-winning performance.

When he was not appearing with an established club, Ward assembled one-time units of the top players available and, billing themselves as Douglas Lake or

Quilchena, Nicola, Grande Prairie or Falkland, his teams went on to win more than their share of tournaments in Kamloops, Vancouver, Victoria, Washington state and California.

Much of the cost of mounting and transporting these one-time teams came out of Frank Ward's pocket and out of the general budgets of the Douglas Lake. Even in the middle of the Depression, when there were deep cuts in every area of the Ranch's operations, Ward kept his string of ponies intact and continued to move a dozen or so of them back and forth to Kamloops. His regular presence on the old reservation field was probably responsible for keeping the club going for as long as it did. Only his annual trips to Calgary were suspended and that was more a consequence of his advancing age and the general state of the game than a diminishing of his passion for polo.

As the Depression loosened its grip on the Canadian West, the Ward family once again began to solicit offers for the Douglas Lake Ranch. Time had taken its toll on the ten original shareholders. The family's connections to the ranch, and to British Columbia in general, had become increasingly tenuous. At sixty-five years old, Frank Ward's days as unchallenged master of the ranch were over and, in 1940, he was pushed gently but firmly into retirement.

Until the day he left the ranch for Victoria, Ward kept up his fierce schedule of travel and meetings on behalf of the numerous ranch and livestock organizations for which he was the principal spokesman and he continued to play as much polo as he could. His wife, Kenny, had stayed at the ranch while Ward ranged freely across the West for three decades. Even his imminent retirement and the prospect of their finally being able to enjoy the fruits of their labours could not undo the damage that had been done to their marriage. She finally left her husband and the Douglas Lake for Eastern Canada where she lived out the rest of her years.

Ward played his last polo at the 1939 Victoria tournament, closing a career that had spanned the whole history of the British Columbia game. Since 1896, he had played more polo for more different teams and engraved his name on more different trophies than any other figure in the history of the western game. Although in a losing cause, it was perfectly fitting that Frank Ward, a sixty-five-year-old man riding a twenty-three-year-old pony, scored the last goal of the tournament.

Ward retired his string of ponies to a life of pampered ease at the ranch and, while he remained a director of the Douglas Lake, its day-to-day operations were put into the hands of his long-time assistant manager. Buoyed by the demands of war-time production and the post-war boom, cattle prices were at an all-time high by 1950. In that year, the Ward family finally saw an offer that it liked and sold the Douglas Lake Ranch, lock, stock and barrel, for $1.4 million.

Frank Ward stayed on as chairman of the board, but took no active part in running the ranch, preferring to remain in Victoria. He died at his home on April 27th, 1953 at the age of seventy-eight.

THE CROSS FAMILY

I n July of 1885, Alfred Ernest Cross filed a homestead claim on a half-section of land in the southern Alberta foothills just west of the town of Nanton.

Unlike most of his neighbours, A.E. Cross was no English remittance man. He was the grandson of Robert and Janet Cross who had left a ruined family fortune in Glasgow, Scotland, and emigrated to Montreal in 1826. Robert was dead within a year and Janet was left to raise eight children. Through her own determination, assisted by her eldest son John who had initially stayed in Glasgow to finish his legal training, the family's small farm holdings and mercantile business prospered and another son, Alexander, soon began to read the law. A shrewd financial manager, Alexander soon established himself as a leading figure in Montreal's business, social and legal communities.

Alexander's son, Harry, was the first to see that his future lay in the West and, in 1874, he left Montreal for the raucous gold and cattle towns of Colorado. By the early 1880s, he had settled in eastern Wyoming's Converse County and, with extensive loans and investments from his parents, he established what would eventually become a huge and influential ranching operation. He named it "Braehead" after the family's old Scottish estates.

Several years younger than Harry, Ernest was sent off for an English education but his brother's letters from the "Wild West" and his constant reading of pulp magazine stories about the western life had him failing his classes miserably. Brought back to Quebec, he tried business school for a year or two with the same result. Still determined to head west, he transferred to the agricultural school at Guelph, Ontario, a favourite stopping place for many of the early remittance men. There, Ernest was reunited with at least one of the cowboy-struck young gentry with whom he had whiled away his time at his English public school.

In 1881, Ernest agreed to his father's request that he attend the new veterinary college at Montreal's McGill University and, although he again proved he was no scholar, he managed to graduate in 1884. At the age of twenty-two, with his new degree but little practical experience, he immediately headed west to become the bookkeeper-veterinarian of the Cochrane Ranche just west of Calgary.

His tenure at the troubled Cochrane was brief and he began to look around for a place of his own. In July, 1885, after filing on his own homestead, Ernest headed back to Montreal to convince his father and his brothers that the time was right for a heavy investment in the coming Alberta cattle boom.

In a move that would be characteristic of the family's business for years to come, the Crosses sought no outside capital to help establish their ranch (even

Ken Woo

The J.B. Cross Trophy – Presented by the Cross family to honour Jim Cross' fifty years of fine play and generous patronage at the Calgary Polo Club.

though Alexander would have had no trouble assembling a syndicate). They decided to begin small and grow more slowly. In the spring of 1886, Ernest and his brother Edmund came back to southern Alberta with a small herd of purebred Shorthorns, a thoroughbred stallion and three fine Clydesdales. On their arrival in Calgary, they added to their menagerie with three hundred head of cattle and one hundred fifty horses. With their animals and a stock of provisions, the brothers headed out to their new ranch. Before leaving, they registered their brand. Advertising the fact they intended to raise only the finest cattle, they applied for the "A-1." When it was denied, they accepted the proffered alternative and the "a7" was born.

The brothers were barely settled when the legendary killing winter of 1886-87 settled in across the plains. The a7 lost sixty per cent of its herd (Harry's losses in Wyoming were substantially worse) but there was never any question of giving up. The herds were rebuilt, largely with the profits from the sale of horses, and the operation cautiously began to grow.

By the end of the decade, with the ranch on solid footing and his Montreal family investing heavily in Calgary real estate, A.E. Cross had begun to build the friendships and business connections that he would keep for the rest of his life. He became involved with a series of civic improvement issues and was an early (and vocal) advocate of protecting the lease rights of ranchers and stockmen against the growing pressure of the homestead movement. He was also the driving force behind the creation of the Ranchmen's Club and a founding member of the Calgary Polo Club.

While he was only an infrequent player in the local tournaments, Cross remained a generous patron of the polo club for the rest of his life. Although he truly loved the game and was a solid presence on the field when he did appear, the reason he did not play more can likely be traced back to a roundup at Mosquito Creek in 1891. His horse took to bucking and, had Cross simply been thrown from his saddle, he might have expected nothing more than a few bruises or a fracture. But his boots caught in the stirrups, jamming his gut, time and time again, against the saddle horn. The injury, for which he refused surgery, would cause him considerable pain for the rest of his life.

The one thing A.E. Cross did not see in the booming new town of Calgary was a decent brewery. Indeed, there was no such thing anywhere west of Winnipeg. Betting that Calgary's growth would continue unabated, he borrowed from the bank, issued some shares and, in December, 1891, launched the Calgary Brewing and Malting Company. Among those present at the first official meeting in April, 1892 were Herbert Samson, Herbert Eckford and Duncan McPherson. They would soon be joined by T.S.C. Lee, H.B. Alexander and the Honorable F.A. Macnaghten. The names of these first investors were the same as the names on the Ranchmen's and Polo Club charters.

Cross took his beer as seriously as he did his cattle. Before launching the enterprise, he had closely studied industrial brewing during a trip home to Montreal and, when the first beer that flowed from the CB&M proved to be horrible stuff, he left for a four-month master brewer course in New York. Despite its rocky beginnings, quality control problems and a mid-decade depression, Cross' beer soon captured a huge share of the western business, heavily marketed everywhere from Winnipeg to Vancouver.

As the century closed, Cross did two things which seemed decidedly out of character. He moved his politics out of the back rooms and ran successfully for a seat in the territorial assembly at Regina. And, at the age of thirty-eight, he got married. A lifelong bachelor with a reputation for high living, Cross married Helen Macleod, the twenty-year-old daughter of Colonel James Macleod.

A.E. Cross watching his buffalo–
drawn wagon (date unknown) –
The wagon was a publicity tool of
Calgary Brewing and Malting which
always sported a buffalo head on
its product labels.

Putting the a7's affairs into the hands of a resident manager, Cross and his wife moved to a house in east Calgary within walking distance of the fast-growing brewery. A small polo field was created just outside the formal gardens. In this home, "Nell" Cross gave birth to seven children, five of whom survived to reach adulthood.

Despite extensive investments in mining, oil and real estate, the brewery and the ranch remained the cornerstones of the rapidly growing Cross family fortunes. Riding an unprecedented boom in the years before the Great War, A.E. solidified his position as one of Calgary's most important and influential citizens. It was Cross, together with three other legendary ranchers (known to every Calgarian as the "Big Four") who underwrote the costs of Calgary's first Stampede in 1912.

And then, in 1916, in the midst of war-time prosperity, Alberta, and eventually every other Canadian province, voted for Prohibition. Although the brewery survived, profits were slashed and, for the eight years in which the province was officially "dry," the business got by on soft drinks, "near beer" and more than a little bootlegging. Cross' problems were only compounded by the post-war collapse of the beef market. There were times in the early 1920s when the whole enterprise was in serious jeopardy.

By the mid-1920s, all of Ernest's early friends (and original investors) were long gone from Calgary. Cross and O.E. Brown were the only founding members of the polo club who still remained in the area. Although

his playing days were over, Cross remained active with the club, always ready to make substantial donations to upgrade the badly deteriorated playing fields or improve the clubhouse and outbuildings. His contributions were crucial to the survival of the club in the lean years immediately following the First World War.

In 1927, Ernest's eldest child, Jim, played his first match with the Calgary Polo Club. James Braehead Cross was twenty-three years old and had just returned from a brewery course in Birmingham, England to become secretary of the CB&M.

Like his siblings, he had been educated at private schools in Victoria and, like his father, gone off to the agricultural college at the University of Guelph. A natural athlete and a fierce rider, he also shared his father's old love of the high life. It was Jim's dream that, one day, he would run the a7. However, when Ernest decided his son would join him in the brewery, Jim went along, albeit grudgingly.

With Jim showing great talent for running both the brewery and the ranch, Ernest was free to travel more widely, revisiting the places and the people that had been part of his life from the very first days. He and Nell sailed for an extended stay in England and Ireland. In 1930, Jim married Eileen Russell and his sister, Mary, married Ford dealer Mel Dover and left for India where Dover ran the company's dealership network. In that same year, Ernest and Nell made their first-ever trip to see his brother's Wyoming ranch. With Ernest only in his late sixties but still suffering from his old roundup wreck of forty years before, their grand tour had a sad, end-of-the-trail feel to it.

The Depression hit the Cross empire hard. The a7's prize cattle, which had regularly brought the highest prices at the Chicago stockyards, were shipped for pennies on the dollar. The brewery's profits (including those from the chain of fifty hotels that were the beer's principal outlet) plummeted and Jim was forced to deal with mounting labour and production problems.

In January, 1932, A.E. Cross took the train from Calgary to Montreal to face another round of major surgery. With him was his seventeen-year-old son, Alexander ("Sandy"), on his way to begin his studies at Kingston's Royal Military College. His youngest child, fifteen-year-old John, was still at school in Victoria.

Ernest Cross never recovered from his operation. He died on March 10th, 1932. His funeral service was probably the biggest Calgary had ever seen. The tributes to his years of contribution to the public life of the city and the Canadian West filled the newspapers for days after his death.

Cross' death left the family's future firmly in the hands of twenty-nine-year-old Jim Cross. Despite his father's substantial estate, the Depression and huge succession duties required that he consolidate the many holdings and investments and concentrate on saving the ranch and the breweries. The family home in Victoria was sold and extensive properties in downtown Calgary were let go in lieu of the taxes owed on them. Oil stocks and a myriad other investments were sold and, with the proceeds, Jim bought all the outstanding CB&M shares that were still held by his father's oldest friends, those few survivors of the Mosquito Creek roundups and founding members of the Calgary Polo Club who had managed to outlive him.

Sandy gave up his dream of mining exploration and went off to learn the brewer's craft while John finished high school and went east to study agriculture at the University of Guelph. Jim and Sandy would run the breweries while John assumed control of the a7.

Through the worst years of the Depression, the Cross' traditional aversion to carrying large debts paid off and the two cornerstones of the family's enterprise managed to survive until the war-time boom brought them back to profitability.

From the time he first appeared with the Calgary Polo Club in 1927, Jim Cross rarely missed a practice or a tournament for the next forty years. While his father's old injury had limited him largely to the role of supporter and patron, Jim's continuing financial support was matched by an intense devotion to the game on the field.

In the hard times of the 1930s, when both the Calgary and High River clubs saw their playing memberships sink well into the single numbers, the enthusiasm of Jim Cross and Kink Roenisch did not waver. They continued to travel in search of a good match, re-establishing the old connections with Spokane and Vancouver, and working to ensure that the Western Canada Championship survived, no matter how few clubs were able to take part. Without Jim Cross and those few other hard-core adherents maintaining the foundation, it is hard to believe that the Prairie game could have recovered from its long war-time hiatus.

Following the second war, Cross resumed his leading role with the polo club, working (and paying) to help put the grounds back into playable condition and even contributing to the purchase of new jerseys. Many of the new, young players who joined the club at the start of its third era first took to the field on Jim Cross' ponies. Although he announced his retirement once or twice and did take a year off in the early 1950s, he could not give up his game.

When Calgary finally joined the United States Polo Association in 1952, Cross served as an informal liaison between the club and the distant executive of the Pacific Coast Circuit. He was playing a good deal of polo at his winter home in Santa Barbara and was really the only Calgary member who had any regular exposure to the players (and the politics) of the California clubs that dominated the circuit. Correspondence from the circuit governors regarding such things as revised handicaps, the granting of tournaments or election of officers were almost automatically forwarded to Cross and the club secretary's formal replies were often verbatim copies of his comments.

Although the club did not travel often during the 1950s, when it did head south to Portland or Spokane, Cross would be there. He also encouraged other members of his family to take up the game. His brother,

James Braehead Cross.

Sandy, and his nephew, Mary Dover's son David, both played a season or two, but neither took to polo with anything like Jim's passion. His son, Donald, however, became a familiar figure with the Calgary club and a regular member of its tournament teams.

As was so often the case with the many father-son combinations that played over the years, Donald found it difficult to develop his own style and strengths. His father was a fierce, all-in player who could dominate a game as much by the strength of his personality as by his considerable skill with the stick and ball. Several members of the club expressed their pleasant surprise at how good a player Donald could be whenever he was not sharing the field with his father.

As the 1950s came in, Jim Cross moved to re-organize and rationalize his family's businesses. The a7 was fully deeded to brother John in return for a herd of purebred cattle which Jim used to stock his new Bar Pipe Farm near Okotoks just south of Calgary. Throughout the decade, he fought an increasingly difficult and expensive battle to keep the big eastern breweries out of his territory. He refused several offers to purchase the CB&M and then paid far too much for a small northern Alberta brewery just to keep it out of the conglomerates' hands.

In 1957, the Alberta government struck a serious blow with its announcement that breweries could no longer own hotels. At that time, the Cross family owned perhaps fifty and had only ten years to sell them off. Jim Cross was forced to accept the inevitable. Calgary

Brewing and Malting was sold to Canadian Breweries in return for a substantial cash payment, millions in stock and a company directorship. The arrangement lasted only a couple of years. The Cross brothers were as uncomfortable working for someone else as any of their forbears. The Canadian Breweries shares were sold, Donald came home from his job with the company in Toronto and Jim resigned from the board.

Advancing age and the cumulative effect of a series of polo-related injuries saw Jim Cross begin to curtail his time on the field, although he continued to be a major source of behind-the-scenes support. When their old Chinook Park grounds were sold in 1960 and the club relocated to a new facility near Okotoks, the land for the new grounds was made available by Jim Cross. When he finally gave up the game for good in 1975, his store of polo tack and travelling gear was auctioned off and the proceeds turned over to the club. Don, with a young family and increasing commitments to the Calgary Exhibition & Stampede Board, stopped playing at about the same time, ending eighty years of the Cross family's presence at the heart of southern Alberta polo.

James Braehead Cross died on February 15th, 1990. His brother, Sandy, still lives in the foothills just south of Calgary. Don is still at Bar Pipe Farm and the children of John Cross still run the great a7.

Joseph Deane-Freeman was born in 1854 at Castle Cor in County Cork, Ireland. The small farming and ranching community of Millarville, Alberta seemed an unlikely destination for one who, upon leaving school, trained for a career at sea.

In 1875 he married twenty-eight-year-old Anna Foley, a widow of some means with three or four children. Shortly after their marriage, they left for a honeymoon in Australia, presumably with an eye to settling permanently in that country. Within a year, however, they were back in Ireland with their first child and remained there for nearly a decade.

In June of 1886, Deane-Freeman filed on a quarter-section of land on the north fork of Sheep Creek near the new hamlet of Millarville southwest of Calgary. His wife, their five children, a nursemaid and a hired boy came out to join him a year later.

Justin Deane-Freeman – Taken soon before his departure for California.

Courtesy of Desmond Deane-Freeman

While waiting for their house to be completed, the family stayed with friends near Calgary and then, in the final months, lived in tents on the Millarville quarter. Their expansive log home was christened "Monea" after a property in Ireland and soon became a focal point in the social life of the new community. It was often home to Millarville's Anglican services until the opening of Christ Church in 1896 and the grounds around the house also boasted a cricket pitch, tennis courts and, most important of all, a polo field.

The Deane-Freemans had seven children in all — the last two being born at Monea — and the family's connections to the Millarville and High River communities were cemented by a series of marriages, with the game of polo involved in many of them. Eldest daughter Mysie married Charles Douglass in the first such ceremony recorded in the Millarville parish register. Charles Douglass (together with his cousin, Cecil,) was a member of the local club. Alice Deane-Freeman married Norman Willans, a Millarville club member. Their son, Trevor, and grandson, Barney, both became players in the Calgary area. In September, 1914, Dolly married legendary Pekisko-area rancher W.G. Hanson, a long-time member of both the Pekisko and High River polo clubs.

But it was through Joseph's three sons — Justin, Willie and Brudenell — that the Deane-Freemans marked their permanent place in the history of western Canadian polo.

It is highly unlikely that Joseph himself ever played the game. He would ride a horse if no other transportation was available, but he was certainly no equestrian. Although the first record of a polo club at Millarville does not appear until 1897, the game had been played there for several years, probably on the field at Monea. That field, although later supplanted by the club's permanent grounds near the racetrack, was probably laid out by the younger Deane-Freemans who took to the game very early in their lives. Joseph certainly encouraged his sons and enjoyed the social aspects of the game. For his continuing support, he was made a life member of the Millarville Polo Club.

Joseph's eldest son, Justin, was born in Ireland in 1882. A gifted athlete, he excelled at cricket and hockey, but it was polo that became the driving passion in his life. Though he held several jobs, including stints as manager of the Cowan ranch at Cochrane and working for the millionaire rancher, Pat Burns, he was never far from a polo field.

His name first appears on the tournament record in 1899 playing for Sheep Creek-Millarville in the annual Calgary tournament. From that moment, the natural brilliance of this homegrown sixteen-year-old would be a source of amazement to his fellow players, to newspaper reporters and to the crowds who watched his steady growth over the next decade.

Just after the turn of the century as Justin continued to lead a series of strong Millarville foursomes to a steady string of tournament victories, he came under the tutelage of George Ross, the district's pre-eminent polo patron and teacher. It was Ross who took the twenty-four-year-old Justin to the Montreal tournament in 1906 and was probably instrumental in his spending the following season in that city, playing with fellow southern Albertans Marston SexSmith and Harry Robertson.

When Ross left High River to settle at Fish Creek and begin that club's brief but impressive life, Justin began to appear less frequently for his home club, preferring to hone his skills with Ross and the strong group of Calgary and Pine Creek expatriates that had gathered around him.

By 1908, George Ross had begun to spend his winters in the employ of the Coronado Polo Club outside San Diego and, until the club was closed in the early 1920s, his presence and patronage made Coronado the winter home for a succession of Alberta players. It was Ross who secured a permanent, professional position for Justin at Coronado beginning with the 1909-10 season.

Deane-Freeman returned to his Millarville club for the 1909 Alberta season, making what the newspapers recognized as a sort of "farewell tour." Certain that Coronado would prove a successful (and permanent) venture, Justin's wife and their two small children were to join him, as were his parents. The senior Deane-Freemans sold Monea to Condie Landale in late 1909 and left for California.

Everything seemed full of promise and, by the end of February, 1910, Justin had established himself as one of the top players on the California circuit. His first handicap rating may have been as high as seven goals.

On March 12th, the team was back on Coronado Island after a successful tournament outing at Riverside near Los Angeles. Along with Justin, there were two other Albertans in the foursome: George Ross and High River's Harry Robertson. They were playing a practice game against a team from the Southwest Polo Club. The *High River Times* reported the result:

Justin Deane-Freeman, one of the greatest polo players that Canada ever produced was fatally injured in a polo game at the Coronado Country Club, San Diego, California, on Saturday afternoon and died on Sunday morning.

Exactly what happened has long been the subject of debate and many different accounts have surfaced over the years. The "official" version appeared in the *San Diego Union* and was reprinted by the *High River Times* under the headline "Tragic Death of Great Polo Player":

[Deane-Freeman] was being ridden off by Reggie Weiss of Los Angeles, a member of the Southwest team [and] the ponies collided heavily. Freeman's mount reared in the air, the back of its head striking Freeman on the forehead as he leaned out of his saddle for a stroke. The blow on the forehead stunned him, and he was dismounted, his foot catching in the iron. The pony became frantic and struck out, the blow catching Freeman on the head.

Years later, a young Desmond Deane-Freeman asked his father, Willie, about Justin's death. The story he was told was quite different.

According to Willie, that last game may have been just a practice, but there was something very real at stake: pride. The Southwest team, comprising four Weiss brothers, had been at the Riverside tournament three weeks earlier and suffered a crushing defeat at the hands of Coronado. The score was 11-4 and the *Los Angeles Examiner* reported the match as follows:

The physical prowess of one man, Justin Deane-Freeman, was responsible for the overwhelming defeat of the crack Southwest Club this afternoon. His drives were simply irresistible and against his terrific onslaughts the Weiss boys were powerless. He won the game for his team and the Frank J. Mackey trophy cup. Demoralization came with defeat, and in the last periods Coronado piled score after score.

It would be natural for the Southwest players to single Justin out for special attention during the practice match, both to exact a measure of revenge and to ensure that he didn't do it to them again. As Willie told it, the newspaper account made no sense. With Justin leaning out to play a shot, his pony's head rearing straight back could not have hit him. Rather, the fatal accident occurred when Justin attempted to play an offside backhand as Reggie Weiss rode in at a rather steep angle from his right. As the Southwest player tried to pull up, his horse's head crashed down onto Justin's. One side of Weiss' long-shanked bit was driven into Justin's temple, rendering him unconscious and dropping him from his mount.

Whatever the truth, the Deane-Freeman family was devastated. Joseph and his wife had sold their beloved Monea, expecting to live out their remaining years in California with their son and his young family. Although they came back to Canada, they never re-established a permanent home, living most of the time with other members of the family. Anna died in 1913 at Salmon Arm, British Columbia, while visiting with a daughter from her first marriage. Joseph lived on until

Willie Deane-Freeman on "Jill" – Although she was small —
just under 14 hands — and had to be played with short sticks,
Jill was Deane-Freeman's favourite horse. Purchased for only
$35 and said to be "half thoroughbred and half Shetland pony,"
Jill was his mount throughout his years with High River. She never
missed a game and was the only pony Willie refused to lend.

Courtesy of Desmond Deane-Freeman

1936. When staying with his youngest daughter, Nora, in Vancouver, he died at the age of eighty-two.

Gertrude Taylor, Justin's wife of only six years, was heartbroken. Leaving their two children — Justin, aged five and May, an infant — with a sister-in-law, she returned to her home in Blackpool, England. Less than a year later, on January 14th, 1911, she, too, would be gone. According to the *High River Times,* "The shock caused by hearing of the sad fate of her husband brought on a lingering illness which culminated in her death."

William Edward was the sixth of seven Deane-Freeman children and the first to be born at Monea. He was twenty-two when his brother Justin was killed. Willie had made his first recorded appearance at a polo tournament in 1903 as a fifteen-year-old with the Millarville Juniors, but for the next eight years he seems to have restricted his activities to the local club grounds. Any fears that Justin's death might dampen the family enthusiasm for the game were answered in 1911 as Willie took his place on the senior Millarville team, beginning a polo career that would stretch well into the 1930s.

In the four years leading up to the first war, Willie starred for a strong Millarville team, drawing a good deal of notice for his play from the local newspapers. In 1912, he joined a High River aggregation for the Western Canada Championship Tournament in Winnipeg. Unfortunately, 1912 was the year that North Fork proved unbeatable, winning the Winterton and Chipman trophy matches from High River by a combined score of 20-2.

Willie married for the first time in 1914 and his wife, Nancy, bore him two sons — Clive in 1914 and Desmond two years later — only to die in September, 1917 giving birth to their daughter, Barbara. Willie could not possibly manage with three small children so Clive and Des were sent to live with their Aunt Dolly on the Hanson's ranch west of High River.

Willie married for a second time in 1921 and another daughter, Margaret, was born the next year. His second wife, Mabel, was the widow of Pekisko homesteader (and Gee-Bung club member) Stanley Rigg. After Rigg was killed in the war, Mabel came back from England to settle his estate and sell their property. She and Willie met (probably not for the first time, given their polo connection) and were soon married.

After living for a short time with his brother, Brudenell, in the Alberta community of Millet, Willie saw the opportunity to purchase his old family home and, in 1922, a Deane-Freeman family was once again settled in at Monea.

There had been no organized polo at Millarville since the outbreak of the war and Deane-Freeman's return apparently did nothing to change that situation. He probably kept a few ponies and may even have practiced a little stick-and-ball on the old short field at Monea, but, with one exception, he does not seem to have travelled to Cochrane or Calgary in search of a game. All that would change in 1927.

That year, Willie Deane-Freeman came back onto the polo field and back to top-flight tournament form, but not for his old team at Millarville. It was for a reborn club at High River.

With the McHughs and Deane-Freeman, High River soon moved back into prominence. Almost from their first tournament, they put together a string of victories that few teams in the Western Canada could match. In the years between the club's revival in 1927 and their final season in 1939, the scarlet jerseys won seven provincial championships and four western Canadian titles.

Willie himself led the team to six of these championships and was runner-up five times. He was formally elected playing captain in 1929, a position he held until at least 1937, though his top playing days came to an end in 1934. Racked by rheumatoid arthritis, particularly in his hands, he could no longer manage the long, accurate shots which were the trademark of both Willie and his brother, Justin.

With his arthritis steadily worsening, Willie Deane-Freeman remained at Monea until the end of the second war when he sold out and retired to High River. He died there in 1953 at the age of sixty-five.

Joseph's third son, and youngest of the Deane-Freeman children, was Brudenell. Born at Monea in 1891, Brudenell, too, played the game, appearing with the Millarville "B" side on several occasions between 1911 and the outbreak of the first war. He enlisted in 1914 and served overseas with the rank of sergeant. He was wounded in action.

While in Britain he became engaged to an English girl named Myra Smith but she did not come to Canada to marry him until 1923. She and Brudenell tried to make a success of the homestead he had shared briefly with Willie but the land at Millett was less than ideal and in 1926 they left Alberta to live on Vancouver Island.

After working at different farms in the Victoria and Duncan area, he settled at Colwood and opened a riding academy. Together with Major A.G. Piddington, Brudenell was one of those responsible for the rebirth of polo on Vancouver Island in the late 1930s.

At the close of the second war, with a desire to return to ranching, Brudenell sold his business at Colwood and moved up to the Cariboo where he secured a half-section near Knight Lake. The operation was enlarged as other members of the family took up adjoining quarter-sections, running cattle and raising hay. Brudenell died in 1950 and the ranch passed to his son.

Willie's two sons, Clive and Desmond, all but grew up with the Hansons, though they both attended prep school in Vernon, British Columbia, before graduating from Banff High School in 1934. Most of their summer holidays were spent at Monea with their father, where they both played polo, but only Des took to the game with the family's traditional passion.

Des went to the Royal Military College in Kingston, Ontario in 1934 and, on his graduation in 1938, joined the Strathcona's. He served with the regiment in war and peace, rising to the rank of colonel before he retired in 1969.

Des began playing polo at High River as his father was reaching the end of his career. He rode out with the High River "Pinks" regularly in 1937 and came close to winning the Western Canada Championship that year, losing only to his clubmates from High River's "Whites" in the final match.

He played with the Strath's in their last two years of competitive polo. Although the regiment had it highest number of players in those years (often sending two teams to tournaments), they had no Harvey or Powell to take them to championship level. Ironically, the team's final achievement was to win the consolation round of the 1939 Western Canada Championship, played during the week that war was declared.

That tournament was the end of polo for the Strathcona's, but not for Des Deane-Freeman.

In 1963, he went to Ghana as military attaché and the commander of a team of some twenty Canadians sent to train Ghana's army. Soon after arriving, he noticed a sign that read "The Accra Polo Club" and met the club captain. Although he was then nearly fifty years old and had not swung a mallet in twenty-four years, he acquired two ponies and all the necessary gear from a player who was returning to England and went back onto the polo field.

Although the grass was poor and the "ponies" actually the slowest thoroughbred stallions from the local racetrack, the Accra club played a regular schedule

Courtesy of Desmond Deane-Freeman

Colonel Desmond Deane-Freeman, 1954.

of chukkers, usually as late in the day as possible to avoid the relentless equatorial heat. Deane-Freeman found himself responsible for handicapping the eighteen or so British, Dutch, Swiss and American members (including four women), umpiring when not playing himself and at least trying to enforce some semblance of the rules. Two teams from Accra (with Des captaining the "B" side) went annually to a tournament in Lagos, Nigeria and both managed to win their divisions regularly.

After two years in Ghana, Deane-Freeman was posted to Vancouver in 1965 where he continued to play the game with the Vancouver Polo Club, usually riding some of the excellent cutting horses owned by department store magnate Chunky Woodward.

Following his retirement from the Forces in 1969, Des moved to Kelowna, British Columbia (where he still lives), staying active in the horse world by training hunters and three-day eventers. When, after a long hiatus, the Kelowna Polo Club started play again in the early 1990s, Des was invited to come out. In his own words: "I was tempted to have a go, but, after one attempt, at age seventy-three, I was too insecure in the saddle ever to play polo again."

So ended the nearly century-long connection between the Galloping Game and the Deane-Freemans of Millarville, Alberta.

In August, 1882, William Duncan Kerfoot was hired as the resident manager of Senator Matthew Cochrane's namesake ranch just west of the town that now bears his name.

W.D. Kerfoot, like many of those responsible for the day-to-day operations of the big English and eastern Canadian-owned ranches, was an American. He was born in 1859 in Virginia's Shenandoah Valley, the son of Confederate cavalry captain J.F. Kerfoot. He had come west to the Montana Territory in the late 1870s and established a cattle operation on the upper Missouri near Fort Benton. It was in that raucous town, at the height of the trouble between the cattlemen and the sheepherders, that he was hired to run the Cochrane Ranche.

In 1884, Kerfoot married Adriana Bell-Irving, sister of the man who had founded one of the earliest of the Grand Valley ranches north of Cochrane. Their first son, Duncan Irving, was born a year later.

In late 1885, following a disagreement with the Cochrane Ranche, W.D. resigned and took up his own homestead in the Grand Valley near his brother-in-law. Five more children followed in quick succession. He continued to live at his ranch until 1908 when he was fatally thrown from his favourite horse during a parade in Calgary.

Kerfoot's four sons all took to the game of polo with a passion. They were probably introduced to the stick and ball by their neighbour, Oswald Critchley, after he bought the Bell-Irving's ranch in 1909. The two eldest brothers — Duncan and Adrian (known to all as "Pat") — began to appear for the Cochrane and Grand Valley teams almost from their beginning in about 1910 and both were listed on the 1914 Hone Cup handicap list with Pat boasting a 3-goal and his brother a 1-goal rating. At this point, they were just beginning to develop their skills and were not yet up to travelling with Critchley and the rest of Cochrane's "A" team to Fort Macleod or Spokane.

After the war, however, the four Kerfoot brothers hit their stride and, together with their brothers-in-law

The Kerfoot's Grand Valley polo team, 1925 – (left to right) Bill Wolley-Dod, Percy, Archie and Pat Kerfoot.

Bill Wolley-Dod and Vic Saunders, they became a driving force behind the Cochrane polo revival of the 1920s and early '30s.

Duncan, Pat, Archie and Percy regularly played together as a team under the banner of Cochrane or Grand Valley. When practice games were needed or a tournament called, they could subdivide into two or three teams, filling out any number of different foursomes with Bill Wolley-Dod, Gordon Hinde, Chappie Clarkson, Laurie Johnson, long-time Millarville and Cochrane captain Condie Landale and his son Alex. They could even occasionally call on skilled semi-regulars like Billy Trevenen or O.A. Critchley's son, Walter. Polo also provided a stage for the Kerfoot's predictable sibling rivalries. One Calgary player recalls two of the brothers leaping from their horses in the middle of a game and getting into a fistfight. They were on the same team at the time.

Even when the game of polo was struggling to re-establish itself in southern Alberta following the war, Cochrane seemed to thrive, despite losing such pre-war stalwarts as Oswald Critchley, the Rhodes brothers and Chester de la Vergne. The strength of the district was perhaps best demonstrated at the 1925 Calgary tournament where no fewer than four Cochrane-area teams attended. In addition to Cochrane itself and Grand Valley, T.B. Jenkinson's Virginia Ranch and a pick-up team headed by Condie Landale also appeared. Probably no other district in Canada was capable of mounting so many fine players at one time.

In their various combinations, the Kerfoot brothers continued to ride out regularly together until about 1926 when the Grand Valley team suspended play. From then until polo ceased to be a part of the life of the Cochrane district, Archie and Duncan remained the most active. Together with Laurie Johnson and Bill

Wolley-Dod, they kept their schedule of regular Sunday practices at the old field inside the Cochrane racetrack and continued to appear for tournaments at the Calgary club's Chinook Park grounds. They played together for the last time in 1932.

For the Kerfoots, it was more than just a love of polo that bound them to their neighbours in the district. They were also major contributors to the long list of "polo marriages" that has marked the Alberta social scene since the game's introduction. Not only were the brothers connected to the Bell-Irvings through their mother, but Archie also wed a member of that family. Both Kerfoot daughters married polo players and Duncan's wife Margaret Melly, was Oswald Critchley's niece. To top it all, youngest brother Percy was married to Condie Landale's daughter, Lucy.

The four Kerfoot brothers remained in Grand Valley for many years, with Archie eventually taking over the old home ranch where he lived until his retirement in 1958.

Duncan established the Providence Ranch, lost one son to the Second World War and saw another, James, seriously wounded. James took over the Providence after his father's death in 1946.

Pat, too, ranched near his brothers, raised a family of his own and eventually retired to Sidney, British Columbia where he died in 1959.

It is nearly one hundred twenty years since W.D. Kerfoot first came north from Montana and more than seventy since a matched foursome from Grand Valley appeared on a polo field. But, though the intervening years have diminished its numbers, the Kerfoot family remains today very much a part of life in the Cochrane district.

THE ROENISCHES

Throughout its century-long history in Western Canada, polo has always been a family affair. As fathers gave way to their children and then to their grandchildren, names like Wilmot, Ward, Willans and Deane-Freeman stretch across six decades and more. Six members of the Kerfoot family played the game, as did five of the Crosses and Hones. But it's unlikely any family will ever match the record of the Roenisches. Beginning in 1933, and continuing until the present day, the family has contributed no fewer than ten players to the rosters of the High River and Calgary polo clubs.

Clinton W. ("Kink") Roenisch was born in Minnesota of German and Swedish stock. In 1910, at the age of twenty-one, he came west with his brother, joining the thousands of other Americans and Europeans then flooding into southern Alberta at the end of the last great homestead movement.

The brothers settled in Calgary and took work shovelling wheat and barley for the Midland Pacific Grain Company. Eventually, the family owned the company.

Although his principal residence was always in Calgary, Roenisch's involvement with High River polo dates from about the time he purchased the "Walking R," a modest ranch just west of the town on the old River Road. His first recorded appearance with the club dates from September, 1933, when, at the age of forty-four, he took part in a pick-up practice match between the senior and junior players. He was a "senior" in age only since there is nothing to indicate he had any previous experience with the game. He had gone out to watch Kamloops at a Western Canada tournament game in Calgary a year earlier and decided that polo would be his sport. He purchased his first two aging, but still playable, ponies from the Strathcona's and joined the High River club.

Courtesy of Rob Roenisch

The third generation of Roenisch family polo at the 1987 Roenisch Memorial, Calgary – (left to right) Rob, cousin Lisa, Julie, Mrs. Clint (Barbara) Roenisch, Rich and Jan.

Courtesy of Rob Roenisch

Rob Roenisch with "Rosita," best playing pony at the North American Cup, San Antonio, Texas, 1985.

move his string of ponies. With few southern Alberta players willing (or able) to travel out of town for a tournament, he joined Jim Cross, Clem Gardner and either Charlie Arnold or Fred Scott for trips to Spokane in 1936 and Vancouver in 1938.

While the war closed the second era of western polo for most teams, High River continued to play well into 1944. By July, 1942, there were four Roenisches on the field. Playing alongside Kink were Clint and his two brothers, Harold and Davis. While Harold's time in the game was brief, Davis went on to play regularly in Calgary until about 1956 when he was carrying a 1-goal USPA rating. He also appeared with teams at Chicago and Oak Brook, Illinois.

Although still in his late teens, Clint had emerged as one of the most consistent players of the late 1930s, riding out both with and against Kink at every major tournament from 1937 until 1939. With organized polo at High River gone for good, both Clint and his father settled in with the Calgary club just after the war.

Nevertheless, the Roenisch family kept its strong connections to the High River district. In 1949, Kink purchased the OH Ranch southwest of the town. Its roots reached back to the earliest days of Alberta's cattle kingdom. At about the same time, he sold the Rocking R and bought the Round T. Although the old Eckford Ranch's sixty-year history as the social centre of High River polo was over, there was always a field at the ranch and the third generation of Roenisches would learn the game there.

Roenisch Senior played with Calgary until past his sixtieth birthday. In what must have been one of his last significant appearances, he joined with sons Clint and Davis to win the 1949 Western Canada Championship. Worsening cataracts forced him from the field in about 1951 and in recognition of his long dedication to the game of polo, he was elected honorary president of the club for 1952 and 1953. Kink died in 1976.

Whatever Kink lacked in experience, he more than made up for in enthusiasm and dedication. From that first appearance on, he rarely missed a game or a tournament and soon took his place on the High River "A" team. As the Depression deepened and players began to fall away, Roenisch and Ellison Capers over at the Round T were probably responsible for keeping the club alive. Among other tangible contributions, it was Kink who paid for the lumber to board the field in 1935.

By the spring of 1935, a second member of the family had taken to the game. Kink's eldest son, Clinton, Jr. ("Clint"), then only about thirteen years of age, was being touted by the *High River Times* as one of the club's up-and-coming young players.

By 1936, Kink was fully committed to the game, playing with High River at the provincial and Chipman Cup tournaments and even building a special trailer to

Clint stayed in the game until well into the 1970s, closing a forty-year career by playing his last polo with his sons, Rich and Rob, and their first cousin, Bob Spaith, the son of Clint's sister, Betty. It was not just advancing age and the steeply rising cost of playing that put Clint on the sidelines. Rather, he remembers it was hearing his sons yelling at him to get out of the way that finally made him hang up his sticks.

By the mid-1970s, the third generation of the Roenisch clan was making its mark on the Calgary tournament scene. Rich, Rob and Bob, playing with Tim Gregg, won the 1974 Calgary Challenge Cup. Rich and Bob repeated as champions the following year. Spaith gave up the game soon after to pursue his career as a sculptor but, before the decade was out, another Roenisch combination — this time Rich, Rob and Rob's wife, Julie — won the cup again.

Rob was also beginning a professional career that continues to this day. His first play-for-pay opportunity came in 1974 with W.B. Wilson of Midland, Texas and this led to a year with the Schlitz beer team in Milwaukee, Wisconsin and at its winter home in Florida. After taking 1976 off to work on southern Alberta's oil rigs, he came back into the game to play with Calgary's Bill Daniels at Eldorado and spent two years with Carleton Beal's B.T.A. team, dividing his time between winter seasons at Santa Barbara and summers in Midland.

Rob had met Julie, the daughter of a local rancher, when she was working in Calgary as a groom for Charles Hetherington and they were married in 1976. They travelled and played together until soon after the birth of their son, Daniel, in 1980 when they settled back in Calgary.

In 1983, they both went to work for Fred P. Mannix as he began to establish his Fish Creek team and, by the end of the decade, Rob could boast a 5-goal handicap, had won several major USPA tournaments, including the 1985 Pacific Coast Open at Santa Barbara, and played with the Canadian team at the 1987 North American Championships.

Julie also developed as a very fine player in her own right and her 2-goal handicap made her the highest rated woman in Canada. In October, 1992, she became the first woman ever to play in the U.S. Open.

Rob's brother, Rich, began playing polo in the early 1970s just before their father retired. He also exhibited a natural flair for the game (achieving his 3-goal rating before his brother did) and went on to play regularly in Calgary and Santa Barbara. He met his wife, Jan, a native of New Mexico, when she was working as a groom and playing some polo in Jackson Hole, Wyoming.

When Rich and Jan settled on their place south of the city near Longview, Jan joined her sister-in-law at the Calgary club and the two were largely responsible for bringing serious women players back onto its fields for the first time in nearly fifty years. Today, fourteen women are playing members at the club.

Although obviously a talented player, Rich never took to polo full-time. He still plays the game occasionally, but works as a sculptor, producing a series of major commissioned bronzes for such places as the Calgary Stampede, the Bar-U Ranch National Historic Site and Indio's Empire Polo Club. He also created the trophy bronzes for the Eldorado club and recently produced a new trophy for the Canadian Open Polo Championship. Jan, too, is an intelligent and gifted artist.

In the year 2000, twenty-year-old Daniel Roenisch, already carrying a 3-goal rating, played his first season as a professional polo player. He has decided to make his life in the game and Kink's great-grandson will easily carry the Roenisch family well into its eighth decade on the polo fields of southern Alberta.